LOOKING AWAY

'A trenchant account of India in the thrall of wealth accumulation and increasing inequality.'
—Deborah K. Padgett, professor, New York University

'*Looking Away* tries to understand how "inequality without outrage" has become a defining marker of Indian society. It describes in searing detail the many forms of discrimination and injustice that result from the absence of empathy for those without the advantages of birth. There are shocking individual stories, but also stories of survival, extraordinary courage and individual compassion that provide some glimmers of hope.'
—Jayati Ghosh, professor, Jawaharlal Nehru University

'Slippage in shared sense of civic responsibility, loss of confidence that government can make a difference, the transit of mass homelessness from scandal to fact of urban life, criminalized indigent survival strategies, vigorous efforts at misery-cleansing of streets before international events, invisible structural violence, class-segregated living spaces, disadvantage that means "exile from hope", waning moral outrage at steadily mounting evidence of social inequality: all these and more make *Looking Away* an instructive, recursive read.'
—Kim Hopper, author, *Reckoning with Homelessness*

'Harsh Mander tells the wrenching story of poverty and exclusion in the midst of plenty, and paints an even more distressing story of the

studied indifferences of India's new prosperous class. The work of a compassionate pragmatist with a lifetime of experience working within and outside the state, *Looking Away* also explores the policies, the politics, the lessons and maybe more importantly, the values that could pave the path for a more inclusive India.'
—Patrick Heller, professor, Brown University

'An important and evocative book, written with passion, about the challenges of rising inequality in India today, which are compounded by the astonishing indifference of people of privilege to pervasive injustice and suffering around them, and the wide sway of prejudice in the middle classes against vulnerable groups.'
—Zoya Hasan, professor, Jawaharlal Nehru University

LOOKING AWAY

INEQUALITY, PREJUDICE AND INDIFFERENCE IN NEW INDIA

HARSH MANDER

SPEAKING TIGER
An imprint of FEEL Books Pvt. Ltd
4381/4, Ansari Road, Daryaganj
New Delhi 110002

Copyright © Harsh Mander 2015

First published in Speaking Tiger in paperback 2015

ISBN: 978-93-85288-00-5

10 9 8 7 6 5 4 3

The views and opinions expressed in this book are the author's own
and the facts are as reported by him which have been verified
to the extent possible, and the publishers are not in
any way liable for the same.

Typeset in Adobe Garamond Pro by SÜRYA, New Delhi
Printed at Sanat Printers, Kundli

All rights reserved.
No part of this publication may be reproduced,
transmitted, or stored in a retrieval system, in any form or by any means,
electronic, mechanical, photocopying, recording or otherwise,
without the prior permission of the publisher.

This book is sold subject to the condition that it shall not, by way of trade
or otherwise, be lent, resold, hired out, or otherwise circulated, without
the publisher's prior consent, in any form of binding or cover
other than that in which it is published.

To
Shahid Azmi,
and to
India's three million street children
who survive our cruelty, betrayal and indifference
with bare-faced courage, cheeky spirit and resilience

~

This feeble blemished light, this dawn mangled by night,
This is not the morning that we had so longed for…
—Faiz Ahmed Faiz

Never, never be afraid to do what is right.
Society's punishments are small compared to the wounds we inflict on our souls when we look away.
—Martin Luther King Jr

CONTENTS

In Feeble Light   xi

MANY EXILES OF INDIA'S POOR

Normalizing Poverty	3
Food and Rage	11
Hiding the Poor	21
What Would You Do with ₹2,000?	24
Rainbows in the Dust	30
Hands, Heads and Hearts	39
The Eklavyas of New India	44
Youth, Jobs and Dreams	59
For the Crime of Destitution	79
'Illegal' Homes and Pickpockets	83
The Indian Help	91
Living and Dying on the Streets	95
The Crime of Falling Ill	105
The Merit of Reservations	115
Farming and the Epidemic of Terminal Despair	127
Is Farming a Dying Civilization?	133
Unequal Destinies: Malnutrition among Tribal Children	138
Two Imaginations of Good Government	147

THE LEGITIMIZATION OF PREJUDICE

Bigotry without Apology	159
Modi's Triumph and India's Scalding Majoritarian Summer	167
The Myth of Violence	187
The Alleged Fifth Column	196
Being Muslim in India Today	200
Prejudice and the Middle-Class Muslim	206
The Mosque in Ayodhya	214
Hindutva Demographics	222
The Improbable Story of 'Love Jihad'	225
Profiling 'Criminals' and 'Terrorists'	233
Competitive Conversion	245
Remembering and Forgetting 1984	261
A Secret Execution	267

THE IMPERATIVE FOR PUBLIC COMPASSION

How Will India Change?	273
Limits to Our Empathy	278
Two Sides of a Red Brick Wall	283
In Shared Spaces	289
Ways of Giving	293
Building Solidarities	300
The Legitimacy of Violence	306
Faith and Forgiveness	317
Of Mercy and Justice	324
Learning from Mohandas	328
Learning from Babasaheb	331
Learning from the Grosmaires	338

Learning from Zakia and Shameema	341
Learning from Yusuf	350
Learning from Those with Nothing	353
Learning from Shahid	358
Epilogue	363
Notes	365
Acknowledgements	413

IN FEEBLE LIGHT

I sometimes wonder how I would describe today's India if I were a historian writing a hundred years from now.

I would write, first, that the paramount marker of the first decade of twenty-first-century India was the extraordinary indifference that people of privilege had for the intense and pervasive levels of human suffering all around them.

In an interview he gave in the middle of 2013, philosopher and public intellectual Noam Chomsky observed that India's 'misery and oppression are so striking, much worse than in any country I have ever seen. And it is so dramatic'.[1] Tellingly, Chomsky also noted: 'What is really striking to me...is the indifference of privileged sectors to the misery of others. You walk through Delhi and cannot miss it, but people just don't seem to see it...they put themselves in a bubble and then they don't see it.'[2]

There is indeed a startling absence of compassion among a majority of well-to-do Indians towards the millions who have no advantages of birth to shield them from hunger, oppression, violence, squalor and humiliation. A dispassionate external observer would be bewildered by middle-class India's capacity to look away when confronted with enormous injustice and suffering; by our society's cultural comfort with inequality. That the accident of where a child is born still determines her chances in life almost irrevocably— whether and how long she would be able to study, and with what quality, the vocations open to her, the limits of her wealth and social standing, even her most basic well-being and dignity—is widely considered unproblematic, even legitimate. Many people of wealth and privilege are convinced that they have what they do because they deserve it, and that those who are in want and need also deserve their lot—because of laziness, addiction to drink, lack of education, lack of ambition, low capabilities in general, and the profligate breeding of large families.

The second-most striking marker of this age that I would record, looking back on India a century later, would be the legitimization of prejudice and discrimination against people of minority faiths and cultures and people whose life choices differ from those of the majority.

Since the early 1990s, there has been an erosion, among significant sections of the middle class, of our traditions of pluralism and the lived acceptance—however imperfect—of diversity. People of minority communities are subjected to bigotry, intolerance and open hostility. Large sections of the elite and middle classes are also unapologetically prejudiced against people of 'lower' castes, residents of urban slums, people from ethnically distinct regions of the country like the Northeast, working-class migrants from poor states like Bihar, coloured people, sexual minorities and many others who differ in whichever way from the 'mainstream'.

The two most formidable challenges that will engage the peoples and governments of all countries on the planet during the twenty-first century will be the ways in which they handle inequality and deal with diversity. Historically, India has culturally sanctioned inequalities of gender, caste and class more than any other ancient civilization. But it has also welcomed and nurtured people of diverse cultures and faiths to a greater degree than any other. In newly independent India, there was a resolve to acknowledge and reverse the country's history of entrenched inequalities, and to build on its strength of effortless diversity. But this resolve has weakened greatly in recent decades. As talk has grown of India's new Tryst with the Market, the number of people relegated to the margins of our society has also grown dramatically. The convergence of the economics of inequality and the politics of majoritarianism has made India a more divided and unequal society than at any other time in its recent history.

~

In Feeble Light

When the dust settled after the general elections of 2014, it was apparent that this had been no ordinary poll. What had been waged was no less than a battle for India's soul. No election in free India's history has left the moral, social and political landscape of India so profoundly divided.

In India's puzzling first-past-the-post election system, less than two out of five voters backed the winning side, which was led charismatically and energetically by the leader of the Right-wing Bharatiya Janata Party (BJP), Narendra Modi. More than three out of five voted against the BJP and its allied parties. Just one in three voters supported the BJP. Yet the BJP earned a decisive majority in Parliament (even without its allies), the political support it received having surpassed all expectations. A wide range of parties retained loyal support in specific regions, but the Indian National Congress which, in a previous distinct avatar, had led India to freedom, was reduced to its lowest seat tally and vote share since it was constituted 129 years ago. The Bahujan Samaj Party led by the feisty Dalit leader Mayawati Kumari won the third-highest vote share but not a single seat in Parliament. The Left parties were humiliated in their erstwhile strongholds.

However, it is important to understand that the election of 2014 was not just the emphatic victory of one political party and the humiliating defeat of others. This has happened many times in the short history of the Indian republic—in 1967, 1977, 1980, 1989, 1999 and 2004—and is indeed the stuff of democracy. What was more significant this time was the rapture, hope and triumphant vindication which significant segments of the population experienced in the victory of Narendra Modi, the highly controversial former chief minister of Gujarat—there can be no doubt that it was significantly his personal victory more than that of the political party which he led, because it was his personality which spurred such adoration among his supporters; but he was buoyed up also by the extensive mobilization effected by cadres of the Hindu nationalist organization, the Rashtriya Swayamsevak Sangh (RSS). Equally stark was the collective sentiment of dread, gloom and hopelessness, as well as a profound insecurity among millions of Modi's opponents. The real story of the 2014 elections is of the social, and not merely the political, winners and losers—one segment of people who felt that Modi's victory signified the glorious consolidation of their own economic and social ascendancy, and another segment who felt devastated by the result, seeing in it a crushing of their dreams for themselves, their communities and their country. For the latter, it was not the parties they supported—which many recognized to have floundered and failed them spectacularly and unforgivably—but they themselves who had been vanquished.

Who are the social winners of the 2014 elections, the people who voted for the BJP and who celebrate its conquests as their own? They include not just large numbers of India's urban, overwhelmingly caste-Hindu middle and upper classes—the most influential cheerleaders—but also people Modi himself describes as the 'neo-middle class'—the new entrants to the middle class—and the aspirational class, those who have not yet entered the middle class but are hopeful and impatient to benefit from India's growth. Many among these are first-time voters between eighteen and twenty-two years of age. In addition, the BJP benefited hugely from a unified anti-minority Hindu vote-bank—there was a striking blurring of most caste lines and a significant recruitment even from among the subaltern castes, including that of Dalits in Uttar Pradesh and Bihar, against the religious minorities, especially Muslims but also of people in tribal areas, many of whom are Christians.

Who are those who perceive themselves to be the social losers of this election, many among the three out of five voters who opposed the victorious party and its allies? There is first the mass of secular Indians. This secular electorate comprises not only people from the numerically small upper-class liberal elite, but millions of ordinary Indians in the small towns and villages of the country who—in the ways they live their lives—oppose ideologies of difference and divisiveness and uphold an intensely pluralist though, simultaneously, a highly unequal civilization. The second set of losers are India's minorities, especially Muslims but also Christians, who are stunned and frightened by the scale of majoritarian consolidation, unmatched even by the aftermath of Partition and the demolition of the Babri Masjid, the two lowest points in communal relations in independent India. Many Muslim friends confessed to having wept when they heard the results. Also in dread of backlash and persecution are India's sexual minorities.

The third and the largest set of social losers are India's very poor people—migrant workers, landless farm labourers, displaced forest dwellers, farmers driven to despair and suicide, weavers and artisans threatened by extinction, women in unpaid or under-paid work, over 200 million people who still sleep hungry, over 100 million people condemned to the squalor of slums, young people who have never had the chance to enter school or continue beyond primary school, and people whom each health emergency pushes further into catastrophic penury or kills outright. They are the twenty-first-century Indians, who cannot even dream of one day entering the golden middle class, people exiled from aspiration. One of India's greatest living writers, Mahashweta Devi, once remarked that the first fundamental right of all is the right to dream. These are people in permanent exile from dreaming.

The emphatic rejection of the outgoing Congress-led government by significant sections of India's voters is also hailed by the winners as a decisive rejection of the ideas of both secularism and the welfare state. But this would be a grave misreading of the message sent by the voters. It is the *performance* of the previous government on these two yardsticks which was rightly and understandably rejected by the electorate. The ideas themselves remain critical for the survival and well-being of a country of such immense diversity of belief systems and ways of life, and of so many million residents who still live in abject want and oppression.

I am convinced that the battle for India's soul will be won in the end by the ideas of justice, equality, solidarity, public compassion and reason. The social losers of the 2014 election are ultimately on the right side of history.

~

Ela Bhatt, one of India's tallest social workers, reminded us in a moving speech delivered at a celebration, organized by NDTV, of the greatest living Indians, that 'poverty is violence'. 'It is violence,' she elaborated, 'perpetuated with the consent of society. A society that is silent, or looks the other way in the face of poverty, [gives] consent to exploitation, injustice and war. Poverty strips away a person's dignity, humanity, it corrodes the human spirit. There is no justification for poverty in India.' And she added, 'Diversity is the key to life. Our world is richer when cultures and subcultures flourish, when faiths and sub-faiths intermingle; when each language, dialect and *boli* have freedom of speech. We need a multiplicity of economies and sub-economies that co-exist in harmony. Monoculture and standardization of practices are nothing but ways of managing Nature or managing people; they are not life-giving forces. India's rich diversity needs the spirit of *bahudha* [multiplicity] to sustain it.'[3]

This is something we expect non-state, social formations to champion and work for. But social formations are today confused by the turbulent upsets not only in Indian politics, but also within their own ranks. Since the early 2000s, 'civil society' has moved Rightwards. Till then, whatever their other differences, it could be assumed that most participants in this space would be broadly Left-liberal. Since the communal violence in Gujarat in 2002, however, and even more after the Anna Hazare-led anti-corruption movement, the centre of gravity, even of civil society, has swung significantly to the Right. In this changed scenario, some social formations believe that they should seek political power and influence mainstream politics from within. Others remain uncertain, worrying about the slippery ethical ground of electoral politics, and the frequently problematic positions of even progressive political formations on issues such as gender, markets and pluralism. Yet others are quietly bracing themselves to survive in a radically altered—more Right-wing and less tolerant—political environment, if not with vocal support, then at least by buying safety with the counterfeit of their silences.

And yet, this is precisely the time when non-party citizen formations must be at their strongest, with conviction and clarity of vision. With one of the weakest political oppositions within Parliament in the history of the Indian republic in 2014, the main opposition to the market-majoritarian-militarist-fundamentalist government must come from outside Parliament, from non-party citizen formations. Their most significant contribution would be to bring ideology back centrestage in political discourse. We need to insist on debating the central questions on which the future of our people rests: How can social and economic equality be achieved even while markets are nurtured? How can India's pluralism be defended against majoritarian assaults? How can public services better and more accountably deliver quality health, education and social security to poor people? How can we defend human rights and dignity in areas where oppressed people or social minorities are battling the Indian state and big industry? How can *all* young people be assured jobs and hope?

~

There were many egalitarian impulses in India immediately after freedom. At the cusp of independence, Jawaharlal Nehru wrote that India 'must aim at equality'. He clarified that this 'cannot mean that everyone is physically or intellectually equal or can be made so. But it does mean equal opportunities for all, and no political and social barrier…It means a faith in humanity and a belief that there is no race or group that cannot advance and make good in its own way, given the chance to do so. It means a realization of the fact that the backwardness or degradation of any group is not due to inherent failings in it, but principally to lack of opportunities and long suppression by other groups.'[4] Soon after, addressing the Constituent Assembly in the opening debate on 22 January 1947, Nehru said: 'The first task of this Assembly is to free India through a new constitution, to feed the starving people, and to clothe the naked masses, and to give every Indian the fullest opportunity to develop himself according to his capacity.'[5]

In these two statements Nehru laid out the basic principles of equality of all citizens in free India, principles that would be embedded in free India's Constitution. The responsibility for drafting this document fell on the shoulders of Babasaheb Ambedkar, the most powerful voice for equality in India's political class in the twentieth century. The Constitution established political equality with universal adult suffrage. By abolishing caste discrimination and forced labour, and introducing legal protections for the rights of minorities, it also attempted to reduce social and economic inequality. It enjoined the state to ensure a social order which promotes the welfare of all people, minimizes inequalities and prevents the concentration of wealth, promotes decent work for all, provides public assistance for the unemployed, aged, sick and disabled, provides maternity relief, and ensures nutrition, education and public health for every citizen. But, prophetically, Ambedkar warned that after adopting the Constitution, 'we are going to enter into a life of contradictions. In politics we will have equality and in social and economic life we will have inequality'.[6] He was convinced that 'political democracy cannot succeed without social and economic equality', and that 'democracy is empty if there are glaring inequalities in it'.[7]

Political democracy took firm root in the first flush of freedom. Political formations that promoted social divisions went on the back foot after the assassination of Mahatma Gandhi by persons and organizations radically opposed to secular democracy. Large estates were successfully abolished, and the state took the lead in reviving agriculture and large industry. But there were also early signs of impending challenges to social and economic equality. School education through a common school system for all was neglected. Caste oppression and debt bondage persisted, as did barriers to equal access to social leadership, jobs and schools; women continued to suffer violence, and corruption spread rapidly like a deadly virus.

Divisive communal organizations also regrouped and gathered new strength.

There was also the failure of the overall project of land reforms. Rural poverty in India is closely tied to conditions of landlessness, or small, unviable holdings. In the first three decades after Independence, land reforms remained high on the stated agenda of governments and state administrations. Success was significant in the abolition of large estates, for which there was high political backing because the zamindars of the past were close allies of the British colonial rulers. However, attainments in redistributing ceiling-surplus land, abolishing or regulating tenancy, and allocating surplus cultivable government land to the landless and preventing land alienation from tribal and other socially vulnerable landholders were much more limited. Large landholders benefited from several exemptions, such as those given to the bogus religious, educational and charitable trusts that they set up. They also distributed land to their relatives—and even cats and dogs—in order to escape the law. The zamindars and other large landholders let go only of their most marginal lands, and they also continued to retain benami possession of most of their lands through fraud and by force.[8] By the end of 2005, state governments across India had declared only 1.8 per cent of India's agricultural land as surplus. Of that land, the governments distributed as little as 1 per cent to just 4 per cent of rural households.[9] Even these efforts were concentrated in a few states—West Bengal, Jammu and Kashmir, Kerala and Assam.

The success was greater, at least on paper, with tenancy rights: 12.4 million tenants, comprising around 5 per cent of the total households in India, were given rights over 15.6 million acres of land, comprising, again, 5 per cent of the total acreage of land under cultivation.[10] But tenancy was also widely subverted by landholders who misused the provision for taking repossession of the land for 'personal cultivation'. There was large-scale trickery and forced eviction of tenants through collusion with local land authorities, who ensured that tenancies were not recorded. P. S. Appu, one of

India's most credible scholars and administrators, estimates that as high as a third of all tenant households in rural India were evicted from the lands that they cultivated, so that landholders could evade the tenancy reform laws.[11]

Among the biggest losers of India's failed land reforms were its tribal people, which I observed first-hand in tribal districts in Madhya Pradesh and Chhattisgarh—Betul, Barwani, Khargone, Rajnandgaon, Raigarh and Bilaspur—where I served as a district officer during the 1980s and 1990s. As I tried determinedly to implement the law to restore land alienated fraudulently or coercively from tribal landowners, I found that statutes protecting tribal ownership and possession of land were among the most unimplemented of all land reform laws. Millions of former tribal landowners remain utterly powerless to engage with the unfamiliar legal system. Only a very small number of tribal people succeed in filing claims for restoration, but even among these, less than 50 per cent of cases are decided in favour of tribals in most states for which data is available.[12] Even when cases were decided in their favour, these rarely resulted in the actual transfer of lands to the legal but powerless tribal landowners. The result has been large-scale loss of land, be it through private transactions or as part of massive, forced displacement for urbanization and industrialization. As the majority of land transfers from tribal people are unrecorded, forced and illegal, there is no official data that provides a realistic estimate of the extent of tribal land alienation, but there is no doubt that it has been catastrophic for the survival and well-being of tribal societies.

It is hardly surprising, therefore, that the cumulative impact of all these measures of land reforms has been negligible even almost seven decades after Independence. Sixty per cent of the country's rural households have rights over only 5 per cent of its total agricultural land; whereas 10 per cent of the population has control over 55 per cent of the land.[13] It is indicative that, for some years now, even the rhetoric of land reforms has disappeared from the country's policy and political agenda as a serious instrument for battling rural poverty.

It has been replaced, instead, by softer options like micro-credit and wage-employment programmes as well as policies which further enable land transfer for development projects, a stated policy of the BJP government at the Centre. According to a report published by the Centre for Science and Environment, 830,244 hectares of forest land has been diverted for development projects between 1981 and 2011, a quarter of which was diverted between 2007 and 2011.[14] The total number of Displaced Persons and Project Affected Persons between 1947 and 2000 was estimated to be more than sixty million.[15] The record of rehabilitation and resettlement, meanwhile, has been abysmal.[16] While more recent numbers are not available, the ongoing drive towards urbanization and industrialization is likely to have resulted in a similar or higher level of displacement in the period between 2001 and 2010.

~

I was born eight years after India won her freedom—a time when the country was much poorer, much hungrier, in much worse health and more hopelessly trapped in historical bondages of caste and gender than it is today. But I remember my childhood as a period defined by a culture of egalitarian and secular idealism. There was an ethos of relative restraint among people of privilege. The excesses of erstwhile maharajas and landlords were rejected as decadent. Conspicuous consumption was considered vulgar in the face of massive deprivation among the vast majority of our fellow citizens. Young people born in wealthy and middle-class homes were taught to live modestly. Children were instructed not to waste food, as there were 'hungry children outside'. I recall getting my first set of new clothes only when I was eight years old. College campuses were sites of socialist stirrings of all shades, including far-Left militancy.

I studied in an elite boys' boarding school with many anachronistic, feudal hangovers, but we were completely oblivious of differences of religion, class and caste between us. For our school prayer, my British school principal chose a song by the poet Allama Mohammed

Iqbal: 'Lab pe aati hai dua'. Today, this dua, or prayer—which affirms that no religion teaches enmity and seeks god's blessings to be of service to the suffering and oppressed—has been ghettoized in India, banished out of the mainstream and restricted to Muslim madrassas. Of course, caste and communal inequalities were rampant even when I was growing up, but airing one's prejudices against people of different religions or the 'lower castes' was neither commonplace nor socially acceptable among the middle classes in the ways that it has become today.

Popular theatre, cinema and film music celebrated ideas of equality. The Left-leaning association of performing artists, the Indian People's Theatre Association (IPTA), constituted in 1942, included in its ranks the best talents of the time: Prithviraj Kapoor, Ritwik Ghatak, Utpal Dutt, Salil Chaudhry, Ravi Shankar, Khwaja Ahmed Abbas, Sahir Ludhianvi, Kaifi Azmi and Balraj Sahni. IPTA and the Progressive Writers' Association had a profound influence on popular Hindi cinema—as did Dravidian political writers on Tamil cinema. Many Hindi films were populated with farmers fighting for their land, factory workers for proletariat rights, and homeless people for dignity and housing. Nargis playing the matriarch bravely battling famine, flood and an evil moneylender in *Mother India* (1957), Balraj Sahni as the farmer pulling a hand rickshaw on the streets of Calcutta in a desperate bid to save his agricultural land in *Do Bigha Zameen* (1953) or Raj Kapoor in the role of a Bombay footpath dweller in *Shree 420* (1955) became part of our collective social consciousness.

Times have changed. If you were receiving an introduction to India through the movies being made in Hindi today, you would imagine that there are no poor people left in the country. Everyone is impossibly rich, living in designer clothes and homes; the indebted peasant, the wage worker, the street dweller have been exiled from our popular cinema. Jyotsna Kapur and Manjunath Pendakur, in an intriguingly titled paper, 'The Strange Disappearance of Bombay from Its Own Cinema', show how, in this period of neo-liberal economic growth, India's biggest metropolis has been erased from the cinema that it is home to, because of the imperative 'to erase history, memory, and render invisible those who are on its losing end'.[17] The same expulsion of the poor occurs also in popular television soap operas, in which the leading ladies wear silk saris and gold jewellery, even to bed.

Yasmin Premji, novelist and wife of IT czar Azim Premji, told me once about how her parents would send her to school in a car, but she would feel so embarrassed that she would stop the car a block away and walk to school. Today, all such constraints and inhibitions have been thrown to the wind. Privilege is considered an entitlement, a sign of personal accomplishment that the world must see and envy.

Poverty and destitution, on the other hand, should be invisible. Teaching a class of more than two hundred first-year college students in Delhi, I asked one morning how many had been inside a slum. Not a single hand went up. I asked how many had at least seen a slum. Less than half the class raised their hands, many very tentatively. I was startled because it is impossible to live in a city like Delhi and not *see* slums. I realized then that many middle-class and wealthy young people are being raised in ways that seal them off in bubbles where the only reality that registers on their hearts and minds is their own. They never encounter poor people, except those at traffic lights whom they have learnt to look at but not see. They live in gated colonies, are transported in air-conditioned cars or buses to gated, often air-conditioned schools and colleges, and they shop, dine out, drink, dance, visit beauty parlours and gyms and watch films in air-conditioned malls. This extraordinary ability to not see what is in plain sight is central to the new society's project of exclusion. If we actively shared spaces—schools, parks, cinemas, public transport—with people who are socially and economically different from us, it would construct grounds for the possible fostering of understanding, empathy, and even friendships across class and caste, which have all but evaporated. As the old adage goes, what the eye cannot see, the heart cannot—or, rather, need not—grieve.

In my father's generation, most people across social classes studied in the same government school (although it is also true that there were hardly any Dalit children in these schools). This would be unthinkable today. In my generation, a vast majority of young people travelled by general public transport, thus sharing space every day with people of diverse backgrounds, but this is no longer the case—the air-conditioned metro network is one of the few democratic spaces in our big cities, but the very rich and the poor don't use it. Unlike many cities in the world, there are no specified cycle paths. Instead, cyclists, cycle-rickshaws and even auto-rickshaws are barred from many sites; for instance, the Indira Gandhi International Airport in New Delhi. In a seminar on smart new cities organized by the London School of Economics in Delhi, Enrique Penalosa, the mayor of Bogota in Colombia spoke proudly of the successful implementation of the first Bus Rapid Transport (BRT) in his city, by creating separate lanes reserved exclusively for public buses, and he remarked, 'When a 100 people in a bus speed past, laughing at a Mercedes stuck hopelessly in traffic on the next lane, this is democracy at work.'[18] Such democracy was a non-starter in Delhi, when the pilot BRT was noisily opposed by the vocal middle class, and had to be eventually abandoned. Sheila Dikshit, the former chief minister of Delhi, lamented repeatedly in the LSE conference that 'the people' of Delhi rejected the BRT. She did not clarify that by 'the people' she only meant the middle classes; the poor do not seem to even qualify as 'the people'.

In the past, cinema halls too were popular, accessible sites where people of different social classes crowded and mingled. Now the scandalous cost of cinema tickets has ensured that few, if any, of India's poorer working-class people will see the inside of a modern cinema hall. Mainstream newspapers and magazines, like cinema and television, further conspire to erase the poor from the consciousness of middle-class children and youth. The only poor people they interact with are their compliant domestic helps and chauffeurs, people created for the sole purpose of serving their needs.

Arundhati Roy, in her scathing essay 'Listening to Grasshoppers', aptly describes 'the most successful secessionist struggle ever waged in India—the secession of the middle and upper classes to a country of their own, somewhere in the stratosphere where they merge with the rest of the world's elite'.[19] This 'vast middle class punch drunk on sudden wealth' has created a kingdom with 'its own newspapers, films, television programmes, morality plays, transport systems, malls and intellectuals'.[20] On the other side is 'a much, much vaster, desperate underclass' of people 'dispossessed of their lands by floods, drought and desertification' and massive infrastructural projects.[21] The era of free markets, she observes, has recalibrated some but reinforced most of the old inequalities of an ancient society. This 'old society has curdled and separated into a thin layer of thick cream—and a lot of water. The cream is India's "market" of many million consumers (of cars, cell phones, computers, Valentine Day's greeting cards), the envy of international business. The water is of little consequence'.[22]

The degree and direction of changes in the material conditions of inequality since Independence can be a matter of debate among scholars, based on differences of definition and calculation. But what worries me more deeply is middle-class India's ethical perception of this inequality as inevitable, logical, or even legitimate, as they believe that people have wealth because they worked hard and earned it, and the poor who are left behind need to study harder and work harder to raise themselves. This belief system seems to have been adopted even by those still aspiring to enter the middle classes—mostly young people impatient to leave behind the depressing darknesses of their origins and to bask in shining India. Inequality without outrage is indeed the defining marker of our times.

~

In this book, I will often talk about India's 'middle classes', and from this title it may seem reasonable to assume that they stand somewhere in the middle of India's wealth and income range. But that is far from the reality. Those whom we describe conventionally as middle-class people in India actually stand in the first two income deciles of the population, not the fourth or the fifth. In fact, even important official statistics such as those reported by the National Council of Applied Economic Research (NCAER) embrace a definition of middle class which includes only 12 per cent of the total population.[23]

Some attribute the wide and popular use of the misnomer as a deliberate attempt by the elite to deny their privilege, much in the fashion of the term 'job-creators' in America.[24] This mainstream idea of the 'middle class' obscures the fact that this segment of the population earns incomes in several multiples of the median income.

A sizeable number of young men and women from the lower end of the middle class, who were able to acquire some education, do long to break out of the limits set by their caste, gender, class, geography and history. These are young men and women with fire in their bellies, many of whom have probably placed their faith in the market and Modi's promise that jobs will be created. However, it would be a huge mistake to assume that all young people in India—in which half the population is below twenty-five years of age and which is home to the largest youthful population in the world—are able to aspire for a new life in the new economy. Only 7 per cent of the youth of India are able to get a college degree, and the quality of these colleges differ widely; further, the numbers are even smaller for young women, and Dalit, tribal or Muslim young people.[25] But even a college degree is no guarantee of a better life; one out of three graduates between the ages of fifteen and twenty-nine years is unemployed.[26] The most disadvantaged, however, are those who were denied schooling in this age group; they have the lowest unemployment rate—implying that they are probably engaged in casual and badly paid work.[27] The government estimates that close to 40 per cent of these youth, from rural areas, is employed as casual labour.[28]

It is important to not ever lose sight of the fact that for a much larger population than both the middle class and the aspiring class—

however expansively defined—youth only means migrating in distress and often bondage to faraway lands to fill the stomachs of their impoverished families if they are young men, of early marriage and motherhood and unending toil if they are young women. These young people subsist in low-end casual jobs, without full stomachs, or with access to clean water, decent work, decent schools and health centres. They are India's millions who are still banished from the shining, individualist, consumerist aspirations which young people with better chances of education and social mobility are able to at least dream of.

~

The Indian middle classes are today socialized in not one but three normative systems which justify inequality. The first of these is the caste system, which validates a social order in which a person's birth legitimately determines her life chances, her access to education and the livelihoods open to her. The second is the British class system, in which people with old wealth, combined with exclusive education, acquire 'refined' lifestyles that mark them out from the 'boorish lower classes' and 'upstart new rich'. And the last of these is the more recently acquired celebration of conspicuous consumption associated with the collapse of the socialist world and the rise of neo-liberal, market-led growth. The dominant value is that 'greed is good'—it is time to liberate oneself from the 'socialist guilt' of the past, to abandon old-fashioned values of thrift, restraint and modesty, and instead to make—or inherit—money and spend on oneself with no restraints or inhibitions.

This is the new India which celebrates when India's richest man, Mukesh Ambani, follows up his gift of a 60-million-dollar jet-plane to his wife with the most expensive residence in the world, a twenty-seven-storey house for a family of four, built at an estimated cost of one billion dollars, which boasts three helipads, four storeys of hanging gardens, and a staff of 600 domestic helpers. This, in a city where at least two hundred thousand people sleep on pavements, and more than 40 per cent of the population lives in shanties. In the 'liberated' climate of today, not just the fifty-five dollar billionaires with a net worth of $193 billion which *Forbes* reports, but numerous middle-class Indians think nothing of organizing weddings in which the cost of each plate is twice, or even six times the monthly income of the majority of Indians.

In the words of film-maker Saeed Mirza, 'large sections of the formerly "stoic" middle class got seduced. It got seduced by all the goodies on display: food, clothes, cars, electronic gadgets, toiletries, beverages, shoes and everything else on display in those incredibly inviting store windows and shelves. It began to party. It was almost as if after years and years of abstinence this solid bloc of sobriety had gone on a binge. What nobody realized was that the centre of the nation had caved in. There was nothing to temper the onslaught of excess. All this was happening in a country where over seventy per cent of citizens lived on less than two dollars a day.'[29]

In 2013, NDTV in its silver jubilee celebrations honoured those whom it regarded as the twenty-five greatest living Indians.[30] Among the large media houses, I feel greater kinship of values and politics with NDTV, but I still found myself in disagreement with much of their selection. Their list of twenty-five included five people from big industry, including Mukesh Ambani and, additionally, numerous popular film and sports stars that have excelled in their fields but lead opulent lifestyles and do little to public service. On the other hand, there was only one name from social movements, Ela Bhatt, and one intellectual champion of public responsibility to the poor, Amartya Sen. The 'power list' which the newsmagazine *India Today* brings out annually is even more crowded with rich captains of industry, and includes even fewer public servants and intellectuals. The heroes of this new India—rich, often second-generation industrialists, cricketers and film stars—flaunt their Ferraris and diamonds with little sense of obligation, both for public restraint and public service.

~

Inequality is not a condition peculiar to poorer or developing countries. It is a global malady. According to a recent study, income inequality in the world has been on the rise since the early nineteenth century and has risen at a much faster rate since the 1980s.[31] A paper presented by Oxfam in Davos in 2013 caught the world's attention when it established the astounding fact that eighty-five people own the same wealth as the bottom 3.5 billion people on the planet.[32] Winnie Byanyima, executive director of Oxfam, declared: 'It is staggering that in the 21st century, half of the world's population—that's three and a half billion people—own no more than a tiny elite whose numbers could all fit comfortably on a double-decker bus.'[33] Oxfam noted in 2014 that, further, from March 2013, these eighty-five people grew richer by \$668 million every day. If Bill Gates was to cash all his wealth and spend \$1 million each day, it would take him 218 years to exhaust his fortune.[34] It noted further that the richest 1 per cent of the world's people owned an incredible 48 per cent of its wealth, leaving the remaining 99 per cent to share (unequally) the remaining 52 per cent of global wealth. The top 0.1 per cent is doing even better, increasing their share of the national income by fourfold since the 1980s.[35] In most of the planet, the share of labour in national income has fallen and real wage levels have stagnated under the impact of neo-liberal policies which weaken labour protections and lower taxes on the rich, reducing resources for public spending and fuelling conflict, war, poor health, mass migration and political corruption.[36]

In his seminal book *Capital in the Twenty-First Century*, which quickly acquired rock-star status since it was published in French in 2013 and in English translation some months later, Thomas Piketty, professor at the Paris School of Economics, demonstrates that the top 1 per cent in the United States enjoy around a fifth of the total income, which reflects a return to levels of inequality that prevailed a century earlier in both Britain and the United States. But even more remarkably, he finds that much of this concentrated affluence is not self-earned but inherited wealth, and is thereby even more ethically repugnant.[37] Children and grandchildren of the rich will largely replace their parents and grandparents on the steep economic ladder, as much as children and grandchildren of the poor will remain impoverished, regardless of their potential and hard work. As Oxfam observes, 'A child born to a rich family, even in the poorest countries, will go to the best school and will receive the highest quality care if they are sick. At the same time, poor families will see their children taken away from them, struck down by easily preventable diseases because they do not have the money to pay for treatment.'[38]

The Oxfam report further calculates that if even a tax of 1.5 per cent was imposed on the wealth of all the world's billionaires, it could get every child into school and deliver health services in all the poorest countries of the world, saving an estimated twenty-three million lives. Nisha Agrawal, CEO Oxfam India, estimates that a wealth tax of merely 1.5 per cent on sixty-five of the super-rich of India could potentially lift ninety million people out of poverty.[39] And if the country could reduce inequality by 36 per cent, it could eliminate extreme poverty.[40]

This said, it must also be admitted that a great deal has indeed been accomplished globally in overcoming poverty. Jeffrey Sachs says in the July 2013 BBC series 'Why Poverty?' that in 1800, 90 per cent of the world's population lived in extreme poverty.[41] By 2015, that number was expected by the United Nations to come down to about 15 per cent.[42] Still, this is little solace to the millions of children, women and men across the world who continue to endure avoidable hunger, sickness and deprivation.

The world today is also characterized by unprecedentedly large movements of diverse populations across borders. Earlier, many countries—especially smaller ones—were relatively homogeneous in terms of culture. Now, every country is being forced to learn ways to coexist with unfamiliar cultures and faiths as more and more people are migrating in search of work, education or to escape persecution. This is why every nation has to fashion its policies—economic, social and moral—to deal with the twin challenges of both inequality and difference.

In Feeble Light

These same challenges confront India, the world's most populous democracy, one of its fastest-growing economies and, historically, the most diverse large civilization in the world. There can be no doubt that since the end of colonialism, India has taken vast strides in battling poverty. Still, even if we were to accept the minimalist official definitions of what constitutes the end of poverty—definitions that many disagree with—the actual number of poor people in the country has grown massively. It is estimated that in 1951, four years after the British colonial rulers left Indian shores, about 162 million people—half the country's population at the time—were poor; the most recent estimates by the National Sample Survey Organization put the level of poverty in the year 2011 at 22 per cent, which is about 269 million people.[43, 44] I'm convinced that if we deploy alternate measures based on a different normative understanding of what constitutes a life of basic dignity, we would agree that the number of poor people in India would be much higher. (I have argued elsewhere that official definitions of poverty are deeply problematic; what the official bodies consider to be the threshold of poverty is actually closer to a threshold of starvation and destitution; therefore, they grossly underestimate the number of poor people in India.)[45]

However, this, too, should not obscure the fact that life has indeed changed for the better for millions of our people. Whatever measure we use, there is little doubt that people on the whole are generally better off than they were, say, even a decade ago. The literacy rate at the time of Independence was around 12 per cent, while life expectancy hovered at about thirty-one years.[46] Today, 74 per cent of Indians are literate—although we can again justifiably quibble about the minimalist definitions of literacy—and life expectancy has risen to sixty-seven years.[47]

These changes are not nearly rapid enough, they have not covered nearly enough people, but they *have* occurred. As Jean Dreze observed at the launch of *An Uncertain Glory: India and Its Contradictions*, which he co-wrote with Amartya Sen, 'If you feel that nothing can change, think about how things were as recently as 10 or 15 years ago, especially in the poorer districts of the country...At that time there were no roads worth the name, no modern communications, no functioning anganwadis [young child care centres], no right to information, no social audits, no sanitation campaign, no Gram Sabhas [village assemblies] (except on paper), no Forest Rights Act, no employment guarantee, no ASHAs [community health workers], no old-age pensions, no ambulance services, no midday meals, no minimum wages, and virtually no public distribution system. And contrary to the impression you may get from the mainstream media, many of these interventions actually have an impact, and could have a much greater impact with more resources, political support and application of mind. So the problem is not that things cannot change, or that they do not change. It is that they are not changing fast enough, even as the rest of the world is on the move.'[48]

The real concern, then, is that while India may be a leader today in spurring global economic growth, it remains a laggard in reducing poverty. A World Bank report published in 2009 estimated that in 2015, nearly 34 per cent of the global population living at less than $2 a day would be doing so in India.[49] Given trends over the last two decades, the projection seems like an accurate estimation of the existing situation. Almost every developing country in Asia—except Timor-Leste and Bangladesh—was able to achieve a greater reduction in the number of people living under $2 per day, in the period between 1995 and 2012, than India.[50] Using even the tight-fisted poverty line of $1.25, it is estimated that the proportion of the world's poor living in India increased steadily from 22 per cent in 1981 to 33 per cent in 2010.[51] If one uses the median developing-country poverty line of $2 per day on purchasing parity, 80 per cent of India's rural inhabitants and just under 70 per cent of urban residents would be recognized as being poor.[52] The big story which these figures tell is that whichever way you define poverty, the largest proportion of the world's poor live in India—a situation that is likely to persist in the near future.

We need to also distinguish between relative or partial accomplishments in reversing poverty and successes in reducing *inequality*. Data from the Credit Suisse Global Wealth Databook 2014 shows that the since 2000, the wealth share of the richest 1 per cent in India has been increasing steadily, in contrast to the rest of the world, and they now hold almost half of the country's total wealth. Similarly, the wealth share of the top 10 per cent has increased by nearly 10 percentage points since 2000. In contrast, the poorest 10 per cent own only 0.2 per cent of wealth.[53] Wealth inequality in the country has actually been rising rapidly, rather than reducing.

The benefits of social development and economic growth—employment, education, nutrition, healthcare, clean water, sanitation, housing and social protection—have reached far fewer numbers of historically disadvantaged groups like women, tribal people, Dalits and Muslims than the rest of the population. The 2011 India Human Development Report shows, for instance, that despite the overall decline in India's poverty rate, the incidence of poverty amongst the Scheduled Castes and Scheduled Tribes is higher than the national average by 8.5 percentage points.[54] And even among these disadvantaged groups, as among others, girls and women have suffered the most, as there has been an increasing feminization of poverty across the country.

Oxfam observes that India's income concentration at the top fell in the first three decades after Independence but, since then, for the top 0.01 per cent, real wages grew annually by more than 11 per cent.[55] In contrast, real household expenditure for the rest of the population rose by only 1.5 per cent.[56] The gap in the share of total income of the top 10 per cent and the bottom 40 per cent of people in India has constantly risen since 1995, sharply aggravating inequality.[57] The report also notes Dreze and Sen's observation on the agricultural sector, 'In agriculture, growth in real wages was 5 per cent in the 1980s, but fell to 2 per cent in the 90s, and virtually zero in the 2000s.'[58] Nisha Agrawal notes that India needs to follow a bottom-up rather than trickle-down approach, 'For one, this would involve stimulating agriculture, which employs a large number of people. Sadly, the current belief seems to be that diluting land acquisition and other laws will lead to growth. Such dilutions will only concentrate wealth in a few hands and impoverish others, leading to more inequality.'[59]

In India, from two resident billionaires with an income of $3.2 billion in the mid-90s, numbers grew to forty-six and combined wealth to $176 billion in 2012, and their share in GDP rose from 1 to 10 per cent.[60] Oxfam notes, tellingly, the identities of these forty-six dollar billionaires—there is one woman, one Muslim and no Dalit or tribal person in the grouping. Each of the other billionaires is from the upper castes, including twenty-eight from the traditional merchant classes.[61] The Hurun Global Rich List states that on 17 January 2015, the number of India's dollar billionaires rose to ninety-seven, with a total worth of $226 billion. India now has the third largest numbers of billionaires among all countries in the world, after the US and China.[62]

The challenges of inequality in India are compounded by the powerful revival of the politics of difference, a new conservatism and the evidence of active social and state hostility towards minority groups and communities, reflected in grossly under-provisioned Muslim ghettoes, religious profiling in both terror-related and other crimes, and the extra-judicial killings of tribals, Muslims and Dalits. There is growing appeal among the middle classes for Right-wing politics that often combines market fundamentalism with hostility towards minorities and India's neighbours. In the general elections of 2014, this mood was best represented by Narendra Modi, who fought a blistering electoral battle deploying 'shock and awe' tactics against his adversaries—who included liberals, socialists, 'secularists' and minorities—whom he felled decisively to become India's sixteenth prime minister.

Of all the major political parties seeking votes in the 2014 elections, the BJP, through its prime ministerial candidate, offered the Indian electorate perhaps the most cohesive, if troubling, vision for the country. Modi offered a combination of three fundamentalisms. First, a market orthodoxy which guarantees unprecedented levels of subsidies to big business in the form of long tax holidays, soft loans, cheap land and electricity, at the expense of public expenditure on education, health, social protection and public infrastructure. Next was communal fundamentalism, constituting barely disguised hostility towards religious minorities, especially Muslims, which was the main rallying agenda on the ground in electorally crucial states like Uttar Pradesh and Bihar. And the third was a militarist fundamentalism, envisioning an aggressive foreign policy, including war with Pakistan. Modi's offer to the voters was a kind of 'buy one, get two free' political bargain, but one in which you cannot embrace one of the fundamentalisms without also accepting the others.

It is important to recognize that the political choice that approximately 40 per cent of India's voters made in the summer of 2014 by voting for the Modi-led BJP and its allies is not unique. Indeed, many countries of the world today, most notably in Europe, even including Scandinavia, show a similar preference for a confident, resurgent and aggressive Right over centrist and Left-of-centre formations that are increasingly defensive and uncertain, with shaky commitments to social welfare and protection. (There are important exceptions in some Latin American countries, like Brazil, and in 2015, Greece.) But in many of these countries, Right-wing politics is mainly about market economics, and does not combine the same open hatred of minorities that we find in contemporary Indian politics (although there is a latent anti-minorityism and, indeed, almost an Islam-phobia in the anti-immigrant stances of many European and North American Right-wing parties). It is little wonder, then, that one of India's foremost thinkers, Amartya Sen, remarked at the Jaipur Literature Festival in January 2014 that as someone on the Left of politics in India, his 'big political wish is to have a strong and flourishing right-wing party that is secular and not communal'. Given his own Left-leaning politics, this sounds paradoxical, but he explained that 'there is an important role for a clear-headed pro-market, pro-business party that does not depend on religious politics, and does not prioritize one religious community over all others'.[63]

But in India, Right-wing market economics has remained—as Sen puts it—'parasitical' on Right-wing religious sectarian politics, as exemplified by the politics of the BJP and even more dramatically in Modi's leadership of Gujarat for a dozen years. This carries today, after Modi's national triumph, the deeply worrying prospect of worsening inequality and social intolerance. There is no necessary convergence between Right-wing economic policies, Right-wing chauvinism and Right-wing militarism. Right-wing economic policies can coexist with liberal and secular policies relating to minorities and restrained defence plans. But where these do converge—as they do in Indian politics today—I believe they constitute a grave threat to secular democracy. The result of the elections of 2014 would not have caused such extensive dismay among many people if it was a victory only of an economic Right formation. It was the convergence of the economic Right with majoritarian and militarist triumphalism, spurred by enormous corporate financing, which caused such disquiet.

~

Many of us have begun to believe that even if India is some years yet from first-world status, it is miles ahead of other developing countries. So how does India really compare with the rest of the developing world in terms of economic and social inequality?

A 2011 World Bank study concludes that 'inequality in India seems to be in the same league as that in Brazil and South Africa, both high-inequality countries'.[64] Agreeing with the report, Amartya Sen and Jean Dreze point to evidence of growing economic inequality in recent decades, because despite highly accelerated economic growth, the decline in poverty has not sufficiently picked up, and the main beneficiaries of economic growth have been the 'comparatively affluent in urban areas'.[65] They write famously of 'islands of California in a sea of Sub-Saharan Africa'.[66] They also affirm that India has 'a unique cocktail of lethal divisions and disparities', and that few countries 'contend with such extreme inequalities in so many dimensions, including large economic inequalities as well as major disparities of caste, class and gender'.[67]

Stephanie Nolen, a Canadian reporter for the *Globe*, at the end of her five-year tenure in India, had many things to say about the country, including: '[I met] families of landless agricultural labourers who lived in windowless, low-roofed mud huts that would barely hold pigs. I saw a young couple sit down to their one meal that day: a pot of insect-speckled, four-day-old rice...In village after village, I met people living in conditions more grim, more horrifying than almost any I had seen in 20 years of reporting that had taken me from the AIDS-ravaged highlands of Lesotho to dust-baked southern Afghanistan.'[68] She goes on: 'There are many places—South Africa and Brazil, for example—where growth has been accompanied by an increase in inequality between the richest and the poorest. But in all those places, the poorest, at least some of them, have seen their own baseline improve. In India, the basic indicators of quality of life—child deaths, maternal mortality, access to clean water and sanitation, quality of housing—have not budged for a vast tranche of the populace. Seventy per cent of Indians still live on less than $2 a day. Less than 7 per cent graduate from high school.'[69] The 2011 census data confirms that 215 million people—nearly the size of India's middle class—have zero assets. They do not own even a bicycle or a radio.

There remain differences among scholars about whether India is indeed among the most unequal countries in the world, and whether and to what extent inequality has grown in the period of market-led globalization. A great deal depends on the measures of inequality we rely on; those that are in widest currency tend to rely on material elements of income, expenditure and wealth, and less on the fractures of gender and social inequalities which specially characterize India. A widely used measure of economic inequality within countries is the Gini coefficient in which 0 indicates complete equality and 100 indicates complete inequality.

India's wealth Gini was estimated to be 66.9 in 2000, compared to 66.0 in Bangladesh, 55.0 in China and 78.4 in Brazil.[70] Wealth distribution takes into account ownership of land holdings and capital and is therefore a better indicator than income distribution for assessing the ease with which the poor overcome poverty. In other words, the nature of economic inequality in India is one that carries within it much weaker potential for poor people to overcome their relative deprivations over time, compared to a country like China or even Bangladesh.

However, the Gini, like most international comparisons, focuses on material inequality of income or wealth, and not social inequality. An exception is the 2013 UNDP Human Development Report that contains an inequality index based on social indicators, which ranks India 135th out of 187 countries, at the lower end of the scale.[71] Given the starkly lower outcomes for minorities of gender, caste, tribe and religious identity, particularly in the areas of health and education, this is unsurprising.[72]

In a telling article in *The Indian Express*, political scientist Ashutosh Varshney observes that India's contemporary economic structure has three pillars. India has the fifth largest concentration of listed dollar billionaires (after the US and China); the third largest middle class (after China and the US); and the single largest concentration of the poor. 'The first two pillars,' he points out, 'are the principal drivers of economic growth. But the third pillar, not an economic driver, is a significant driver of politics. The bottom third of India does not get enough calories per day...Being underfed, the bottom third is also routinely sick. The hungry and the sick can't be productive workers, even if they want to. Markets can't help them all that much.'[73]

~

Both the outcome of and a driving engine for the increasing normalization of inequality and poverty are dramatically new ideas about what constitutes the 'good state'. When I entered the civil service in 1980, there was no doubt that the theory of good government was that its first duty was towards people of disadvantage—the poor, the hungry, the landless, the homeless, the sick, Dalits, tribal people, women, minorities, the disabled and so on—and that the primary yardstick of its success was how effectively it protected them from exploitation and violence, and ensured their dignified survival and progress. The practice of government did frequently fall substantially short of this goal, but this failure was at least acknowledged to be a deviation from the ideal. This changed dramatically from the early 1990s when, in the wake of liberalization and market reforms, the theory of government was completely turned on its head in just a few years. Now the main duty of governments was seen to be to create a 'market-friendly environment', to facilitate private investment and fuel market-led growth. This implied a de facto devaluation, if not a full-scale abandonment, of the goal of promoting social and economic equality. Even where there was some acknowledgement of the fact that market-led growth had its shortcomings, the argument, as social and political commentator Pratap Bhanu Mehta notes, was that 'at least it is more effective at reducing poverty' and that 'it is also creating the conditions for a more durable equality of opportunity, by providing the resources for things like education'.[74]

But, as Mehta points out, the kind of economic growth India has experienced since the 1990s has not dented old forms of social inequality and has, in fact, aggravated economic inequality. It is impossible to actually achieve greater equality without accepting that the poor will need more resources than the non-poor to achieve the same outcome as the non-poor. And yet, the new, market-fuelled imagination of good government continues to prevail—that its primary duties are not to the weak and the dispossessed but to big business. This has profoundly altered both the culture and practice of government at all levels. Many Directive Principles of State Policy in the Constitution have been quietly buried, especially those related to reducing inequality and preventing the concentration of wealth. The state has withdrawn from the 'commanding heights' of the economy, making way for large global private industry giants.

Successive governments have rapidly transferred vast reservoirs of natural resources like coal belts, minerals and natural gas to private industry in opaque ways, resulting in a succession of mega-scams and a pervasive culture of crony capitalism which dominates almost all political formations. This has replaced the older forms of cronyism—the politician–bureaucrat alliances that characterized the licence-permit raj.

A conscientious district officer, posted in one of the many tribal forested regions of India where vast coal and mineral reserves are located, would in the past have regarded her major duty as being to ensure that the local people, especially tribal communities, are not dispossessed unjustly or forcefully, and that forests are protected even as industry expands its footprint and profits. Today, she would be genuinely confused, because the dominant political mandate—in almost all regimes, but more openly and urgently in governments led by avowed champions of large private industry like Narendra Modi—is to ensure that industry acquires these private and forest lands as swiftly as possible, with the least impediments. The protection of the legitimate rights of local communities and the fragile ecology must be subordinated to the new project of nation-building, which has become synonymous with galloping profit for private enterprise.

There is open influence of large industry on decision-making in the government, particularly on matters related to the economy. Dreze and Sen point to 'revenues forgone'—through policies and processes designed to benefit the private sector—to the tune of ₹5,300 billion in 2011-12, amounting to 5 per cent of the GDP.[75] (These are not revenues actually earned, but estimations of what could have accrued to the public exchequer had certain taxes been imposed.) Of this, just exemptions on diamond and gold imports are estimated at ₹570 billion, twice the estimated additional cost of the National Food Security Law, but whereas there has been vocal outcry about the unaffordability of the Food Law, there is virtually no public debate, let alone protest, about the revenue benefits to influential groups. In Gujarat under Modi, as we shall see, unprecedented public funds at rates of interest as low as 0.1 per cent repayable after twenty years were given to Tata Motors to relocate their small car project to Gujarat from West Bengal, along with 1,100 acres of fertile land at ₹900 per square metre and exclusive power and water supply. Despite protest from farmers' groups, media attention and ensuing controversy, the state government repeated this public largesse to big business with Ford and then the Adani group, which was awarded land at shocking, rock-bottom rates of ₹1 to ₹32 per square metre.[76] Not surprisingly, Gujarat's investments in education and health in the same period were among the lowest in the country.

Contrary to the widely propagated belief that fighting inequality would damage the pace of economic growth, Oxfam points instead to evidence to the contrary that extremes of poverty are bad for growth. Robust and lasting growth requires the reduction of inequalities, which otherwise undermine the productivity and morale of working people, and limit the number of people who could participate in the market.[77]

Many people believe that inequality is an inevitable outcome of the surge of economic growth and globalized technological progress. The Oxfam report underlines instead that inequality 'is the product of deliberate policy choices', of which the two biggest drivers are market fundamentalism and the capture of power by economic elites.[78] Market fundamentalism, much in favour with successive Indian governments since the 1990s, insists that growth requires reduced government interventions and the further freeing up of markets. This militates against public investments in education, nutrition and health; labour protections and progressive taxation, the decline of which further fuel inequality. Economic elites buy political clout, which in turn purchases tax exemptions, land concessions, subsidies on electricity and water, and reduces public expenditure in the social sector. In India, the tax exemptions granted to corporates in every recent budget could substantially finance gaps in India's monetary requirement for education, nutrition and healthcare.

Popular philosopher Michael Sandel reminds us of the dangers of becoming not just a market economy but a market society, in which private profit determines important social choices.[79] Max Lawson of Oxfam recalls Sandel's lesson that 'the more that things are only valued by price, the more important wealth becomes. If this only applied to luxury goods—champagne or private yachts—then perhaps it would not matter that much. But when you can use your money to buy political influence, safety and security or superior education and healthcare—then the distribution of wealth becomes more and more important'.[80]

The ways to dam the surging tides of inequality are well known: raising and enforcing statutory wages, expanding taxation of the rich, enhancing public investments in education and health, enlarging social protection for the aged, infirm and disabled, and enhancing benefits for children. But in India, as in much of the world today, market fundamentalism and powerful economic elites still determine state priorities and resist policies aimed at creating a more equal world. The world therefore remains one in which poor people, women and members of disadvantaged communities remain in status quo, however hard they may toil.

~

Jean Dreze compiled an interesting count of key terms in Finance Minister Arun Jaitley's budget speech in July 2014, the first after the installation of the new government. Investment was mentioned thirty-four times and growth thirty-one times. In contrast, sanitation was mentioned three times; food security, nutrition and employment guarantee, twice each; and social security just once. Terms which never made it to the speech included child, pension (for the unorganized sector), the National Health Mission, Integrated Child Development Services (ICDS), school meals and maternity entitlements.[81]

A great deal of the movement of the Indian state away from high public investments in health, education and nutrition of its disadvantaged populations, and from redistributive taxation, since the 1990s, was driven by the 'Washington Consensus' of the World Bank and the International Monetary Fund (IMF). Therefore it is extraordinary that very recently, these very institutions have begun to acknowledge that they may have been wrong, and drastically so. 'In far too many countries the benefits of growth are being enjoyed by far too few people. This is not a recipe for stability and sustainability.'[82] These are not the words of a Left-wing ideologue, but of Christine Lagarde, managing director of the IMF.

She goes on, 'Let me be frank: in the past, economists have underestimated the importance of inequality. They have focused on economic growth, on the size of the pie rather than its distribution. Today, we are more keenly aware of the damage done by inequality. Put simply, a severely skewed income distribution harms the pace and sustainability of growth over the longer term. It leads to an economy of exclusion, and a wasteland of discarded potential.'[83] She compares rising inequality in the US and India. 'In the US, inequality is back to where it was before the Great Depression, and the richest 1 per cent captured 95 per cent of all income gains since 2009, while the bottom 90 per cent got poorer. In India, the net worth of the billionaire community increased twelvefold in 15 years, enough to eliminate absolute poverty in this country twice over.'[84] She argues that distribution of wealth matters, and contrary to prevailing economic orthodoxy until now, redistribution policies are not counterproductive for growth, 'because if you increase the income share of the poorest, it has a multiplying effect on growth...but this does not happen if you do so with the richest'.[85]

There is a steep slope of unlearning that the elite and the policy-makers they influence—across the world as much as in India—need to come down. The good state is not one that works only for markets, but one that redistributes resources and invests in education, healthcare, nutrition and social protection for the benefit of millions of people at disadvantage. A state that, in the immortal words of modern India's greatest son, Mahatma Gandhi, wipes every tear from every eye.

In 1947, one of the subcontinent's most loved poets, Faiz Ahmed Faiz, lamented in his iconic poem 'Yeh Daagh Daagh Ujala' the betrayals and disappointments of our Independence. As I write this sixty-seven years later, the anguish, loss and longing he gave words to still echo in many hearts:

> Yeh daagh daagh ujaalaa, ye shab-gazeeda sahar
> wo intezaar thaa jis kaa, ye wo sahar to naheen
> Yeh wo sahar to naheen jis ki aarzoo lekar
> chale the yaar ke mil jaayegi kaheen na kaheen
> falak ke dasht mein taaron ki aakhari manzil
> kaheen to hogaa shab-e-sust mauj kaa saahil
> kaheen to jaa ke rukegaa safinaa-e-gham-e-dil...

> This feeble blemished light, this dawn mangled by night,
> This is not the morning we had all so longed for,
> Not the dawn in quest of which those comrades
> Set out, believing that in heaven's great void
> Somewhere there must be the stars' last resting-place,
> Somewhere, the verge of night's slow-washing tide,
> Somewhere, a harbour for the ship of heartache...[86]

MANY EXILES OF INDIA'S POOR

Normalizing Poverty

Anthropologist Akhil Gupta poses a vexing question: why does a state whose legitimacy should derive from bettering the lives of the poor continue to allow between 250 and 427 million people to live in desperate poverty, and deny them food, shelter, clean water, sanitation and healthcare?[1] He suggests that poverty is a form of 'structural violence'; that there is little substantive difference between genocide and simply allowing poor people to die. He calculates conservatively that about 2 million people have died of malnutrition and preventable diseases every year in post-colonial India.[2] The total number of people who died in India's last major famine, the Great Bengal Famine of 1943, was three million.[3] The annual number of India's hidden, avoidable deaths dwarfs the annual loss of human life resulting from all natural disasters globally, estimated at about 300,000.[4]

The reason why the preventable deaths of these many millions year after year is not 'considered exceptional, a tragedy and a disgrace', according to Gupta, is the *normalization* of poverty. He illustrates this with an interview that P. Chidambaram, then finance minister, gave the BBC in 2007, in which he declared his confidence that by 2040 India would wipe out poverty.[5] What is noteworthy, firstly, is that the poverty of which he promised erasure is closer to near-starvation-level ultra-poverty, not poverty as defined by the global norm of $2 income per day; and, secondly, that he did not regard this timetable problematic in any way. The deputy chairperson of India's Planning Commission during the United Progressive Alliance (UPA) years, Montek Singh Ahluwalia, also went on record with the same time frame for urbanization.[6] Gupta observes: 'By the time the

Indian government plans to wipe out poverty, very few of the poorest people living today will still be alive. Such a statement makes sense...only against a backdrop in which high rates of poverty are taken as normal.'[7]

Indeed, for most people in India, just as there are hills, valleys, deserts, rivers and forests in this teeming, ancient country, there is also poverty. There has been poverty in the past, it exists in the present, and it will endure long into the foreseeable future. The social acceptability of letting people stay poor, therefore, is not considered problematic. Not providing food, clothing, shelter and healthcare to people in dire need is not seen as killing them. This social violence is rendered invisible so that poverty does not constitute a scandal and the preventable deaths of masses of the poor does not provoke soul-searching or public outrage.

This is Gupta's invaluable insight, one with which I am in complete agreement—although, incidentally, there are other elements in his book that I contest.

It explains, also, why there is resistance among people of relative privilege to legislation which aims to make access to food, shelter, education, work and healthcare the fundamental right of every Indian citizen. Or to efforts to implement policies of affirmative action for historically disadvantaged groups. There is, in reality, a hierarchy of citizenship under the thin veneer of equal citizenship guaranteed by the Indian Constitution. Full citizenship is enjoyed only by the middle and upper classes—and even within these groups, it is enjoyed much more fully by urban, upper-caste, Hindu, non-tribal, able-bodied, heterosexual men. Today, the neo-middle classes and the aspirational classes are now knocking on the doors of these dominant groups, hoping not to change the status quo but to share its privilege.

Social commentator Pratap Bhanu Mehta also speaks of normalizing poverty through stratagems of avoidance. He writes that the 'experience of inequality—and its associated indignities—is commonplace and visceral. To confront it fully is so existentially disturbing that it is often kept at bay by a whole series of interdictions and stratagems...'[8] He adds that 'the sheer scale of human suffering leads one to naturalise it. It is hard for individuals to bring about change. You don't mind change, but you just hope someone else, perhaps the state, brings it about with the least pain possible. In the meantime, the best you can do is erect barriers that allow you to escape your bad faith.'[9]

This culture of social avoidance, of 'invisibilizing' the poor, afflicts both people at large as well as the state. A government steering rapid market-led growth is impatient with reminders of the large unfinished business of mitigating the suffering of the huge underclass. It deploys many strategies. It counsels patience—markets take time but they will finally deliver to all; wait until 2040 and you will see the end of poverty. It is also in denial—people do not die of starvation, but of deficient health and carelessness; children are not malnourished because they lack food and clean water, or because their parents lack decent work, but because of irrational and foolish child-rearing practices; and that people are not impoverished and excluded because they have been oppressed, denied equal opportunities and have been subjected to violence, but because they are lazy, unenterprising, partial to drink, and reproductively irresponsible. For decades, all governments have reported that debt bondage has ended, despite extensive evidence of persisting 'un-freedoms' in employment in many sectors like agriculture, stone quarries and brick kilns, and the surge of what Jan Breman calls neo-bondage.[10] (These newer forms of bondage continue to barter debt for slavery-like conditions of work, even as the old feudal obligations of the employer to the bonded labourer and his family have declined.) The scandal of farmers' suicides is increasingly dealt with by instructions to police stations to refuse to register debt as the cause of suicide.[11] Similar devices are deployed to seriously under-record crimes of violence against women and girls, and almost completely blank out violence against sexual minorities.[12] All states report the end of the outlawed practice of manual scavenging—people of designated castes being employed to clean dry latrines and carry excreta in baskets on their heads—though thousands are forced to earn a living as scavengers across the country, many of them even as contract labour hired by the government-run Indian Railways.[13] The same casual disregard for human dignity makes municipalities continue to require men to clean sewers manually; many of whom die because city governments do not invest in technologies to ensure their safety.

Successive governments have also underestimated the extent of poverty, by fixing unconscionably low 'poverty-lines'. Such low interpretations have been a standard and recurring routine of planning and budgeting in this country for several decades. Many official committees have published voluminous and learned reports, difficult to understand by anyone who has no formal training in economics. Not surprisingly, debates about these reports and their conclusions remain confined largely to opaque academic literature; lay people accept them at face value. One of the more recent of such reports was the Tendulkar Committee Report, on the basis of which the Planning Commission submitted to the Supreme Court in 2011 that if a city dweller earns more than ₹32 a day and a villager ₹25, she is not

© *The Hindu*

poor.[14] This claim was so outlandish that it troubled even the middle classes.[15] The Planning Commission's affidavit to the court was widely reported; therefore, not just judges but ordinary citizens understood, for the first time, in simple language, how governments estimate poverty in India. This resulted in national outrage. John Harriss, in a paper, underlined the absurdity of this approach by citing this cartoon (p. 6) which had appeared in *The Hindu*.[16]

The crux of the problem goes back to how poverty is defined and measured, and where that phantom, the poverty line, is fixed. When the Supreme Court asked the government in 2011 to explain how it estimates the numbers of poverty-stricken households in the country, the Planning Commission replied that ₹25 and ₹32 a day for rural and urban households respectively, 'ensures the *adequacy* of actual private expenditure...on food, education and health'.[17] My core disagreement here relates to how the Tendulkar Committee, on whose report the Planning Commission bases its current estimates, calculated what expenditures are 'adequate' for a household to live on. There is an extraordinarily circular argument used to justify the computations. The committee first calculated how much households in urban areas spend on food, education and healthcare. They then went on to make the critical assumption that these median levels of expenditures for urban areas are 'adequate' for any household to live on with dignity. If you actually explain this assumption, it means, for instance, that the committee regards as adequate less than one rupee a day for health expenditure, barely enough to buy an aspirin. The word used by the committee to explain its assumption is 'normative'. In economics this means something that involves a value judgement, as opposed to matters of facts. In simple words, the learned committee, and the government which accepted its findings, makes the value judgement that such abysmally low expenditures are sufficient for the poor to live on.

The Rangarajan Committee report of June 2014 raised the urban poverty line to ₹47 per day per capita, and the rural poverty line to ₹32 a day, both significant increases. The numbers of the poor have thus swelled in its estimate, but the basic infirmities of the methods and calculus remain fundamentally unaltered.[18] Even working with the Rangarajan Committee figures, we would arrive at an incredibly callous idea of what constitutes a life of bare survival and very basic security and dignity. Let us take the case of a person earning ₹47 in an Indian city today—in Delhi, for example. She would earn ₹1,410 per month to live on. Rent, even for a single room in a slum would not be less that ₹1,000-2,000 a month. Therefore, if she spent half her earnings on any kind of roof over her head—even a mere plastic sheet—it would not get her a corner of a tiny shanty. She would have to make compromises on the quality and quantity of food each day; a kilogram of rice costs ₹20-30; a weeks' worth of vegetables, at least ₹200; milk would be completely unaffordable, at over ₹30 a litre, as would any form of animal protein. Further, what would she spend on travel, when a single bus ticket costs a minimum of ₹15 these days? How would she send her children to school? Even if fees are waived in government schools, there are many other costs. And, god forbid, if any of her family was to fall ill, she would have nothing to spend for healthcare which, even in overcrowded government hospitals, entails steep out-of-pocket expenses on drugs, diagnostics and hospitalization.

In 2011 I was part of a dharna outside the Planning Commission protesting this 'poverty line'. Young protesters had tried to pack into cardboard boxes—to be gifted to members of the Planning Commission—what they could buy with one day's income as dictated by the poverty line. The contents of these boxes—which the police ultimately prevented from reaching the members' hands—was instructive: one box had just two bus tickets costing ₹15 each; the cost of travel to and from work. This would leave nothing for food or any other essentials. Another box contained half a pencil, 25 grammes of beans, four pieces of okra, 25 grammes of flour, and one arm of a shirt. In another were stuffed 50 grammes of dal, half a shirt for a child, beans for one meal and 50 grammes of washing powder. One more box had half a bar of soap, half a banana, five pieces of okra, half a notebook, and half a toothbrush.[19]

It is this assumption—that it is all right for the poor to live with so little—that is also my problem with the estimates of declining poverty in India's high-growth years. On the one hand, middle-class aspirations of living levels 'adequate' for us have climbed to global standards, but we believe it is fine for the poor to subsist on cheap, rough food and foul drinking water, live on the streets or in sub-human urban slum housing, defecate in the open and have near-zero access to public healthcare. Only when people are able to access decent wages, pensions, maternity benefits, healthcare, sufficient food and every other necessity that an average middle-class person takes for granted, should they be deemed to have been freed from poverty. That is yet a very distant mirage for millions of Indians, including a vast number of those whom official planners and economists would want to count among the non-poor.

Jean Dreze and Amartya Sen remind us that among the consequences of 'great economic and social inequalities are major asymmetries in the opportunities that different sections of the population have to participate in democratic institutions'.[20] They give many examples of 'elitist biases' in public priorities and policy. These include 'the orientation of the news media (dominated by middle-class concerns), parliamentary debates (now heavily geared to business-oriented legislative reforms), the legal system (far from impartial between different classes), foreign policy (strongly influenced by the superpower aspirations of the Indian elite), and so on'.[21] They also note that 'the low priority attached to basic needs fits into this general pattern. India has world-class institutions of higher education (especially in fields such as management and engineering) side by side with ramshackle primary schools in disadvantaged areas. This contrasting pattern has much to do with the disproportionate influence of privileged classes on public policy. Similarly, the fact that the government spends about three times as much on "defence" as on healthcare is not unrelated to the lobbying powers of the military establishment, especially in comparison with those of underprivileged hospital patients'.[22]

India's poor face many exiles. They are exiled from the consciences of the people of privilege and wealth. They are exiled from our cinema, television and newspapers. They are exiled from the priorities of public expenditure and governments. They are exiled from debates in Parliament and offices. They are exiled from institutions that could offer them some basic security through education, healthcare and social security. And they are exiled from the hope that their children or their grandchildren will one day escape a life of back-breaking toil and social humiliation. This last is the most profound of their exiles.

Food and Rage

In the autumn of 2013, the Parliament passed a law to guarantee food security to every resident of the country. The Food Security Act legally binds the government to provide very cheap foodgrain to two-thirds of the country's households, school meals to all children in government and government-aided schools, feeding programmes for children below six years of age and pregnant women, and near-universal maternity entitlements.[23] For the state to become legally bound to undertake these many responsibilities for millions of its poor and malnourished citizens was a momentous development in the nation's history. However, I was stunned by the ferocity of upper-class rage that followed.

Almost every day for a week I found myself facing television cameras—and in front of anchors, many of whom would not bother to conceal their bias and their anger—trying to defend the idea of such a law. I argued why I believed it was imperative that there should be mandatory and enforceable duties for governments to provide food to ensure that all people—especially in a country that is home to a third of the world's hungry men, women and children—have access to sufficient food.[24] Tempers were even more frayed because, by chance, the consideration of the Food Bill in the Parliament coincided with a sharp decline in the value of the rupee. Commentators ran banner headlines saying 'the food bill famishes the rupee', suggesting—completely irrationally—that a law which was still being debated and had not yet been implemented had led to the crash of the rupee.[25]

I recall one particular debate in which an otherwise enlightened leading businesswoman of the country, whom on other occasions I have found reasonable and measured, asked in exasperation, 'Why should people who have worked hard to earn their wealth, and who have done nothing to damage the economy, be taxed to feed the poor?' I replied, 'You would agree that the poor also work hard, harder than the wealthy? And that they have done even less than the wealthy to harm the economy? And, further, that in a good society, people of wealth and means are happy to share with people who live with too little, so that they can have a more decent life?' I was surprised and dismayed that we had arrived at this point in our public debates, a point where we were interrogating on national television the most elementary principles of the social contract of community living in an unequal society.

The language used by commentators to describe the Food Security Act was telling. Based on where they stood on the political, economic and, indeed, ethical spectrum, they variously described it as a freebie, a dole, a hand-out, a give-away, a subsidy, an investment in human capital or a moral obligation. Industrialist Rahul Bajaj declared that 'all such give-aways are populist measures'.[26] Journalist Sadanand Dhume, in a particularly withering article in the *Wall Street Journal*, compared the 'harebrained' law to 'something cooked up by a Soviet planner on a bad day', derived from 'the limitless imagination' of 'a gaggle of activists and do-gooders' and 'leftist intellectuals who have never encountered a government handout they didn't like'.[27] Dhume's rage was spectacular, as he ranted against other rights-based welfare programmes, such as the 'expansive rural employment guarantee scheme' (which he described as a 'right to dig ditches') and a 'right to education policy that has sunk India's already abysmal math and reading scores (teachers aren't allowed to fail students)'.[28] He concluded: 'But even by these exalted standards, the food security bill marks a new low.'[29] Full disclosure here requires me to place on record that as a member of the National Advisory Council of the former prime minister, Manmohan Singh, which was chaired by Sonia Gandhi, I convened the working group that drafted the early versions of the Food Bill. Therefore, Dhume's scathing indictment of people he described as 'do-gooders' and 'leftist intellectuals' was directed squarely at people like me.

Author and columnist Gurcharan Das described the law as 'bribes for votes', suggesting that 'giving away virtually free food and power, waiving loans to farmers, creating "make work" jobs, as the UPA government has been doing, has undermined the social contract' and 'contributed to inflation in our country'.[30] Yashwant Sinha, finance minister in the previous National Democratic Alliance government, dubbed it 'senseless welfarism'.[31]

The basic premise of such visceral critiques was that a morally and intellectually bankrupt government was desperately using the honest taxpayers' hard-earned money to bribe impoverished voters with freebies. Economist Pranab Bardhan, one of the minority of prominent economists who spoke out against this dominant pro-market discourse, protested this description of public moneys being spent on anti-poverty programmes as the 'politics of dole'. 'Most of the subsidies of the Indian government,' he pointed out, 'are actually to the business class and middle and upper classes, but that is not regarded as dole. Giving help to the poor for education, health, food or employment is called dole, and to me, this is really tendentious. This serves to distract from the huge amount of subsidies and handouts of the government to better-off people in the form of petroleum subsidies, diesel, fertilizer, LPG and several other subsidies. There are estimates that suggest that the amount of subsidies for better-off people is about three to four times more than the money the government spends on anti-poverty programmes.'[32]

Indeed, every time a middle-class person buys a cooking-gas cylinder, or fills up the tank of a diesel-guzzling SUV, or switches on an air-conditioner, he or she consumes more subsidy than a poor homemaker will take home when she buys her monthly entitlements of subsidized grain under the Food Security Act. The additional cost of the Food Bill, over existing schemes of subsidized foodgrain distribution, was ₹250 billion; in the year 2012-13 the petroleum subsidy was estimated at ₹968.8 billion, and the subsidy for fertilizers was at ₹659.74 billion.³³ (The bulk of the subsidized fertilizer is picked up by rich farmers, because small and marginal farmers own just 37 per cent of farm land; much of this land is rain-fed and those who farm it cannot afford chemical fertilizers.)³⁴

Commentators who are profoundly dismayed by the Food Security Act often take pains to point out that they do not deny that poor people in India deserve a better deal. But they are convinced that the law is disastrously ill-conceived. Much of their criticism focuses on the public distribution system (PDS) segment of the law that guarantees cheap rice, wheat and millets to 66 per cent of the population—around 800 million people. They do not explain their rejection of many of the other, equally significant elements of the law, such as near-universal maternity entitlements, universal feeding for young children and pregnant women, and school meals.

They also do not consider the critiques of those of us who welcome the law as a long-delayed, potentially beneficial statute, but are contrarily concerned that it does not go far enough. Left critics of the law are convinced that subsidized grain under the law should be universally available to all who seek it, and not restricted to 66 per cent of households as prescribed in the law, because when the state targets only those whom it identifies as poor, it tends to leave out in practice those who are most in need. Beneficiaries cannot access foodgrains through the PDS without a ration card, which automatically disqualifies millions of migrant labourers who have no proof of residence outside their state of domicile, as well as homeless people. Earlier drafts contained provisions for the feeding of the destitute and soup kitchens for migrants and homeless persons, but these were deleted in the final law, and we find a paradoxical law on food rights which eliminates provisions for those who are most vulnerable to starvation. Further, nutrition is related not just to the amount of food one eats, but how nutritious this food is. For this, some nutrition activists and professionals wanted to include dals— which supply non-meat based proteins—in the PDS package. Nutrition also depends on how much of the food you eat your body can absorb. If a person, especially a child, is exposed to foul water and unsanitary conditions, this leads to repeated infections; therefore, the food the child consumes cannot be absorbed; for this reason, some would have wanted the act to guarantee not just food but also nutrition security. In summary, Left-leaning food and nutrition activists would have liked the Food Security Act to be even more expansive than it is.

On the other hand, critics of even the watered-down law which was ultimately passed, like the economists Jagdish Bhagwati—who launched a very visible and excessively personalized attack on Amartya Sen for his advocacy of the food law—and Arvind Panagariya believe that the answer to hunger is not for the state to feed people, but to stimulate economic growth.[35] They argue that if large public resources are expended on food subsidies, it will impact investment and growth negatively, damaging the prospect of accelerated growth, increased job creation and people's capacity to earn enough to buy (or grow) their own food. Panagariya explains: 'Our differences with Sen also extend to how the government should deliver nutrition, education and health to the citizenry… Sen firmly believes that the state must directly deliver food, employment, education and health through its elaborate bureaucratic machinery. So he passionately advocates the food security bill and employment guarantee scheme and rejects cash transfers, vehemently opposes education vouchers in favour of government-run schools and slams the door on private health services. Under Track-II reforms, we advocate an approach that empowers beneficiaries instead of public providers. We argue that revenues must be redistributed to the beneficiaries through cash, school vouchers and health insurance, allowing them to decide whether they want to buy food, education and health from private or public providers.'[36]

David Pilling of the *Financial Times* pithily summarized their dispute: 'Bhagwati accused Sen of prioritising redistribution in poor countries such as India. Bhagwati argued that only by generating sufficient growth to begin with would there be enough wealth to spread around. "Sen puts the cart before the horse; and the cart is a dilapidated jalopy!" he wrote last year in *Mint* magazine. Sen, he said, paid lip-service to the idea of growth "much like an anti-Semite would claim that Jews are among his best friends!".'[37]

Those who regard the Food Security Act as profligate populism point also to the high cost of the law. The measure is attacked for being 'unaffordable'; what the *Economic Times* describes as 'money-guzzling': an estimated annual burden of ₹1,250 billion, they argue, will inflate deficits and fuel inflation.[38] These figures, as I argued in an article in *Mint*, need to be taken with a pinch of salt.[39] First, what is relevant is not the total cost but the marginal increase in public expenditure that the Food Bill entails. This amounts to ₹250 billion, which seems a reasonable expansion if we are convinced that what the law offers is a useful public investment. Second, we can manage public deficits if we are willing to tax wealthy people more. India's tax to gross domestic product (GDP) ratio is lower than that of most industrialized market economies, as well as other developing countries like Brazil. Further, it is excessively reliant on indirect instead of direct taxes, which burdens the poor disproportionately.

We also need to weigh the costs of not making much larger public investments in the nutrition, health and education of the poor. These are the enormous effects of hunger, preventable diseases and deaths on the morale and productivity of several hundred million working people and growing children. Economist Sabina Alkire, in an article published in *The Hindu*, offers a telling global comparison.[40] She points out that India 'has a higher proportion of stunted children than nearly any other country on earth, yet spends half the proportion of GDP that lower, middle-income Asian countries spend on social protection and less than one-fifth of what high-income countries in Asia spend'.[41] In lower-middle-income countries, social-protection spending is 3.4 per cent of the GDP. India's is a mere half of that at 1.7 per cent and even this low level is reached largely because of the rural jobs guarantee programme that ensures 100 days of paid work to all poor households in villages. The average for social welfare expenses in upper-middle-income countries is 4 per cent of the GDP and 10.2 per cent of the GDP for high-income countries. Japan spends 19.2 per cent and China, 5.4 per cent. Even Singapore spends more than twice as much as India, at 3.5 per cent of its GDP. In the words of Jean Dreze, the 'mythology of social policy' fostered by a section of India's media hides the truth that 'if anything, India is among the world champions of social underspending'.[42]

Further, it is not right to assume that the pot of public revenues is fixed and given—that if we spend more on food, we will either have to pull back on other important expenditures or raise deficits. There *is* a third option, and that is to raise our tax revenue. In 2012-13, the revenue lost because of exemptions on customs and excise was worth 5.7 per cent of the GDP.[43] UNESCO estimates that if 20 per cent of this had been spent on education, the sector would have received an extra US $22.5 billion in 2013, an increase of 40 per cent over what the government was then spending.[44] India's former finance minister Chidambaram has himself admitted that, 'In 2011-12, the tax-GDP ratio was 5.5 per cent for direct taxes and 4.4 per cent for indirect taxes. These ratios *are one of the lowest for any large developing country* and will not garner adequate resources for inclusive and sustainable development' (italics mine).[45] But, as pointed out by one of India's most insightful commentators on poverty and the agrarian crisis, Palagummi Sainath, Chidambaram did nothing to correct that by raising revenue, and instead balanced his books only by curbing expenditures in the social sector.[46] We need to demand greater integrity in India's efforts at taxation, rather than a moratorium on more public spending for the poor.

Exemptions on corporate taxes, excise and customs duty in 2011-12 and 2012-13 amount to over ₹5,000 billion each year, and this is sought to be justified as being necessary for wealth and job creation.[47] However, as we shall see later in this volume, this rationale for offering tax holidays to the super-rich is not borne out by the overwhelming evidence from high-growth years, which is that this has been a period of virtually jobless growth. This fact underlines the principle that there is no substitute for public investment to enhance the livelihoods of masses of poor people. There is also an urgent need to enhance the integrity of India's tax efforts. All of this confirms that there is considerable scope for taxing the rich to ensure the investments required by India's large population of disadvantaged people.

The third cluster of criticisms of the Food Security Act is that it is not implementable; that state administrations lack the capacity to actually deliver the promises of the law, as even official studies confirm enormous leakages of grains, provided to the public under the PDS scheme, into the black market. There is no doubt that runaway corruption and inefficiencies greatly cripple the state's capacity. But it is important to remember that both corruption and its debilitating impacts on governance are not restricted to programmes for the poor. They apply also to defence deals, for instance, or to urban infrastructure development (as the CWG Games scandal demonstrated), or to the allocation of natural resources like coal mines. But there is no one saying that, because of corruption, we should place an embargo on defence purchases, or stop developing our cities, or cease mining coal. Then why should we selectively apply corruption as a reason to veto investment in programmes for the poor?

And, as Jean Dreze again reminds us, 'The critical importance of mass education for economic development and the quality of life is one of the most robust findings of economic research. From Kerala to Bangladesh, simple public health interventions have brought down mortality and fertility rates. India's midday meal programme has well-documented effects on school attendance, child nutrition and even pupil achievements. Social security pensions, meagre as they are, bring some relief in the harsh lives of millions of widowed, elderly or disabled persons. The public distribution system has become an invaluable source of economic security for poor households, not just in showcase states like Tamil Nadu but even in states like Bihar and Jharkhand where it used to be non-functional. Of course, there is some waste in the social sector, just as there is much waste in (say) universities. In both cases, the lesson is not to dismantle the system but to improve it—there is plenty of evidence that this can be done.'[48]

Gurcharan Das feels that cheap food will disincentivize work.[49] But the belief that impoverished people will work less if their bellies are fuller is deeply problematic in many ways. It fails to acknowledge both the hard toil—often in lands distant from their homes, with little social protection—that characterizes the lives of millions of India's poor, and the fact that like all of us, the poor aim for much more than a full stomach. Poor people are not another species who, merely if they have more rotis or rice in their empty stomachs, will stop working because they have no desire for a better life for their children, or to build some savings and acquire a decent house instead of a hovel. Das fails to recognize that poor people have the same dreams as anyone else, including him, you and me.

It is not my suggestion that the answer to mass hunger is that the state feeds people in perpetuity. Far from it. We need a range of measures to tackle the causes of poverty and end hunger, and these include stimulating economic growth, but many other steps as well, including public measures to accelerate sustainable agricultural growth, ensure sanitation, clean water, healthcare, social and gender equity, and decent and assured employment, among much else. But while all of this unfolds, it is unacceptable for people to have to live with hunger and its consequences. Therefore, the state must provide food for as long as it is necessary.

Moreover, spending on food is not a populist dole but an investment in India's greatest economic resource—its vast young population who are in the productive age group. It is imperative for consolidating the gains of India's demographic dividend. Every second child in India is malnourished, which means that nearly every second young adult who enters India's workforce does not develop to his or her full potential. What hope can there be, then, for not just equitable but also sustained economic growth?

Also, with the state ensuring food security, the savings on the cost of cereals would place more disposable income in people's hands, and this enhanced spending by millions would stimulate growth from the grassroots. And we also need to factor in the spin-off benefits to the largest group of food-insecure people who are, ironically, those who grow food: our small famers, land tenants and farm workers. The assurance that the state would purchase foodgrain to distribute to two-thirds of India's households would create a publicly guaranteed, assured market for millions of these food growers, and would thereby protect them from food insecurity.

I have also often stuck my neck out to try to make a moral case for the Food Security Act. In an article in the *Economic and Political Weekly*, I wrote that in a country that allows great suffering and inequality to continue, mainly because of the lack of outrage among the middle and upper classes and the lawmakers over such a tragic state of affairs, the greatest imperative for a food security law is to breach our collective indifference.[50] Editor and columnist Siddhartha Singh specifically countered my moral position in an article in the *Mint*, speaking of the fragility of moral reasoning and arguing that rationality imposes strict limits on morality. 'While the government will have acted in a moral manner, how moral is it for officials to steal food meant for the poor? If one examines the entire distribution chain, one "moral" act by the government will unleash immoral behaviour by many.'[51] Gurcharan Das also made a similar argument.[52] I am not claiming that the law will impose a perfect morality on public actors. But it will establish both a legal and a moral benchmark; one that states how suffering associated with hunger should be utterly unacceptable.

Even those of us who are convinced about the efficacy of markets to ultimately end poverty should not fail to see that, at least in the medium term, there is no substitute for large state investments to ensure that all people have work, food, education and healthcare.

Growth cannot be sustained much longer on the thin shoulders of hungry people, of unprotected migrant labour, or those enfeebled by poor health or held back by lack of educational opportunities. There is a great gaping hole in our collective soul which we must mend.

Hiding the Poor

In a country of global aspirations, the persistence of extreme and widespread poverty causes embarrassment, leading to official knee-jerk instincts to hide the poverty-stricken. This was literally the strategy adopted during the Commonwealth Games in Delhi in 2010.

Driving to work each morning, I pass by some slums. In those untidily laid out, makeshift homes, with mud walls and roofs of plastic or tin sheets, live an assortment of waste pickers, domestic workers, street vendors, and casual, daily-wage workers. Electric wires are strung dangerously across the settlement, and black sludge gathers in open drains. I see men and women bathing alternately under open public taps. Half-clad children with begrimed faces and laughing eyes spill on to the pavement and play. Some, with plastic bags larger than their bodies slung over thin shoulders, pick waste. Few go to school.

These are not unusual sights in Delhi, or any other Indian metropolis. But a week before the Commonwealth Games began, I was startled to find one morning that I could no longer see the slums. Instead, I saw purple and indigo posters erected on bamboo scaffoldings, with pictures of a cheerful tiger cub, the mascot of the Commonwealth Games. These were strategically—and unsubtly—placed to hide the slums from view. I felt a deep sense of shame.

The official efforts to cleanse the city of its poor had begun much earlier. In the run-up to the Games, the government demolished 350 slum settlements. One of the colonial Anti-Beggary Laws, which criminalizes destitution, was deployed to send thousands of people living on the streets of Delhi to beggars' homes. This law, as recounted in a later chapter, gives little opportunity for the accused to defend themselves, and forces them to spend up to ten years hidden in filthy prison-like poor-houses. Impatient to banish from sight the city's most wretched people, the government set up eight mobile courts in which magistrates would be driven to locations where people would allegedly beg, and many would be rounded up and immediately sentenced by a judge, who was simultaneously witness, prosecutor and adjudicator.

As the dates of the Games drew closer, the police rounded up homeless people in camps in public parks, again camouflaged by festive posters, assuring them that they would be housed and fed there for the duration of the Games. But they were then herded into trucks and forced on to packed trains to leave the city, their palms marked with official purple stamps which do not wash off for several days. If they returned, these people were warned, they would be despatched to jails or beggars' homes. Police also descended on slum shanties and 'advised' residents to leave the city at least until 17 October, when the Games would end. Only those with 'identity cards' would be 'allowed' to remain, and panic-stricken people formed serpentine lines in front of police stations, vainly seeking some kind of proof of identity. Many finally left the city, forgoing precious wages and spending their sparse savings on travel, desperate to avoid police custody.

This official shrouding of the poor from sight is not unusual. In preparation for the 'Vibrant Gujarat' summit in Ahmedabad, in 2015, for which potential global investors and wealthy non-resident Indians gathered in large numbers, the municipal corporation again hid the slums which the overseas guests were likely to drive by on their way to the summit venue, with large hoardings celebrating the achievements of the state government. Earlier, when the Chinese President Xi Jinping visited the same city in 2014, an energetic drive was undertaken to 'cover-up' slums located near the Sabarmati Ashram with green curtains.[53]

The government is ashamed of the poor ostensibly because they are 'dirty and unhygienic'. But, as I shall observe in the next section, living the way they do is not a choice for the poor. It is the direct outcome of the failure of governments to provide them affordable, legally sanctioned housing—or set up hostels for the working-class poor—and to extend public services like sewerage, piped water supply and drainage to indigent settlements. Innumerable studies show that slums are less effectively served by local bodies. Around a third of India's slums have no access to tap water or drainage. The figures are much higher for unrecognized slums, and slums in poor states like Bihar, Uttar Pradesh and Madhya Pradesh. Nine out of ten non-notified slums in Bihar, Madhya Pradesh and Rajasthan and eight out of ten in Chhattisgarh and Odisha have no latrines. The shame then is not that the poor are unclean, but that governments have forced them to be so. The urban poor and slum dwellers, who constitute between 25 and 65 per cent of the population in most Indian cities, rarely occupy more than 3 to 5 per cent of land; yet the dominant middle-class sentiment is that they are crowding the city; they must be driven out and their houses demolished.

Governments claim that the poor need to be ejected not just to clean up the city, but also to make the city safe both from terror-related and 'regular' crimes. Once on a night round on the streets, I saw a posse of policemen thrashing sleeping homeless people with their batons. I asked a policeman why he was beating them. 'We have instructions,' he told me, 'to flush terrorists out of the city.' I replied, 'I have never heard of a terrorist who was homeless. Have you? Where would he hide his RDX and his bombs? If you have to randomly look for terrorists, there is greater chance that you will find them sleeping in a five-star hotel than on the streets!' And there is no evidence, either, to show that homeless people commit other crimes more than any other segment of the population.

When I hear glib talk of building 'smart cities' across India, I know things will get much worse for those who are economically disadvantaged. The 'smart city' or 'world-class' city of the official and middle-class imagination is one that is cleansed of its poor. The middle class aspires to a city in which the poor are ejected from their slum homes, barred from begging at traffic lights and from vending on the streets, and slum and street children are prevented from playing in public parks. The poor are even being pushed out from public roads. City roads are increasingly perilous for the cyclist or the pedestrian. For people without private transport, daily travel frequently involves crowded, slow-moving, intermittent buses, or a daily risk to one's life. (The Delhi Metro is one bright glimmer in this hopeless story.) The share of buses, as a proportion of all registered vehicles has decreased from 11.1 per cent in 1951 to 1.1 per cent in 2011.[54] On the other hand, just between 1991 and 2011, registered motor vehicles have increased from twenty-one million to 142 million and two-wheelers from fourteen million to 102 million.[55]

Ironically, as our cities get wealthier—at the top, of course—the number of those who fall hopelessly and invisibly through the cracks increases. There is no space today for the construction of a different, more compassionate imagination of a 'world-class' city. Of a city that includes its disadvantaged residents with respect and justice. Of a city that banishes poverty, not the poor.

What Would You Do With ₹2,000?

In the winter of 2013, close to 500 aged women and men, nearly all destitute and from rural backgrounds, camped for a month in Delhi barely a couple of kilometres from Parliament. They were demanding a decent pension for all old people, something that those people who retire in the formal sector take for granted.

But few heard or heeded their voices; certainly no lawmakers did. In the din of the election campaign that soon followed, they were even more completely forgotten. In the development model proposed by the elected government, the feeble voices of the elderly have become even more marginal, even though people over sixty years old constitute 7 per cent of the population.[56]

Their demand for universal old-age pensions was not as charity but their due as unorganized workers. Unorganized workers grow food; they are engaged in manufacture; and they build, clean and provide services for the general population in a myriad different ways. In the years between 2000 and 2010, the annual growth rate was more than 7.5 per cent, but the annual growth of employment in the formal sector was less than 0.3 per cent.[57] Therefore, the greatest contribution to India's economic growth came from workers in the unorganized sector.

Formal-sector workers are assured a pension of around half their last pay drawn, indexed for inflation. Approximately 93 per cent of the workers in India are employed in the informal sector, and 99 per cent of them have no pension arrangements. The only pensions that they can access are the meagre ones provided by the Centre.

The Central government pension scheme, launched only in the mid-90s, provides a monthly payment of an incredibly meagre ₹200, and that, too, to only one out of five of those above the age of sixty and ₹500 to those above eighty years of age.[58, 59] Even this small cash support is restricted to those older persons who are *officially* identified as being below the poverty line (BPL), and BPL lists are notorious everywhere for leaving out a large number of those who are very poor.

This central pension amount is topped up unevenly by various states. Even this paltry amount is delivered irregularly in most states. Central and state governments together spend ₹143.7 billion annually on pensions for unorganized workers, who form 93 per cent of the workforce.[60] There are large variations on a state-by-state basis. Interestingly, Gujarat spends the least per capita on pensions (just ₹31) compared to Rajasthan's high of ₹400, a telling disparity within their development models.[61] In contrast, for those 5 per cent of workers who are in formal government employment, annual pension spending is ₹1661.69 billion.[62] The Centre for Budget and Governance Accountability calculates that public spending, annually, per old person, in the unorganized sector is ₹124 rupees as against ₹19,051 per government servant for government pensions.[63] In other words, governments spend around 153 times more on pension per capita in the organized public sector compared to the unorganized sector.

~

More gravely, the lists of poor households compiled by the government ignore poverty *within* families. Studies estimate that nearly three out of four aged women and one out of three old men are fully dependent on others for sustenance. Aged persons within families who are entirely dependent on the support of their older children widely suffer humiliation, neglect and abuse.

We often assume that our greatest dangers are from strangers on dark streets or from violent men who might break into our houses. The sad truth is that the highest perils of brutal and persistent violence actually lurk within the intimate spaces of our homes, from those to whom we are closest.

Little illustrates this with more poignancy and immediacy than a twelve-city study conducted by Helpage India.[64] Its stunning principal finding was that *every second* elderly person suffers abuse within their families.

The abuse elders reported were common across social classes and cities, although there were differences between cities. Bangalore and Nagpur reported the highest instances of elders being abused and Delhi and Kanpur the least. Four out of ten old people testified to verbal abuse, three to neglect, and a third to disrespect. One out of five recounted enduring such abuse almost daily, a third around once a week, and a fifth every month. Six out of ten reported against their daughters-in-law and an almost equal number reported against their sons. However, only 7 per cent of the people surveyed reported against their daughters, and no one said that their grandchildren were abusive.

Nearly half the old people interviewed in the study identified one common reason for their abuse at the hands of their children: that they must depend economically on them.

Motilal, an ageing plumber in East Delhi reported being unable to earn enough for his basic needs even after performing backbreaking labour. At the same time, his son denied him adequate food and money for medicines. Mansi, an unlettered widow in the same city, was given only two chapattis a day by her daughter-in-law, and her son refused money for her cataract operation. A flower-seller in Bangalore, Ramanna and his wife, moved in with their son as his health declined and he could no longer bear the daily rigours of street vending. But both old people were forced to work all day, 'worse than domestic servants', and even their simple needs were refused.

In another irony, nearly a third of the elderly people surveyed felt that their abuse did not stem from their economic dependence on their children, but from the dependence of their adult children, mostly sons, on their small incomes.

Ramiah in Bangalore had a reasonable income by way of rent from his house, but this income became the bone of contention between him and his son and daughter-in-law. And since he was forced to spend a major part of his money on medical care, he was harassed constantly.

Mohinder from Delhi owned a shop, which gave him a decent income, as well as the house in which his two sons lived. But the elder son would still harass him for money to spend on alcohol, and was rude and disrespectful. A Railways pensioner in Chennai, Manilingam, could not handle constant abuse from his daughter-in-law and chose to move out and live a lonely, separate life. But many old people cannot bring themselves to take this terminal step: they report that even more than their economic dependence, it is their emotional dependence on their children, and most of all their love for their grandchildren which binds them to their sons' homes, despite the abuse and neglect they suffer. These were the ties which weighed down Lata, a widow in Nagpur incessantly abused by her daughter-in-law, whenever she considered leaving her son's home to live by herself.

In many villages, I have seen desperately poor households migrating for work in the cities, leaving their old parents behind to beg or starve to death. I try not to judge them, and their parents mostly do not as well, because of the desperation of their children's want.

Our self-image in India is of a people who lay less store on material pursuits and uphold the institution of the family. The

Helpage report is an unhappy reminder of how distant from this are the realities of changing India. The melancholy stories which the Helpage report brings to us are of desperate want and material greed, of economic dependence and disputes over property and income resulting in the growing abuse and neglect of aged people within our homes.

~

Health activist Vandana Prasad undertook a health survey of around a hundred of the old people who had gathered in Delhi in the winter of 2013 to demand a decent pension for all old people. She found their average weight was only 46.7 kilogrammes; 39 per cent were significantly underweight and 13.7 per cent were in conditions not merely of 'thinness', but starvation. These were old people fit enough to participate in the harsh, weeks-long winter demonstration; she warned that those left behind in the villages could be even worse off.[65]

Formal-sector workers receive pensions of around half their last pay drawn. Using this as the yardstick—the government's own—the indigent old people who gathered at Jantar Mantar in the winter of 2013 under the banner of Pension Parishad demanded a universal pension equivalent to half the statutory minimum wages of unorganized workers, which is roughly ₹2,000 a month. ₹2,000, incidentally, is a fraction of what many of us in the middle classes would spend in an evening outing with the family, watching a film in a multiplex, and then some dinner afterwards.

Talking to some of them about what they would do if they actually got the pension was both educative and heart-breaking. Suhagan Devi of Muzaffarpur, Bihar, said, 'I'll use the money to get treatment for my filariasis, because of which my son keeps me out of my house.' A lady sitting next to her nodded and added, simply, 'If we get this pension, our children will take care of us.'

One old couple told us, 'Out of this ₹2,000, we'll spend money on food, medicines, rent… And if we are able to save some money then we'll set aside ₹100 every month for our cremation.' Others made even more specific plans: 'If we get this money, we won't sit idle, we'll buy a goat, and that goat over a period of time will become a source of income and we'll live a better life.'

For some who were fighting disability and disease, the ₹2,000 would only make bare survival possible. 'I'm handicapped, so I'll spend this money on arrangements for me to move around. And I can afford the medicines I need.' An old woman said, 'We are a family of seven, my husband is a cancer patient; my son is disabled and his wife is a TB patient. Even basic needs like food cost much more than ₹2,000 rupees every month. We are under heavy debt. I don't know what I'll do with these ₹2,000.' An elderly widow said, 'I have two sons. One of them is deaf and mute and the other is a drunkard. Food, clothes, water—all of it costs much more than ₹2,000.' Another put things in perspective: 'Maybe we can survive on ₹2,000. But who can live a life of dignity on this money?' And yet, even for this she would have to sit on a dharna far from home, braving the winter chill.

But one old woman was more expansive in her day-dream, 'If I get this pension, I'll use an auto-rickshaw to travel to hospital and get my medicines. I'll be able to eat good food. This much money will satiate my soul. And most importantly, I won't be a burden on my family anymore.'

On the last day of the dharna, an old widow from a village in Bihar looked very distraught. Shankar, a compassionate senior activist helping the elderly on their dharna, comforted her. 'Don't worry, amma, you will be back in your village soon.'

'That is what I am worried about, son,' she replied. 'Here in the dharna at least I ate three meals every day. How will I fill my stomach when I'm back in my village?'

Rainbows in the Dust

Freezing winter nights on the streets of Delhi. On pavements, side streets, road dividers, under bridges, in subways, shop fronts and lofts of staircases, in railway platforms and bus stations, one can dimly make out the huddled forms of sleeping children. If one cared to count, the numbers on any night would cross fifty thousand; children who live, work, play, eat, fall sick, fight and love, despair and dream, all under the open sky. They are typically reluctant to speak candidly of their lives to adult strangers, because they have encountered few adults who they can trust. But when they do, the stories they have to tell are harrowing.

~

Raju Das, a boy barely a teenager, sleeps with other homeless children around a water tank in the New Delhi Railway Station. For most of the years since he left his home in Shantipur, a small town in the Kamrup district of Assam, this has been his only home.

Like many children who flee their families to escape intolerable abuse, Raju is unwilling to talk about precisely what drove him from his home. But one night, at the age of seven, he walked away decisively from his truck-driving father, mother and two younger brothers, never to return. It was an act of incredible courage for a child so young, echoed and repeated in the lives of tens of thousands of street children who decide at very young ages to bravely escape violence and abuse in their homes by fending for themselves, at whatever cost.

Raju walked along the railway track near his home and boarded the first train that he could. He alighted in Alipurduar in Cooch Behar. He had ₹200 which he had stolen when he ran away from home, and bought food on the railway platform. He lingered there, and watched children, some older, some younger than himself, earning money by selling water to passengers in plastic bottles which they filled at the public taps in the station. Their clothes were grimy;

often oversized shorts or trousers held up by little more than a string tied around their thin waists. They seemed carefree, with ready laughter, and they walked with a swagger.

Raju's money quickly ran out, so he decided to try his hand at selling bottled water. Some of the boys in the station beat him up but an older boy, their leader, restrained them and said that he was like one of them. They then welcomed him into the gang, and taught him their trade. The bottles sold at ₹5 each, and he easily earned around ₹50 a day. At that time, around 2007, a child living on the streets could earn up to ₹150 a day in Delhi, recycling waste. At night, they slept on the platform, and three or four boys would share a sheet to cover themselves. They gave their savings to the stall owners for safe keeping. There was no place to store their clothes, so they would wear the same clothes until they became thoroughly filthy, throw them away, and buy a fresh set.

A couple of months later, some of the boys in the gang decided to travel to Delhi; for the adventure, and because the earnings were better in the metropolis. Raju decided on impulse to accompany them. They first took a train to Howrah, and then to Delhi.

Before long, Raju learnt to earn his living by rag-picking, starting out in the early hours of the morning with a huge sack often bigger than his own small frame, with separate pockets for bits of paper, cloth, plastic pieces, scraps of iron and other trash. At the end of the day, he would sell his daily foraging to wholesale waste traders near the Sheila Cinema Bridge, located very close to New Delhi Railway Station, who, in turn, would sell to recycling units.

Some of Raju's friends would also take up other seasonal occupations. They would work with caterers in the wedding season; they would reserve places for passengers in trains during rush hours; they would black-market cinema tickets; they would clean commercial and private vehicles, even trains; they would work as vendors for tea and food stalls, or as apprentices in roadside automobile repair garages; they would even carry loads as porters or work as shoeshine boys. Contrary to common prejudice, only one out of ten children on the street begs for a living, and most of these are very young. Even fewer beg as part of organized gangs.

Raju and his friends would mostly buy food from itinerant food stalls. On bad days, some would eat at dargahs or temples, and younger children would even forage for food in rubbish heaps. Not surprisingly, they would frequently fall sick. Illness is a time of trial, because no government hospital will admit these urchins in filthy clothes. But they do not go hungry in these times, because others in their gang invariably buy them food and take care of them.

Raju and his friends don't have designated playgrounds, but have always found ways of having fun. Street entrepreneurs set up makeshift video parlours, especially on lanes where they sell their rags and waste. These are nothing more than spaces marked off by faded saris, hung as curtains, with a television set. For ₹5, one can watch as many films as one likes. The parlours are packed with the rejects of the city—boys like Raju and his gang, lonely migrant workers, rickshaw pullers, porters, construction workers—raptly watching Hindi movies interspersed with pornographic shorts.

Raju, like most street children, was introduced to the easy but deadly escape from pain and loneliness offered by soft drugs early in his days on the streets of Delhi. Paint thinners are readily available at any stationery shop for ₹25 a bottle. Shopkeepers know that the children who buy these chemicals are not using them for art, but do not hesitate to sell the narcotic to the street urchins who flock to their stores. Two bottles are enough for a day for one child. They soak a rag and inhale the fumes of the paint thinner, and it transports them to a world free from hurt and violence. But it also destroys their lungs, rendering them vulnerable to tuberculosis. Many children graduate to hard drugs like smack, but Raju steered himself away. He knew that for those who succumb to smack, it is virtually the end of the road.

I asked Raju who was the finest adult he knew. He did not hesitate. It was Sachin-bhai, a pickpocket operating in the New Delhi Railway Station. I must confess to have been startled by his choice. Raju explained: 'He protects us from older bullies, buys medicines for us when we are sick, and discourages us when we inhale solution and other drugs.' 'I was on this platform since I was younger than you,' Sachin-bhai would tell children like Raju. 'I know this world. If you take to drugs, you will never escape to a better life. You will die here. I will not let this happen to you.'

A few years later, Raju told me that Sachin-bhai was dead, probably from drug overuse.

There are winter nights when all of us drive past the huddled forms of children sleeping on the streets without a thought, let alone a word of love or dreams for the children's future. I realize then that Raju was probably right when he chose the pick-pocket over all of us.

~

A sullied hand tugs insistently at your clothes. You turn to see a little arm outstretched—at once peremptory and tentative—a small head of tousled, matted hair, patchy and pallid skin coated with many days of unwashed dirt, bare sprightly feet, and a loose, faded frock almost slipping off the little girl's slender shoulders. On those shoulders rest the burdens of survival of a large destitute family. And yet what shines through the grime, like a miracle, is the most beautiful pair of sparkling black eyes.

There are fewer girls on the streets of Delhi than boys, but they must negotiate the metropolis at its predatory worst, every day. Unlike the majority of street boys, like Raju, who courageously negotiate lives alone on the streets, rebelling against abuse and neglect in their homes by severing links with their families, most girls we encounter on the streets of Delhi continue to live on pavements or in slums *with* families, who send them out to earn money to support their siblings and parents. This they do stoically and bravely, but with much less of the reckless joyfulness that street boys craft out of their hard-won freedom. In their early years, girls mostly beg. As they grow older, the majority rag-pick in waste dumps and markets, earning more than a hundred rupees daily. Often bullied and molested, they learn to shout swear words and grapple with their fists. Many chew tobacco or sniff adhesive solutions. And, either through their parents or on their own, many soon learn ways to furtively earn larger sums from older men who seek casual sex with children.

In 2006, when we first began work with homeless children, we met a few such girls outside Hanuman Mandir in Delhi, not far from Yamuna Pushta, an embankment along the Yamuna in Delhi adjoining the Nigambodh cremation grounds, home to thousands of homeless people.

Farah, delicate and fragile underneath her grubby exterior, was barely ten years old. She came from a family of migrants from a village near Kolkata. She could not hear or speak, nor could her younger sister. Their father was addicted to smack and would spend his time in a drugged haze. His two daughters would beg, with wordless insistence, at the Hanuman Mandir where many homeless children and women garther for food and alms. Devotees at the temple distribute bananas and other fruit; others bring cooked kulchas and kachoris with halwa; many give away sweetmeats as prasad. On festival days or in memory of loved ones, some even distribute clothes. But the day's work for the sisters would not be complete until they had collected a few coins from the worshippers at the temple. Their mother would sit on a side lane, and the girls would run up to her periodically, deposit their collections, and run back for more.

A group of volunteers were sitting outside the temple gates, talking to some of the girls, when all at once Farah tensed, visibly wilted, and tried to hide behind one of the young women volunteers. An older girl, Shabnam, ran up and fiercely grabbed the shirt of a disabled old man who was walking past. He, too, was mute, but he angrily gesticulated and threatened the girls. Shabnam protectively embraced the younger Farah. Gradually, the sordid tale unfolded.

Farah's mother had sold her to this old man. He would rape her regularly and, in return, give money to the family. We located

Farah's mother and angrily urged her to let us take the girl under our care. She declined sadly. 'I love my daughter. But if I let her go, how will the family live? He will not allow us to beg here, and we will all starve.' While we tried to get the police to rescue the girl, I struggled to not judge the utterly defeated older woman, but could not quite succeed.

Shabnam, Farah's protector, and her family migrated years ago from Bihar to Yamuna Pushta, from where they were banished to Bawana by the government. Each day, the family of six would take a two-hour, crowded bus ride, costing ten rupees each way, to reach the Yamuna Pushta area. Their father used to ply a rickshaw in Chandni Chowk but after they were banned by the traffic police, he was unemployed.

~

Sita was fourteen, and would often be detained by the local police who had her labelled as an incorrigible thief. Her family had been sending her out to earn for years together, and would usually beat her if she returned with less than ₹150 each evening. Usually, this was not difficult, as she was an expert rag-picker. But she was not just her family's principal bread earner, she was also a child, and on some days she and her friends lose track of time playing games in public parks. On her way back, fearing punishment at home, she would break into homes and steals whatever she could sell on the black market. On other days, Sita would find a man who wants sex—men all too easily found. She would take the money in advance, and they would quickly conclude their liaison in a dark corner of a park. While there were times when she ran away with the john's money, such luck was rare.

Many of the girls living on the street have single mothers. Rehana's husband left her a decade earlier, and her sons had grown up to become vagabonds. Her two daughters would keep the hearth going with their earnings from rag-picking. To add tragedy to destitution, the man whom Rehana lived with killed one of her sons in a fit of rage when she refused to part with her life's savings of ₹4,000. The man was in in jail and Rehana was surviving on the pavements of Bawana.

Astha's father also left home, leaving behind six children: three brothers and three sisters. Her mother started living with another man, who would drink away all the money that the children brought home.

Seema's blind mother had begged all her life but heroically taken her five daughters through elementary school. Proud of her Class 7-level education, Seema would insist on speaking with us in broken English. But most girls pounding the city's streets are not so fortunate. Every single girl we have met on the streets longs to study, but this will be possible only if the government opens hundreds of residential schools for them. After a great deal of lobbying, the Delhi government finally agreed to work with us to open three such residential schools for street children since 2006, and forty-five across the country. Soon after, many more homeless mothers offered to send their children into our care than we have space for, ready to sacrifice the earnings of their girls so that they live safe and happy childhoods illuminated by learning. Within a year of care and protection, most girls blossom extraordinarily—they heal, forgive, bridge their lost years of schooling, enter regular schools, and are often at the head of their classes.

~

Thousands of children like Raju, Shabnam, Sita, Astha and Seema, in every city in India, are forced to make the rough and cruel streets their home. They are plucky, yet profoundly vulnerable, survivors. They defy and endure, usually with other children, the harsh adult world of the streets. Like miniature adults, they negotiate with spirit and audacity the brutalized life of pavements, public parks, railway and bus stations, and waste dumps.

Many children and youth of the street enjoy no protection from adults, especially at an age when they are at their most vulnerable. A study conducted in 2007 found that about 34 per cent of the children surveyed lived away from their families.[66] Other children and youth on the street have families in the city, on the street or in slums. However, because of the extreme destitution and vulnerability of single homeless mothers, or because parents use drugs or are otherwise unable to care for their children, they are left largely to their own devices. There are no official surveys of the numbers of children living on the streets of the country, but their numbers are likely to be close to two million.[67]

A pioneer in work with street children, Sister Cyril Mooney, called them 'rainbow children'—for the colour and verve of their fragile little lives. I find this name suits them well because while rainbows are enchanting, they can never be held in the palm of one's hand. These children are free spirits and hate being kept cooped up, or supervised closely, or constantly corrected. Therefore, they need intelligent and understanding guidance from adults that comes only with love. But this is rare, and most state and many non-state efforts instead choose to lock these children up in jail-like, loveless institutions which crush their spirits.

And while they are often extremely resilient, they carry within themselves, always, a well of emptiness because the significant adults in their lives have failed them. These children build shells around themselves which they don't allow others easy access to.

Children living on the street see violence, betrayal by adults, death and more suffering than many of us experience in an entire lifetime, and survive it all.

~

A film that affectionately celebrated the spirit of the boys and girls living on our city streets—*Slumdog Millionaire*—unexpectedly caught the imagination of the entire world.

More than two hundred of the sort of children who played such important roles in the movie had, by the time of the film's release in Delhi, become an important part of my own life and those of my young colleagues. We met them over many months on the streets—on pavements, under bridges, in market and temple courtyards, at traffic signals—and, over time, they agreed to leave the streets behind them and begin a new life with us in three homes we run for them in Delhi. It was in the company some of these children that I wanted to see the film.

One evening, I went to a cinema in west Delhi with thirty of these boys. The children were scrubbed, they were in their best clothes, and were very excited. Before the film started, we gathered in the yard outside the cinema and I explained to them why we were watching the screening. A foreigner had made a film about their lives, I said, therefore thought we would enjoy seeing it together.

As the film unfolded on the screen, they watched rapt, between mouthfuls of popcorn and samosas. We had a couple of rows to ourselves and others in the audience were curious as one child would run across and lean his head against my shoulder, and then another. Some children became pensive, saddened by memories, but most seemed infected by the film's celebratory mood which lauded their resilience and hope in the hardest of times.

Later, when we discussed the film, what most boys said they liked best was how the younger street children had been portrayed in the film; their cheeky attitude and the ways in which the film affirmed that they could never be crushed by the grimmest of trials. A favourite moment for many was the one in which one child suspends another from the roof of a running train with a rope, to steal food through a window. For another, it was the defiant retort of the children even as they were being thrown out of the speeding train: 'What do they think? Is this train their fathers' property?' Yet another recalled with laughter how, even when trapped by a sinister beggars' mafia, a boy refused to sing unless the leader gave him fifty rupees.

The train sequence reminded me of a conversation with a group of boys in Hanuman Mandir in Delhi. They had decided to take a vacation in Hardwar, and said that they had travelled by train, without buying a ticket, dodging the ticket checker throughout the journey. One said he had a poem to describe their situation. 'Aana free! Jana free! Pakde gaye to khana free!' (We go free of charge! We return free of charge! If we get caught, we get food free of charge [in jail]!).

They thus survive the most brutal violence and want which the streets inflict on them, mainly with the weapons of their laughter, comradeship and nimble feet. *Slumdog Millionaire* has many flaws, both as a film and as social documentation; it did not ring true in many of its literal portrayals, and even less in its political and social analysis; but it is completely truthful in one thing, its re-creation of the spirit of the children who make the streets their home.

Hands, Heads and Hearts

Otherwise well-meaning friends often say to my young colleagues and I: 'We appreciate your efforts to educate these street children in the best schools you can find for them. But, realistically, you must plan to get them into vocational courses as soon as possible. After all, in the end, they will be working with their hands.'

I try not to be prickly, but I cannot stop myself from responding, 'The day *you* decide to put your own children into vocational classes instead of institutions of formal learning, I will do the same with mine.' I fully and deeply respect the dignity of labour, but bristle at the assumption that merely because children are born into situations of disadvantage, they *must* be taught to work with their hands, and children born to privilege will *naturally* learn to work with their heads. This is, in essence, the idea of caste which endures robustly, often just below the surface, in modernizing India. I believe that every child must be taught to work with her hands *and* her head, and indeed, also with her heart. We need to learn to respect labour, the way Japan, for instance, treats its master craftspersons as national treasures. But we cannot persist with the accepted wisdom that where children are born must determine where they will eventually work as adults: as labourers in fields, on construction sites, in quarries or factory floors; or sit behind a desk, in a science laboratory, a corporate boardroom, a hospital ward, or in front of a group of students.

The same acceptance of dual standards for rich and poor children also underlies debates on abolishing child labour. While children with middle-class upbringing attend school, others, not so fortunate, herd cattle; weave carpets; forage on city waste-heaps; beg at traffic lights; wait at roadside eateries; labour on farms and in factories, in brick kilns and coal mines, in brothels and in our homes. What is remarkable is not just our collective acceptance of such diverging destinies of children merely because of where they are born. I find astounding that the law—the Child Labour [Prohibition and Regulation] Act, 1986—in India, until very recently, permitted most children of any age to work, except in a relatively small band of prohibited 'hazardous' occupations, such as in foundries, fireworks factories, mines and kilns.[68] Even these limited prohibitions were rarely enforced; no more than a few thousand prosecutions every year, and even fewer convictions were reported in the entire country.

Legislation has been unsuccessful in stopping child labour even in hazardous industries. A third of all acknowledged child workers are found to be in hazardous occupations. Around half the total number of children working in hazardous occupations are employed in the paan, bidi, and cigarette industries, in construction, and as domestic help.[69] Seventy-two per cent of recorded child workers are in farming and constitute almost 9 per cent of all agricultural workers.[70] These children work long hours on farms and face the harmful effects of pesticides and other chemicals. Many girls are subject to the hazards of physical and sexual abuse at work even at ages as young as ten or twelve.

The 2011 census reported that over four million children between the ages of five and fourteen were engaged in various forms of work.[71] According to World Bank data, in 2010, an estimated 2.1 per cent of all female children between seven to fourteen years of age were in employment as were 2.8 per cent of all male children in the same age bracket.[72] If individuals up to eighteen years old are counted as children, as they should be, then the proportion of children at work would be even higher.[73]

Child-rights activists believe that the actual numbers are still much larger, because every child who is not in school is a hidden child worker—rearing younger siblings, tending the home, or supplementing the family's income. These are called 'nowhere children', and the India Human Development Report 2011 estimates that there are four times as many nowhere children as compared to recognized child workers.[74] The National Sample Survey Organisation (NSSO) data for 2007-08 shows that working and nowhere children still constitute 15.4 per cent of children in the under-fourteen age group.[75]

There are encouraging reports of growing numbers of children in school, and declining child workers during the last decade.[76] But we need to view these figures with caution, both because enrolment figures are grossly swollen by children who never attend school, and also because there is growing evidence of the informalization of the work force concurrent with rapid economic growth.[77] Work is often sub-contracted to home-based workers by big companies to evade regulations which protect labour, and this work is transferred also to the children working from home; as a consequence, children may be inducted into the labour force at ages as low as five or six years. Such child labour is invisible to the census enumerator.

When, inspired by child-rights activists, I proposed a total legal ban on child labour as a member of the National Advisory Council, I had expected wide and ready support from the government. But I was surprised by the kinds of strenuous arguments put forward in favour of legally permitting the children of the poor to work instead of being in schools and at play. The official explanation of why it is acceptable for children to work—summarized in the Gurupadaswamy Committee Report, 1979—is that 'as long as poverty continued, it would be difficult to totally eliminate child labour and hence, any attempt to abolish it through legal recourse would not be a practical proposition'.[78] I find that this 'pragmatism' continues to dominate the government's stand on child labour. Even many progressive activists and thinkers are uneasy about a complete ban on children being allowed to enter the labour force because they see few options for an impoverished family who would rather send their children out to earn than to school.

There is no doubt that desperation drives indigent parents to send their children to work at a young age. Under no circumstances, therefore, should any law penalize parents for the hopeless cycles of hunger, unemployment and debt in which they are trapped. However, this cannot be an alibi for the state, freeing it from its duty to ensure that children are not at work but in school. I learnt from child-rights activists, like my friend Shantha Sinha, that child labour is not just the outcome of poverty but also its cause. It is only by escaping work and, instead, entering and remaining in school that a child has any hope of escaping the inequality, drudgery and want that her parents and grandparents suffered. Labour takes a permanent toll on a child's body, mind and spirit. Without education, chances are high that a landless agricultural worker's child will remain a labourer, and a rag-picker's child, a rag-picker. And the experience in districts where child labour is effectively eliminated is that when child workers are unavailable, adults are employed instead, getting higher wages than children, and the entire family is better off than when children worked. Myron Weiner, in his 1991 book *The Child and the State in India*, has made a similar point.[79] He uses examples from Scotland, China and Africa to show that the expansion of education to excluded groups does not *follow* higher incomes of poor families, as is often assumed, but actually precedes it. The state does not have to wait for the rise of households out of poverty to ensure that people send their children to school; on the contrary, the extension of education to such households creates conditions in which families are able to escape the poverty-trap.

Some suggest that child labour is necessary to enable artisanal, farming and fishing communities to teach their skills to their next generation. Children can learn these traditional trades even after school hours, or during vacations. But stretched beyond a point, this argument can become a disguised rationalization of the caste system. Why should the child of a weaver, ironsmith or paddy cultivator necessarily be taught to follow the vocation of his or her parents when he or she grows into adulthood? The arguments of dignity of labour are again valid only if middle-class children are taught, equally, to work with their hands.

An even more worrying defence of child work mounted by government departments is that banning child labour would make several Indian exports uncompetitive, because adults would have to be paid more for the same work and children are more productive with their 'nimble fingers'. I have heard EU government officials openly admit openly that they support programmes against child labour to make European products, which do not employ children, more competitive. Empirically, only a small proportion of Indian exports employ child labour; the largest majority of children who are employed work in agriculture. Even if they did not, surely India's economic growth cannot be built on the frail shoulders of the youngest segment of our population.

~

I have been privileged enough to work directly with a few hundred children who, until only a few years earlier, begged in temples and dargahs, recycled trash from trains or waste dumps, or picked pockets. While we knocked on the doors of many schools to get them admitted, only a few opened up to us. These children excel among their classmates today. They sing, dance, play, and enjoy the childhood long denied to them. When these children go 'home' for Eid or Diwali to be with their parents, it means mostly going back to sleep beside their parents on the streets. But when they grow into adulthood, I am certain that they will not beg, or rag-pick, or sleep on city pavements, as their parents did and still do. This is why child labour must be fully outlawed. It is not tenable for the Indian middle classes to maintain that whereas they will purchase the best schooling and recreation which money can buy for their own children, a childhood of toil is sufficient for the children of the poor.

Not sufficient also—as I shall argue in the next chapter—are poorly functioning, poorly staffed, poorly resourced and discriminatory schools.

The Eklavyas of New India

I have never worked as a full-time teacher, but many times over my adult life, I have enjoyed the privilege of teaching young people. I instructed young recruits to the Indian Administrative Service (IAS) and other higher civil services in the mid-90s; and, since 2002, after I left the IAS, graduate students in my alma mater, St Stephen's College, Delhi; post-graduate students in IIM Ahmedabad and Jamia Millia; and my young students who spent much of their childhoods on city streets and in children's jails. Over these many years, as I came to know these children closely, to love them and to believe in them, I began to observe clearly that at the core there is very little intrinsic difference between those three groups of young people—those who were selected to the elite civil services, those studying in the country's most prestigious institutions of higher learning, and my children who learnt life on mean city streets. They have the same range of talents, temperaments and possibilities. I can only conclude that were they given the same life chances, *there would be no difference between them.*

In the epic Mahabharat, Eklavya, a tribal boy, learns to become a finer archer than even Arjun, the most accomplished archer of the five Pandava princes, merely by secretly observing the guru, Dronacharya, as he trains the princes in the use of weapons. But when Eklavya reveals himself to pay homage to his teacher, he is commanded by Dronacharya to sacrifice his right thumb, so that he may never surpass any prince. This story, which brings to focus the savagery of caste barriers, continues to have painful relevance in contemporary India where caste still determines a child's destiny, and where elite schools stubbornly resist entry to children born in disadvantaged families. Eklavya is a painfully contemporary story.

The richest families send their children overseas, to the world's best schools and universities. Next come the children who are raised in elite, exclusive private schools. Children from the lower middle class and poorer urban areas can, at best, aspire to municipal schools, which typically have far inferior outcomes. This bars them from admission to better colleges, and they cannot afford the fees of private universities. Rural children may be crammed into unequipped classrooms, with one or two teachers—often absent, poorly trained and monitored. And, of course, the homeless, migrant, working and disabled child may never see the inside of a school, and will remain trapped in the hopeless poverty of her parents.

Outcomes in the lesser well-off schools, not surprisingly, are dismal and seem to be getting worse. For instance, the number of children in Class 8 who could perform a simple problem of division has dropped from 68.3 per cent in 2010 to 44.1 per cent in 2014.[80] Math learning levels have been declining in every state, except Tamil Nadu, Andhra Pradesh and Karnataka. English learning has either remained unchanged or gotten worse; between 2009 and 2014, the number of children in Class 5 who can read simple sentences of about five words each is practically unchanged. In 2009, over 60 per cent of the children surveyed could read sentences in Class 8, which dropped to 44 per cent in 2014.[81] A study of learning outcomes in urban municipal schools by Pratham and UNESCO found that approximately 44 per cent children in Class 3 and 32 per cent in Class 4 could not even recognize numbers; less than 1 per cent in Class 3 could perform simple division.[82]

Education, therefore, has profoundly failed to open up avenues of social mobility. Instead, the education systems in this land actually closely mirror the vast inequalities of our society and reinforce them further. If you are born into a Dalit, tribal or Muslim household, or are disabled, there are much higher chances than you will not enter school, or if you do, you will face discrimination and drop out early; you will also have much fewer chances than other children to reach high school and enter college. If you are a girl among all of these groups, your chances would be even slimmer. Among children between the ages of six to thirteen from Dalit, tribal and Muslim households, 5.96, 5.9 and 7.67 per cent respectively are out of school, compared to 2.67 per cent for the remaining population.[83] In other words, children from these socially deprived communities are two to three times more likely to never enter school compared to other children. Likewise, fewer children from these groups complete schooling: 56 per cent of Dalit and 70.9 per cent of tribal children drop out of school by Class 10 compared to 49.3 per cent for the overall population.[84]

The Sachar Committee—appointed in 2005 by the prime minister, Manmohan Singh, to map the socio-economic status of Muslims in India—found that 25 per cent of Muslim children aged six to fourteen had either never attended school or had dropped out.[85] UNESCO reports that in 2005, 28 per cent of Muslim children had less than two years of schooling; 33 per cent had less than four years; and the mean years of schooling was also lowest for Muslims—6.11 years against an average, for all children, of 7.29 years.[86] A later investigation by the principal author of the Sachar Committee Report, Abusaleh Shariff, found that for the period between 2004-05 and 2009-10, improvement in rural literacy, compared to urban, has been higher for all social groups, except Muslim OBCs. Matriculation levels overall were also lowest amongst Muslims—years after the Sachar Committee recommendations were made.[87]

The Centre for Equity Studies (CES) brings out the 'India Exclusion Report' each year and, in the first report for 2013, we chose to focus a major segment on school education. Many writers collaborated to piece together a profoundly disturbing document.[88] In 2009, the Parliament passed the Right to Free and Compulsory Education Act 2009—hereafter called the RTE 2009—guaranteeing every child the right to free and compulsory education up to the age of fourteen years, and laid down standards for every public provided school. The moral case for such a public duty lay in the grim and dark reality of millions of children being deprived of education due to a myriad reasons, and the inequities and poor-quality education which dogged those socially and economically deprived children who did join school but could not remain in it. The CES report establishes why India's children need the right not just to free and compulsory but also *equal* education.

The report notes that although it is officially reported today that enrolment in elementary schools is nearly 100 per cent, sizeable numbers of children who are completely invisible to the state remain neglected. UNESCO reports that in 2011, 1.674 million children were out of school, as were 20.270 million adolescents in the same year.[89, 90] The 'India Exclusion Report' notes how the invisibility of children out of school is particularly remarkable for one category: urban street children who are physically visible to policy makers every day. Additionally, an estimated thirteen million childhoods are stolen in farms and factories, eateries and domestic workplaces. There are 100 million migrant workers, and many children who migrate with their families suffer interrupted and abruptly terminated schooling. In conflict zones, children often cannot attend school because school buildings are occupied by security forces, or because there is general insecurity, or because parents have lost their lives or have disappeared. In some cases, children have also been recruited as soldiers. Children of sex workers or of parents living with HIV-AIDS and leprosy, as well as children from nomadic and de-notified tribes also face severe barriers to schooling.

The educational accomplishments—including literacy, school enrolment and retention—of women and girls, Dalit, tribal and

Muslim children, and children with disabilities, have all improved over the last decade, but all still remain well behind the general population. Fewer, but still not insignificant, numbers of these children never enter school. But for those who do, as the report indicates, the experience is often one of humiliation and discouragement. Among our many failures as a people, the most unconscionable is the way we treat our children. Large numbers battle homelessness, stigma, violence and hate, and many more continue to perform labour meant for adults instead of attending school. But as our report demonstrates, even among those who do enter school, millions of children, born into disadvantaged castes or stigmatized faiths, or with disabilities, suffer humiliation and neglect within the classroom. Unequal India will also change only when our classrooms become more egalitarian and humane.

Dalit children report that they are made to sit separately during classes or during meals and are compelled by their teachers to perform humiliating chores like cleaning toilets; they also report disrespect and unjust punishment at the hands of their teachers. The 'India Exclusion Report' finds: 'With regard to SC or ST children, teachers also allude that they do not need to study well and attain good marks, because the government has already made reservation provisions for them in education and employment. Teachers perpetuate caste-based discrimination by questioning the value of education for children from "low" castes who they (teachers) believe will move on in life only to undertake menial, traditional caste-based occupations. Teachers stereotype Muslim students as children who will gravitate towards violence and terrorism in the future and it is therefore believed that investment in education for them is worthless. A similar attitude affects children with disability. Government expenditure on children with special needs, teacher time and learning for them is all considered to be an undue burden on the State. Principals and teachers often complain that disabled children are taking away the space and opportunity of others.'[91]

The CES report observes that teachers tend not to look at classroom diversity as a learning resource, but as a limitation and distraction and a drain on teachers' energy and resources. For children who spend a greater part of the day in school, experiences of discrimination, neglect, active biases or prejudices and ill-treatment from teachers and peers often result in them dropping out or frequently absenting themselves out of fear or psychological hurt. In an atmosphere where their identity, based on caste, religion, tribe, gender, or disability, is mocked at, the school, instead of a nurturing space, becomes a place that is feared. 'Often the internalization of prejudices affects the psyche of children to arouse feelings of self-blame and to limit their participation, aspirations and potential, thereby denying them the equal chance at growing diversely at par with others. The perception that they lack opportunities…acutely constrain their opportunities and agency. This translates into unequal learning achievements and social capital in future and further interlocks with the marginalised backgrounds of their parents, who are often unable to assist them in coping academically while simultaneously striving to earn a livelihood.'[92]

Nagraj Manjule's 2013 Marathi film *Fandry*, which means Wild Pig, should be compulsory viewing in every school and college. No other motion picture I have seen evokes the torment and shame of growing up as a member of a stigmatized caste in contemporary India as poignantly as *Fandry* does. A teenaged boy, Jabya, belongs to a Dalit family which has been forced over generations into the despised caste vocation of rounding up wild pigs. Jabya develops a secret love for an upper-caste classmate. He watches her in wordless devotion as she studies at her bench in class, or walks the dusty pathways of the village. She is not deliberately unkind to him but, as a boy from a lower caste, he hardly exists in her consciousness. The boy still hopes that one day she will return his affections, and dreams endlessly of it. But in a heart-rending climax, she joins her classmates in mocking Jabya when he is forced to help his family capture some wild pigs in the village. As his fellow students watch him undertake work which they regard as most unclean and humiliating, he painfully realizes that his country may give him the right to study today alongside other children, but the stubborn inequities of caste still mark him as separate and lowly because of the accident of his birth.

In a study of rural untouchability in ten states a few years ago, in which I worked closely with four leading social scientists and several Dalit field activists, we found that in one in three and, sometimes, even one in two rural schools, even today, Dalit children are forced to sit separately at the back of the class, and eat from separate plates in separate lines from other children.[93] Some teachers even ask these children to clean school floors and toilets, chores never assigned to upper-caste children. *Fandry* offers, in Jabya's longing and ultimate humiliation, an affecting glimpse of what transpires in the hearts and minds of children who study beside children marked as socially superior because of their caste.

'Despite the gravely adverse consequences,' the writers of the report conclude, 'the resilience of school children across the country, to brave all odds and walk or cycle to school needs to be applauded and encouraged by initiating immediate reform.'[94] Marathi Dalit poet Waman Kardak writes:

Send my boy to school
Lord and Master
I tell you
Send my boy to school

We may be terribly poor
Famine may knock at our door
I'll see that he gets to school
Send my boy to school...

If my clothes are torn, what do I care?
My boy must never go bare
What use do I have for a jewel?
Send my boy to school...[95]

~

In the summer of 2013, twenty-two children in Chhapra in rural Bihar died after eating school meals in a government school, an event which briefly shook the public conscience. But the incident could have happened almost anywhere in the countryside, and probably does, but invisibly, on a smaller scale. For many reasons, this was a tragedy waiting to happen. This calamity was the outcome of something much larger than mere local neglect by junior officials as many commentators described it. It was the result of how poorly welfare programmes for India's poor, even our children, are organized, resourced and monitored.

The primary school in question did not have premises of its own and was being run in a local government office building. There was no store, therefore rations for school meals could not be purchased in bulk and safely stored. There were just two teachers to teach five classes of children; one was on leave, and the only one holding fort was a low-paid, unqualified para-teacher. She purchased the provisions required for each day's meals from a local store. A container in which cooking oil was stored had possibly been used earlier to keep insecticides.

It was not she who was culpable for the children's tragic deaths. She was doing her best in a system which places no value on her and the indigent children she taught and fed.

School meals across the country are grossly under-resourced. Allocations for cooking costs have not been enhanced despite runaway food and fuel inflation in recent years. Many schools have not been invested with the basic infrastructure for cooking and storage, utensils, a clean eating space and potable water. Cooking staff is poorly paid. For a programme as scattered as this, the most effective systems of monitoring are always those which are also decentralized. We need systems of social audits, we need to hear the voices of children, and effective systems of regular monitoring by parent committees, school management committees and local panchayats.

Much of this would entail additional public money, but also far greater political prioritization, administrative will and the willingness to be accountable. But we should clamour to muster both the resources and will required for this, because what can be a higher priority for public investment and attention than the health and futures of our children? All our children.

~

There are many who believe that education will reform best if the public sector gives way to private schooling. Even poor families are opting for private schools because public schools just do not function. But a truly egalitarian educational system can be built only with a common school system in which children in a neighbourhood—rich or poor—attend the same publicly funded school. Private education will only enhance inequality. This is the experience globally. Max Lawson of Oxfam observes, 'The World Bank Group has in the past been a great champion of universal free primary education, but it has now started to get much more excited about private education instead, promoting this in Pakistan and elsewhere. Yet UNESCO research shows that for the poorest 20 per cent of families in Pakistan, sending all children to a private school would cost approximately 127 per cent of that household's income.'[96] The situation is not very different in India.

This does not mean that as long as they exist, private schools should remain exempted from social responsibilities to children whose parents cannot afford their fees (or children without parents to take care of them). Although the RTE 2009 fittingly placed primary responsibility for the right to free and compulsory education on the public sector, it also legislated for modest duties for private schools, by reserving 25 per cent of their seats at entry level for disadvantaged children (reducing the earlier proposal of 50 per cent), for which they would be compensated by the public exchequer. Only 17 per cent schools today are private, and even among these, only around 2 per cent are elite, therefore the numbers of deprived children who would enter privileged schools is microscopic. Private schools can and should never replace public schooling, and that is not the intention of RTE 2009. The small supplementary role assigned to private schools cannot and should not in any way free the state from its obligation to provide high quality education to all children.

The momentous import of the reservation of seats for disadvantaged children in elite private schools lies elsewhere, that it could create, for the first time in India's millennia-long history of structured inequality, spaces where children of the rich and the poor study, eat, play and grow together. In a country which for centuries has blocked educational opportunities to millions of children only because of the chance of their birth (which some describe as 'ovarian roulette'), this recent piece of innovative legislation offers a rare opportunity for belated civilizational atonement to millions of India's Eklavyas. Ending the educational apartheid of centuries by democratizing our classrooms with the entry of children of disadvantage to elite private schools could mark a watershed in our country's history, in the way that desegregating schools did in the US during the Civil Rights movement of the 1960s.

The arguments which were put forward against the desegregation of schools in America in 1960s strangely—even eerily—mirror what we hear in India today in the opposition to this reservation of seats in educational institutions. Some decry the encroachment of the government into the private sector; some say that economically or racially disadvantaged students would simply not be able to cope in an integrated environment and should be kept apart; others make the most arrogant argument of all, that poor children will dilute the 'merit' of elite schools.

Instead of accepting and embracing the modest social responsibility entrusted to them by the law, India's elite schools employed a battery of the country's most expensive lawyers to challenge, in the Supreme Court, the constitutional validity of the law which mandated compulsory admission of deprived children.[97] They argued that it is the state's duty to provide public services like education to the disadvantaged, and it should not shift its burden to private enterprises.

They claimed that the government had no right to interfere in enterprises in which it did not invest, implying that there is no difference between selling soap and selling education.

The law commits governments to reimburse private schools for every disadvantaged child, at an estimated ₹10,000-20,000 per child per year. The elite private schools claimed that these amounts are too low, and would force them to raise fees, lower standards or reduce profits. They claimed that their right to preserve the 'special' (read 'exclusive') character of their schools would be violated if they were forced to admit children from poor and disadvantaged backgrounds.

In its affidavit to the Supreme Court, the union government eloquently explained the rationale of the new law. A private school is not just a for-profit 'occupation'. As an education centre, even if unaided, it is integral to its social responsibility to contribute to 'the development of more heterogeneous and democratic classrooms, where children of all social groups and categories learn to interact with each other, develop respect for diversity and differences, and move towards building a more tolerant and humane society'.[98] It affirmed evidence that heterogeneous classrooms provide better learning to all children, both privileged and disadvantaged.

The entry of children of disadvantage, the managements of private school also alleged, would dilute quality because of the poor merit of these children, suggesting that underprivileged children are intrinsically less meritorious. But how do they compare the merit of a well-nourished, protected child of wealthy, highly educated parents, employing expensive tutors; and a girl who grows up in an unsanitary and cramped slum, both her parents non-literate daily-wage workers, with nowhere to study and no one to help her with her homework, bathing under an open tap, and with the additional burdens of cooking, fetching water and taking care of her younger siblings?

Another perverse argument offered by elite schools is that admitting poor children into privileged schools would harm the *disadvantaged* child. The principal of a south Mumbai school questioned how a student from an economically weaker section would adjust to a school in an affluent area (Cuffe Parade, in Mumbai, in this instance).[99] An article in the *Hindustan Times* quoted educationist Basanti Roy as saying, 'A child living in the slum will find it difficult to adjust to his peers from well-to-do families. He will remain a misfit in the bigger group...There will always remain a cultural difference.'[100] In *The Hindu*'s Sunday Magazine, the principal of Rishi Valley School A. Kumaraswamy made the case that 'children who lack academic support from their families are likely to remain low performing, and may suffer by comparison. Apart from this they would be faced with difficulties that stem from the contrast in social markers such as dress, possessions, parental profiles etc. All this could seriously affect the self-esteem of underprivileged students.'[101] Therefore, he suggested that instead of integrating children from disadvantaged backgrounds in 'elite' schools, these 'well-endowed' schools should establish separate schools for poor children.

This was exactly the stratagem adopted by the elite schools in Delhi to deal with the Delhi government's dictum in 2012 that all schools must reserve 15 per cent of their seats for poor children. They established afternoon schools for under-privileged students which had much poorer educational standards than for regular students. These afternoon schools are run in the Hindi medium, and after the regular-fee-paying, 'English-medium' students have safely left, ensuring that the two sets of children never even meet, let alone mingle and become friends.

To take advantage of the quota in Delhi, I have knocked on the doors of many highly respected schools to admit the former street children we take care of, but have mostly been refused, or offered a few seats in these segregated afternoon schools.

The untruth—and injustice—of the claim that disadvantaged children will not be able to 'adjust' to schools which include children of privilege has been disproved by the manner in which our former street children have adjusted in the few schools in Delhi which offered them admission—St Mary's, Jamia Millia Islamia School and Balwantrai Mehta School. Our children have been found to quickly grow academically, often leading their classes; they display a range of other talents in sports and dance, and make friends easily with their more privileged classmates. The transition has not been painless. Cultural barriers between classes do exist, and our children are socially at the bottom of the social heap, with no parents or with parents who still beg or pick rags on the streets. But we find that sensitive teachers and sensitive school leaders like Annie Koshy and Admiral R. H. Tahiliani can and do a great deal to smoothen the transition, and help children of disadvantage bridge cultural barriers.

However, the burden to adjust to the environment at school—much like for African Americans in segregated America—still remains mainly with disadvantaged children. Why can this burden not be borne, or at least shared, by children of privilege?

In this context, we can learn, most of all, from the work of Sister Cyril Mooney, an Irish nun who, for nearly two decades, admitted street girls to study in the elite Loreto Day School, Sealdah, with fee-paying parents subsidizing pupils without parents. She carefully nurtured an environment in which girls from diametrically opposed opportunities and backgrounds studied together with mutual respect and understanding. This was accomplished in small and big ways. She found that children from poor backgrounds were initially uncomfortable wearing closed shoes, so she made it a rule that all students should walk barefoot in school until Class 6. If a child wore a particularly glitzy wristwatch to school, she would call the child to her office and ask why she thought that her peers would admire her only if she showed off expensive belongings. I met many girls, who were formerly from the streets and who studied in Loreto, and found them poised, confident and hopeful. I also met many former and current students of the same school from privileged homes, who were proud that their school uniquely offers equal spaces for the poorest children to study and grow. Sister Cyril asks: 'It is fashionable to teach "hands-on computers", "hands-on problem solving", then why not "hands-on compassion"?'

The most sensitive commentary that I read on this contestation—

which mirrored the mores of unequal India today—was by television newsreader Sonia Singh in *Outlook*, writing as the mother of a five-year-old son who was in an elite school which admitted poor children.[102] At a parent-teacher meeting, she easily spotted the father of a disadvantaged child. She asked him how his son was coping. He replied that all was fine, except for a problem created by a rich classmate's birthday. His son was also invited, and was really excited about attending. But his father was worried about one problem—his wife would have to accompany his son to the party as he was too small to go alone. There are two kinds of escorts of the young children in any party, he explained. One is the domestic help—the ayahs and chauffeurs—and the ayahs are seated in a segregated room, and the chauffeurs left outside. The other are the parents, who are welcomed to another room in the main part of the house.

The father of the young child was worried about how his son would feel if his mother would be seated, as was most likely, with the ayahs.

In 2012, the Supreme Court upheld the validity of the provision guaranteeing 25 per cent reservation to children from weaker socio-economic backgrounds under the law guaranteeing the right to education. But elite schools have continued to subvert the law through a variety of shameful subterfuges. *Outlook* carried the story of Prakash, a milkman in Bangalore who was elated as his daughter was admitted under this reservation into an international school, and who was asked to pay £48 every month—in pound sterling, as this was an international school. The school staff explained to him that education was free only with regard to tuition fee; the £48 was for all the 'other' fees, ₹5,000 at the day's conversion rate, and 90 per cent of Prakash's monthly income.[103] These other 'heads', compiled painstakingly for several schools by Nagasimha Rao, convenor, RTE Task Force in Bangalore, included ₹7,000 a year for handwriting improvement and calligraphy in one school, ₹1,500 for star-gazing tutorials in another, ₹4,000 for computers or ₹2,000 for swimming.[104] This, of course, in addition to the nearly ₹8,000 that parents across the country are forced to spend on books and uniform, despite the RTE mandating schools to provide them free of cost to children from disadvantaged backgrounds. 'From "cautioning" poorer parents about the "high level" of education their children might not be able to cope with to demanding up to Rs 3,00,000 for international trips the schools organise, elite private schools do everything they can to eliminate children from weaker sections,' reports Nagasimha Rao.[105]

At the heart of the resistance to admitting disadvantaged children to elite schools in India is the unwillingness of middle-class Indians to accept the idea that their child, the children of their domestic help, and a child from the streets will sit on the same school bench; study, eat and play together, and even become friends. This is compounded by the fear that, perhaps, your domestic help's child may actually fare better at school than your own, much like Eklavya out-performed the Pandava princes!

I have already spoken of our work—with many idealistic young colleagues—with around 300 Eklavyas (more girls than boys) in Delhi, and they work with a larger number of around 3,500 former street boys and girls in Hyderabad, Patna, Chennai, Kolkata and Bangalore. These are girls and boys who were found begging or picking rags or pockets for survival on pavements and railway platforms. With just a couple of years of care, they came to terms with their abuse and trauma, healed, forgave, gave up drugs, and entered regular school. In these private and government schools, they have blossomed, studied hard, displayed many talents, and been found to really value education; indeed, more than most children who take it for granted.

Five years after we began work with these children, in 2011, ten of them in Delhi passed their 10th Board examination and half a dozen their 12th Board. For children who had spent most of their childhoods on pavements, railway platforms or in children's jails, this was a formidable achievement. I wonder how many children from elite private schools can match this. I do not understand how private schools claim that the entry of disadvantaged children will dilute merit; all that it will do is to breach the complacency and conceit of privilege.

There are young adults among the former street children in our care who are now studying for their Bachelor's degrees in social work, or learning to be chefs, software technicians—one boy, who was born to a homeless mother, is learning to be an animation filmmaker. I hope I live long enough to see them grow into fine, happy, contributing citizens, each living testimonies, both to the intrinsic equality of all children and to the enormous loss our country inflicts upon itself by depriving millions of our children equal, common, decent education.

Youth, Jobs and Dreams

Never before in history, and probably never in the future, will any country be home to as many young people as India is today. Every second Indian alive today is less than twenty-five years old. Two out of three Indians are below thirty-five years of age.

A promise which helped sweep Narendra Modi to power in 2014 was that he would help create jobs for millions of India's restless young people and enable them to share in the country's growth story. Modi's success in 2014 was hitched to the soaring dreams of this large mass of restive young people, many of them first-time voters between eighteen to twenty-five years of age, often described by commentators as new India's aspirational class.

What is often overlooked is that this aspirational young population did not constitute all, or even a majority, of India's young people. In its ranks were only those young men and women who were able to enter and stay through school, and the even smaller numbers privileged enough to enter college. What were their numbers? Data published by the NSSO in 2009-10 shows that in rural areas, only 3.7 per cent men and 1.6 per cent women—between twenty to twenty-four years of age—were graduates or above. The corresponding figures for urban areas was 15 per cent men and 11 per cent women.[106]

A report—based on figures published by the NSSO for 2007-08—showed that large regional variations also existed: in the age group between twenty-two to thirty-five years, less than two out of ten in the northern and southern regions of the country and less than one out of ten in the north-central and north-eastern regions had access to higher education. The numbers were even far fewer—often around half—for young women as compared to men.[107]

It was these youths who were able to access higher education who desperately—and legitimately—longed to escape the drudgery and want, the toil and thrift, and the burdens imposed by gender, caste, class and religious identity which trapped their parents. They believed that they could indeed realize their soaring dreams, in ways which would have been unthinkable when their parents were of their age.

It was these young people who filled the grounds when India against Corruption, a movement led by Anna Hazare, signalled a popular uprising against the venal and corrupt political leadership whom they held responsible for holding them back from realizing their impatient dreams. It was they who stormed the streets in protest against the gangrape of a young woman in the winter of 2013, whose own life-journey from working-class and slum origins to a confident paramedical student, represented the grit and the dreams of the great new aspirational middle class. It was these same young people who voted enthusiastically in 2014, raring to be admitted into the glitz embodied in the lifestyles of the new middle class.

There are many ironies of history here. The young people who voted so emphatically against the UPA regime in 2014 were the children of its own policies of economic reform, the evidence and symbols of its success. This aspirational class would not have surged without globalization, the first steps to which were taken by Rajiv Gandhi, and which was spurred by market-led growth introduced in 1991 by Narasimha Rao and nurtured in its peak years, 2004-09, by Manmohan Singh. But not only did the dizzy pace of economic growth falter in the last few years of the UPA government, inflation peaked too, and the rupee crashed. Even more damagingly, the high noon of the growth years did not yield jobs in the numbers that aspirational young Indians had clamoured for. Modi promised young people that he would correct this; he would steady and steer the country back to high economic growth on the back of policies designed to bring back massive international capital inflows into the country. This in itself was expected to yield jobs for our eager, youthful millions.

But I worried, and for many different reasons. I worried at one level about the failure of Left-liberal political formations to capture the imagination of the young with ideas of social solidarity, of aspiring for a better life not just for oneself but for *all* people, especially the wretched and the oppressed. It is perhaps natural for greying, balding men like me to be nostalgic about my youth. But I recall that when I was young, our dreams in college campuses and coffee houses were for a better world for *all* people, especially for those left behind and dispossessed, and not just for ourselves. It is not a failing of young people today that their dreams are centred on themselves. I continue to carry robust faith in young people, and indeed because of them I still nurture hope for the future of my country and my world. The betrayal, I believe, is of our generations which immediately preceded them. It is our cynicism and opportunism, the brittleness and shallowness of our convictions, and our financial, intellectual and moral corruption which left a vacuum, which the consumerist aspirations of our times filled.

But I worried even more for the impetuous young people who nurtured these brilliant dreams as they voted in droves in the 2014 elections, because I could see no pathways by which the economy could accomplish the explosion of jobs which Modi's leadership promised. This was because the course correction he offered was to steer India back to policies of 'reform' of the high-growth years of the previous government, but untrammelled by the red or green roadblocks put up by the Left or the champions of the environment.

He also ignored that the reality of what had been accomplished in the years of highest economic growth in India was the accelerated but unequal expansion of wealth, certainly, not the expansion of decent work for India's poor. On the contrary, we had seen the reverse; the shrinking of decent work in the sunshine years of high growth. Coen Kompier contributed a harrowing essay to the 'India Exclusion Report' compiled by the CES.[108] He established that 'very few jobs have been added, mostly of low quality, whereas employment opportunities in public enterprises, the formal private sector, and agriculture *actually declined'* (my emphasis).[109] In the decades between 1999-00 to 2009-10, 'while GDP growth accelerated to 7.52 per cent per annum, employment growth during this period was just 1.5 per cent, below the long-term employment growth of 2 per cent per annum, over the four decades since 1972-73. Only 2.7 million jobs were added in the period from 2004-10, compared to over 60 million during the previous five-year period.'[110]

Employment in the organized sector actually went down after 1997, while that in the unorganized sector rose.[111] In fact, employment growth in the organized sector has registered a continuous decline between 1972-73 and 2004-05. Kompier cites the 2009 report of the National Commission for Enterprises in the Unorganized Sector, which found that the 'vast majority of jobs created in recent years have been in the informal sector, in the absence of a legal framework for labour protection and social security. Out of every 100 workers, the report revealed, around 90 per cent work in the informal economy producing half of India's economic output. This implies that out of a current total workforce of around 475 million, around 400 million workers, considerably larger than the total population of the US, are employed with little job security or any formal entitlements to call upon the protection of the labour law regime.'[112]

Industry continued to chafe at the Indian government's failure to introduce what it called labour 'reforms', and labour reforms were one of the promises of the avowedly industry-friendly government led by Modi. I find the use of the term 'reform' disingenuous, because what is sought is not a better deal for the labouring class but, rather, the further weakening of the already infirm framework of labour regulation in our country. This would perhaps attract more investment (but even this is arguable), but would further damage the promise of assured, dignified and safe work for the aspirational young. Leo Panitch noted in *The Guardian*: 'For most of the 20th century, the word "reform" was commonly associated with securing state protection against the chaotic effects of capitalist market competition. Today, it is most commonly used to refer to the undoing of these protections.'[113] He was referring to a *New York Times* article about how many European countries were now 'furiously dismantling workplace protections in a bid to reduce the cost of labour', which 'further eroded worker protections, fuelling a boom in low-paid, short-term "mini-jobs"...'[114] The contemporary Indian story is very similar.

High among the expectations from the new government was that it would muster the political will to 'reform' labour laws to render these more 'flexible'. The rigidities of the current labour regulatory regime, it was alleged, were major hurdles to attract private investment into manufacturing. Greater freedom to hire and fire workers, a less intrusive labour welfare supervisory regime and the reduced power of labour unions would, it was argued, actually benefit workers, as greater private investment would result in higher economic growth and, therefore, more jobs.

Many problems and untruths beset these arguments. Firstly, as already observed, between 2004-05 and 2009-10, when growth averaged 8.43 per cent, only a little over two million new jobs were added for the fifty-five million people who joined the workforce. In 2014, one million new young people joined the workforce every month. Second, although labour laws prohibit the appointment of contract workers for perennial tasks, these years saw a sharp growth in contract and casual work, at the expense of regular employment. Atul Sood, Paaritosh Nath and Sangeeta Ghosh demonstrate that the share of contract workers in total organized employment rose from

10.5 per cent in 1995-96 to 25.6 per cent by 2009-10, while the share of directly employed workers fell from 68.3 per cent to 52.4 per cent in the same period.[115] Even regular workers were increasingly appointed on short-term contracts, with little or no social security, as the termination of their employment was not legally barred. The increasing informality in the organized labour market had, in turn, blurred distinctions between formal and informal labour.

In this way, fewer and fewer workers could enjoy the protections of secure employment and social security which the letter of the law intended. This unstable employment landscape was further stymied by a poorly staffed, badly trained and loosely supervised labour department, notoriously prone to rent-seeking. The high-growth sector of construction was almost entirely powered by unprotected, unorganized workers working at dirt-level wages and in unhealthy, unsafe environments, in open violation of the law. Likewise, a greater part of factory-floor work has transformed into home-based work, where low wages are paid for long hours of labour, with no social protection; the work environment is extremely unhealthy and hidden and uncounted child labour has burgeoned.

In this light, labour law amendments introduced in June 2014 by the newly elected Vasundhara Raje government in Rajasthan caused me deep disquiet. These amendments firstly reduced the application of the Contract Labour Act to companies with more than fifty workers, against the then current twenty. This statute prohibited engagement of contract labour in tasks requiring perennial work in the production process, and prescribed a mechanism for the registration of contractors. The amendments likewise reduced the protections of the Factories Act only to units employing twenty workers with power supply and forty workers without power supply, down from the existing norm of ten and twenty workers respectively. This, in effect, reduced health, safety and welfare standards which employers were earlier legally bound to ensure.

The legal changes further exempted factories employing 300— up from the current 100—workers from the Industrial Disputes Act, which protects the right of collective bargaining, and raised the minimum numbers of workers required to register a trade union from 15 to 30 per cent. Labour economists estimated that after this amendment, around 57-60 per cent workers in the formal sector could be fired, or be made subject to suppressed wages and degraded work conditions.[116]

The cumulative impact of these amendments would be to free more employers from even the poorly enforced and modest obligations they currently have to ensure the job security, health and social protection of their workers. I am not convinced either that this dilution of labour protections will indeed spur economic growth, or that this is an ethically just social bargain even if it does. And there is even less evidence that this is an assured pathway for the creation of millions of jobs which India's teeming youth legitimately aspire for.

What is more, even the inadequate, fast-eroding and poorly enforced protections extended by India's labour laws exclude nine out of ten workers who toil in the unorganized workforce. The only guarantee that these workers enjoy is of uncertain, sporadic, low-paid, often unhealthy work, without social protections for health and old age. K. P. Kannan, labour economist, writes that he earlier believed that the major problem of construction workers was the payment of minimum wages, until he realized that their predicament was more often the payment of any wages at all, as every other worker he met in construction sites had not been paid any wages for long durations.[117] Jan Breman, who has tracked the conditions of unorganized workers for three decades, poignantly records the plight of millions of footloose workers—whom he describes evocatively as 'hunters and gatherers'—who seek work on any terms, anywhere in the country, in an unending struggle to keep their families afloat.[118]

~

When I travel to any site of big industry, I ask local young people about what they have gained from it and the answer is, invariably, a bitter negative. Indeed, their only stories are of irreparable loss.

Owners of modern industry tend to opt firstly for technologies which displace labour, rather than enhance it. And the men and women they do employ are usually from outside, people with better educational and technical qualifications (and easier to control than locals).

The majority of schools in the country teach young people little which makes them employable in the new job market. The quality of education, overall, is abysmal. The influential annual study conducted by the Annual Status of Education Report (ASER) showed that in 2012, more than half of all children in Class 5 could not read a Class 2-level text, and nearly half could not solve simple, two-digit subtraction problems.[119] ASER 2013 found that, compared to 2012, there was virtually no change in the percentage of children from Class 3 in government schools who could read a text from Class 2— around 32 per cent. Among children studying in Class 5, the percentage of children enrolled in government schools who could read a text from Class 2 decreased from 50.3 per cent in 2009 to 43.8 per cent in 2011 and to 41.1 per cent in 2013. Comparing children enrolled in private and government schools, this percentage decreased from 52.8 per cent (2009) to about 46.9 per cent (2012) and did not change in 2013. The ASER reports showed that educational outcomes in private schools were not much better than government schools, but the gap was widening with time and overall decreases in learning levels could be attributed to further lowering of learning outcomes in government schools. In the period after 2010, as mentioned above, when the percentage of children studying in Class 5 who could read texts from Class 2 dipped, the percentage of readers in private schools held at 63.3 per cent, whereas readers in government schools had decreased to 41.1 per cent. In 2014, this figure increased marginally for government schools (42 per cent) and declined slightly in private schools (62.5 per cent).[120] The 2013 survey found that 33.2 per cent of children from government schools, studying in Class 3, could perform basic subtraction, compared to 47.8 per cent in private schools; 18.9 per cent in government schools could perform exercises in subtraction, compared to 44.6 per cent in private schools; 20.8 per cent in Class 5 in government schools could do simple division, compared to 38.9 per cent in private schools.[121]

Although 70 per cent children are today completing primary school, the completion rate in the lower secondary levels is considerably lower. In 2005, 56 per cent children completed lower secondary school but, in the poorest quintile, the rate was 21 per cent. In other words, in the lowest 10 per cent, only one out of five children were completing Class 10. In 1998, the completion rate for the poorest quintile was actually higher, at 31 per cent. In this poorest quintile, less than 13 per cent girls completed lower secondary school. The mean years in education for the poorest quintile also fell from 4.35 years in 1998 to 2.88 years in 2005. It was the lowest for Muslim girls, at 5.33 years, compared to 6.92 years for males.[122]

The future looks different to different young people based on the accidents of their birth: as a boy or as a girl; in a high-caste or low-caste household; in a village or in a city; in a hut, shanty or pavement or an expensive nursing home. Some can look forward confidently to secure, well-paid, dignified and decent work, and a comfortable retirement; a much larger number to uncertain, low-end, low-paid, unsafe, humiliating work, with no pensions or social security, and vast, ever-looming interludes of unemployment. But in between are a new mass of young people, still left out so far from decent employment and high consumption, but who are pushing at closed doors and who aspire to enter this shining club. This young aspirational population is not willing to wait any longer for the life of consumerist fulfilment which it has been promised.

The chasms which separate the destinies of young people in India is illustrated by a study of key transitions experienced by 50,000 young people in six states—Andhra Pradesh, Bihar, Jharkhand, Maharashtra, Rajasthan and Tamil Nadu.[123] The study found that while youth in the country were better educated than the general population, schooling was far from universal among them. Almost one in ten young men and one in four young women had never attended school. In this, young women in rural areas and married young women were particularly disadvantaged; one-third of rural young women and almost two-fifths of married young women had never been to school. Just two out of five young men and one out of three young women had completed high school. The rates were particularly low among several subgroups—young women, married youth, rural youth, those belonging to poor households, Muslim youth and those belonging to scheduled castes and tribes. Similarly, far smaller proportions of youth in the northern states than those in Maharashtra and the southern states had completed ten or more years of education.[124]

Three out of five young men and women said that they could not enter or stay in school because of the poverty of their families, because they had to work on the family farm or trade, or migrate for wage work. More than half of the young women additionally reported reasons related to housework. For women, another major reason for dropping out of school was early marriage. Moreover, most lacked the skills needed for employability. Just one out of five young men and one out of four young women had attended even one vocational training programme.

In a paper, 'Decent Work for Youth in India' the International Labour Organization warns that, globally, youth are three times more likely than adults to be unemployed.[125] It points out that 9.7 per cent of young men and 18.7 per cent of young women in India were unemployed in 2009-10, against unemployment rates for Indians between thirty to thirty-four years of age reaching only 1.2 and 3.4 per cent for men and women, respectively. It underlines that young people around the world were hit hardest during the global financial crisis due to their precariousness in the labour market, and that young women typically experience higher rates of unemployment than men. Most young people in developing countries such as India cannot afford to remain unemployed for long because they have to bring food to their older and younger dependents. They struggle to find decent jobs in the formal economy. Consequently, most youth are underemployed and exploited and eke out a bare living in the informal sector.

~

There is indeed an urgent need for labour reforms, but not in the form it is commonly understood, ensuring the dilution of the few labour protections which still survive in India's statute books. Instead, what is essential is the rationalization and codification of all labour protections into a single law, and the commitment of employers and governments to adhere to this law and extend its coverage resolutely to every worker in the country. What is also urgently needed is a common school system assuring equal, quality education and opportunities for higher and technical education to all children regardless of class, caste and gender.

It is only the assurance of decent work to all workers and equal education to all children and youth which will ensure that households can afford the food, education, healthcare and housing necessary for a life of basic dignity for all, a promise withheld too long from too many of our people.

Millions of young people today are not in the ranks of those who can realistically hope for a 'good life' during their youth—or even their lifetimes—or to force open the doors of the life which is possible through secure and decent employment. Far from aspirational, they still walk the thin and precarious road to uncertain survival. Sajjad Hassan writes movingly of one teenaged Dinesh Manjhi.[126] His 'life has run in fast motion—at 19, he is brother to two sisters and a younger brother, son to his 55 year old mother, and the breadwinner to all. Father died a year ago, to sudden disease, that the family is still unclear about. But Dinesh's early tryst with adulthood began much before his father's demise. It was at least seven years ago that—forced by dirt poverty at home—his father first took Dinesh along to Gurdaspur, in the western state of Punjab, to help with errands on the farm that he himself worked on as seasonal worker. Work was hard, but it added the valuable extra to what the father saved to bring back home every season. When Dinesh is not labouring on farms in Punjab, he is at home, in Dumri village, eking out a living as a construction labourer, in neighbouring Muzaffarpur town (in Bihar), earning between Rs. 100-150 a day, on days he is able to find work. His younger brother, Mukesh, 15, is following in Dinesh's footsteps—picking up the skills of construction labour, even though the work is hard and hazardous. But that is still better than opportunities in Dumri itself, as farm work is available at most for 15-20 days a year, during (paddy or wheat) harvest time, at about Rs. 100 a day. There is no other source of income...'[127]

This life—of wretched poverty and hard, soulless, low-paid labour, often in unfamiliar lands—is what millions of young people of nineteen or even fifteen years of age still look forward to. Decades of freedom and high growth have done nothing to change the destinies of young people like Dinesh Manjhi. The world for him is not shining or aspirational. And there is little successive governments are doing—or even promising to do—to ensure that Manjhi's daughter or son can look forward to life with more robust hope.

Therefore, it would be a great mistake and injustice to imagine that all of India's young population realistically aspire to a better life. The majority still remain tied down to the hopeless lives of their parents and grandparents. Millions of young men still have no option except to join the enormous labour force and be tied down to bare survival through distress migration. No official data exists on their numbers—another deliberate invisibilization—but estimates vary widely from ten to 100 million; Jan Breman and Kavita Srivastava suggest that the most reliable numbers are somewhere between thirty and fifty million people.[128] I have tried to track the journey of just a few of these people. More than a hundred thousand people migrate every year from the hunger belt of Bolangir, Odisha, after taking a small monetary advance from local labour contractors. I found that most end up annually in brick kilns on the outskirts of Hyderabad city, which has an insatiable appetite for building materials. The whole family works for up to eighteen hours a day; housing, childcare and educational services are negligible; wage arrears are paid only at the end of the year to prevent escape, and any assertion is met with outright violence.

The CES report also underlines that boundaries and distinctions between the organized and the unorganized sectors are gradually blurring. Informal employment is rising in the formal sector, and the formal and informal economies are firmly intertwined. In India, the informal economy has swollen to 93 per cent of all economic activities, accounting for half of India's gross national product.[129] It notes that the labour market in India is organized more along social lines than according to legal precepts, in which a strong overlap exists between caste and class. 'Persons from marginalized groups, particularly Dalits and Adivasis, form the bulk of the workforce at the bottom of the informal economy as well as in the factories of the formal sector.' Indeed, low in caste is low in class. Dalits form the bulk of the workforce at the bottom of the informal economy as well as in the factories of the formal sector. Many Dalits are at work, firmly restricted to the lowest jobs available.[130]

The report further observes that 'workers with formal jobs enjoy a certain status in life. Their jobs are secure, their payments sufficient to maintain a family, send their children to school, live in a decent house, and keep time to spend leisurely with friends or family. But this security breaks down when employment security ends, or when slums are being torn down, or when people are evicted from (semi) public spaces for beautification or other purposes. In other instances, male migrant workers leave behind their families, also leaving behind the hope fixed upon him of family members in want of his remittances. High costs of living in towns and cities reduce remittances. When one fails to live up to these expectations, workers may turn to petty criminal behaviour or run away, leaving behind broken families with reduced income. Saving some money is out of the question as every penny is invested in the hope of getting at least one square meal every few days. With no money for rent, housing conditions constantly deteriorate until one possesses nothing but some plastic sheets covering branches or abandoned pieces of wood. Fuel is expensive too. Poor health resulting from this poverty is shortening lifespans.'[131]

The result is that new categories of people are created who are considered a burden. People once labelled 'paupers' are now termed 'disposable people',[132] 'nowhere people',[133] 'surplus people',[134] or 'labour surplus'.[135] Scholars like Jan Breman find that new forms of hidden debt bondage have appeared, with intermediary labour contractors mediating between large formal industry and impoverished, unprotected, and often desperate workers in India's vast rural hinterlands, from which young people are trying to escape in hordes as though from a doomed and dying civilization.[136]

~

In 2010, Delhi was in the final stages of frenetic refurbishment, for display to 5,000 sports competitors and an expected 1.2 million spectators from eighty-five countries, who were to gather for the Commonwealth Games, the third largest international sporting event of the world.[137] In preparation for the Games, scheduled in October 2010, an estimated ₹260 billion had been spent in Delhi over the previous three years. The investments included a Games Village in the ecologically fragile bed of the river Yamuna, eight international sports stadiums—many of which were likely to remain unutilized after the Games—twenty-five under-bridges and over-bridges, underground parking lots, an extended metro line and eight-lane highways, and a sparkling new international airport. The operative, over-used words deployed by public leaders and officials to describe the city of their aspirations were 'world class'.

Forgotten in the shadows of this feverish new glitter were the men and women whose toil had made the garish makeover of this city possible. At its peak, in 2008-09, an estimated one hundred thousand workers had converged on the metropolis, driven often by desperate poverty from several of India's rural backwaters: Bihar, Jharkhand, eastern Uttar Pradesh, Madhya Pradesh, Odisha, West Bengal and Chhattisgarh. It was with the cheap sweat of India's poorest people that this 'new' city was being built. Government agencies were cynically complicit in withholding from them their legal rights of fair wages, decent living conditions and safe and secure work conditions. These agencies contracted the construction to multinational construction firms, and these sub-contracted to a series of intermediary agencies which, in turn, further continued downward cycles of sub-contracting. At the bottom of this pyramid were the labour contractors who recruit desperately poor workers from India's impoverished rural backwaters. Rarely were these workers employed for more than a few months, after which they were replaced by a fresh batch from an unending army of impoverished men in a stagnant, dead-end rural economy. It was a clear strategy to not allow them to organize or demand their elementary legal rights.

During the Asiad Games in 1982, the infrastructure of the city had been built by numerous, exploitatively low-paid workers. In 2010, more than a quarter of a century later, pre-fabricated structures and capital-intensive technology enabled shorter completion cycles and a reduced demand for labour, but the conditions of the workers remained as exploitative as ever. The Supreme Court, in its significant judgement in the Asiad Workers' case in 1982, had ruled that 'when a person provides labour or service to another for a remuneration which is less than the minimum wage, the labour or service provided by him falls within the ambit of forced labour'.[138] By these standards, the stark truth is that the manicured glitter of Delhi, manufactured for display to international guests, was constructed by forced labour.

What is unconscionable is that Central and state government agencies and officials, who are themselves the principal employers, or are responsible for the implementation and enforcement of the legal rights of the workers, refused to do so despite continuous and exemplary vigilance by various non-official groups and judicial interventions. The Commonwealth Games-Citizens for Children and Women (CWG-CWC), an alliance of twenty-two organizations mobilized by Mobile Creches and the People's Union for Democratic Rights (PUDR) painstakingly documented serious and pervasive legal violations of the rights of workers to minimum wages, decent living and work conditions, and social security. PUDR filed a petition with the Delhi High Court to enforce the law and ensure better conditions of work and residence for the workers. The High Court, in turn, appointed a Monitoring Committee which included Arundhati Ghose, a former diplomat, and Lakshmidhar Mishra, Special Rapporteur of the National Human Rights Commission. The committee visited ten work sites and labour colonies, and confirmed in a damning report most of the charges made by the petitioners to the High Court.[139] But the months passed and, in the countdown to the celebrated Games, little changed in the lives of the workers and no one I know was punished for these violations of the law of the land.

The workers were housed, on all sites, in sub-human tenements. Makeshift rooms were assembled from asbestos sheets, typically without windows and other ventilation—oppressively hot in summer and freezing in winter. Four or more workers were lodged in small spaces of around 15 square metres. The few common toilets were rarely cleaned and, mostly, open taps substituted for bathing spaces. There were no arrangements for sewerage and drainage; therefore, when I visited the camps after the committee's report was submitted, I found in many colonies that the tenements were surrounded by vast, stagnant, stinking cesspools, infested with mosquitoes and flies. The settlements were located too close to the construction sites and were therefore always covered with thick dust. There were few crèches or schools for the children of the labourers. The colonies defied with comfortable impunity all prescriptions made by labour laws for the welfare of workers.

A study of the Commonwealth Games construction projects by the CWG-CWC found that 64 per cent of the workers were casual and 10 per cent were on contract.[140] This meant that three out of four workers were bereft of the obligations that their employers would owe to their regular employees. Most workers reported being paid well below the statutory minimum wages, let alone fair wages.

The minimum wage prescribed by law is ₹151 a day for unskilled workers, but they were paid an average of only ₹114. Many worked extra hours, but almost none reported getting double wage payment for over-time as prescribed by law. They were paid in cash, illegally and without pay slips, so there was no record of their employment or wages. This resulted in massive unrecorded gains for the employers. Activists calculated, for instance, that in the CWG Village alone, employers earned an extra ₹60 million by withholding minimum wages. Workers were paid only for the days they actually worked, and they were denied paid weekly holidays. Wages were often paid late, and a part of the wages were withheld by contractors to prevent workers from leaving employment prematurely. Women were rarely employed, and where they were, they were paid less than men. We even found teenaged boys on some sites.

The law requires construction workers and inter-state migrant workers to be registered for them to be eligible for social security and other benefits. But very few were actually registered and, instead, there was a systematic effort to not maintain any record of a worker's identity. Thus, in the event of an accident, injury, fatality, or any other claim, it became easy for employers to escape their legal responsibilities.

The nature of construction work is that it is short term, and therefore workers and their families are unprotected. To remedy this, a significant law was passed in 1996 called the Building and Other Construction Workers' Act.[141] It requires all workers to be registered, and imposes a cess on employers. The cess is to enable workers to receive scholarships for their children; health, accident and death insurance; retirement and disability pensions; and loans to build houses. In Delhi, up to 2010, ₹3,500 million had been collected as cess from builders under this law, but only around two thousand, of an estimated eight hundred thousand construction workers in the city, are actually found on live registers. It is incredible that until January 2010, only *one* worker had received an accident claim from this cess, and 100 children received scholarships out of it. Three crèches had been established until then. This was the sum total of expenditures for the workers so far from the cess. Large sums of money are also available for the welfare of construction workers and their families with the government of Delhi. Yet no political leader or official in government seemed interested in enabling those whose hands build this city to lead a life of a little more security and dignity. The fact that the law obliges them to do so seems irrelevant to those who are themselves charged to enforce the law.

Workers often laboured without elementary safety precautions like helmets, masks and gloves. If workers were given boots, the costs were occasionally deducted from their wages. Accidents happened and almost all the sites, but they were rarely reported to the commissioner, Workmen's Compensation, and legal reparation was withheld or diluted. No medical services were available on site, beyond a basic first-aid kit.

I spoke with many of the young men in the sub-human labour camps that hid behind the opulent constructions. They accepted the grime of their living spaces, their exploitative twelve-hour shifts, their illegally low wages, and the loneliness of their uprooting with not just stoic resignation, but something that even resembled gratitude. They were grateful that the city's profligate aspirations had allowed them to survive, even amidst its inhospitability and cynical exploitation.

There are more than 260 laws on the Indian statute books designed to secure fair wages, decent work and living conditions for workers, but none of these illuminated the lives of the workers who rebuilt the capital city. Well before the glittering launch of the Games, their ramshackle labour settlements were cleared and the workers despatched back to the hinterland from which they had been recruited.

This cynical, wilful subversion of basic labour law protections, even by global formal industry which I observed directly during the Commonwealth Games in Delhi is not the exception but the rule. Kompier, in his report for the CES, documents that even in the formal sector, over half the workers are informally employed, in that they do not have a secured tenure of employment, social security and other protections.[142] Further, even more shockingly, the proportion of informal workers in the formal sector has also risen over time, from 42 per cent of the total formal-sector employment in 1999-2000 to 51 per cent in 2009-10. Such trends, Kompier explains, can be understood by the increasing move towards the use of contract labour within the formal sector in order to increase profits and avoid adherence to labour laws.

Sehba Farooqui, who heads the Delhi unit of the All India Democratic Women's Association—the women's wing of the CPI (M)—has found that Delhi's slums are full of women who undertake a range of tasks on piecework from major garment, toys and cosmetic companies.[143] They work bent over in dimly lit and ill-ventilated, crowded shanty rooms for ten hours each day, roping in their children and aged parents. She reported—and we confirmed in our own visit to their homes—that what they collectively earned was sometimes as low as ₹30 a day, on an average, sometimes an eighth of the statutory minimum wage. Indeed, every labour law—governing wages, hours and conditions of work and social security—was brazenly violated in these tiny shanties and child labour had returned through the backdoor. But no company was held responsible by a supine, indeed, complicit state.

~

Instead of adhering to the letter and spirit of labour laws, large corporations contribute to what is described as corporate social responsibility (CSR). I was once invited by a leading television business channel to judge which companies should be awarded for their CSR work. I found the company leading the shortlist was one of those which had evaded all labour laws through the system of sub-contracting during the Commonwealth Games, and I argued strenuously to ensure that the company was not given the award.

I agree with Kompier when he observes that, 'Social responsibility can only follow when "legal responsibilities" have been fulfilled. We already observed that labour laws are generally being circumvented, and that the corporate private sector greatly benefits from its cheap linkages with their suppliers in the informal economy. This by itself is a circumvention of labour laws and coming on top of the direct evasion of labour laws to employees in their enterprises. As long as production by these companies remains unethical, or worse, illegal, this by itself directly contributes to larger corporate profits. Instead of CSR, they can opt for paying higher wages, which would not only reduce the need for their social charity, but also expand demand for their goods...From a worker's view, it would be more effective to abolish social corporate responsibility and start respecting legal requirements first. In this case, corporate social responsibility could become a matter for only those companies having the moral courage to respect rights at work.'[144]

The promise that massive inflows of international capital will ensure decent work for millions of our people lies in a shambles, exposed as an elaborate falsehood. What remain amidst the ruins of this promise are runaway profits for private industry built on exploitative labour practices reminiscent of another darker age, enabled by a complicit state. Kompier concludes: 'Since the abolition of slavery and servitude, labour has never been cheaper than it is today, resulting in a labour market flooded with working poor...To make matters worse, stagnant wages, combined with high levels of inflation have rendered them unable to sustain a basic standard of living. For the working poor, the lack of implementation of laws on minimum wages and labour protection standards result in exponentially higher levels of exploitation and high vulnerability to exclusion from decent work.'[145]

Every young person, even the most dispossessed, is dreaming dreams, for which regime can imprison the flights of hope of the youth? But a world which expects large private businesses, untrammelled by the legal and moral claims of the men and women they employ, to transform these dreams into reality, is ultimately betraying the dreams of our young. And I worry that these dreams of millions of young people will simply crash in an indifferent world.

For the Crime of Destitution

A bench of the Delhi High Court, on 7 February 2007, directed the Delhi government to clear beggars from the streets of the capital and to confine them in beggars' homes. This ruling was passed in response to a Public Interest Litigation (PIL) filed by the New Delhi Bar Association. Lawyers darkly alleged harassment and threats to their lives by 'lepers and beggars' who 'try to extort money' and 'keep on knocking at the window of cars in crossings' with threats of 'dire consequences' in case money is not given. Their petition repeatedly referred to a particularly diabolical 'leper in a blue lungi' who is said to have 'told our member to give him money otherwise our member would be kidnapped and taken to a Basti of lepers where our member would be touched by the lepers so that our member would be affected by the disease of leprosy'![146]

It is extraordinary how, in this matter, the New Delhi Bar Association and the Delhi High Court effectively turned the idea of the PIL on its head. Justice P. N. Bhagwati, who pioneered the PIL in India, envisaged it as an instrument using which the most disenfranchised and powerless citizens of India—people he describes as the exiles of civilization[147]—could access justice.[148] But in this case, influential members of the middle classes were using the PIL *against* some of the most disenfranchised people in the state. And what is more, they did so with almost illiterate prejudice about a fully curable ailment, associated with poverty, which is also among the least communicable. The High Court directed the state government to act more effectively against beggars. The PIL has been used on occasion against slum dwellers and street vendors as well.

Middle-class people—as well as governments—often blame the poor for their living conditions: for being lazy, lacking enterprise, being unreliable, or passively awaiting state largesse. There are many ways that the law of the land empowers state authorities to lock up and, indeed lock away, our most vulnerable people. Most jails are packed with impoverished and socially disadvantaged people, held for prolonged periods without being convicted, and frequently for petty offences. Children without adult care and protection are housed sometimes for the entire duration of their childhood in jail-like, state-run juvenile homes. Girls and women deemed by the state or judicial authorities to be 'in moral danger' because they are rescued from sex work, are incarcerated in custodial women's homes, often confined all day in small spaces with no opportunities for any entertainment and privacy.

But most dramatic are the anti-beggary laws and official campaigns against beggars. It was in the 1920s that begging was first declared a crime in British India, and the law was updated as the Bombay Prevention of Begging Act in 1959, and extended to eighteen states, including Delhi.[149, 150] The definition of begging even includes simply 'having no visible means of subsistence'. In other words, the law makes destitution a crime, punishable by incarceration. Since many beggars suffer from various diseases, both bodily and mental, it implicitly criminalizes ailments as well. It even criminalizes traditional artists, because 'singing, dancing, fortune-telling, performing or offering any article for sale' are deemed offences of begging under this Act.

Any police officer is authorized to arrest, without a warrant, any person who is found to be 'begging', under this wide legal ambit. This draconian power is used routinely by the police to reduce all homeless people to a continuous state of fear and insecurity for the mere fact that they lack 'visible means of subsistence', for which 'crime' they can be beaten, abused, chased, rounded up or arrested. The police tends to use these powers against the softest of targets—destitute women and men—with routine excess and brutality.

Based on usually summary trials, a person found to be a beggar may be detained for a period not less than one year, but which may extend to three years, or even ten years in the case of second and repeated 'offences'. Beggars are not detained in jails, but in what are called beggars' homes. These are abysmally worse than even jails because of the powerlessness and stigma faced by their hapless residents. They are usually restricted most of the day in small, airless, unsanitary halls. They have to contend with watery food and confinement in dormitories that reek of excreta and unwashed human bodies. There are no recreational or rehabilitative services, and significant numbers die lonely deaths. Many have no families to visit them, others are too poor, and yet others are ashamed to let their families know that they have been incarcerated for beggary.

It was in one of these beggars' homes that I met sixty-year-old Abdul who had travelled to Delhi from his village in Assam in a heart-breaking search of his wandering, mentally ill son; he was rounded up and sentenced for three years on the charge of beggary, but had not informed his family about his incarceration. 'If it was jail, I would tell them,' he explained to me. 'But if I contact them from this beggars' home, they may actually believe that I was begging. I can bear almost anything, but I would not be able to bear that.'

In Chennai, I found that government spent ₹3.6 million in 2006 to confine 116 alleged beggars in sub-human conditions, of which 86 per cent was expended on staff salaries.[151] It spent ₹27,000 per inmate annually, or nearly ₹100,000 on three years of their confinement. The government did not find it fit to spend a fraction of this on the rehabilitation and social security of these, the most wretched of our earth.

In my discussions with officers of the Department of Social Welfare of the Delhi, they often complained that beggars' courts were too lenient to the beggars who are rounded up in large numbers. The department installed hoardings in the city which proclaimed that alms-giving weakens the receiver as well as the country. A half-page newspaper advertisement sponsored by the Delhi government dramatically and expansively educated its citizens that their 'alms may cause traffic jams, accidents, illiteracy, inconvenience, unemployment, biri, cigarette, alcohol, bhang, ganja, charas, heroin…mandrax, robbery, rape, sex, theft, murder, prostitution, handicapped, assault, hooliganism', and then, even more mysteriously, 'slums, poverty, debt, ignorance, aggression, encroachment, molestation, mugging…'[152]

Much of this uneducated, middle-class bigotry against the outstretched hand is fuelled by the conviction that beggars choose this as an easy and lazy option, and that begging is organized by mafias, a myth further cultivated by films like *Slumdog Millionaire*. The film depicts, with Dickensian overtones, street children being kidnapped, maimed and forced to beg. But in an unpublished sample survey undertaken by the CES in Delhi, we found that, on the contrary, it was extreme poverty, disability, disease, no social security, the absence of or abandonment by family, and unemployment to account for more than 90 per cent of begging. Children report coercion by parents to beg because their families are unable to feed them but, hearteningly, we also some found a few instances of children with homeless families who beg while also attending school. The survey did not find a single case of beggar mafias. Remarkably, the Delhi High Court was officially informed that a study by the Crime Branch confirmed that there was indeed no such mafia operating in Delhi. Justice Manmohan Sarin also disagreed with the directions of the High Court and their endorsement by the Delhi government that stricter penal action should be taken against beggars, maintaining that detaining beggars was 'nothing short of dehumanising them and they should be let off after an admonition'.[153]

Most beggars are cast away by members of their families, some beg to not be a burden on those who feed them, and almost all have struggled through many low-end professions before they resorted to begging. In a study in Chennai, it was found that 68.75 per cent of the beggars surveyed were disabled or diseased. Nearly half were aged. Many women beggars had been deserted; they were sometimes with children and had no roof over their head.[154] The stigma of leprosy and mental illness, and many forms of disability, makes employment almost impossible, many vocations like street vending are barred by the government, and the meagre state pensions still cover a very small population of the aged and disabled. Many traditional arts now have no market. Community support systems have also decayed.

It is time that we recognize that begging is mostly the last desperate resort for barest survival by people who are the rejects of our glittering world, cast away due to disability, disease, stigma and old age, and a government that refuses to care enough to ensure basic social security for all its citizens.

'Illegal' Homes and Pickpockets

His mother delivered him under a plastic sheet, in a dusty makeshift tent strung on land adjacent to a construction site in the Indira Gandhi International Airport in Delhi, which his parents had laboured to construct for many years. He does not know the date he came into this world: 'We workers do not write our histories.' He smiles sardonically. For his school certificate, his father chose, as his date of birth, Independence Day. So, officially, Pramod Kumar was born on 15 August 1974.

A few months later, his parents returned to their native village in Bhagalpur, Bihar. It *was* home, but for low-caste, landless agricultural workers such as they were, there was rarely any work and every few months, his father would take a fresh loan from the local moneylender and disappear to the city for several months at a stretch. As Pramod's mother gave birth, one after another, to three sons and one daughter, she stopped travelling with her husband. Later, when Pramod's father aged, he also lost the spirit to bear the rigours of long lonely passages to distant work sites. Instead, first, Pramod's elder brother and, then, Pramod dropped out of school and made the same journey to Delhi that their parents had made so often in their lives. They did this so that their families could survive. Pramod was then ten years old.

Pramod's first job as a child migrant to Delhi was as a helper to a mason on the Mehrauli-Gurgoan Road. The wages he earned in 1984 were ₹11 and some paise a day. Survival for him meant sheltering precariously under a soiled plastic sheet, where he was to live for another ten years. The worst months, he recalls, more than even the biting cold of winter, were those of monsoon, in which they would have to wade for days in their hovels in slush, and were forced to mount their stove on a string cot so that they could cook their meals. He lived among others from his village who took care of the growing boy. He loved to study and carried his school books with him from the village. Each year, he would return to his village school for the annual examinations and his teachers would overlook his absence from classes. Eventually, he passed Class 9.

In time, he joined an electrician in Delhi as an apprentice. He learnt the skills of wiring newly constructed homes: the hours were long, the work dangerous for a novice, but the money was better. His wages mounted rapidly to ₹28 and, eventually, to ₹88. He was now able to regularly set aside money to send home to his ageing parents.

On one of his visits to Bhagalpur, his parents wed him to a young girl from a nearby village. The gauna, a ceremony in which the bride moves to her husband's home, took another two years. When Pramod brought his bride to Delhi, he was unwilling to subject her to his harsh life under a plastic tent, so he bought a piece of land from a contractor he worked for in Patparganj in East Delhi. The sale was illegal, because the contractor did not own the land. But there was no legal land offered by the government. It was a low-lying bog clogged with sewage from surrounding areas and infested with mosquitoes, behind the high-rise apartment buildings where he was employed to lay electrical lines. Pramod, his young wife, as well as others who had been illegally sold the land by the contractor, toiled for months to clear and level their plots. The contractor gave them bricks and tin sheets to fabricate their tiny, tenuous houses. Eventually, 430 shanties came up around his, which sheltered around 2,000 migrants like Pramod, and their families, from Bihar, Odisha, West Bengal, Rajasthan and Uttar Pradesh. There was no piped water supply or drinking water and they had to collect water from a leaking pipe 2 kilometres away. The only toilet available to them was the continuously shrinking open spaces around. 'Who could we complain to?' Pramod asked bitterly. 'The contractor? He would have simply packed us off and then what would have become of us?'

When their first daughter was born, Pramod resolved that they could not live like this all their lives. A contractor recruited him for employment in Dubai where he worked for eight years. He left his wife and children in Delhi so that they could attend good schools. His employer took his passport from him as soon as he arrived at the airport, as he did for all his fellow workers, and he worked almost all his waking hours. He never enjoyed his years in Dubai. But he put aside enough to send money to his parents in the village and to his wife in the slum in East Delhi. He visited home every few years, and left his wife pregnant each time. He has three daughters and a boy.

When Pramod finally returned to India, he found that almost all the small building contractors had been driven out of business—a result of globalization. The foreign companies employed only people with formal degrees, something that Pramod could never acquire despite his love of books. This deepened his resolve to educate all his children in English-medium schools, whatever it cost him. The fees in Bal Nikunj Public School was ₹200 every month for every child, but he felt that the school was better than those run by the government, where children could barely write their names.

I asked Pramod's little son what he learnt in school. He thought for a while and then replied gravely, 'Achchi batein! (Good things!)'

One day, residents of the high-rise buildings—which residents of Pramod's slum had toiled to build, and where their wives and sisters washed dishes and floors—decided that they did not want to live next to a slum any longer. Its squalor offended them, and they were convinced that it housed people with criminal tendencies. They filed a complaint in court, stating that the slum residents had violated 'green belt' regulations, and the court ruled against the shanty dwellers without hearing them. On the night of 23 February 2006, a head constable from Delhi Police informed them that demolitions would start the next morning. They huddled helplessly in their homes as, just after dawn, bulldozers appeared. The roads were blocked on both sides. People desperately retrieved what they could in the blur—TV sets, some boxes of clothes, favourite toys—but everything else was crushed by the relentless bulldozers.

They lived desolately under the open sky for the next two months. Some like Pramod moved into tiny rented tenements which they could ill afford. The court which had ordered the demolition had not instructed rehabilitation. Many demonstrations and gheraos of the officers of the Delhi Development Authority (DDA) finally yielded the reluctant offer of undeveloped plots in Bawana, 20 kilometres from their present dwellings, but only if they made a down payment of ₹5,000. Even this offer was made to only ninety-two of the 430 resident families deemed by the officials to be 'eligible'. Of these, forty-eight families took loans from moneylenders at 10 per cent compound interest *per month*, to pay the authorities. For the rest, the only prospect was homelessness.

Pramod took me to see the site where their homes had stood barely months earlier. The DDA had hastily constructed shops on the part of the plot that adjoined the road (where Pramod recalled that they had struggled most to fill the low-lying slush pits). Around the rest of the plot, a wall had been constructed. Through a small gap in the wall, he pointed out a madhumalati vine. 'That is precisely where my home stood,' he said. 'I had bought the madhumalati for ₹25. It soon grew all across the roof of our home. It gave off such a beautiful fragrance at night that it was the envy of the entire colony. It was crushed under the dozers, but revived in the monsoon. It stands there alone. My heart breaks whenever I look at it.'

~

As law scholar Usha Ramanathan observes, for at least 30 per cent of people in any city, a slum is simply 'home'. But for those who do not live in slums, 'Epithets such as "squatters" and "encroachers", and attributes such as "illegality" and "ineligibility" characterise perceptions about the lives and habitations of slum dwellers. While casting the slum dwellers into a stereotype, dirt, criminality, pilferage and their abetment of slumlords to prise public lands for unconscionable gain, are most routinely caricatured.'[155] In this vein, in the Almitra Patel case of 2000, the Supreme Court likened slum dwellers to pickpockets.[156] It 'castigated the process of resettlement as amounting to rewarding a pickpocket, for the slum dweller would be getting an alternative site in place of public land they had been using "free of cost".' But, as Ramanathan continues, 'An alternative adjectival construction of the slum dwellers would represent them as service providers who keep urban inhabitants in home, health and happiness; persons and communities aspiring to fuller citizenship by seeking to utilise the economic, educational and social opportunities that exist in the cities. Slum dwellers can be described as migrant workers who build up cities for those who can afford to buy what they build…industrial hands, whose labour is recognised, but not their need for residence when a city is planned, or the plan is implemented.'

The city's poor are regarded by people who live in settled homes to be illegal, illegitimate residents of the city. This is particularly ironic because the growth strategies adopted by successive governments are pushing people from the countryside in droves to the city. Former finance minister, P. Chidambaram, is reported to have said that his dream India is one in which 85 per cent of the people would live in cities.[157] The puzzle is why the state then makes migrants so unwelcome, treating them as unlawful and potentially dangerous populations. More than half of India's population depends on agriculture for a living, yet public investment in agriculture is down to about 5 per cent of total public sector investment.[158] It is not surprising—as I will describe later—that an estimated 2,000 people abandon the countryside every day. As farmers are crushed by debt and many are driven to suicide, farming families are encouraging the young to escape a dying economy and, indeed, a way of life, while they still can. But the city to which they flee treats them as unwanted, illegal residents.

The Constitution guarantees people the right to live and work in any part of the country. Yet in cases such as Hem Raj versus the Commissioner of Police, challenging the demolition of slums in an area called Nagla Machi near East Delhi, the Supreme Court was explicit that people should not come to Delhi unless they can afford to live in the city. Most of Delhi's middle classes are migrants, but no one is asking them to leave. The poor are seen as burdens on the city, ignoring that they provide inexhaustible supplies of cheap labour to build the city, cook and clean homes, recycle waste and deliver the cheapest retail as street vendors. The lifestyles of the middle class would be impossible without the army of the poor who are so unwelcome in the city.

In Delhi, nearly 50 per cent of the city's residents live in slums and unauthorized colonies which occupy barely 3 per cent of the city's residential land.[159, 160] And yet we clamour that these lands should be freed of the encumbrance of 'illegal' populations living there. Political leaders of every hue, and not just openly chauvinistic parties like the Shiv Sena, rage against migrants who clog up and dirty the city. In a television debate I once participated in, where slum migrants were being demonized and the popular clamour, supported by many, was that they should be blocked from coming into cities, I asked who in the audience had grandparents who were born in Delhi. The only hand which went up in the TV studio belonged to anchor Vikram Chandra. Middle-class Indians can legitimately migrate to any part of the country to pursue a better life, but not poor people.

The Amitabh Kundu Committee set up by the Planning Commission estimated that the housing shortage in India is to the tune of 18.78 million units.[161] Gautam Bhan and his colleagues from the Indian Institute for Human Settlements, writing for the 'India Exclusion Report 2013-14', observe that '95 per cent of the shortage in housing is for families classified as either from the Low Income Group (household income between Rs 5,000-10,000 a month) or Economically Weaker Sections (household income under Rs 5,000 a month). The increasingly commonly heard refrain that, "even middle class and working households cannot afford adequate housing" in Indian cities is untrue. The housing market does not, as is commonly believed, exclude large number of middle and working class communities from adequate housing though it may well exclude them from the kind of housing stock they want.'[162, 163]

Most middle-class people blame slum residents for living illegally and in squalor, as though they choose to live this way. Bhan explains why many residents in Indian cities live 'illegally', by occupying and building settlements on public or private land—they do so because of the state's failure to keep to its own stated commitments to build low-income and affordable housing; because of the inadequate notification of urban, residential land in planning documents that could provide space for legal housing to be built; the skewed structure of our urban land and housing markets that makes entry into the formal housing market nearly impossible for most urban residents; and the absence of sufficient investments in regional and urban infrastructure to expand settlement structure and accommodate migration as well as natural growth, among many others.[164]

The answer, some believe, is to 'resettle' slum residents outside the city. Gautam Bhan, along with Kalyani Menon-Sen also studied the deleterious impact of state slum relocation to 'legalize' illegal slums by eviction and peripheral resettlement from the old city of Delhi to Bawana in its distant periphery. This causes what they call 'permanent poverty', as 'a generation is prevented from development by a depletion of assets, a breaking of livelihoods, increased costs due to the distance from work and the city, increased violence, the fracturing of long-built community ties, as well as large-scale dropouts from school education'.[165]

Life in most slums in almost any Indian city is hellish. Typically, people live amidst sludge and waste, without sewerage and functioning toilets, without clean drinking water, in houses which get partially submerged in the rains because the natural drainage outlets have been built over, and often with excreta and plastic waste strewn in every direction. In his report, Bhan notes that data from the 2011

Census shows that 63 per cent of all households recognized or notified as 'slums' have either open or no drainage for waste water.[166] About 34 per cent of slum households have no latrine on the premises, and the residents of over half of such households defecate in the open.[167] Almost 43 per cent of slum households do not have a source of drinking water within the premises.[168] But these figures are likely to be considerable underestimations, because the most vulnerable urban poor communities live in slums which are not notified or recognized, or even mapped by the state. In these, there are fewer toilets and no sewerage arrangements. People therefore defecate everywhere into open drains or in almost any open spaces available. There are no facilities to dispose off solid waste, therefore large waste heaps abound; in fact, many slums are actually built on or near landfills. Many slums grow along lowlands, including the beds of city drains carrying untreated refuse, and there are slums in which people walk during monsoon months in knee-deep, filthy water. There are few if any public stand-points for potable water, and people spend hours in queues to fill water; in several cities, people buy water from private vendors.

In a slum I visited in Pune, 5,000 families actually live *on* the tracks in the railway shunting yard. Sixteen times each day, they jump off the tracks as the trains approach, and return when the locomotives have passed. The slums I went to in Patna were so filthy that I wondered how people could live and survive in them. Women in both the Pune and Patna slums spoke of how their children were always sick. How could anybody expect any different?

The illegality of slums makes the residents dependent on slum mafias, which foster a climate of regular extortion, violence and crime. And the perpetual threat of demolition by the state contributes to a fragile life of unrelenting uncertainty. And yet, middle-class Indians believe that people choose to live these lives, as though they had any real choices, and that for this crime they should be penalized and packed away somewhere, anywhere, but not where their daily, 'in-everybody's-faces' poverty offends them.

The Indian Help

In her extraordinary novel *The Help*, Katherine Stockett writes about the lives of black women domestic workers in a small town in Mississippi in 1962.[169] At the time in which the novel is set, the civil rights movement was yet to alter the unequal social relations between races in this small, conservative settlement. Stockett observantly recreates the segregation, distrust and disrespect which African American women workers routinely endured while working in middle-class white households. In the novel, three women lead a secret rebellion by anonymously writing about their experiences with their employers.

What deeply troubled me after I read the book was that the humiliation and exploitation suffered by domestic workers in southern US half a century earlier was, in fact, in many ways less oppressive than the daily lived experience of an estimated three million domestic workers in middle-class homes across urban India in the second decade of the twenty-first century. And that this causes us so little outrage.

Behind the walls of Indian middle-class—and even many lower-middle-class—houses, unequal India is constantly produced and reproduced in the way employers treat their domestic help. This is where children of relative privilege learn early to accept and normalize inequality, lessons they learn for life. When a small boy of four is asked to touch the feet of all his elders, how does he know so early that he is expected to touch the feet of all older people—except the domestic help? How does he learn that domestic workers are the only elders he can command, call by their first names, and speak rudely to without being corrected?

In the American novel, one African American help raises seventeen white children in her lifetime of employment. She has to sacrifice the care-time she wanted for her own son so that she can earn the money to tend to him. As long as they are babies, many white children love her more than their own mothers. Her heartbreak comes when they grow up, and treat her with the same casual disrespect and condescension, and acquire the same prejudices, as their mothers. How many of us urban, Indian, middle-class adults have been similarly raised by women who neglected their own children, women we have forgotten as we grow and they age?

In *The Help*, the 'rebellion by writing' of domestic workers in Mississippi is spurred by the decision of some employers to build segregated toilets for their helps, which they find insulting. But in middle-class Indian homes this is routine. A study in Delhi conducted by Jagori, an organization working primarily with women, found that in 30 per cent of the homes surveyed, part-time domestic workers had no access to toilets at all, and of those who did, used segregated toilets in 40 per cent of the homes.[170] In *The Help*, domestic workers ate at dining tables but at different times from their employers. But in Indian homes, there are often separate plates for the help to eat from, and they almost never eat at the same table as their employers. They are usually made to sit on the floor for their meals. They are not given the same food as the employers, but rationed quantities of coarser, cheap food, or leftovers.

The domestic help as portrayed in the book, in the 1960s, were modestly paid and worked eight hours with weekly off-days. Studies confirm that live-in Indian domestic workers today toil almost every waking hour, often seven days a week.[171] An official study estimated in 2004 that there were around 4.75 million domestic workers in the country.[172] Since domestic workers are mostly unregistered and are an invisible workforce, the actual numbers may be much higher. For instance, the study estimated that households in Delhi and Mumbai employ six hundred thousand domestic workers respectively, but activists place the numbers at one million in each city. There are three categories of domestic workers: residential workers who work 24x7, many of who are recruited through placement agencies; full-day workers who work from morning to evening for nine hours or more; and part-time workers who carry out specific tasks in more than one household and are normally recruited directly from and reside in slum areas. Additional tasks range from washing and ironing clothes, walking the dog, cleaning cars, mopping floors and toilets, and many others. Wages paid to domestic workers tend to be very low and are arbitrarily fixed well below statutory minimum wages and paid in recompense for much longer hours than prescribed. They spend many hours, often without breaks, sweeping and swabbing floors, washing clothes, cooking and taking care of the aged and children.

Part-time helps are paid so little that they work in multiple houses, which adds up to inordinately long working hours. Both full- and part-time helps have few, if any, paid holidays. They are protected by no labour law regulation and no social security contributions. Salaries are cut if they damage property, some workers report being denied their earnings by deceitful calculations, and they are often accused of stealing. Their work of sweeping, cleaning and cooking entail numerous health hazards, compounded by poor and irregular food and little rest and recreation. Aged domestic help are routinely dismissed from service to fend for themselves, with no question of any pension.

Left feminist economist Jayati Ghosh maintains that, 'Inequality is the cause of lower wages for domestic workers in India. Inequality in India permits lower wages for domestic work.'[173] She observes that despite the huge contribution made by domestic workers in society, they remain largely invisible and undervalued, which reflects the low value India places on social reproduction. She affirms that domestic workers should have equal rights for reasonable hours of work, weekly rest of at least twenty-four consecutive hours, a limit on in-kind payment, as well as clear information on the terms and conditions of employment.[174]

It is extraordinary that such a large and vulnerable workforce still lacks a specific protective legislative framework. The majority are women—often children—and migrants, which anyway renders them especially vulnerable. Compounding this problem is the fact that workplaces are hidden away within people's homes. As Ghosh observed, the greater part of the work performed by household help is underrated as work because, in most homes, it is considered unpaid and unacknowledged 'women's work'.[175] Since most middle-class enforcers of legal protections for domestic workers would themselves be employers—often on very similar exploitative terms—of domestic workers, there is built-in bias against domestic workers in enforcement. In the high-profile run-in of Indian diplomat Devyani Khobragade with her domestic help, Sangeeta Richards, which made international headlines for many weeks during 2013 and even strained Indo-US diplomatic relations, it is remarkable how unanimous public sympathy—in the media, the diplomatic services, the bureaucracy and even across political parties—was for the employer rather than her domestic help. Few were concerned with Richards's side of the story.

The dependence of urban middle-class households on domestic workers has grown further because of the entry of much larger numbers of educated women into the formal workforce. They depend critically on domestic carers to enable them to work and earn yet, as Sujata Ghotoskar again observes, contributions made by women domestic workers to the economy are grossly underrated, partly because domestic care-giving work by women is both devalued and taken for granted.[176] The growing economic dependence on them has increased their bargaining power a little, but this is limited because they are mostly unorganized. Domestic help assert their power today mainly by changing employers more freely than they did in the past, and addressing their employers not as sahib and memsahib, but as uncle and aunty.

Middle-class India's greatest shame is its employment of underage children as domestic workers. This is an invisible and powerless category of workers and, therefore, there are no reliable estimates of child domestic workers. The official study conducted by the National Commission for Enterprises in the Unorganized Sector (NCEUS) estimates that 20 per cent of all domestic workers are under fourteen years of age.[177] That is a shocking one in five. A quarter of all workers are between the ages of fifteen and twenty years. If you total both these figures, this means that an unconscionable two to three out of every five domestic workers are toiling for wages in homes when they should be studying and playing in schools and colleges.

Children who need protection and need to be rescued from hazardous conditions are the responsibility of Child Welfare Committees, constituted for single or groups of districts and comprise five members (including one woman) who are nominated by the government. In our work with street children, Child Welfare Committees also frequently refer to us children rescued from trafficking; we find a large number of young girls who have been trafficked from states like Jharkhand for domestic work. Parents battling hunger and debt in the teeming Indian countryside, reeling from endemic agrarian crisis, especially in tribal regions like Jharkhand, often surrender their children to agents who traffic them for domestic work in cities. Children are preferred over grown-ups because they are submissive and uncomplaining.

These children's stories are devastating and shaming: of criminal neglect, slave labour and violence, utterly forgetful of childhood. A girl of seven told me how her angry employer in Delhi just dismissed her and turned her on to the streets alone one day, and of the many horrors of her wanderings until she was rescued by the police and ultimately came into the care of my colleagues.

Unequal India will begin to change only when we teach our children to treat people who care for us in our homes as equal human beings, commanding the same worth and dignity.

Living and Dying on the Streets

It is a harsh unforgiving winter each year for homeless people who survive Delhi's streets. Through long foggy nights, bleary-eyed with sleep, they squat around tiny fires, desperately trying to keep the chill out. Many curl up together, sometimes under a single thin blanket, bony bodies pressed against each other, some along with stray dogs, all sharing body warmth. But we also encounter the stiff sleeping forms of single, lonely people, almost frozen in the cold. Every wintry night leaves behind more bodies—anonymous, dispensable people; rickshaw-pullers, balloon-sellers, women thrown out on to the streets by violent spouses, children who have escaped abuse, abandoned old people, all of whom could not battle any further. There are still no shelters of any kind for more than 90 per cent of over a hundred thousand men, women and children in the nation's capital for whom the open sky is the only roof.

Entrepreneurs in the walled city around Jama Masjid have learned to profit from the failures of the state to provide for its most dispossessed citizens. They hire out quilts to homeless people at ₹10 a night, and mattresses for an additional ₹10. They also occupy open tracts of government lands—where the government could have built many shelters—on which they erect makeshift private 'shelters', with plastic sheet roofs but no walls. Under these, they lay small cots with blankets and mattresses which they rent out to the homeless people who can afford to pay ₹30 rupees a night. A bonus of sleeping in these privatized 'shelters' is that the police are paid off to not harass the people who pay to sleep here.

Winter forces homeless people to make difficult choices. If you want the warmth of a quilt to keep out the cold, you may have to give up a meal. But people exposed to extreme temperatures require even more calories simply to maintain body temperature.

One late night in 2010, making the rounds of Old Delhi, we found Mohammed Shareef plying his cycle rickshaw, looking for passengers. He told us, 'I am hoping to earn another ₹20 so I can hire a quilt and mattress for the night. I earn ₹150 a day, sometimes less. Of this, I give ₹45 to the rickshaw owner. Each meal costs ₹40. I have to pay even for the water that I drink, and for the bath I take. Everything here costs money. Sometimes I don't have any money to buy food. Sometimes I cannot hire a quilt, and it is very hard to sleep in the cold.'

That same night, we also found a woman who would go on to die on the very streets where she lived. When we found her, she was starving, and seemed frighteningly close to death. It was the daily-wage workers who sleep at Jama Masjid who had spotted her a few days earlier. She had walked a few steps and then collapsed. They had fed her, and she had revived, but could not speak a single word. A compassionate relief worker, Deepak Das (who was once a street teenager and was raised by us), called a mobile police van. To their credit, they arrived promptly, and agreed to transport the destitute woman to a government hospital. The presence of Deepak, who has fought with hospital staff to accept many destitute homeless people, ensured that they admitted her. But we walked away with the cold, unspoken knowledge that most people in her place in the many harsh streets of Delhi would simply die.

Then, in Nizamuddin, we met a middle-aged homeless man whose self-chosen, principal vocation is to dispose off unclaimed dead bodies. Sometimes he is informed by the police; at other times, other homeless people call him to take away rotting human bodies off the streets. He tries to enquire about the religious faith of the dead person. If the person is Hindu, he transports the body to the cremation grounds; if Muslim, then to the cemetery. Local people, mostly homeless, pool money to pay for these last rites, and if there is some money left over, he uses it for food. In one of the coldest winters in the city, he recalled collecting ten bodies in a single night. There is rarely a post-mortem and many deaths are not even recorded. The lives of the destitute are extraordinarily cheap in our land.

On our tours across the city we have found that a large number of people were rendered homeless because governments demolished their hutments, and never provided them alternative accomodation. There were over 250 such families who slept in a public park in Nizamuddin. One of these families was headed by Kusoom, a woman who migrated from Assam decades ago in search of work. She had built a small shanty over time, which had been pulled down many years ago and, since then, she had slept in the park—summer, winter or monsoon. It is difficult for a woman to live alone on the streets, therefore, like many single homeless women in Nizamuddin, she accepted a series of homeless men as transient partners, each of whom left her even more wounded in body and spirit, and sometimes with children to raise. She tried to find work as domestic help in people's homes to feed her two surviving children and herself, but could rarely earn more than ₹600 rupees every month, barely enough to live on. She and her children often begged and ate at dargahs. However, she was spending a precious ₹120 every month to send her son to a private school, and was preparing to send her daughter as well.

Many homeless people, including children, survive the rigours of the cold and rain by using drugs. You find them glassy-eyed and dazed—impervious to the suffering, loneliness and shame of fighting nature and an uncaring city. We ask homeless people which season they find the cruellest in Delhi. Many say it is winter, because it threatens life. But others say the monsoons are the worst. When it rains at night, it is impossible to sleep, or cook, and their few belongings are soaked.

Yet there are little slivers of hope in all this despair. We met a woman who had lived for seventeen years on a traffic island in Nizamuddin, under a plastic sheet. But she had adopted an abandoned boy and had elected to raise him even though she was herself utterly destitute. The boy had grown up, and was more devoted to her than any child she would have carried in her womb.

And Shareef, the cycle-rickshaw driver, told us in Old Delhi, 'This is the story of the poor. But I work very hard, and therefore, however difficult my life is, I know I live it with dignity.'

~

In the winter of 2010-11 we decided to investigate how many homeless people die each day in the capital city of India. This morbid quest turned out to be deeply unsettling for each of us who engaged with it. We discovered that every day, an average of at least ten homeless people die desolate, lonely deaths on the streets of Delhi.

Why did we undertake this grisly investigation? It began when, that winter, the public conscience of even the normally morally insulated middle classes was stirred briefly by media reports of homeless people dying in the winter cold. Many of those who succumbed to the fierce winter chill were young working people: balloon-sellers, rickshaw-pullers, casual workers and street vendors.

The Delhi government's record, all these years after Independence, in setting up even elementary shelters for homeless people has been dismal—although governments in many other cities have failed the homeless even more comprehensively; several, like Mumbai, have no government-run shelters for the homeless at all. Even while Delhi was witnessing in 2010 some of the coldest temperatures in a decade, the government, until 2010, had not been stirred to take steps required to protect the people living on the streets from extreme weather. It offered shelters to not more than 3 per cent of the homeless people of the city until then but, in the winter of 2010, even these few shelters were reduced, presumably because of more pressing priorities. The closing down of even the few basic shelters which existed had been going on for some years. During the earlier year, there were forty-six shelters for the homeless during winter—which included seventeen permanent and twenty-nine temporary shelters. The number was then reduced to thirty-three.[178] Matters came to a head when one of this small numbers of temporary shelters was pulled down one near-freezing December night in 2010, to make way—according to municipal officials—for a park, and homeless people began to die at that very site.

Once core temperature falls, a person requires ever higher calories just to maintain body temperature. People die on the streets in winter simply because they are denied food and shelter. Malnutrition and hunger are the underlying causes which make people susceptible to extreme weather conditions. Therefore, as commissioners of the Supreme Court in the Right to Food case, N. C. Saxena and I wrote to the judges of the Supreme Court soon after the deaths, in December 2010, of the homeless precipitated by the closure of shelters, that many of the deaths could have been avoided had the government provided shelters to people living on the streets and implemented food schemes for them. The judges of the Supreme Court, Justices Dalveer Bhandari and K. S. Radhakrishnan took urgent cognizance of our letter and directed the government of Delhi to immediately provide as many shelters as possible. An angry High Court, led by Justice Ajit Prakash Shah, simultaneously took suo moto notice and summoned officials of the Delhi government.[179] In compliance with the firm dictates of the courts, the Delhi government doubled the numbers of shelters that it had established since Independence within two nights.

These events raised many questions for us. We wondered how many people die every day on the streets of Delhi and, indeed, every city. Was it a problem only of winter? Who were these people, and why did they die?

The government keeps no records which could give us clear and direct answers to these questions. Therefore, my young colleagues Smita Jacob and Asghar Sharif set out on an investigation of crematoriums, graveyards and police stations. At the end of a protracted, painful search, they came up with many disquieting findings.

Neither police nor hospitals keep records of people who die on the streets. But we found that police does keep records of 'unclaimed dead bodies', on their Zonal Integrated Police website.[180] These are records of people who die on streets, and sometimes hospitals. Police confirm that these bodies are mostly of single, destitute, homeless people who have no family who can claim their bodies and dispose them off with dignity. We felt that these records would give us some indication of how many *single* homeless people die.

These police records showed that between 1 January 2005 and 31 December 2009, 12,413 unidentified dead bodies were recovered in the state of Delhi. This data for sixty months indicates an average of about seven unidentified bodies per day. This implies that the Delhi Police recorded at least seven solitary homeless people dying every day on Delhi's streets.[181]

However, not even all single people who die on the streets enter the police's records. Some bodies are taken directly to crematoriums and cemeteries. Smita and Asghar learnt from homeless people that it was the electric crematorium at Sarai Kale Khan and the Muslim burial ground of the Delhi Wakf Board which makes arrangements to dispose off unidentified bodies. They requested the managers of the crematorium and the cemetery to share their records for the first four months of 2010. Poring through these registers, they found evidence of many more unidentified deaths than were recorded in police records. These averaged 306 dead bodies a month—or more than ten, daily.

But even this is not the full story. In the many years that I have worked with homeless people, I have observed that neighbours and others who shared space with the homeless dead routinely raise donations from among themselves. From their meagre means, they try to ensure that the dead find dignity. None of these people who are beneficiaries of neighbourly charity enter police or cemetery records as 'unclaimed bodies'. Also excluded are people whose death rites are taken care of by their families. We concluded, therefore, that probably even more than ten people die, per day, on the streets of Delhi.

Then, we wanted to compare our findings with other city residents who die in the normal course. The CIA Factbook estimates 7.35 deaths per 1,000 in 2014, which translates to 735 deaths per 100,000—roughly, two deaths a day.[182] Delhi's homeless population is estimated at 100,000, therefore the death rates for the homeless is at least five times the average national death rate. This means that easily five times more homeless people die, per day, compared to people who live in houses.

Our gloomy pursuit threw up still further surprises. We had assumed that homeless people would die mainly in the cold. An analysis of the police figures revealed the contrary, that deaths peak not in winter, but in the summer months, followed by the monsoon. The summer heat is relentless and unforgiving, and homeless people have no escape or respite from it, by day or night. It is this which probably claims most lives. Each monsoon deluge also carries along its deadly burdens of refuse, waste and infections.

We had also assumed that it would be the aged, the infirm and the disabled who would be amongst the dead. We were shocked to learn that about 94 per cent of the dead were men, and the average age of the dead was forty-two years. It was, therefore, principally the labouring men who were dying, and not just the aged and the destitute.

We looked closely at the records of one police station, Kashmere Gate, to collate the officially recorded causes of death. We found that only 8 per cent of the deaths were attributed to accidents, suicides or murder. The remaining 92 per cent were listed under 'natural causes': hunger and thirst, extreme heat or cold, diseases of poverty like tuberculosis, and a curious category reflecting the government's contempt for the most destitute of our people: 'beggar type'. It was chillingly evident that most of these large numbers of young men were dying, ultimately, because they were underfed and homeless.

I take some solace that—through judicial, civic and media activism—we have been collectively able to ensure some visibility for homeless persons. In the elections to the Delhi assembly in the winter of 2013, and again in early 2015, political parties like the Aam Aadmi Party focused some concern for the homeless. The police and state government officials, in the winter of 2014-15, started forcing homeless people to enter shelters, ignoring not just the deplorable conditions of many of these structures, but also that shelters can still house only less than a tenth of Delhi's homeless population. As a result of this attention, ironically, homeless people had to flee the most visible highways of the city for small bye-lanes where they hoped not to be found by policemen forcing them to sleep in homes which often do not work for them or do not exist at all!

~

One more blood-drenched road accident. Another soul-numbing statistic. A drunken man, driving at night at deadly speeds, loses control and crushes thirteen sleeping men. The driver is arrested but released on bail next day. People forget, until the next accident. In Delhi, there were three accidents involving homeless men in one week in the month of August 2014.

The thirteen men pounded by an SUV on the night of 17 August 2014 were just settling down to sleep at around 10 p.m. on a road divider a few hundred metres from a shelter at Yamuna Pushta which my young colleagues run for destitute homeless men. Gautam, a forty-five-year-old house painter from Rajasthan recalls that shortly after he had eaten his evening meal, 'I had almost fallen asleep when I heard a loud noise and before I knew it, something rock solid came and hit me. I was one of the first to be hit. Fortunately, my left leg was folded, not stretched. I am grateful to God that nothing worse happened. A few others were very badly injured.' Vipul, a thirty-year-old casual labourer from Assam, added, 'I don't remember what happened. I heard a loud noise and after I got hit I could not get up.' Vipul's right foot is badly damaged.

Gautam recalled that the driver tried to run. 'The car was still not stable, and the man ran in the direction of the road on the other side. However, the police had already arrived, and he could not cross the road, perhaps in panic.' A social worker from the shelter had by then called the police, and they arrived within minutes. In the next half hour, three police vehicles and an emergency ambulance rushed the thirteen injured men to various public hospitals. The following day, thirty-six-year-old Ekraj died, and six other men battled long for their lives. The ones who pulled through were permanently disabled.

Who were these men, and why did they risk their lives sleeping on the road divider of a busy highway? Almost all were men who, at some point in their lives, came to Delhi to seek work to feed their families back in their villages—elderly parents, siblings, wives and children. The work they found was casual, intermittent and so poorly paid that there would be nothing left to send back home after they had spent money on their basic needs. Therefore they chose the hard life of sleeping rough on the streets, so that their families could survive.

In our work, we also encounter homeless men who fail to regularly find even such low-end work, and who save little to send home. Their self-esteem plummets, their bonds with their families fray and sometimes snap, and they gradually slip into a life of hard drugs, food charities, and occasional work in wedding parties or rag-picking.

Around 4,000 of these lonely, destitute, homeless men have made Yamuna Pushta their home. It is only because this stretch of land is so inauspicious and inhospitable that the city has ceded it to the city's dregs. Our shelters, and those run by other organizations, rapidly fill up every evening, and thousands of men still sleep in the open every night.

Homeless people explain why, especially in the summer and monsoon months, they choose to sleep so dangerously on pavements and road dividers. Anywhere else, such as in parks or parking lots, sleep is almost impossible because of swarms of mosquitoes. Near a highway, sleep becomes more possible because automobile fumes drive away pests. The stark fact is that these men risk their lives every day, and indeed critically damage their lungs with vehicle emissions, because it is the only way that they can sleep every night.

The solutions are not so hard to find. Each city should construct large numbers of hostels for working men and women, with inexpensive rooms and dormitories which make sleeping on the streets unnecessary; and invest in affordable rental and self-owned social housing and thousands of community kitchens supplying affordable, nutritious food. If building contractors are forced to establish decent worker-camps for all their workers, with water, sanitation and child-care services, before they begin long-term projects, a significant number of potentially homeless poor people could be housed. But the stark truth is that these public investments are not made, and avoidable deaths continue just outside our doorsteps, daily, because they are people who are too poor to matter.

The Crime of Falling Ill

We will call the boy Rajesh. He had a shy, winning smile, a lanky frame and rakish hair. Picked up repeatedly for housebreaking, the teenager spent many years repeatedly running away from various observation homes created in Delhi for children in conflict with the law. We offered to take care of him instead in our children's home, on the condition that we refuse to lock him up because we oppose the incarceration of children. A compassionate magistrate agreed.

He chose to stay with us, although our doors are always unlocked in the day, and we all grew fond of him. He spoke little about his family, except to say that his father was dead. We heard that he had a mother, but she seemed to have despaired of raising him well. His brother drove a bus, but he had broken ties with him. As he grew into adulthood, he shifted into a home for young adults, Unnati, which we run for young homeless adults whose higher and technical education we try to support. Unlike most other former street youth in our care, he was reluctant to study, and still unclear about what he would do with his life.

Quite abruptly, Rajesh's behaviour changed dramatically. His housemates reported that he became suspicious of them and accused them of plotting against him. He started hearing voices. It quickly became apparent that he was engulfed in an acute episode of full-blown schizophrenia. My colleagues took him to the Institute of Human Behaviour and Allied Sciences (IBHAS) in Shahdara. The doctors examined Rajesh in their outpatient department, prescribed medicines, but couldn't admit him because they had no beds to spare.

He returned to Unnati, where his housemates and the staff tried to engage him. He played a game of chess, but was mostly quiet. The next day, no one quite knows what exactly happened. He fell from a height, got burned by an electric line next to the apartment, and badly hurt himself. The staff in Unnati called an ambulance which took him to the emergency unit of the All India Institute of Medical

Sciences (AIIMS), the country's premier tertiary-care and research public hospital. The doctors worked on him diligently, and declared him to be out of danger. Eight hours later, after midnight, they asked that he be shifted to the neurosurgery department of Safdarjung Hospital which is just across the road from AIIMS. His housemates, former street boys themselves, kept continuous vigil by his bedside, more caring than brothers.

The boy was obviously in great pain, groaning continuously, and still hallucinating, lashing out at the doctors. But to our surprise, within another eight hours, the doctors at Safdarjung discharged him, saying that home care would be sufficient for Rajesh. In desperation, we returned to IBHAS. I had to intervene personally at senior levels of the hospital administration for the boy to be given a bed. He responded to the treatment and improved visibly in a couple of days; he was calmer, and his pain became more bearable.

However, after two days, the IBHAS doctors again asked for Rajesh to be sent to AIIMS, because of neurological complications. AIIMS refused to admit him, and asked that he be returned to Safdarjung, which had discharged him earlier. We pleaded that they had already refused to admit him, so they, instead, referred him to the other major public hospital in Delhi, the Ram Manohar Lohia Hospital. We took Rajesh there; the doctors gave him some medicines but again refused him a bed. Finally we took him back to IBHAS, and requested again that they admit and treat him there. I personally pleaded with the senior officials of the hospital because without treatment the boy's entire life could lie in ruins, and they finally consented. He spent a month there. My colleagues finally found his mother, and she took the boy back home when IBHAS discharged him. They rebuilt their broken relationship, and she returned with Rajesh to their village in Bihar to help her boy heal.

~

I feel an intense disquiet about the fate of young people like Rajesh, who can experience mental illness like anyone else. Recent advances in medicine have ensured that most mental illnesses can be treated professionally and compassionately, therefore patients have a chance of recovery and a life of relative peace. What is critical in mental illness is early intervention, which gives better results. But if the illness remains untreated, patients can either harm themselves or others grievously, or the illness will cause patients to lose livelihoods or relationships. Gradually, such people join the ranks of the numerous mentally ill who populate and are abused on the streets.

Caring for persons with mental disorders has always been a challenge, both in rich and not-so-rich countries, even for well-resourced and expensive private mental health clinics, but much more so for public health systems. However, over the last two hundred years, care systems in India have gradually improved. Where, up to the eighteenth century, the 'cure' for mental illness was incarceration in jails, in the nineteenth and early twentieth centuries, patients were confined to care and control in asylums. In the late twentieth and twenty-first centuries, conditions bettered and patients began to be taken care of in general hospitals and by the community.

This progress was also reflected in the changes to the laws relating to mentally ill people—from the Indian Lunacy Act of 1912 to the Mental Health Act, 1987, to proposed legal changes currently on the anvil. The Lunacy Act 1912 laid down guidelines—solely for institutionalization in an asylum—of a person who is proven to be a 'lunatic' by an examining medical officer and magistrate. The stigmatized term 'lunatic' was used unproblematically, and was vaguely defined by the law to even include anyone who 'causes a nuisance' or is deemed to be dangerous, and who could be incarcerated under its provisions. The Mental Health Act, 1987, sought, in contrast, to protect the rights of those who were institutionalized either voluntarily or against their will; prevent unnecessary institutionalization; regulate the powers of the government in controlling psychiatric institutions; and also provide for guardianship of patients without support and legal aid. A more progressive law to protect persons with mental illness was approved by the UPA government in 2013, but this was not passed by Parliament. However, there is a group which remains outside the gamut of all changes—homeless people and people without families and economic means when they become mentally ill.

Thirty years earlier, what would have happened to Rajesh? Instead of the modern and improved IBHAS, there would have been the primitive mental hospital in Shahdara, in which patients were once chained, mostly naked, given electroconvulsive therapy and detained, often for years. Rajesh would not have been turned away, he would not have been left to cause harm to himself, but the treatment would have broken both his dignity and his spirit. He would have stayed in hospital for many, many years, lost to himself, his mother and the world.

Human rights concerns are rightly pushing such closed and custodial mental hospitals into history. But what have these been replaced by? In the case of Rajesh, no one was willing to take responsibility for his care. Despite many efforts and the goodwill of carers, he was shunted from hospital to hospital even though he was acutely ill and needed medical care for schizophrenia, along with treatment for injuries sustained during his fall. He also showed that people with mental illness can harm themselves, as a part of the illness response, unless treated and relieved of the distressing delusions and hallucinations. Yet none of our major public hospitals was willing to take him into their care. And while we managed, with enormous difficulty, to get him treatment, the prospect that Rajesh needs life-long care worries me.

Even middle-class caregivers of patients of mental illness find it hard to access treatment, particularly when the patient herself refuses treatment. I have found that mental health professionals do not want to take responsibility for involuntary care, even though it may be critical for the patient's own protection. But these problems become greatly compounded if the caregivers are poor, because they cannot afford the costs of repeated hospital visits and long bedside care at home, especially if the patients are difficult or unruly.

Public hospitals are typically most reluctant to admit homeless patients because they are unwashed, lack a residential address, cannot afford medicines and tests, and do not have anyone to provide bedside care. Homeless patients are even more unwelcome if they are mentally ill, because they are challenging to manage. Rajesh did not have many of these disadvantages; he had people by his side who loved him, and we also exercised some middle-class influence, yet he still was being tossed from hospital to hospital. The situation is even more hopeless in private hospitals, even though they have a legal duty to provide some beds for free.

There is clearly a deep ethical crisis in care-giving professions, in medical care in general and mental healthcare in particular, as well as in the idea of a caring state. For people in distress who have no money to offer, there is an unconscionable abdication by professionals, both public and private, and by the state. It is as though there is an unstated consensus that patients with limited or no means of support should be allowed to suffer untreated; as though they do not matter at all. However, the right to receive care cannot be left as a function of one's wealth or power.

~

I spent the early years of my working life as a civil servant in remote rural and tribal districts of Chhattisgarh and Madhya Pradesh. I observed how, often, large numbers of tribal and other villagers in rural hinterlands would die in multitudes in localized epidemics of gastroenteritis or malaria, which would be barely reported even in the state media. These areas were meagerly served with any kind of primary health services. The major concern of most of the scant public health staff that was deployed was to find 'cases' for family planning, all preferably by terminal methods. Child health was reduced to polio drops, not comprehensive healthcare, sanitation, nutrition and clean drinking water; and maternal health to contraceptives.

After returning to Delhi, over the last decade, I began working with urban homeless people. I found that many homeless people give up seeking treatment because they cannot afford the services even of public hospitals, with devastating outcomes on their health, livelihoods, and survival with dignity. Homeless people die of aliments like tuberculosis because they have no place they can rest in, eat nutritious food and be cared for. I found that the situation is little different for residents of urban slums as well. Most cities have virtually no public primary healthcare services, except a few maternity clinics, focused mostly on family planning. The few that exist have virtually no allocations for drugs and diagnostics. In many cities, slum dwellers I met spoke of the disrespect with which they were treated by the health personnel; doctors wouldn't even touch them for a physical examination because they found them unclean, and often taunted them for producing too many babies. Public doctors would demand that they buy not just most drugs, but even consumables like plastic gloves, before they could be treated. They would have to wait long hours in queues, mostly in the mornings; therefore visiting a public health clinic would mean sacrificing the day's earnings. They therefore found visiting a private practitioner more economical, who even if he was often unqualified, and would also charge them money, but would treat them with a modium respect. Sadly, the treatment they would prescribe would be frequently irrational and inappropriate. Those who could not afford the private practitioners would go directly to the pharmacist and take whatever drugs he would suggest. Others would just live with their ailments, enfeebled, and ultimately die.

Public health scholar and paediatrician Vandana Prasad undertook a study to understand the barriers faced by adult street dwellers in Delhi in accessing healthcare in Delhi.[183] The people investigated included able-bodied casual workers, rag-pickers, women who had escaped or had been expelled from violent and abusive homes, and people suffering from a variety of disabilities, including mental illness. One of the most important findings of Prasad's study was that catastrophic illnesses most commonly tipped poor people into homelessness.

The study also found that uppermost among the many barriers faced by the homeless in attempting to access public healthcare services was, simply, the lack of money. They lacked BPL cards which would otherwise make them eligible for free medicines and were forced to buy medicines and pay for tests. Many gave up because they could not afford the services of even public hospitals, which had a devastating effect on their health and livelihoods, and impacted their survival with dignity. The research also encountered three invalids who had once been able-bodied, working homeless men and had suffered treatable injuries from road accidents or at work. But since they could not afford government hospitals, they were permanently disabled, and were forced to beg life-long.

Another prominent barrier to accessing healthcare were the delays and 'shunting' experienced by the participants in busy public hospitals, which led many participants to give up before their problem could be addressed. A young homeless woman spent two years begging doctors in four tertiary-care public hospitals in Delhi to treat her young baby, all of whom kept insisting that there was nothing wrong with her. It was only her persistence—she describes it as 'haath pair jodna', or extreme supplication in front of the doctors—which led them to recognize that the girl was suffering from a congenital intestinal blockage and agreed to operate on her, thereby saving her life.[184]

These myriad problems are further compounded by low literacy, isolation, unfamiliarity and stigma. Other barriers include elementary infrastructure problems such as the lack of a place to safely store medical records.

In Prasad's study, not a single homeless respondent possessed a BPL card or any other automatic proof of their status as being 'poor'. Thus, no one could access the social security entitlements meant for them. They also lacked physical addresses which could be quoted on medical records as well as attendants to help them in hospital. Many homeless people do not have attendants—in most cases, family members—who are expected to cater to all the needs of patients because either they are alone on the streets or anyone who could accompany them is usually out on the streets, trying to survive.

Vandana Prasad's rigorous and empathetic study documents, in painful detail, how hard it is to be homeless and require healthcare. She concludes that it is only a comprehensive, universally free public system of healthcare, one that does not require any cash transactions between the service providers and the users, which can enable the homeless to surmount the prohibitive costs of care.

They would require, in addition to universal healthcare, comprehensive social protection, residential shelters, recovery shelters, and support for their particular needs as homeless persons, such as nutritional support and paid attendants, for the periods when they need to be hospitalized. But in a country where even existing public health services are being downsized and privatized, there is little room for optimism that citizens will secure the dignity of healthcare if they have the misfortune to be houseless, alone, and unwell.

~

During my childhood, many like me in the middle classes went to public hospitals when they fell sick, and the services offered in these public institutions were completely free. Today, every Indian city is dotted with expensive super-speciality private hospitals which closely resemble five-star hotels. The illusion is complete with an elaborately moustachioed doorman opening the doors of your car as you drive into many of these hospitals. As with government schools, the middle classes have completely abandoned—for the poor—public hospitals (except some tertiary-care hospitals); part of the 'secession' by the middle classes observed acutely by Arundhati Roy.[185] The quality of services in public hospitals has declined since people of influence no longer have any stake in their effective functioning but, even more gravely for the poor, care in the public hospital may be cheaper than in the private sector—but it is no longer free.

The average per-hospitalization cost *in a public hospital* is estimated to be as high as ₹3,000—and the poorer the state, the higher the costs are likely to be because there are fewer private providers for many categories of services. Some of the expenses in public hospitals are in the guise of user fees or services charges—for registration, for admission, for diagnostics, and even as consultation fees. However, a major part of the charges are due to drugs and diagnostics that are prescribed but not supplied, and instead have to be purchased outside the public hospital from private pharmacies and laboratories. This is the outcome of the policy introduced in the 1990s as part of a wide battery of market reforms. But now that many pharmacies and laboratories have mushroomed around public hospitals, there is also a nexus and a new culture encouraged by sales representatives that encourages government doctors to prescribe more drugs and diagnostics for outside purchase rather than provide them free within the hospital. The expenses which have to be borne by impoverished sick persons could be so high—as we shall observe—that they could become a barrier to seeking care. I am convinced that a fully cashless and paperless system (requiring no records to qualify the patient for care), in which all the Ds—doctors' fees, drugs, diagnostics and diet if hospitalized—are free, supported entirely by public subsidy, can protect the healthcare of impoverished patients, and not just save their lives but also protect them from pauperization.

But India's indifference to the survival of the poor is reflected in the abysmally low public investments in health in India. Public funding on health is barely 1.2 per cent of the GDP (with the Central government's share as low as 0.3 per cent), around a third of the average of 2.8 per cent in low- and middle-income countries, and much lower than industrialized countries.[186] The country spends three times as much on defence. Even more distressing is that most of this public expenditure is on tertiary care, because this is the only segment of public health services in which the middle classes still have a stake, but the poor are not major beneficiaries of these services. Public expenditure on health would benefit the poor if it focused on preventive, promotional and primary curative healthcare, which are starved of resources. Families meet about 70 per cent of health-related costs through out-of-pocket expenditure, most of all on medicines. This is increasingly pushing poor families into deeper poverty. A study based on NSSO 2004-05 data estimated that out-of-pocket health expenditure pushed nearly thirty-six million people into poverty, compared to twenty-six million in 1993-94.[187]

It is not surprising then, that one of the leading contributors to poverty is the rising cost of healthcare. The World Bank estimates that one-quarter of all Indians fall into poverty as a direct result of hospitalization.[188] A study conducted by *The Lancet* estimated that more than sixty million people in India, or almost 5 per cent of the population, were forced below the poverty line by healthcare costs in 2011.[189] A much larger section had to take a deep reduction in their quality of life because they had to give up many essential comforts to cover their health costs.

Another significant population which became more vulnerable to other financial stresses because of healthcare costs was that of farmers. Thus, in rural areas, a lot of farmer suicides happened because risks in agriculture were compounded by the risk of having to incur costs for healthcare.

The greatest reason for people's impoverishment and death due to high health costs is the move—by institutions like the World Bank and the International Monetary Fund (IMF)—to replace free public health services with user costs, making not just private but also public health costs unaffordable for the poor. Therefore, it is very significant that, in 2014, the president of the World Bank, Jim Yong Kim, admitted that the assumption that people in poor countries should pay for healthcare was wrong; 'There's now just overwhelming evidence that those user fees actually worsened health outcomes. So did the bank get it wrong before? Yeah. I think the bank was ideological.'[190] This admission that the Bank's influential pressure on many governments to pull back on public health provisioning and replace it with for-profit private health services was 'ideologically' driven, is belated but very welcome. But many governments, including our own, seem to be still influenced by this same market fundamentalism.

~

My mother passed away in 2014. In the four years preceding her passing, my ageing parents—both in their eighties—were in very frail health, with many life-threatening conditions. We were in and out of an array of expensive private hospitals, each of which was staggeringly expensive, and was paid for by my father's UN-provided health insurance. But they were always crowded—there was clearly no shortage of people who could afford the astronomical fees. My mother had twenty-four-hour nursing at home for three years preceding her passing away. I realized soberly that had we been less privileged—like the large majority of Indians are—my parents would not have remained alive for as long as they did.

In a sobering counterpoint, a few years ago I saw a television report which continues to haunt me. A man in Uttar Pradesh unsuccessfully tried to drown his nine-year-old daughter. His daughter was devastated and bewildered, because she knew her father to be a loving and responsible parent. The broken man explained that his daughter's kidneys had given way and, for the past two years he had spent all his savings and sold all his belongings for her treatment. But, as a result, his other children were pauperized, struggling even for their basic needs like food. He felt he had no option except to drown his beloved sick child to save the rest of his children.

To be poor in India is a crime. To be poor and also gravely ill is a crime deserving only the death penalty.

The Merit of Reservations

Indian democracy is dishonoured from time to time by brutal massacres of the country's historically oppressed communities—mostly Dalit and Muslims. But an even greater disgrace is that mass killers who periodically target people only because of their religion or caste are rarely punished. This legal impunity springs from the deep institutional prejudice which scars India's otherwise independent judicial system.

It is for this reason that the judgment passed by the Andhra Pradesh High Court in April 2014—ignored in the heat and dust of the general elections—which acquitted all twenty-one men who were serving life sentences for the massacre of Dalits in Tsundur, should have shocked and grieved observers much more than it did.

In 1991, a minor altercation in a cinema hall spiralled into a terrifying massacre. A high-caste Reddy man was enraged when a Dalit college student, Ravi, rested his feet on his seat. In reprisal for this impudence, Ravi was first attacked in his village, Tsundur, then charged with theft, and then arrested. Following this, the upper-caste community fell back on old weapons commonly deployed by higher castes through the ages to subdue disadvantaged communities: an economic boycott was imposed to break their backs, as upper-caste farmers refused to employ the landless Dalits as farm labour or tenants.

Emotions, already raging, were further fanned when a false charge was levelled at a Dalit youth, that he was sexually harassing local Reddy girls. (This allegation is chillingly similar to the one made twenty-two years later in Muzaffarnagar, Uttar Pradesh, which again was later proved false, but which similarly led to violent reprisal against local Muslims.) Mass rage gripped the surrounding countryside and resulted in a well-planned attack on the Dalits. As they desperately tried to flee the village they found it surrounded on every side by Reddy men in tractors armed with daggers and iron rods. They were brutally assaulted, and many mutilated bodies were flung into the Tungabhadra canal. This caste-fuelled assault left eight men dead and three badly injured.

What followed was a rare judicial victory, heroically won after many years of struggle by the Dalit survivors of Tsundur village, who braved boycott, violence, and social and state intimidation in an epic battle for justice. Determined that the perpetrators of these atrocities should not go unpunished, like they always had in the past—as Subash Gatade recalls in an article in Kafila—the survivors refused to accept summons or to appear in court until the government agreed to appoint a special court to hear the case and, for the first time, to conduct the special court in their village.[191] They also demanded and ultimately secured both a public prosecutor and judge with reputations for fairness.

Typically these cases drag on for years, and witnesses and survivors are wearied and coerced into rescinding their statements. But not in Tsundur, where victims did not allow their poverty and centuries of social oppression to break their resolve, resisting powerful attempts to buy their submission with threats, money and jobs, and raising the slogan 'justice not welfare'. Young Dalit men abandoned their education and refused to marry until justice was won for the survivors of the butchery. Gatade recalls many people who stood tall for justice.[192] Merukonda Subbarao, a daily-wage worker became a local hero after he identified and named forty of the accused in the courtroom from among the 183 accused. It took great courage for him to resolutely identify powerful men in court who, earlier, he could never walk alongside or even look in the eye.

But their epic resistance and success in securing justice from a criminal justice system infamous for its anti-Dalit bias has been today reduced to nothing. More than two decades after the crime, the Andhra Pradesh High Court ordered that twenty-one men serving life sentences for the massacre walk free (one of them even joined Jagan Reddy's election campaign).

The High Court ruled that 'the prosecution failed to prove the exact time of the death of the deceased and place of occurrence and the identity of the persons who attacked them'. It found further fault with the prosecution, because no complaint had been filed about the attacks, and the judges rejected the witnesses's statements because of 'contradictions'.

In doing so, the High Court ignored the formidable challenges of fear and loss faced by survivors of caste and communal mass crimes when confronting an openly partisan police system. The Tsundur Special Court, which had severely indicted the police for its anti-Dalit bias, had rightly acknowledged that a defective investigation could 'naturally' lead to 'contradictions and omissions' from prosecution witnesses. Therefore it had accepted a certain amount of omissions in statements, rightly noting, 'Every omission is not a contradiction.' Indeed, the Supreme Court, in many rulings, has held that it is unreasonable and unjust to expect the same standards of evidence in mass crimes as in regular individual crimes, because of embedded institutional bias.

The rejection of the veracity of the statements which the Dalit survivors courageously made in open courts, battling violence, intimidation and boycott, was therefore a grave setback to the greater idea of justice. It was unjust for the judges of the Andhra Pradesh High Court to close their eyes to the larger context of economic and social violence and power imposed by caste superiority and ownership of large land holdings in rural India, and the close nexus of rich, upper-caste landed communities with the police and the ruling establishment.

The survivors of the Tsundur Dalit massacre chose to fight the injustice and bloodbath to which they had been made subject not by picking up arms and joining the Maoist rebellion, which had already struck deep roots in the surrounding countryside. Instead, they rightly placed their faith in the ponderous processes of a democratic state and its criminal justice system. But by letting them down so profoundly, India's superior courts further fuelled the despair which is gripping the younger segments of Dalit, tribal and Muslim populations, confirming to them once again that justice and security is hard to secure for India's historically oppressed people.

~

India leads most countries in its policy of affirmative action for historically disadvantaged groups, the Scheduled Castes and Tribes. The implementation of this policy in the decades since Independence has ensured that young people from communities which were barred from education and dignified public employment have been able to enter professional colleges, and also the civil services and elected seats of office. As Jean Dreze and Amartya Sen observe, 'India was also among the first countries to include legislation aimed at affirmative action to combat the lasting influence of past social inequalities. The "reservations" and other priorities for scheduled castes (formerly, the "untouchables") and scheduled tribes expanded the horizon of legal support for social equity, no matter how we judge the exact achievements and failures of this early departure. Affirmative action would not become a serious possibility in the US for many years after the Indian constitution (which had many affirmative provisions) came into effect in 1950.'[193]

There was relatively greater consensus for these measures among people of higher castes and classes in the early decades after Independence. But this consensus has all but crumbled since the early 1990s, when the rage of young people from the higher castes spilled on to the streets as they bitterly battled this measure through various emotive measures, including by setting themselves on fire. There are few issues which continue to divide the country as deeply as the question of reservations. India's new middle class, and even upper-caste members of the neo-middle class and aspirational middle classes, refuse to accept that this measure is but a small but just recompense for the violent injustice and denial to generations of Dalit and tribal people for many centuries of our troubled and unequal history.

If young people privileged by caste admit to such a violent and unjust antiquity at all, they suggest that this injustice has long passed into history, and young people born in new India should not have to pay the price of inequities, which they believe have long been overcome by the influences of modernity and democracy. Most urban upper-caste Indians remain unaware or in active denial of untouchability. If they consider it at all, they regard it as a rapidly disappearing vestige of the past. Many ask: surely untouchability is now no longer widely practised? Surely Dalits are now treated just like everyone else? Aren't the atrocities against Dalits that are reported in the news simply aberrations that depart from a generally more positive picture of social progress? Isn't the problem of untouchability limited to so-called 'backward' states like Uttar Pradesh and Bihar? Haven't government policies and programmes helped Dalits overcome the stigma of caste? The subtext of this denial of the contemporary reality of untouchability is to also demolish the moral and political rationale for affirmative action in favour of Dalits, such as reservations in jobs and educational institutions.[194]

These were arguments I heard regularly in classrooms in the Lal Bahadur Shastri National Academy of Administration in Mussoorie where I trained young recruits to the civil services during the mid-1990s. I worried about the tenor of these classroom discussions because in the same classrooms were an equal number of young people who had entered the civil services through reserved quotas. Many of the latter remained silent during these discussions but were deeply hurt and quietly indignant as I tried to convince the upper-caste students that caste discrimination and untouchability remains a reality for millions of people of disadvantage. In classes in which reservations were discussed—sometimes bitterly such as when Arun Shourie, a powerful Right-wing intellectual opposed to reservations and, indeed, Ambedkar's entire legacy, spoke to trainees—I noticed that students unconsciously rearranged how they sat in class, with the quietly angry and defensive students belonging to the Scheduled Castes, the Scheduled Tribes and the Other Backward Classes ranged defensively on one side, and openly angry and assertive upper-caste groups on the other.

This denial that untouchability is still a part of India's contemporary reality was also what motivated me to work with some of the country's finest social scientists—Ghanshyam Shah, Sukhadeo Thorat, Satish Deshpande and Amita Baviskar—and undertake a massive field study of rural untouchability in 565 villages in twelve states: Punjab, Uttar Pradesh, Bihar, Madhya Pradesh, Chhattisgarh, Rajasthan, Maharashtra, Odisha, Andhra Pradesh, Karnataka, Kerala and Tamil Nadu. This became the largest study of untouchability in modern India.[195]

I have written about the findings of this landmark study elsewhere, but they need to be briefly reiterated in a book about inequality in India. The study 'shows that contrary to popular belief among urban, upper-caste people, the practice of untouchability has translated in the modern socio-economic milieu and still defines the experience of Dalithood in the country. Not only does it manifest in subtle forms, but active discrimination of Dalits persists'.[196] Despite being charged with a Constitutional mandate to remove inequality and promote social justice, the Indian state tolerates and even facilitates the practice of untouchability.

Among the disturbing findings is the fact that in more than one out of three government schools, Dalit children were made to sit separately during meals. A fifth of the Dalit children were not even permitted to drink water from the same source. A quarter of all the children were prevented from entering police stations and ration shops. One in three public health workers refused to visit Dalit homes, and a quarter of the Dalits surveyed still did not get letters delivered to their residences. Dalits were seated separately in nearly a third of self-help groups, cooperatives and panchayat offices. In 15 per cent of the villages surveyed, Dalits were not even permitted to enter the panchayat building. They were denied access to polling booths, or were forced to stand in separate queues in 12 per cent of the villages surveyed.

Dalit settlements are most often segregated from the main village, and these traditions are reproduced even by the government, when building Indira Awaas housing colonies for Dalits, or by NGOs engaged in reconstruction programmes after the 2001 earthquake in Gujarat. In nearly half the villages surveyed, Dalits were denied access to water sources. In over a third, we found that Dalits were denied entry into village shops. They had to wait some distance from the shop; the shopkeepers would keep the goods they bought on the ground and would accept their money similarly, without direct contact. In tea-shops, again, in about one-third of the villages, Dalits were denied seating and had to use separate cups to drink from.

The study found violent opposition to public displays of well-being—upgrades in housing and clothes, or even public celebrations—by Dalits. In nearly half the villages, bans operated on wedding processions on public—upper caste by assumption—roads. In 10 to 20 per cent of the villages, Dalits were not allowed even to wear clean, bright or fashionable clothes or sunglasses. They were barred from riding their bicycles, unfurling their umbrellas, wearing footwear on public roads, smoking, or even standing with their heads held high.

We found that Dalits were restricted from entering, on an average, two-thirds of Hindu temples in eleven states, ranging from nearly half in Uttar Pradesh to 94 per cent in Karnataka. The research established that such restrictions endured even after the conversion of Dalits to egalitarian faiths. Forty-one of the fifty-one villages surveyed in Punjab reported separate gurudwaras for Dalit Sikhs, and even where Dalits worshipped in gurudwaras frequented by upper-caste Jats, they were served in separate lines at the langar, and were not permitted to prepare or serve food. In Maharashtra, despite social movements spurred by Ambedkarite social movements and the mass conversions of Mahars to Buddhism, Dalits were denied entry to temples in half the villages surveyed. State reports from Kerala and Andhra chronicled divisions in the church between Dalit converts and others, and even discrimination against ordained Dalit priests.

Untouchability persisted even into death; in nearly half the villages surveyed Dalits were barred access to cremation grounds. In Maharashtra, even where Dalits had their own cremation grounds, these were permitted only on the eastern side of the village, so that the upper castes would not be polluted by the offending winds blowing from the west to the east.

The study reported discrimination against Dalits even in the labour market. Although Dalits were normally coerced into agricultural labour in unfavourable conditions, sometimes even of bondage, they were excluded in the lean agricultural season, when work is scarce for all; that was when upper-caste workers were preferred. In a quarter of the villages surveyed, Dalits were paid lower wages than other workers. They were also subjected to much longer working hours, delayed wages, verbal and even physical abuse, not just in 'feudal' states like Bihar but also, notably, in Punjab. In more than a third of the villages, Dalit workers were paid wages from a distance, to avoid physical contact. The study also sadly found evidence of discrimination between non-Dalit and Dalit workers, evidence of caste surmounting proletarian solidarity.

Although the large majority of Dalits are landless, even in the few cases where Dalits were landowners, they were denied access to water for irrigation in more than one-third of the villages. In a fifth of the villages, they were denied access to grazing lands and fishing ponds, and violent upper-caste opposition was reported when Dalits encroached on or were allotted government lands for cultivation, or even housing.

Untouchability was found to extend even to consumer markets, with Dalit producers in more than a third of the villages barred from selling their produce in local markets. Instead, they were forced to sell in the anonymity of distant urban markets where caste identities blur, but this imposed additional burdens of costs and time, and reduced their competitiveness. Caste taboos applied particularly to products like milk, so that in nearly half the villages with cooperatives, Dalits were not allowed to sell milk to the cooperatives or even private buyers. In a quarter of the villages, they were prevented even from buying milk from cooperatives. Dalits were therefore not only disproportionately burdened with poverty to start with, caste discrimination in labour and consumer markets condemned them to lower wages with harder work in uncertain employment, and imposed restrictions on their access to natural resources as well as markets for their products.

Even more than in secular and religious public spaces, the practice of untouchability endured most in rural upper-caste homes, in what people regard to be their private sphere. Our study confirmed that in as many as three quarters of the villages surveyed, Dalits were not permitted to enter non-Dalit homes, and 70 per cent would not eat together with Dalits. Even Dalit researchers engaged in this study were denied entry into upper-caste homes.

Some opponents of caste-based reservations argue that reservations should be made for poor households regardless of caste. They fail to recognize that the rationale for reservations is not only the indigent circumstances of a household, but a history of generations being denied the chance to read and study or change their occupations, improve their social situations, and achieve their actual potential, and of humiliation and violence. These are households in which no one could read a book until the coming of democracy. These are households which suffered across generations—indeed, across centuries—intense social humiliation, being treated as though they were born lesser human beings—unclean, uncouth, fit only to handle the waste of society, and for unskilled, unpaid or low-paid labour. They also fail to recognize the enormous, additional burdens of poverty borne out of being a Dalit or a tribal. If you are born into a Dalit or tribal home, there is a much greater chance that you will not be able to enter school, or to remain in school and enter college, that you will sleep hungry and be under-nourished, that you will be landless, that you will be in debt bondage, that you will be forced into distress migration, and that you will have a home unfit for human habitation. And if you are a girl or woman in these historically oppressed groups, the chances of being unschooled, in poor health and nutrition, under-paid and landless, and sexually abused would be even higher. Six decades of affirmative action are too few to correct these monumental wrongs of history.

~

Long before the massive draw of the anti-corruption movement of recent years, which brought the usually politically apathetic youth of the elite classes to the streets, there was one issue which roused these young people from time to time. This was the issue of reservations in government employment and higher technical education—such as medicine and engineering—for students from historically disadvantaged groups. In 2006, they raised a banner called Youth for Equality, bringing together upper-caste, middle-class Indian youth from medical and engineering colleges across the country to protest the affirmative action reservation policy for lower castes and tribal communities, and gathered on the streets.[197] Their website even today extols what they call a 'national movement', which builds on the 'idealism, passion and courage' of youth. That year, I felt compelled to write an open letter to them:[198]

> Throughout history, in every country and every culture, it is young people who have been at the forefront of struggles to fight for and build a more just and humane world. Therefore, stirring images on the front pages of newspapers of young people stoutly defying police batons, riot shields and water cannons in defence of what they believe, should normally seize the imagination and lift the heart. Yet they inspire in me instead a deep reflective sadness.
>
> I personally believe strongly in affirmative action for people who have historically suffered discrimination and a systematic, comprehensive, often brutal and savage denial of their rights to education and to respected livelihoods. Many young people who have taken to the streets believe that such discrimination, as may have existed, has passed into history. Yet a recent study in 10 states of which I was a part, confirmed that humiliating practices of untouchability and structured discrimination against people of so-called 'lower' castes continue to be widely practiced in most parts of India, barring their access to dignified livelihoods, public services like water, even sitting with others in school or in tea-shops.
>
> I find the debate on merit, raised also by senior influential supporters of your campaign, spurious and demeaning to people who live with injustice, suggesting not that they lack fair opportunities, but that they intrinsically lack worth. We need also to reassess what we mean when we speak of merit. I would see immeasurably more merit in a doctor who scores lower grades in medical college, but is willing to serve in deprived villages and slums, than one who tops the 'merit' list, and applies for the first green card that transports him to privileged and well-paid jobs in the United States.

Still, I do not intend to enter here into a debate on reservations. I agree that the modes of designing and implementing affirmative action, including reservations, can legitimately be contested and reformed, and we owe it to the young people who have taken to the streets to listen and debate with them.

Yet the anguish is because middle-class, upper-caste youth take to protest for the first time in years in our country, ultimately for what they must recognise to be the preservation of their privilege. It is more painful when they do so using slogans of equality, unity and justice. These words caught the imagination of many of us as we grew up, and are far too precious to be squandered and devalued in battles for defending the rights of those that already have better chances than millions in the country can ever dream.

But I grieve most when they choose to protest by holding brooms and posing for photographers, claiming that they will be 'reduced' to sweeping the streets if reservations in institutions of higher education are extended. It is an insult to the dignity of labour, a mockery of generations of people who are confined by the cruelty of caste to the work of scavenging, often carrying human shit in baskets and buckets on their head, people whose work ensures that we have cleanliness and comfort in our worlds.

I long for the day when the same young people spill on to the streets because two hundred million people in our country go to sleep hungry, despite the fact that we grow enough food to fill every stomach. Because fifty thousand homeless children are forced to sleep under the open sky in the capital city of Delhi, hungry, abused, at freezing winter temperatures. Because more than two thousand people were brutally massacred in Gujarat and over a hundred thousand are unable to return to their homes even four years later, only because they happen to worship a different god. Because Dalit children are still made to sit separately in several rural schools. Because there is an epidemic of despair in the countryside, as thousands of farmers feel compelled to take their lives. Because as many infants and children die of malnutrition and infection in slums in our country as in the poorest countries of sub Saharan Africa.

Earlier generations such as mine may have failed you profoundly.

Fight them if you feel you must, and lead them to reclaim lost, betrayed, almost forgotten dreams of a world of peace, equality and justice.

The Marathi poet, Suresh Kadam, laments:

The sunset does not bury our sorrows
Nor does sunrise bring new hopes.
Everything continues relentlessly.
Society bound by her rituals of ages.[199]

Farming and the Epidemic of Terminal Despair

His son Babu found him dead in the cowshed behind their home. Kusara Mallagaud had drunk pesticide late the previous night, and quietly lay down for the last time in the shed where no one could hear him as he writhed alone in pain in his last hours. He clearly wanted to die the way he had tried to live his life, enduring his suffering himself, always trying to shield his family. But even though he fiercely protected them all his life, in the manner of his death, he profoundly and permanently abandoned them.

Kusara succumbed to the deadly epidemic of despair that is stalking rural India, which has already taken what some experts estimate to be more than 200,000 farmers' lives in the period between 1995-2007.[200] As governments hotly contest these figures, this epidemic of terminal despair shows no signs of abating. Palagummi Sainath calculates that 'suicide rates among Indian farmers were a chilling 47 per cent higher than they were for the rest of the population in 2011'.[201] In some states, they were well over 100 per cent higher. A farmer in Andhra Pradesh is three times more likely to commit suicide than anyone else in the country, excluding farmers. And he is twice as likely to do so when compared to non-farmers in his own state. The odds are not much better in Maharashtra, which has recorded the maximum number of farmers' suicides for over a decade. He reports further that the adjusted farmers' suicide rate for 2011 is in fact slightly higher than it was in 2001, and that too after the numbers of persons in agriculture has declined, and after states have tried hard to fudge numbers.[202]

Babu, barely nineteen, suddenly found himself the oldest male member of the family. He bravely tried to hold back his tears, as his grandmother and aunt wept inconsolably around him. His mother had gone to her parent's home in the ritual of mourning, and his younger siblings were still numbed and stunned. 'If only he had spoken to us, we would have sold everything to pay off his debts,' Kusara's sister kept wailing. The villagers who had gathered around added, 'It was he who would give strength when others would lose heart. We never dreamed that one day he would go this way.'

It was only to his son Babu that Kusara had occasionally confided. Babu had observed his father's progressive retreat into his silences. Babu had himself opted to drop out of school to share his burdens. A month before he died, Kusara had spoken to his son about the hopeless enormity of his debts: ₹300,000. Every day, he had to hide furtively from the moneylender and, in doing so, was forced to feel a deep sense of shame. But for how long could he avoid him? Babu suggested that they sell off their home and their two-and-a half acres of land. His father did not agree.

In six consecutive years of drought in their village, Pallepahad, in the Medak district of Andhra Pradesh, they could extract virtually nothing from their small plot of land. Kusara had taken a loan from the village moneylender to dig a borewell three years earlier, in 2003. It was dry. Desperate, he took more loans. Four more borewells failed as the water table fell dangerously low.

Every year, the farmer had to beg for loans for other purposes as well, to buy seed, fertilizers, pesticides, and other inputs. Earlier, nationalized or cooperative banks would give him credit, today he was turned away from their doors. The private moneylender charged

3 to 5 per cent rates of interest compounded monthly, but at least he was there in Kusara's time of need. Much of the credit he extended was in kind, as seeds and other agricultural inputs. These were often spurious or overpriced, but he had no option but to buy them.

Earlier, farmers would store their own seeds, but today, hybrid seeds and commercial farming no longer enables them to do this. The new technology also impetuously demands ever-mounting applications of chemical fertilizers and pesticides. Earlier, the main fertilizer used to be animal dung. Today, few can afford to feed bullocks throughout the year; it is cheaper to hire tractors for ploughing, but that too costs money. Fertilizer, electricity and water subsidies for farmers have shrunk in compliance with the prescriptions of the World Bank and the IMF and, therefore, input costs for farmers soar even higher.

In a good year, the farmer makes a profit. But what happens in a bad year? It is not just the monsoons that can fail him. Farmers have been thrust into the harsh winds of global markets. Even a good harvest can be calamitous for them, if global prices, of which they have no advance knowledge, let alone any kind of control over, unpredictably crash. In theory, the government still guarantees procurement of their produce at a minimum assured price but, in practice, mandis only purchase from large farmers in prosperous regions. The small farmer, desperate for cash, is forced to sell his harvest to the moneylender who purchases at whatever price he chooses, often reselling later at much higher prices in the mandi or on the open market.

The moneylender does not need to use brute force to reclaim his loans. It is enough to stand in the village square and shame his debtors by talking loudly of their unpaid debts. This humiliation itself drives peasants—proud, stoic, still immersed in traditional values of faithfulness and honesty—to desperately sell all they own; land, jewellery, cattle, their homes, to repay their debts. Or else, to escape the shame, take their own lives.

One of Manmohan Singh's first engagements as prime minister

after the UPA came to power in 2004 was to commiserate personally with the survivors of farmers who had committed suicide in Andhra Pradesh, and to promise a 'new deal' to Indian farmers.[203] And yet, all that they got was a 'relief package' of soft loans to which they would qualify only after the farmer has committed suicide, and a 'moratorium' on past loans that is unenforceable because the farmers remain dependent on the same usurious private sources for credit in the future. It seemed that even the state would extend some relief only to farmers who proved their eligibility for support by taking their own lives!

Sainath contends that 270,940 farmers have committed suicide between 1995 and 2013, relying on official data gathered by the National Crime Records Bureau.[204] There is irony in that it is the National Crime Records Bureau which collects data on these deaths of terminal desperation because, up to late 2014, all these persons were criminals—attempting suicide is a crime under law. The yearly average between 2001 and 2011 has been 16,743 or around forty-six farmers per day. Farmer suicide rates were 47 per cent higher than the rest of the population in 2011, with the rate at 16.3 per 100,000 farmers, as opposed to the national average of 11.1 per 100,000.[205] Even if it is assumed that some farmers commit suicide for personal reasons, independent of farming, the higher rates clearly suggest that many of their acts of suicide are a response to the mounting hopelessness of their vocation. The suicide rate in 2011 was slightly higher than in 2001, which was at 15.8 per 100,000.[206] Farmer suicides did cause some public anguish a few years ago, even among urban middle-class people; now we seem to have become inured to the news, despite commentators like P. Sainath who indefatigably remind readers that farmers in India continue to take their lives, and nothing that the government does or does not do seems to alter this reality.

It is extraordinary that this was not a major issue for any political party in the general election of 2014. The rate at which farmer suicides occurs shows no signs of declining, and deaths remain concentrated in five states most heavily engaged in agriculture, where two-thirds of all suicides occur.[207] The states are Maharashtra, Andhra Pradesh, Karnataka, Madhya Pradesh and Chhattisgarh; outside of these five states, five more show higher suicide rates in 2011 than in 2001, including the breadbasket states of India, Punjab and Haryana.[208] But like poverty, caste and gender oppression, the epidemic of terminal despair in India's countryside has become normalized as one more unfortunate but unchangeable reality.

The causes of these suicides have ranged from untenable debt burdens through exploitative private credit, forcing farmers to sell their land, to the unprotected integration of Indian agriculture with the global economy and cost-intensive agricultural technologies leading to high costs and low wages. The 2011 census shows that the percentage of the country's population engaged in agriculture is shrinking but, still, 58 per cent of the country is employed within the agricultural sector.[209] Urban migration will see more than half of India's population living in cities by 2050.[210] As agriculture plays an increasingly small role in the GDP of India (it contributes only 14 per cent), there are fewer incentives for farmers to stay in agriculture, and as the costs of inputs increase, agriculture is increasingly narrowed to a small group of landholders who have the capital and the influence to afford to remain in agriculture. On the other hand, 84.87 per cent of the total holdings belong to marginal and small farmers.[211] The rural poor, as well as marginalized and smallholder farmers, mainly live in resource-poor areas where there are also concentrated occurrences of malnutrition. These farmers find it difficult to access agricultural inputs, loans and credit, farm extension, and marketing opportunities for their output.

The Green Revolution helped the country expand food production by many times but also brought along certain costs, both environmental and social. Water aquifers are falling alarmingly, with estimates in Punjab showing that 75 per cent of available ground water has been overexploited;[212] chemical inputs and industrialization has caused harm to the natural environment; soil has become increasingly saline, and less fertile;[213] land degradation in general is high due to erosion and waterlogging.[214] Arable land, soil, water and biodiversity have been rapidly shrinking because of the pressures of pollution, population growth, urban sprawl and climate change.[215] The Indian Council of Agricultural Research estimates that out of a total geographical area of 328.73 million hectares, 120.40 million hectares is affected by various types of land degradation.[216] Chemical fertilizer use has increased from 1.1 million tonnes in 1966-67 to 27.7 million tonnes in 2011-12.[217] But while fertilizer use increased by over twenty-five times, the gain in foodgrain production was only threefold.[218]

Matters are aggravated by private ownership of seeds and an unequal market where farmers are forced to take loans to pay for agricultural inputs, including genetically modified seeds, fertilizers, chemicals and the like. Due to the higher costs, the ownership of farms has become more concentrated, with farmers who face poor years unable to repay loans and being forced to commit suicide.[219, 220]

Not surprisingly, then, farmers' suicides continued unabated during the decade when the UPA government was in power, from 2004-14. It was—and still is—only with the massive expansion of rural credit for small and marginal farmers; with protection from the vagaries of global markets; with expanded subsidies for agricultural inputs; with the promotion of watershed development for rain-dependent farmers; with the adoption of appropriate, low-cost and low-risk agricultural technologies; with assured procurement from small farmers at support prices; and the protection of incomes that the farmers' despair could be alleviated. But of none of these were seriously attempted, nor was the all-important statespersonship, compassion and courage, which was needed to pull back rural India from the brink, in evidence. For the new Bharatiya Janata Party (BJP)-led government, farmers and their plight is not even on the list of its high priorities.

Kavita Bahl and Nandan Saxena's documentary, *Candles in the Wind*, is a portrait of the women left behind after despairing farmers, crushed by debt, take their lives in Punjab. For these women, the option of departing from the world does not arise because there are children to be raised. The film pays homage to the spirit and courage of these heroic single women as they battle impossible debts and the doomed vocation of agriculture, to endure, persevere and nurture a new generation.

~

In Kusara's home, fragments of a shattered life remained scattered poignantly around us, in photographs and memories which his family shared with us. We picked up a few fragments of his life: we learnt of Kusara's devotion to the deity Hanuman; his delight in his friends, his love for his family, his enormous pride in his daughter's achievements at school, and his resolve, now lost like so much else, to send her to college.

Marginal and small farmers are increasingly abandoning their holdings and migrating in desperate search for wage work. Indeed, well over two thousand people are quitting agriculture every day. But not young Babu. With interest mounting inexorably with each passing day, and pressures from the restless moneylender, he had no idea how he would repay the loan of ₹300,000 which his father had left behind. But whatever had happened, he was clear that he would remain a farmer. 'This alone is what gave meaning to my father's life. It is what gives meaning to mine.'

Is Farming a Dying Civilization?

Back in 2009, I lost a very dear friend, Narendranath Gorrepati, to brain cancer. In life, as in death, my friend taught me many lessons in human goodness. I also learned from him the impossibility of life as a farmer in new India.

Naren was in university in Delhi with me in the 1970s, a few years my senior. He joined as an officer in the State Bank of Hyderabad, but was restless from the start. He resigned in five years and initially worked for Lokayan—a forum established by political scientist Rajni Kothari for dialogue between intellectuals, practitioners and political activists for alternate development and politics—in Delhi in 1980 at half the salary he was receiving from the bank. He voluntarily reduced his salary further because of the financial difficulties the organization was facing. He then moved to Hyderabad, with his wife and lifelong soulmate Uma Shankari. A series of personal tragedies—the loss of Uma's father, and Naren's mother in an accident—pushed them to take the next decision, changing their lives forever. Uma recalls, 'Somehow death became certain, life very, very uncertain. We realized that life may be short, and whatever good things we want to do we should do today, now. We planned therefore to follow our hearts: to go to our village, to look after the lands with organic farming, and continue Naren's social work.' So in 1987, the family returned to Naren's ancestral village, Venkatramapuram, Andhra Pradesh, where they lived until Naren took ill in 2009.

Naren was born into a family of landlords. His father, unwilling to alter the rules of caste observed in the village, was against allowing Dalits to enter the kitchen or sit with them at the table. Naren too was stubborn, but in his own gentle way. The solution he crafted was uniquely Naren's: in all the years that he lived in the village while his father was alive, he ate his food on the kitchen floor, not at the dining table, and when there were Dalit visitors, they ate with him on the floor. His wife and two young daughters joined him in this practice. Naren would sit with his father at the table when he had his meals, but not eat at the table himself. Later, he would sit on the floor with his food. This was Naren's daily satyagrah for social equality in his home.

A firm believer in organic and eco-friendly farming techniques, Naren experimented a lot by cultivating his own fields with organic technologies, without chemical fertilizers and pesticides. He also wrote extensively on his observations of the agriculture sector, especially of the travails of dry-land farmers. He contributed to village self-rule by reviving and participating in the internal settlement of family and land disputes. He fought the destruction of crops by elephants in ways that would protect both the elephants—by creating a corridor for them—and the victims by repeatedly pleading with government officials for enhanced compensation. He resisted and helped reverse heavy electricity tariffs on farmers.

Much more important than what he contributed to his people was how he related with them. Dalit families recall how Naren used to routinely visit their homes, eat with them and wash his own plate. He helped educate many Dalit children and youth, and encouraged inter-caste weddings. In his own home, everyone was welcome and fed generously, even as Uma sometimes argued with him about how they would make ends meet. He sent out mangoes from their orchard every year to all: to comrades and officials, but never forgetting all the poorer people who had no mango gardens of their own—the washer-folk, barbers, potters, smiths, carpenters, mechanics and school teachers. Our friend Rajni Bakshi recalls how he uniquely crossed all boundaries; everyone was his friend—the police, government officials, Naxals, the RSS, Communists, Ambedkarites, Dalits, casteists, even the very people whose lands they were claiming to hand over to the poor. Human rights activist K. Balagopal, who himself passed away soon after Naren, recalled when Naren died, 'To Gandhians he spoke of class struggle. To Naxalites he spoke about the immorality of violence.' Both mourned him inconsolably when he died.

Uma returned to their village after Naren's passing away, determined to continue their experiments with sustainable and just farming. Feisty and determined as ever, although touching sixty, she persevered bravely for many years in a near solitary struggle. But then in 2013, she made an announcement to her family and friends, which left all of us pensive and grieved. She had resolved to return permanently to live in Hyderabad with her daughter and son-in-law, and leave behind in the village a hired hand to look after their fields.

Uma wistfully described to us emptying villages, hollowed out of their young people, leaving behind only those too old to move, or those with whom their grown children in cities were unable to share their poverty. The government schools in the villages Uma left behind were closing down one by one because there were fewer children left; all of whom were moving in droves to residential schools in towns, their parents convinced that they had no future in the countryside. Venkatramapuram was once served by a decent public bus service, making five to six trips a day. Within a decade, these were reduced to two trips and, by the time Uma left, there were none. There weren't enough passengers to justify a service.

Until the 1970s, a third of the farmers irrigated their fields with water from wells that were merely 9 to 15 metres deep, or that which collected in small tanks. The rest relied on rain-fed agriculture, and the soil was moist. But since then, the electric pump literally became a watershed in the history of their village. People started drilling borewells, and dug deeper and deeper to access ever-receding water. In Venkatramapuram today, almost all the borewells have run dry. Some people, in insane desperation, have gone down to 200 metres without striking water.

'Agriculture is firstly about food,' says Uma, a truism which nearly everyone has forgotten. 'Farmers, planners, consumers have all come to believe that farming is mainly about making money. Money is of course important, but it is a by-product of agriculture. The primary goal of agriculture is to provide ourselves with good, nourishing, safe variety of foods. But no longer!'

With electrification, pumpsets also introduced the epochal, life-changing idea of cropping for cash. In Naren and Uma's region, sugarcane, milk, meat and mango became the main generators of cash. In the past, people would grow a wide variety of crops on both wet and dry lands—paddy, millets, pulses, oil seeds, sugarcane, coconut, vegetables, herbs and spices. Meat, fish and milk were all a part of the diet, even for the poor, because little was sold in the market. Cash payments to workers were rare; they were mostly paid in kind—grain, clothes and the like. There was year-round farming.

Farmers and farm workers, for the first time in history, are today forced to buy much of their food, dependent on a creaky and corrupt PDS, or volatile and inflationary private food markets. The largest numbers of persons who sleep hungry each night are, ironically, food growers. When people grew the food they ate, there was also more sharing of food.

Uma says, 'The first thing people would say at any time of the day to a visitor is, "Come and eat." There was enough food left over to give to beggars, cows, dogs, cats, birds and so on. These days, women calculate and cook just enough food for the family, because everything has to be purchased and the incomes are meagre and uncertain. Beggars have become rare; they too seem to have moved greener pastures, to the traffic signals in the cities...'

Even as the groundwater was steadily receding, disaster struck. In the seven years between 1997 and 2004, four years were officially declared drought years all across India, and the other years also saw severe rainfall shortages. This further spurred mass migration. Farmers and farm workers became convinced that there was no future in agriculture or in rural areas, and started sending their children away to urban residential schools. Committed family labour became scarce.

Since 2006, the Mahatma Gandhi National Rural Employment Guarantee Act helped double agricultural wages.[221] But it would offer employment in Venkatramapuram for hardly twenty to forty days in a year; and the scheme in that village was riddled with corruption and delays, with a lot of uncertainty about when and whether people would receive work. Therefore, landless agricultural workers fled even faster than the farmers to the cities, as they cannot live or work on hungry stomachs. Even the drinking-water bore-well had dried up; they received a small amount of water in tankers once every two days, and Uma could not carry water every day from the tanker to the house. She was alone most of the time and felt lonely. And unlike when Naren was around, she found herself unable to enthuse the people of the village to work together to battle the challenges of water and land. 'Even now people have not lost hope,' she told me, 'it is just that their hopes have shifted to urban areas and urban jobs; people are educating their children and moving to cities. If people lose hope, then what is left?'

Uma was saddened but in no way vanquished. In Hyderabad, she began volunteering time with the Kisan Swaraj movement to demand a Farmers' Income Commission and resist genetically modified seeds and the corporatization of agriculture. She engaged a worker for a monthly salary to look after a few head of cattle and grow some rainfed jowar and horse gram on their land. In 2013, she spent ₹11,600 rupees to grow groundnut and received ₹6,000 worth of product and fodder in return!

This generation will pass somehow, but what about the next? The Indian countryside has transformed into this wasteland of near-terminal despair and increasingly impossible survival, by new technologies, forced integration with globalized markets, and an uncaring state. For a sector which employs half the population, contributes a sixth of the GDP, the state allocates as little as a twentieth of total public investment. It is no wonder, then, that tens of thousands of farmers each year poison or hang themselves; and millions of the young flee, when they can, to wherever they can, while they still can.

Unequal Destinies: Malnutrition among Tribal Children

Among India's most dispossessed children are those who are born into tribal homes. Often raised close to or within increasingly threatened and rapidly depleting forest habitats, they are more likely than most other children in India to be hungry and malnourished, to not receive healthcare when they are sick, to not enter or remain in school, and to die too early, as compared to other children, including disadvantaged children who are born in other historically oppressed groups.

In the year 2000, a distressing 47 per cent children overall were underweight in India, almost one out of two children.[222] But the story was far more troubling for India's subaltern social groups: the corresponding figures for the proportion of underweight children among the Scheduled Castes was 54 per cent, and for Scheduled Tribes an even higher 56 per cent.[223] This means that 27 per cent more ST children were underweight compared to non-ST children.[224] 53 per cent ST children were stunted, 29 per cent severely, compared with 48 and 24 per cent respectively for all children.[225]

Not only is an unconscionable proportion of tribal children grossly malnourished, their condition is improving at a very tardy pace compared to the rest of the child population. During the 1990s, the nutritional status of non-SC and ST children improved annually at 2.36 per cent, compared to just 1.02 per cent for SC and only 0.24 per cent for ST children.[226] This means that even as other children in India are slowly—indeed, far too slowly—becoming healthier and well-nourished, tribal children are being left further and further behind other children.

Such high levels of malnutrition are associated closely with a much higher probability of illness and death as compared to other children. Ninety-six tribal children under the age of five years die out of every 1,000 live births, compared to seventy-four children out of all populations segments. Rural tribal children constitute 12 per cent of all rural children between the ages of one to four years, but contribute 23 per cent of deaths in this group.[227]

After they cross their first birthdays, tribal children face twice the chances of dying than non-tribal children.[228] What is striking is that at birth until their first year, tribal children have almost the same survival chances as non-tribal children. The early parity in survival chances between tribal and non-tribal children is probably the result of healthy breastfeeding, weaning and feeding practices prevalent in most tribal communities.[229] But these initial advantages slip very rapidly because of the intense poverty of tribal households, low food intakes and very poor access to healthcare.

This pervasive malnutrition of tribal children is embedded in the ubiquitous and stubborn poverty of tribal communities. In 1983, it was estimated using NSSO data that almost 46 per cent of all Indians were poor, but the numbers of STs who were poor were much higher, at 63 per cent.[230] (As stated earlier, these estimates are based on very minimalist definitions of poverty, closer to a starvation line than a poverty line, but are still useful for comparative purposes, across groups and over time.) By 2005, whereas poverty by these estimates fell by 40 per cent for the overall population, it fell only by 31 per cent for STs.[231] This slower decline of poverty among STs resulted in an even greater concentration of tribal people in the lowest income deciles. Although they constitute only 8 per cent of the population, their share in the lowest-wealth decile rose from 22 to 25 per cent in these two decades.[232]

Given this dense and persistent concentration of poverty among tribal populations, it should not be surprising that studies confirm widespread hunger among these communities. A study conducted in 2009 by the National Nutrition Monitoring Bureau (NNMB) of 40,359 tribal households in 1,032 villages of nine states, found that their mean intakes of most foodstuffs were considerably below the Recommended Daily Intake (RDI), which is the daily intake level of a nutrient that is considered to be sufficient to meet the requirements of healthy individuals.[233]

The study confirms that routine hunger is part of the lived reality of the majority of tribal children. More than 70 per cent of the pre-school and school-age children were found in the NNMB study to consume less than adequate levels of both protein and calories.[234] In other words, the evidence is that in seven out of every ten tribal households, children are unable to ingest enough proteins and calories.[235] For children between one and three years of age—the most critical years to build nutritional foundations—their average intake of cereals and millets was 149 grammes per day, against the suggested level of 175 grammes. The average consumption of pulses and legumes, 16 grammes, was even lower, less than half the suggested level of 35 grammes per day. The average consumption of fats and oils was very low, at 4 grammes, against the suggested level of 15 grammes per day. The intake of sugar and jaggery was 6 grammes, against the suggested level of 30 grammes per day. Although their consumption of protective foods, such as green leafy vegetables, milk and milk products, fruits, sugar and jaggery increased marginally, their consumption levels were grossly deficient compared to recommended levels. Even more gravely, among pregnant and lactating women, the median intakes of all nutrients were below the RDI.[236]

It is evident that the nutritional deprivations of tribal children are substantially rooted in the high levels of poverty and absolute hunger of the households into which they are born. But their nutrition is further imperilled by the very rudimentary—and often completely absent—public health services in areas where tribal populations reside. Forty-one per cent of the tribal children who fall prey to fever and coughs receive no treatment, compared to 27 per cent children from the Scheduled Castes, 28 per cent children from the Other Backward Classes and 25 per cent children of other castes.[237] This means that even the inadequate quantities and quality of food which tribal children are able to eat is often not absorbed by their frail bodies because of untreated aliments. Not just tribal children, but mothers, too, are much less likely to receive healthcare; for instance, the National Family Health Survey-3 (NFHS-3) reported that only 40 per cent of tribal women receive three or more ante-natal care visits, as compared to 63 per cent for non-SC, ST and OBC women.[238] This, too, has adverse implications for the health and, ultimately, the nutrition of the children.

Even this sombre story of the hunger, malnutrition and health neglect suffered by tribal children hides the enormity of distress and want endured by children in several million tribal households in many parts of the country, because of heterogeneity between and within the tribal population in India. The NNMB study referred to earlier points to great variations in the food intake of tribal populations between states, with tribal communities in Kerala reflecting some of the lowest food intakes. Not surprisingly, tribal populations in Kerala have been in the news because of malnutrition deaths, which is shocking in a state otherwise noted for its high human development indices.

In 1993, the government of India notified seventy-three tribes as 'primitive tribal groups', based on extreme vulnerability: most of these were hunters and gatherers and practised shifting rather than settled agriculture. The official terminology has since been amended to the more politically correct 'particularly vulnerable tribal groups', but their conditions continue to be even more fragile than that of tribes which are engaged in settled agriculture. It is among the particularly vulnerable tribal groups that I have witnessed the highest levels of starvation deaths among children during nearly a decade of work as Special Commissioner of India's Supreme Court, related to the right to food.[239]

~

This barely changing, grim destiny of tribal children—of persistent hunger, gaunt bodies, easy susceptibility to illness and a higher likelihood of early death—is not just the outcome of enormous state neglect. These are the cumulative wages of something much more culpable—their condition results from the active pauperization and dispossession of tribal communities by state policy itself, and by the state's dominant models of governance and development. This systemic and systematic deprivation and oppression began in early colonial times, but persisted seamlessly in the policies introduced by the Indian republic after Independence, despite the sensitivity of India's first prime minister, Jawaharlal Nehru, to tribal 'welfare'.

Early tracts by anthropologists and colonial administrators describe these isolated communities, mostly living in remote hills and forested regions, as distinct, relatively homogenous and self-contained social and cultural entities. These studies were mostly preoccupied with their cultural and social arrangements, and dwelt less on their material conditions of poverty, illness and hunger. However, as sociologist Virginius Xaxa observes, although their housing and clothing were very elementary and their survival basically at subsistence levels, desperate poverty as indicated by starvation-related deaths was generally absent, except for episodic famines and epidemics.[240] Apart from these calamitous mass deaths from time to time, Xaxa points to evidence that food and survival were not a problem in tribal society and there was a general increase in the population. In fact, the proportion of the tribal population rose significantly from 2.26 to 3.26 per cent between 1881-1941 whereas the population of Hindus steadily declined from 75.1 per cent to 69.5 per cent during this period.[241]

Despite their isolation and subsistence-level existence, tribal communities probably benefited from their free access to a wide variety of forest produce—plants, tubers and animals—and their healthy child-rearing practices, therefore individual hunger and malnutrition of the kind visible in tribal communities today were rare. Over the years, sitting among people in remote tribal communities, I have heard old men and women wistfully recall that when they were children, men and women used to be much sturdier.

Some of my fondest memories of my time as a civil servant in Madhya Pradesh and Chhattisgarh are of the treks across the hills and forests to reach remote hamlets. My father was a civil servant in Northeast India. I have many childhood recollections of several proud and beautiful Arunachal and Naga tribal peoples, and the many tribal groups in the Andaman and Nicobar Islands, where my father also headed the civil administration. I am convinced that India's many tribal groups are the most civilized peoples in our large and vastly populated country. There is far less social and economic inequality within their societies, they cooperate rather than compete, they choose harmony with nature over domination, and they find deceit hard to practise even for bare survival.

And yet I find these little civilizations almost doomed, as they are unable or unwilling to negotiate the world on terms set by non-tribal state and society. Development has only meant brutal dispossession from their lands, forests and traditional ways of life; it has meant mounting hunger, displacement and disease. Many tribal regions are also caught up in the throes of violence—visited upon them by Left-wing and separatist militants and, more recently, the insidious social intra-tribal hatred spread by Right-wing communal organizations. These atrocities complete the devastation mounted on these civilized peoples for centuries by both the colonial and republican Indian states.

The greatest blow to their survival—and communal dignity—was the colonial policy of introducing state control over forests, thereby depriving them of their traditional sources of nutrition and livelihood. As sociologist Amita Baviskar describes, from community owners of their forests, they have become encroachers, tenants and poachers.[242] This policy was unchanged after India became free—of all government departments in independent India, the Forest Department most retains its colonial culture. It is little wonder then, that Verrier Elwin famously recounted that paradise for a tribal person is miles and miles of forests with no forest guard.[243] The forests became major sources of revenue for the state, and tribal people found themselves increasingly debarred from hunting and gathering in the forests, and from their traditional systems of shifting cultivation. Forests themselves dwindled. As they could not gather or hunt in the forests, or grow food, hunger and penury were natural outcomes.

Matters were further aggravated by their forced displacement from their homelands, again as direct consequences of state policy. In the early decades after Independence, the state invested in large irrigation, thermal and steel plants, resulting in enormous displacement of rural populations, with no policies for their rehabilitation. The government of India, in its Tenth Five-Year Plan, itself estimated that between 1951 and 1990, more than twenty-one million people were displaced by large projects, of whom 40 per cent were tribal people.[244] Scholars estimate displacement to be probably thrice this number, and maybe even more if one includes people who were not legal owners of the land and forest on which they depended for their food and livelihoods. Alex Ekka, academic and current director of Xavier Institute of Social Study, Ranchi, for instance, estimates that in Jharkhand, between 1951 and 1995, 90 per cent of those displaced by big projects were tribal people.[245]

The fact that STs are just around 8 per cent of the country's population, but probably more than half those displaced from their lands and livelihoods, is not just a technical accident of geography and engineering. It is the direct outcome of their intense political powerlessness, which nurtures a dominant public discourse in which their dispossession is seen as a legitimate cost which must be paid for the 'country's development'. Clearly, this discourse of development excludes tribal people—and, even more, tribal children—from the imagination of a 'developed' country. It is only as late as 2013 that rehabilitation was legislated as a legal right for those who lose both land and livelihoods to compulsory acquisition, but within a year of the passage of this law these protections were being eroded by the newly elected government. I have served as a civil servant in the areas in which enormous swathes of land were acquired for both the Narmada mega-dams and the Singrauli super-thermal power projects and have studied these projects as a researcher subsequently as well. I have not encountered a single example of resettlement and rehabilitation in which any community of displaced people has been successfully assisted to reclaim the levels of livelihood and habitat which they lost to development projects.

Sadly, the displacement of tribal communities has also been hastened, to a degree, by many environmental activists who support the expulsion of people from their traditional habitats for the creation of sanctuaries and national parks. I find the binary opposition that is sometimes constructed between wildlife conservation and tribal survival to be spurious. Wildlife is not threatened by tribal forest dwellers. They have coexisted through centuries without destroying each other.

State policy also introduced the policy of individual land ownership, which was alien to traditional community land ownership practices. Tribal landowners have lost their lands precipitously to non-tribal outsiders, who have used fraud, usury and intimidation to dispossess them and reduce them to landless workers, often in debt bondage. Most states with large tribal populations passed laws to prevent fraudulent and forced land transfers from tribal to non-tribal hands and, indeed, to restore land illegally and exploitatively expropriated in the past. But most of these laws have been singularly ineffective in protecting the land rights of tribal communities, because of pervasive administrative bias and corruption, and because tribal landowners are completely unequal to the challenge of working the legal system to secure their rights.

And now, in the decades after India opened up to global, market-led growth since the early 1990s, it is large and powerful for-profit corporations which have penetrated tribal habitats for mining and extractive industries. It is the abiding—and probably fatal—misfortune of tribal people that their traditional homelands sit upon the country's richest reservoirs of coal and minerals. The new government elected in 2014 promised an even more investor-friendly regime, which included the probable dismantling of the few, still very inadequate but hard-won protections for people who lose their lands and livelihoods to powerful large corporations.

In the face of such insurmountable odds, there seems little hope that the causes of hunger and malnourishment of tribal children can be removed in the near future, and probably not even in the medium term.

Unless this changes dramatically and soon, millions of tribal children will continue to suffer the highest burdens of hunger, malnutrition, illness and early death in the country. And with its insatiable hunger for more electric power, consumer goods, new glittering cities and untrammelled economic growth, a young and restless middle class is unable or unwilling to make the direct connection between its glitzy malls and bulging shopping bags, and the malnourishment and early deaths of many million tribal children.

Two Imaginations of Good Government

Varied imaginations of what constitutes a good state competed in the national elections of 2014, especially in the prime ministerial candidature of Narendra Modi. There were some who believed that Modi was India's most capable leader; his influential cheerleaders included several captains of Indian industry, senior academics, serving and retired civil servants, professionals and traders. There were others who were equally convinced that his continuing ascendancy would be profoundly dangerous for democracy, pluralism and social and economic equity.

Both assessments were based on evaluations of the results of Narendra Modi's leadership of the state of Gujarat, where he was chief minister from 2002 to 2014. It was extraordinary that the same administration should be evaluated in such irreconcilably divergent ways. These oppositional assessments reflect the two diametrically contradictory ideas of good government. One view is that governments must, first and foremost, effectively facilitate market-led economic growth, and their success should be measured against this yardstick. The contrary view is that the performance of governments should be assessed by what they deliver for the most disadvantaged citizens of the country. For people who adhere to the former imagination of government, Modi is the most successful administrator in the country; whereas for the latter, he is the most failed of our leaders.

After the clamour of the 2014 general elections ended and the new government led by Modi stepped in confidently, the public debate about which development model is best suited for a country of vast economic potential and embedded historical impoverishment became of even greater import for India's future and the destinies of its people. In his energetic campaign, Modi downplayed—but did not erase—his earlier hostile discourse about the country's religious minorities in favour of one which promises 'development' based on the 'model' of Gujarat. His promise was that all of India would benefit from the verve and pace of economic growth derived from high private investment which he claimed that his leadership had accomplished in Gujarat. Modi's reputation for national leadership of the world's largest democracy was indeed minted in the dozen years of his stewardship of the state, and by his forging of what is touted as the 'Gujarat model' of development.

Modi's leadership style is aptly described by social commentator Tridip Suhrud as 'hyper-masculine': divisive, pugnacious, authoritarian and surgically efficient.[246] A report published by a research wing of the US Congress portrays Gujarat under his leadership as 'perhaps India's best example of effective governance and impressive development...where controversial Chief Minister Narendra Modi has streamlined economic processes, removing red tape and curtailing corruption in ways that have made the state a key driver of national economic growth'.[247] India's wealthiest man Mukesh Ambani described Modi's leadership as 'visionary, effective and passionate'.[248] His brother Anil saw in him a 'role model' for other states to emulate, and hyperbolically claimed that he is the best leader Gujarat has had after Gandhi. He declared that Modi makes him proud to be a Gujarati and an Indian. 'Imagine what will happen if he leads the country?' he gushed.[249] Ratan Tata lauded Modi's track record as an 'exemplary' leader: 'Today there is no state like Gujarat. Under Mr Modi's leadership, Gujarat is head and shoulders above any state.'[250] Telecom giant Sunil Mittal likewise endorsed Modi's elevation as the CEO of the entire nation. These men, who own some of the largest business empires in India—and indeed, the world—chose to leave no doubt who their national icon was.[251]

Modi also has many supporters among the country's intellectuals. One of the best-known Indian economists, Jagdish Bhagwati, crossed swords with Amartya Sen as he celebrated the Gujarat model. He declared that 'Modi has the vision to take India to the next level.'[252] 'The Gujarat model,' Bhagwati said, 'was not just about "creating prosperity". It (the Gujarat model) is also about using the wealth that is created, to increase social spending.'[253]

Arvind Panagariya, who was appointed by Prime Minister Narendra Modi in 2015 to head the official policy think-tank, Niti Aayog, which replaced the Nehruvian Planning Commission, summarized Amartya Sen's rejection of Modi's model of development and his very public differences with Bhagwati.[254] Amartya Sen was critical of the Gujarat model because he felt that Modi laid much higher stress on physical infrastructure than on health or education.[255] 'Sen thinks,' according to Panagariya, 'that the starting point for achieving the desired goal (of battling poverty) must be an immediate massive attack on illiteracy and ill health. This would not only directly contribute to better education and health, it would also bring about faster growth by producing a healthier and more literate workforce. Higher growth would in turn yield larger revenues, allowing further attack on illiteracy and ill health. A virtuous cycle will thus emerge. In this story, growth automatically follows improved literacy and health.'[256] Bhagwati and Panagariya countered Sen by suggesting that Modi was on the right track in accelerating the liberalization of foreign trade and investment, facilitating private players in infrastructure. 'Our view on development policy,' Panagariya explained, 'is almost the opposite of Sen. Track-I reforms provide the true starting point for any poor country. On the one hand, rapid growth directly empowers the citizens through increased incomes that they can use to buy high-quality education and health in the marketplace. On the other hand, it gives the government ever-rising revenues to further enhance public expenditures on health and education.'[257]

The twentieth century saw the massive expansion of the growth of the state in most parts of the world. In diverse political systems, the state derived its legitimacy mainly from what it pledged to its ordinary and, especially, to its impoverished citizens. What states actually delivered to them was very often paltry and deceitful, but they still continued to accept the political and ethical premise that the primary duty of governments was to deliver services, or protect the rights, of common people. This changed dramatically from the last decade of the twentieth century, when agencies like the World Bank and many economists influentially propagated the view that a good government was one that facilitated the functioning of private markets, and not one that directly provided to its dispossessed and socially oppressed peoples. It is by this measure that Modi's administration in Gujarat could be arguably elevated to a model of good (the best?) governance (even though its glittering claims of double-digit growth and millions of dollars in investment were possibly exaggerated).

Modi's claims of his leadership of Gujarat establishing the gold standard of good governance raised many pertinent questions. One was whether Gujarat under Modi indeed outpaced other states in economic growth and private investment. The second was the terms on which this private investment was encouraged, and whether this indeed was for public good. And, finally, was there evidence that people who are economically and socially disadvantaged benefited significantly from this economic growth?

If the yardstick of successful governance as creating a business- and investment-friendly environment is accepted, Modi's government in Gujarat seemed, at least on the surface, to have performed creditably. Gujarat achieved double-digit growth at rates higher than most other states. With just 5 per cent of India's population, it contributed 21 per cent to India's exports and 13 per cent to its industrial production in 2009. Yet, as Lyla Bavadam in *Frontline* observes, nearly thirty years before Modi's dispensation Gujarat was among the three fastest-growing states in the country in 1980. Since then it has more or less occupied that position.[258] This suggests that Modi's policies were not decisively responsible for this good performance. It is also pertinent that growth rates were higher in states like Maharashtra and Tamil Nadu. Gujarat's performance as the most attractive destination for private investment is also overstated. Its share in FDI in 2102-13 was 2.38 per cent, placing it at a distant sixth position among the states of India. In contrast, Maharashtra's share was just under 40 per cent.[259] Economist Atul Sood also reminds us that of the total memoranda of understanding (MOUs) signed at successive high-profile investor summits, the proportion of projects actually realized fell precipitously from 73 per cent in 2003 to 13 per cent in 2011.[260]

Even more pertinent are the terms on which Gujarat attracted private investment. Its sterling reputation as an investor-friendly government derived greatly from the alacrity with which it provided land in Sanand to Tata Motors to set up a factory to manufacture the Nano, the company's small car, after the company had publicly failed to set up a manufacturing unit in Singur, West Bengal. But much of the land handed over to Tata Motors was already controlled by the Gujarat Industrial Development Corporation, while a small chunk owned by farmers was bought at above-market rates with little opposition.

The government gifted unprecedented tax concessions to the Tatas and other big business houses. Paranjoy Guha Thakurta, based on an internal document of the Gujarat state government, reported that the total subsidies given by the Gujarat government to Tata Motors added up to more than ₹300 billion.[261] A Right to Information application revealed that Tata Motors invested ₹29 billion while the state government awarded it a loan of ₹95.7 billion at an incredible 0.1 per cent rate of interest, repayable on a monthly basis after twenty years.[262] All the charges which are normally levied when transferring land from agricultural to non-agricultural purposes were completely waived. Registration fees, too, were not charged. The state government met the entire infrastructure cost of developing roads, provided electricity and gas supply, and allotted an additional 100 acres of land on the outskirts of Ahmedabad to build a township for Tata Motors employees. The Gujarat government also met the cost of shifting the project to the tune of ₹7 billion—this amount included expenses for bringing machinery and equipment from Singur to Sanand. The Centre for Science and Environment calculates that the total subsidy element of the 'cheap' car is half its total market price.[263]

This is all an astonishing exercise in turning on the head the principle of equity that it is the rich who must always subsidize the poor. What we saw in Gujarat was the exact reverse; of contributions made by the ordinary taxpayer—which, because of a significant proportion of indirect taxes, includes payments by the poor—subsidizing the super-rich. It is no wonder that Ratan Tata went on record to say that it would be stupid not to invest in Gujarat. From his perspective as a businessman, of course it would be. In an interview to a news channel, Tata praised Modi's capacity to deliver what he promised, such as land, which his peers were unable to accomplish. 'We are in a democracy,' said Tata, and other elected heads of government 'do not have the capacity to make things happen' in the way that Modi does. In other words, Modi in his stewardship of Gujarat demonstrated the capacity to deliver state support for market-led economic growth *without dissent*. This is his major selling point to attract private capital investment, along with astounding tax benefits, which amounts to the subsidizing of large industry by the ordinary taxpayer.

Noted feminist economist Indira Hirway regards the Gujarat government's policy of spending more on incentives than on development a kind of 'crony capitalism', in which industries set up bases in Gujarat because of the concessions given to them.[264] This was the basic template of the policies of Modi's government for other large industrial houses as well. Apart from the Tatas, there are reports that the Gujarat government had to forego revenues of almost ₹1.29 billion for land sold to Larsen and Toubro at concessional rates;[265] that land was sold to the Adani Group at the incredible price of ₹1 per square metre;[266] to the Rahejas at ₹470 per square metre;[267] where the minimum price fixed by the government was ₹19,000 per square metre. A PIL alleged that this sale led to a loss of ₹11 billion for the public exchequer, and so on in a long list. Besides, under all the hype, only a quarter of the promised investments have actually been realized. Economist Atul Sood also worries about the implications of completely handing over both investment and decision-making regarding all new infrastructure projects—ports, highways, rail—to profit-led large industry, which would naturally prioritize the infrastructure needs of big business over those of ordinary people, and that Gujarat now has among the worst records of labour unrest among states in the country.[268]

But political scientist Ashutosh Varshney regards Narendra Modi's massive victory as a 'game-changer, profitably using the term "critical realignment", a concept that basically depicts a radical shift in the social bases of political power, a shift that is not transitory but long term. A second way to explain the significance of Modi's rise is to deploy a more colloquial term: capitalism with Indian characteristics.'[269]

Those who oppose Modi's Gujarat model of development advocate an alternate, if you like, more feminine idea of good government, which is nurturing and caring.

In terms of this alternate touchstone for assessing a government's worth by its success in battling poverty, discrimination and want, the Gujarat administration dramatically slips from leading the country to being a conspicuous laggard. Between 2005 and 2010, poverty in Gujarat fell by 8.6 per cent; well behind states like Odisha (19.2 per cent), Maharashtra (13.7 per cent) and Tamil Nadu (13.1 per cent).[270] The International Food Policy Research Institute (IFPRI) found the Hunger Index of Gujarat 'alarming', the lowest among all high-income states, and below even Odisha which is notorious as India's hunger epicentre, and impoverished and poorly governed Uttar Pradesh.[271] Forty-five per cent of the children below the age of five in Gujarat are malnourished.[272] Infant mortality among girls, at fifty-one per 1,000, is higher than the national average of forty-nine.[273] The sex ratio fell from 920 to 918 females for 1,000 males between 2001 and 2011, well below the national average of 940.[274] Hirway concludes that 'the growth story of Gujarat is not inclusive, sustainable, equitable or environment-friendly', and that 'there is a disconnect between economic growth and developmental growth'.[275]

While the state gave unprecedented incentives to large businesses, there was a marked decline in investments in the social sector. In

2011-12, Gujarat ranked seventeenth among Indian states in development expenditure as a proportion of total public expenditure.[276] Only 1.09 per cent of public expenditure in Gujarat was on education and health, well behind states like Rajasthan (3.09 per cent); a trend which dismayed and worried Amartya Sen.[277] Shipra Nigam points to the inevitable consequences of this neglect. Between 1999-00 and 2007-08, the proportion of children between six and fourteen years attending school in Gujarat was fewer than the national average.[278] Even more worrying, the proportion of girls, Dalits, tribal Muslims and other children of the minorities who attended school was much lower than national average.[279] Gujarat is again below the national average and also compares unfavourably with other high-growth states such as Tamil Nadu, Haryana and Maharashtra in infant mortality, mortality under the age of five, and mortality rates for women.[280] It is no wonder that in the India Human Development Report 2011, Gujarat ranked a lowly eleventh in 2007-08.[281]

Gujarat's hunger story is even more damning. A survey conducted by the NNMB in 2012 showed that 53.7 per cent of the children under five in Gujarat were stunted (of low height with respect to their age).[282] Stunting is an indicator of chronic malnutrition, mainly caused by repeated illness and lack of access to nutritious food. About 43 per cent of adult men and women have a low body mass index. Time trends from data gathered by both the NNMB and the NSS show that the average calorie consumption and cereal consumption is also falling. There was also a decline in consumption of other nutrients such as proteins, calcium and iron. While many states were improving their PDS over the last five years, Gujarat was one of the worst-performing states on two aspects of the PDS: it has a low and falling per capita PDS consumption, and among the highest rates of foodgrain diversion.[283] Over half of those in the poorest quintile in Gujarat reported that they did not get any subsidized grain, nearly 10 percentage points higher than the national average, according to the 2009-10 National Sample Survey.[284] BPL lists had not been updated since 1998, when the poverty line was fixed at ₹11 per day.

From the benchmark of social equity, the gravest culpability of the Modi government was its openly hostile relationship with its minorities. I will return to the question of the alleged complicity of Modi and his government in the slaughter of Muslims in 2002 later. What is less noticed is the administration's refusal to extend equitable development services to the minorities. Muslim ghettoes are conspicuously under-serviced with roads, sanitation, drinking water and electricity, compared to their glittering neighbours. Gujarat was the only state government in the country which, during the UPA years, refused to contribute its share to a Centrally sponsored scheme of scholarships for children from minority communities, although 36 per cent Muslim children were out of school in that year.

Beneath the bluster and hyperbole of political claims, the choices before the country as it went to the polls in 2014 were stark. Could markets alone deliver a better life for people of disadvantage, or must caring states play a more active role? Would ordinary people, and especially the millions who live in poverty, benefit from a model of development in which huge public funds are committed to supporting large private corporations while investments in education, healthcare, nutrition and social infrastructure remain neglected?

Enough numbers of Indian voters voted in support of Modi's leadership, and pitched their hopes on the premise that the country would gain if it follows the Gujarat model of development as envisioned by Modi. But it worth heeding the warning of Martha Nussbaum, the widely respected American philosopher. She observes that 'although the growth-based paradigm does indeed give Narendra Modi high marks, the Human Development paradigm, by contrast, shows his record as only middling, far worse than that of states such as Tamil Nadu and Kerala, which have been preoccupied, rightly, with the distribution of healthcare and education. Given the high economic status of Gujarat, one might conclude that Modi's record is not just middling but downright bad.'[285] She quotes distinguished economist Mahbub Ul Haq: 'The real wealth of a nation is its people. And the purpose of development is to create an enabling environment for people to enjoy long, healthy, and creative lives. This simple but powerful truth is too often forgotten in the pursuit of material and financial wealth.' She concludes: 'India will not shine without great strides in education and public health. More or less everyone knows this, even when they talk only about growth most of the time. A nation needs a healthy and educated work force if it is to do well into the future. But of course health and education are more than tools for business: they are also essential tools of democratic self-governance. A leadership with a bad record on these issues—and, what's more, with no shame about this record or public resolve to improve things—is likely to prove disastrous for India's future.'[286]

Gandhi, nearly forgotten in Gujarat, was guided by a talisman in moments of confusion. He would remember the weakest person he knew. In Gujarat today, she would almost certainly be female: maybe a girl without food, a riot victim, a displaced tribal, a fisherwoman, a street vendor, or a salt pan worker. Would she seek a government which cares, which affirms her dignity, which partners her efforts to find for herself and her loved ones food, work, healthcare and education? The middle class, the aspirational and neo-middle class, and those subscribing to majoritarian Hindu domination in India may choose in one way. But her choice, if she could make it, and if she could find political parties who could credibly promise her these, could alter the further course of the collective destinies, of both India's middle classes and the multitudes of its poor.

THE LEGITIMIZATION OF PREJUDICE

Bigotry without Apology

In our world today, there is much which has become globalized—the clothes we wear, the food we eat, the films we watch, the songs we dance to, and the social networking sites on which we compulsively exhibit our lives in real time. But, in my travels during the past decade, I have discovered something else which has also become globalized—prejudice. Specifically, prejudice in drawing-room conversations among middle-class people about Muslims. In every city in every country in the world, where Muslims are not in a majority, be it Copenhagen, New York, London, Delhi or Ahmedabad, the conversation over dinner is likely, at some point, to veer to the subject of Muslims. And the dominant view of many people—otherwise affable, educated and liberal—is that Muslims mean trouble, big trouble!

Above all, according to this new globalized 'common sense', Muslims are sympathetic to violence. Indeed, they are the most violent people in the world. People admit that not all Muslims actively engage in violent activities, but they insist that all—or almost all—'within their hearts' subscribe to bloodshed and revenge. They are convinced that most Muslims are fundamentalist by socialization and teaching. Their religion teaches violence. It is ferociously intolerant and hostile to every other faith. It is also regressive, and subjugates women behind veils and encourages families to breed large populations to ultimately submerge the peaceable communities in which they live.

These 'global' conversations not only make such sweeping, profoundly unjust and false generalizations, they also homogenize a vast segment of humanity, failing to recognize enormous differences of gender, class, nationality, language and ethnicity among Muslim people in every country and on the planet. Even an otherwise liberal Barack Obama reaches out to address what he describes unproblematically as the 'Muslim world', this fictionalized homogenized entity which is believed to think and act in unison, and mostly in ways which are dangerous for the rest of the world.

It is for this reason that if I was writing a history of the new India of today, I would regard its second defining feature, apart from the exile of the poor from the conscience of people of privilege, to be the legitimization of prejudice among the middle classes. This display of open bigotry in many ways would have been unthinkable during my childhood and youth. In another dramatic overturning of long-held collective beliefs, just like 'greed is good', it is as though, now, 'prejudice is fine'. After Narendra Modi's election in May 2014 to India's prime ministerial office, a friend wrote to me, 'I thought up to now that the middle class felt entitled to aspiration, learning from diasporic fantasies. But what I did not know was how there is a sense of entitlement about Hindutva. I find that chilling.'

~

There are many targets of the new unapologetic and vocal chauvinism of urban, middle-class people in India today, and these are not just Muslims—slum residents, migrants from Uttar Pradesh and Bihar, domestic helps, the undifferentiated underclass in general, 'reservation-wallah' upstart Dalit officers and leaders, people from ethnically diverse parts of India like the Northeast and Africans residing in India, are some of their easiest marks.

I have watched the shallow cosmopolitan veneer of India's capital city, Delhi, where I live, mouldering and peeling, and reveal an ugly, chauvinist, majoritarian population uneasy with difference. Young people from distant corners of the country—and, indeed, from far countries of the world—converge on the metropolis to study and find work. But they have to soon learn to live with suspicion, hostility, condescension and stereotyping as a way of life in this unwelcoming city of opportunities.

The Legitimization of Prejudice

On a cold winter night in mid-January 2014, a minister in the Delhi government, Somnath Bharti, led a group of citizens into the houses of African women in Khirki Extension, a crowded, inexpensive settlement in south Delhi, claiming that they were peddling drugs and running a prostitution racket. The women were manhandled, searched and humiliated. Brenda Semakula, a twenty-six-year-old Ugandan hairstylist speaking to Aditi Malhotra of the *Wall Street Journal*, said heartbreakingly, 'I feel like we are not liked in this country.'[1]

The bullying of the African women and the police by the minister won him a great deal of support, feeding into racist stereotypes of drug-using and sex-selling immigrant Africans.[2] It is little wonder that a disturbing study by two Swedish economists on racial tolerance in countries around the globe—in which they asked respondents if they would be willing to live with a neighbour who is racially different from them—found India the second-most racially intolerant among the eighty countries they surveyed.[3]

The cosmopolitan veneer of the capital cracked one more time on 29 January 2014 after the murder of Nido Taniam, a young first-year graduate student from Arunachal Pradesh, by men in a Lajpat Nagar marketplace who were taunting him for his appearance and hairstyle. This tore open, like a festering wound, the long-suppressed, collective anguish of young people from Northeast India. They staged angry demonstrations before police stations and at Jantar Mantar, speaking out about rampant sexual harassment and violence faced by young women from the Northeast, random hate-fuelled violence against Northeastern young men, barbs by classmates, work colleagues, landlords and strangers, and bias in police stations, classrooms and, surprisingly, hospitals. The cold, uncomfortable word they used to describe the discrimination that they routinely face was 'racism'.

Their grief mounted further when a fourteen-year-old Manipuri girl working as a domestic help was raped in Munirka in south Delhi as she was returning from a medical store. The rapist, her landlord's son, was photographed by some private closed-circuit cameras as he cruelly dragged her along, and led to his arrest. But we soon discovered to our dismay that Munirka has a khap panchayat which met along with members of the local Residents' Welfare Association and, instead of condemning the rape perpetrated by a young man of their community and finding ways to make the colony safer for women, decided to evict tenants from the Northeast. Their resolution was reportedly to clean up the colony by throwing out from it the Northeastern 'trash'—the word used was 'gandagi'. The hurt and anger of the Northeastern residents of Delhi were doused by diplomatic interventions by the local police, who organized meetings between residents who come from the Northeast, members of the khap panchayat, and the Residents' Welfare Association, who finally agreed to not evict peaceful and law-abiding Northeastern tenants. But the fear remained that there would be a low-key 'cleansing' of the area in the way that Khirki Extension was cleared of most of its African residents just months after the racist attacks visited upon them by vigilante residents led by the minister.

The anguish of migrants to the city from India's Northeast is firstly about the stereotyping to which they are subject. All women from the Northeast are believed to be sexually promiscuous. All men are believed to be drug users and hard drinkers. In Munirka, it was claimed that young men from the Northeast indulge in regular, boisterous, heavy drinking, and use drugs. It is as though people from other communities, including the local Gujjar and Jat youth, do not drink or abuse drugs. Leading newspapers and TV news channels thought nothing of prominently carrying speculative news reports after Nido Taniam's killing (subsequently proved false) that he may have died not because of assaults fuelled by hate, but the overuse of drugs.

Young people from India's Northeast also feel wounded by the routine ignorance of mainland Indians about the area, and how they are not regarded as Indians. Classmates and colleagues do not take the trouble to learn and pronounce their names correctly; some assume they are Chinese or Nepali, sometimes actually asking if they need passports to 'visit India'. Meitei Vaishnavite Hindus from Manipur dream of the day when they can make a pilgrimage to Brindaban in Mathura, but the priests there often bar their entry into the temple, dubbing them 'malaich' or unclean foreigners. Textbooks very rarely carry the histories of the Northeastern states. A teacher in a south Delhi college asked how many students had heard of Rani Lakshmibai, and every hand went up. When she asked how many had heard of Rani Gaidinliu, the Naga heroine of India's freedom struggle, hardly any student responded.

People also bunch all eight states from the Northeast into one, ignoring the enormous linguistic, cultural, ethnic and religious diversity within these states. Arunachal Pradesh alone is home to 150 tribes and more languages than any other state in the country. Yet for mainland Indians, all Northeastern residents are just 'chinkies'. What is long overdue is for all textbooks to include the histories and cultures of the various states in India's Northeast, underlining their contributions to India's rich diversity.

The country's many minorities—religious, ethnic, caste, disabled and sexual, even single women—require a comprehensive anti-discrimination law, one of the many unfulfilled promises of the UPA government which went out of power in 2014. But more importantly, residents of Delhi need to reflect on ways that this city, which welcomed millions of refugees during India's Partition a few generations ago, should now learn to welcome with friendship and open hearts other peoples from India and the world who come with their dreams to this city and make it their own.

~

There is not a great deal which daunts me but, more than almost anything else, the one thing which still drives me to anxiety is the prospect of spending an evening with people of my social class—with the extended family, associates of my parents and parents-in-law, friends from boarding school, and former colleagues from the civil service. Because of my decision to leave the Indian Administrative

Service after the carnage of 2002 in Gujarat, and my articulated, public positions on secularism and the rights of minorities and the poor, I find that my presence in these gatherings almost invariably spurs discussions around both Muslims and the poor, and the tenor of these conversations is rarely friendly. I try to respond in measured ways; I tell myself that I should be willing to listen and engage, but I find the arguments so rooted in prejudice that reasonable debate becomes impossible. I sometimes find myself unreasonably angry and defensive.

These social schisms went so deep and were so dramatic that, autobiographically, my life falls into two phases, one before and one after 2002. After my public denouncement of the communal carnage of 2002, I lost close to three quarters of my friends and associates of my life before 2002—childhood friends from school and college and from the Indian Administrative Service (IAS) and some members of the extended family who knew me from my boyhood. So many of them simply cancelled me out of their lives; presumably, they were aggrieved by my public life-choice of joining the 'wrong' side. The personal became political, but in an inverse way from that advocated by feminists. So many segments of India's middle class felt so implacably hostile to the Muslim 'enemy within' that defectors to the 'other' side were no longer tolerable even as friends who are beyond politics, if such a thing is possible. Of course, the vacuum in my life after 2002 was filled by a magnificent new set of friends and comrades, and my loneliness has healed in part and with time. But the result of the general elections of 2014 has spurred a revival of all the old schisms, this time with an even greater sense of triumphalism.

Sometimes I would appeal in these unsociable social gatherings, especially to elders in the extended family—many of who lived through the trauma of Partition and the 1984 anti-Sikh carnage—that they, better than anyone else, should understand what it means to be members of a demonized minority only because of one's 'different' faith. But they were not convinced; I had sided with the enemy.

~

In 2005, I shifted to Ahmedabad for nearly a year to work more closely with survivors of the carnage because I saw that their conditions and their access to justice had not altered despite all efforts. This became one of the loneliest phases of my life, because bigotry was flaunted even more openly in the middle classes in that claustrophobically fractured and bigoted city. I survived emotionally because of the affectionate comradeship of my colleagues, the aman pathiks and nyaya pathiks, or peace and justice workers, who were mostly working-class survivors of the carnage, or caring working-class women and men from the Gujarati Hindu communities who chose to stand in solidarity with the survivors.

I realized that the other face of the coin of prejudice, in places where it becomes the common currency of social transactions between dominant and minority communities, is fear. There may or may not be open violence, but pervasive discrimination becomes a way of life, as does an invisible dread. In my record of the carnage, *Fear and Forgiveness: The Aftermath of Massacre*, I have described that however cruel and brutal the violence which unfolded over those terrible weeks and months in 2002 was—local survivors call it the toofan, or storm—what has been immeasurably more terrifying for me is what followed in the years later.[4] Through sustained social and economic boycott, and geographical and social segregation, the Muslim community has been 'tamed' into adjusting to new social relations; to get used to fear and social subordination every day; and forced to settle for second-class citizenship. It was a kind of Dalitization of the Muslims. An unspoken message seemed to have been sent out: 'We will permit you to live here, but your settlements must be separate, the services in your habitats meagre, and we do not want to hear the sound of the azaan or witness signs of your religious or cultural assertion.' The ordinary markers of identity of Muslims in mixed public places have been erased. In Ahmedabad, I can easily identify any autorickshaw I am travelling in as belonging to a Muslim because it will not carry any of the religious markers which are so ubiquitous in rickshaws anywhere in the country.

I recall a story which filmmaker Saeed Mirza relates about Bombay in 1984. His mother was in hospital when Indira Gandhi was assassinated by her Sikh bodyguards. The killing resulted in violent reprisals against the Sikh community. Returning from the hospital even as the city was tense, Saeed hailed a taxi and sat in the front seat. He noticed that markers of religion had been recently uprooted from the dashboard. He looked at the taxi driver whose hair was cropped, and asked him if he was Sikh. The old man shook his head vehemently. But Saeed looked more closely at his forehead, and it clearly showed the tell-tale, inverted 'V' of lighter skin; proof that until recently, the man wore a turban.

'I am a friend,' Saeed said to him gently. 'Don't be afraid of me.' The old man began to weep. He spoke of how frightened he was. 'What kind of country is this,' he sobbed, 'where I am afraid to be myself?'

Modi's Triumph and India's Scalding Majoritarian Summer

At the peak of campaigning for elections in 2014, further heat was generated by an open letter published in *The Guardian*, signed by some of the most respected global intellectuals of Indian origin, including sculptor Aneesh Kapur, writer Salman Rushdie and filmmaker Deepa Mehta.[5]

They warned that if Narendra Modi was elected India's next prime minister, it would 'bode ill for the country's future'. 'Without questioning the validity of India's democratic election process, it is crucial to remember the role played by the Modi government in the horrifying events that took place in Gujarat in 2002,' the open letter stated. In particular, it held him culpable for the massacre of Muslims under his watch when he was chief minister in 2002.

'Although some members of Narendra Modi's government are now facing trial, Modi himself repeatedly refuses to accept any responsibility or to render an apology.' It went on to declare that 'such a failure of moral character and political ethics on the part of Modi is incompatible with India's secular constitution, which, in advance of many constitutions across the world, is founded on pluralist principles and seeks fair and full representation for minorities. Were he to be elected prime minister, it would bode ill for India's future as a country that cherishes the ideals of inclusion and protection for all its peoples and communities'.

Another signatory of the letter, Chetan Bhatt, professor of sociology at the London School of Economics, said: 'Modi perfectly embodies a callous, dangerous and authoritarian ideology that stands opposed to genuine liberal, democratic and secular values that founded the modern state of India.'⁶ Writer Amitav Ghosh said that to have Modi at the helm would be very 'destabilising' because the 2002 carnage happened under his watch.⁷ Salman Rushdie also described Modi as a 'highly divisive figure...accused of being responsible for an anti-Muslim pogrom in 2002 in the state of Gujarat...a hardliner's hardliner'.⁸

Amartya Sen also stuck his neck out in a newspaper interview to declare that he did not want Modi to become India's prime minister as he did not have credible secular credentials. 'As an Indian citizen I don't want Modi as my PM...He has not done enough to make minorities feel safe,' he said, referring to his 'terrible record' in which 'the minority feel insecure and could legitimately think that there was an organised violence against them in 2002'.⁹ Economist Jean Dreze wrote, 'Narendra Modi's personality...has been repackaged for mass approval. From an authoritarian character, steeped in the reactionary creed of the Rashtriya Swayamsevak Sangh (RSS) and probably complicit in the Gujarat massacre of 2002, he has become an almost avuncular figure—a good shepherd who is expected to lead the country out of the morass of corruption, inflation and unemployment. How he is supposed to accomplish this is left to our imagination—substance is not part of the promos. The BJP, too, is being reinvented as the party of clean governance, overlooking the fact that there is little to distinguish it from the Congress as far as corruption is concerned.'¹⁰

Within India, writer U. R. Ananthamurthy went so far as to remark that he would not like to live in an India whose prime minister was Narendra Modi.¹¹ For the first time in its history, sixty people connected with the film industry in Mumbai, including many respected names like film directors Govind Nihalani, Vishal Bhardwaj, Imtiaz Ali, Zoya Akhtar and Mahesh Bhatt, actor Nandita Das and singer Shubha Mudgal, signed an open letter which they said was 'a collective appeal to the citizens of India to vote strategically to protect our country's secular character'.¹²

The BJP was predictably furious. Its spokesperson Ravi Shankar

The Legitimization of Prejudice 169

Prasad reacted caustically. 'These comments are prejudiced, biased and some of these people have entertained a pathological hatred towards Mr Modi for years.'[13] Many film actors and technicians rose in support of Modi, and criticized those who had signed the open letter against him. BJP member of Parliament Giriraj Singh exhorted all those who opposed Modi to migrate to Pakistan.[14] The climate was so charged that after Modi's triumph, U. R. Ananthamurthy was sent a one-way ticket to Karachi in Pakistan, and a police picket was posted outside his home in Bangalore. When he passed away some months later, firecrackers were lighted in celebration, even though he was one of the tallest sons of Karnataka.

Both anger and hope peaked, and catapulted Narendra Modi to the seat of power. 'In small towns and villages,' Mihir Sharma reported, 'the most aggressive pro-Modi voices are young men brimming over with anger. Modi speaks to these young men in a way nothing in their lives ever has. He speaks of an India where there is no unemployment, which some of them believe is already banished from Gujarat. He speaks of an India which is so intimidating that China and Pakistan will not dare cross it...He speaks of an India that does not feel the desire to visit America, because Americans will wish to come here...It is middle-caste, even some Dalit men, in smaller towns, anxious to leave their past behind them, who see in Modi something—a will to power perhaps—that transcends origins. Who holds out to them the possibility that their sordid present will become a glorious future—because that future already exists in glorious Gujarat. It is not all about jobs, as some would claim; it is about self-respect. Waves always are...And it is an entire generation of upper-caste, influential, "middle-class" young people in cities, too. Young people who despise reservations, and see Modi as the only leader "untainted" by identity politics, for Hinduism is not an identity for young Hindu people. Young people who feel a quiet approval of the possibility that this incoming Lok Sabha will have the fewest number of Muslims in India's history. Young people convinced their state is not run for them, but for faceless people in villages...Young people who think that hate is what Modi endures from liberals, not what Muslims endured in Ahmedabad, and still do.'[15]

Although Modi greatly toned down his trademark divisive rhetoric and communal hectoring in his campaign, he still refused to apologize for the carnage of 2002 which occurred under his watch. In fact, after the carnage, Chief Minister Narendra Modi had led a triumphant Gaurav Yatra, March of Pride, across the state, referring to his now proverbial chhappan-inch ki chhati.[16, 17] The subtext was that he alone was man enough to fell and tame the Muslims and to show them their actual place. This is why it took him until 2013 to express any regret for the carnage; and, even then, to only awkwardly say that were his car to run a puppy over, he would feel sorry![18]

Two questions are pertinent here. The first is whether India's courts have actually cleared Modi of charges of criminal culpability in the mass crimes of 2002 in many parts of Gujarat. The second is whether the vote Modi sought in 2014 and the vote he received was exclusively for his avatar as a mascot of no-nonsense, market-led economic growth in the fabled development model of Gujarat, or whether it was partly or even wholly a vote for majoritarian Hindu domination and against India's minorities, especially Muslims, but also, to some extent, Christians. I will take up each question by turn.

~

Given Modi's own discourse—until he was chosen as the BJP's prime ministerial candidate eight months before the elections—of barely suppressed triumphalism surrounding the carnage of 2002, his transition to secular statesmanship required the erasure of his culpability. This erasure had been successfully accomplished earlier for the hawkish BJP leader Lal Krishna Advani to pave the way for his prime ministerial ambitions. The trail of blood which followed his Rath Yatra in 1989 and his robust contribution to the movement to violently pull down the Babri Masjid in 1992 were substantially expunged from public memory by a systematic campaign of his willing re-invention as a moderate statesman.

A similar exercise was undertaken in India's most expensive political campaign ever—in which the BJP reportedly spent close to what Obama spent in his election campaign, although the US has a per capita income thirty times higher than that of India.[19] Except for his core Hindu nationalist constituency, Modi was reinvented as the avuncular messiah of market growth.

Given Modi's public position on the 2002 massacre, the obliteration of his role in it was even harder to accomplish than the reinvention of the two earlier prime ministerial candidates fielded by the BJP. But the leaders of industry, as much as large segments of the middle classes impatient to see his installation as the one man who could accelerate economic growth, rejected the idea that his ambitions to attain the highest post in national politics were disqualified by his alleged role in one of the most brutal communal massacres after Independence. They counselled that we should focus on the 'big picture' of growth, as though the violent suppression of minorities is but a minor blemish. Many European ambassadors lined up at his door in the hope of participating in Gujarat's growth story. All of them needed a fig-leaf to cover the nakedness of their choices.

This fig-leaf came was provided by the closure report filed by the Supreme Court-appointed SIT (Special Investigation Team) which absolved Narendra Modi of any role in the carnage, concluding there was no 'prosecutable evidence' against the chief minister. These findings were endorsed by the 'clean chit' given by the lower court which heard Zakia Jafri's petition of 15 April 2013, who had alleged that a high-level conspiracy had been hatched to manipulate the Godhra tragedy so that the carnage which followed could be organized and fuelled. The first name among the fifty-nine accused in Zakia Jafri's petition was that of Chief Minister Narendra Modi. Zakia's lawyer Mihir Desai argued in court that the political head of the state, the home ministry and the administration had sanctioned the 'build-up of aggressive and communal sentiments, violent mobilisation, including carrying of arms, and a general outpouring against the minority community...'.[20] Relying on documents collected by the SIT itself, Zakia's petition attempted to establish that there was a conspiracy at the senior-most levels of the state administration, not just to generate hatred against Muslims, but also to target Muslim people and their property and religious places and 'aid and abet this process by acts and omissions of persons liable under law to act otherwise'.[21]

How much does the SIT's closure report and the lower court's 'clean chit' to Modi really free him from taint? At best, they suggest that there is no irrefutable, *direct* evidence that, as chief minister, Modi actually directed that the slaughter of Muslims be allowed to continue, giving free rein to enraged 'Hindus' to violently vent their rage. The SIT chose not to give credence to the statements of one serving and one retired police officer that he indeed issued such instructions. But Manoj Mitta, in his carefully researched book, *The Fiction of Fact-Finding: Modi and Godhra*, writes that the SIT treaded carefully around the powerful politician. At no point did the SIT file an FIR against him. He was not held accountable for his uncorroborated, public statement, characterizing the train burning at Godhra as a 'pre-planned inhuman collective violent act of terrorism', which incited public anger and which continues to be used to justify the massacre.[22] It likewise did not question him about his claim that he first heard about the Gulbarg Society massacre, in which former Congress MP, Ehsan Jafri, lost his life at 8:30 p.m.— a timeline first established by Mitta in his book—on 28 February 2002, until many hours after the slaughter. By its own admission, the administration was monitoring events and Modi was holding a law-and-order review meeting even as the massacre unfolded, just a few kilometres away at the Circuit House Annexe.[23]

Senior advocate Raju Ramachandran, amicus curiae appointed by the Supreme Court to investigate allegations of Narendra Modi's complicity in the Gujarat riots, also disagreed with the conclusions of the SIT. His opinion, reported to the Supreme Court, was that 'the offences which can be made out against Shri Modi, at this prima facie stage, included promoting enmity between different groups on grounds of religion and acts prejudicial to (the) maintenance of harmony'.[24] He believed also that there were grounds to not dismiss the version of suspended police officer Sanjiv Bhatt out of hand by the SIT. According to Bhatt, on 27 February 2002, hours after fifty-eight passengers were set on fire in a train near the Godhra station, Modi held a meeting at his residence with senior police officers and told them that Hindus should be allowed to 'vent their anger'.[25] Ramachandran states: 'I disagree with the conclusion of the SIT that Shri Bhatt should be disbelieved at this stage itself. On the other hand, I am of the view that Shri Bhatt needs to be put through the test of cross-examination, as do the others who deny his presence.'[26]

Ramachandran also pointed to evidence that two senior ministers were placed in police control rooms on 28 February as riots raged in Ahmedabad and across the state. The SIT did not find evidence that they interfered with the police's independent functioning, but stated that 'there is the possibility that the very presence of these two ministers had a dampening effect on the senior police officials'.[27] He concludes, 'While there is no direct material to show how and when the message of the Chief Minister was conveyed to the two ministers, the very presence of political personalities unconnected with the Home Portfolio at the Police Control Rooms is circumstantial evidence of the Chief Minister directing, requesting or allowing them to be present.'[28]

People who organized and actively participated in the massacre were rewarded. Chief Minister Modi appointed Maya Kodnani as his minister for women and child welfare, after she was charged with leading the mob which brutally killed more than a 100 people, including many women and children, in Naroda Patiya. Maya Kodnani was subsequently convicted and punished with imprisonment for her entire life for her part in the crimes.

However, Narendra Modi's culpability, as chief minister, for the carnage of 2002 should not hinge, in the end, on proving beyond doubt that he directed police officers to allow Hindus to 'vent their anger', or that his ministers and MLAs were obeying his commands by interfering in the independent functioning of the police force or leading murderous mobs. The fact that the carnage continued not just for days but for weeks should be evidence enough of the criminal complicity of senior state authorities, and so should Modi's intemperate statements, and the parading of the charred bodies of the people who died on the train in Godhra. Similar guilt should be attached to those who allowed other communal carnages to continue, whether on the streets of Delhi in 1984 and Mumbai in 1992-93 or the killing fields of Nellie in 1983 and Bhagalpur in 1989.

The 'clean chit' given to Modi is, at best, a technical clearance in the absence of cast-iron evidence, although even this is disputed by experts.[29] But I believe that there can be no doubt of his grave culpability for inflaming sectarian passions by holding Muslims guilty for an offence without evidence, and for the conduct of his government which allowed, including through unconscionable inaction, the continuance of the carnage for many dark days and weeks in 2002.

~

Despite the clouds that hung over Modi's head due to his refusal to express public remorse for the carnage of 2002, it is true that 'development' in the 'Gujarat model' and the failures of the 'maa-beta Sarkar'—the ruling government commonly perceived to have been steered by Sonia Gandhi and her son, Rahul Gandhi—dominated a great part of his message to the electorate in far corners of the country.

Strident anti-Muslim rhetoric—dominant in his rallies in three successive election campaigns for the Gujarat assembly in and since 2002—was keyed low in his triumphant bid for the country's leadership. But still, many persistent undertones reflected his hostility towards India's minorities. He referred to the UPA government in the capital as the Delhi Sultanate and to Rahul Gandhi as the 'shehzada'—imagery which harked back to medieval domination by

Muslim rulers. He donned every kind of headgear to build rapport with culturally diverse populations in all corners of the country, but refused to wear a skullcap. Even though Muslims form 10 per cent of Gujarat's population, Modi never put up a single Muslim candidate in successive polls in Gujarat. His policy was little different for the national elections, which is why the BJP does not have a single Muslim MP in the Lok Sabha—although Muslims constitute more than 14 per cent of the total population of India—a dubious first for any ruling government since Independence.

There is indeed no ambiguity in Modi's politics, no recourse to poetry and equivocality, unlike the last prime minister to be elected from the BJP, Atal Bihari Vajpayee. Vajpayee himself was not above articulating anti-Muslim or anti-Christian rhetoric from time to time. Yet many still regarded him to be a leader of relative moderation. For instance, Vajpayee wrote an open letter as prime minister to his 'Muslim brothers and sisters' in the Urdu edition of the *Rashtriya Sahara* on 25 April 2004, in which he exhorted Muslims to join the mainstream of Indian life: 'I say to Muslims that they should not consider themselves apart. We have to live together. We have one future.'[30] In seemingly conciliatory tones, he endorsed both the myth of homogeneity and the deliberate separateness of Muslims from other Indians. However, his communal pointers would always be cloaked in a garb of moderation.

Through most of his vigorous and meteoric political career, Modi has worn no fig-leaf of moderation, although during the run-up to the national elections, he did cover his majoritarian convictions with his promises that he would ensure miraculous economic growth.

One can speculate about how much of the middle class supported him for his promise of growth, his decisive leadership, or his communal hyper-nationalism. And even if we accept that there were many who backed him for his growth agenda, we must also accept that all these people were not uncomfortable with a leader who was openly hostile to India's constitutional pledge of equal citizenship to all persons regardless of their faith. This reflected at least a passive condoning of aggressive communalism, if not active support for his deeply divisive brand of politics. Journalist Javed Anand observes, 'The real secret of Modi's success lies in a happy coalition of those who adore him for what happened under his watch in Gujarat in 2002 and those who simply "don't care" what he did then because he promises unbridled growth.'[31] Filmmaker Saeed Mirza lamented at the Idea of India Conclave, held in New Delhi in July 2014, that 'a man vilified within the country and around the world for presiding over the mass slaughter of innocents…uncompromising on the RSS's ideology and firmly grounded on its perception of history' was elected because 'it didn't matter to…very large sections of the middle and upper-middle class because they had been either sufficiently polarised over the years or had been sucked into the world of consumerism and self-preservation. As for the youth from the middle and upper-middle class it also did not matter because to them history didn't matter…'[32]

On the back of unprecedented and unimaginable levels of corporate funding, and fuelled by the media, both social and others, Modi's message reached almost every home. Academic Kanti Bajpai noted, 'The media has probably never been as one-sided as it was during this election campaign. So much for its role as the fourth estate; it acted more like the Modi estate. Media studies groups have already shown that Modi benefited from roughly three times the coverage of any other leader. A content analysis will also show that the media said almost nothing negative about Modi's record in Gujarat and almost nothing positive about Manmohan's record at the Centre.'[33] Siddharth Mazumdar reported the unprecedented use of technology: approximately 200 out of 800 million people have access to the Internet, including via mobile phones, many of them young voters, and Modi was in touch with them continuously throughout his campaign.[34] Using 3D rallies, Modi also managed to reach out to thousands of remote villages by addressing them simultaneously from a remote location. Similarly, through his now fabled 'Chai pe Charcha' or 'Discussion over Tea', Modi interacted with an incredible million people at a time, using a hybrid combination of broadcast and webcast.

But the real muscle of Modi's electoral success was in his sweep of seats in the Hindi heartland, especially Uttar Pradesh and Bihar. RSS volunteers shed all pretence of being 'distanced' from politics and joined hands with BJP workers to ensure Modi's victory. Most commentators agree that the dramatic resurrection of the BJP from being a distant fourth contender in 2009 in Uttar Pradesh, after the Bahujan Samajwadi Party, the Samajwadi Party and the Congress, to the victor, reflected a significant majoritarian consolidation. This same majoritarian storm swept neighbouring Bihar, where Nitish Kumar had to bite the dust even though it was perhaps he who was then offering a real model for inclusive growth to the country.

Many believe that this majoritarian consolidation was carefully and skilfully crafted by Modi's closest aide Amit Shah who, soon after the national triumph, was made president of the BJP. The tide turned decisively in favour of the BJP with the party's success in polarizing Hindu voters across caste lines against Muslims by manufacturing hatred against them, beginning with Muzaffarnagar in Uttar Pradesh, a story to which I will return later in this book. Both Uttar Pradesh and Bihar were embroiled in the throes of more than a hundred riots in 2013-14, transforming—in the hearts and minds of Hindus—Muslims into hated 'others' who must be shown their place and taught a lesson.[35] There are many constituencies in which Muslims form a sufficient number of voters to be able to influence electoral outcomes. Amateur political commentators have long described this as the 'Muslim veto'. But almost all of these constituencies fell to the BJP wave. Neutralizing the Muslim influence in these constituencies would have been possible only if *all* other castes and groups joined hands against the political choice of the Muslims. In Uttar Pradesh, Mayawati's loyal caste base of 20 per cent did not desert her; still, she won no seats despite capturing the third highest vote share (both in Uttar Pradesh and the country as a whole). Even so, it is apparent that many Dalit voters and a larger number of OBC voters were drawn to the majoritarian consolidation represented by Modi and the BJP.

I speculate that the parents of many of the first-time voters in Uttar Pradesh, Bihar, Madhya Pradesh and other Hindi-speaking states who voted for the BJP were activists or supporters of the Babri Masjid movement, and it was into this form of politics that these children were socialized—they would have no memory of Gujarat burning in 2002. The first riot they would remember is from Muzaffarnagar, where victimized Muslims were painted as devious villains lusting for and humiliating Hindu women, who needed to be shown their place. This was their primary politicization. The seeds of divisive messages against the looming 'Muslim' threat therefore fell on fertile soil.

Jay Mazoomdar recounts a telling conversation he had with three young men in Varanasi after the elections. "'More than Muslims here, now Pakistan and China will be scared," one of them said disarmingly. Why, was Modi going to fight a war? "No, no, he need not. But they (neighbours) will know they cannot take us for granted anymore," he explained quickly. His friend nodded in agreement before adding: "And there will be riots no more. They (minorities) won't just dare". Weren't they looking for jobs, development? "Of course, there will be good work all around, also employment, and prices will go down. We will see better days," assured the third friend. "But how can one serve the country unless one serves one's own religion uncompromisingly?"'[36]

Many more openly communal statements were made, not just by common people but also by Modi's aides. Modi himself said nothing of the sort but also, at the same time, never publicly reprimanded his aides or distanced himself from their comments. He was happy to reap the political benefits of majoritarian consolidation spurred by these remarks, but freed himself from taking responsibility for them. Amit Shah said, openly, that the vote should be used for revenge in riot-ravaged Muzaffarnagar.[37] Sangeet Som, notorious for uploading a fake video, purportedly showing Muslims killing two Jat brothers in Muzaffarnagar, which fuelled the ensuing riots, was feted on the same political stage where Modi later addressed a rally.[38] Praveen Togadia exhorted his followers to violently prevent Muslims from buying houses in Hindu-majority neighbourhoods in Gujarat. Bajrang Dal activists were protesting against a Muslim family which had bought a house in a Hindu-dominated residence in Bhavnagar in Gujarat. Togadia joined them, suggesting that the protesters should give the occupants forty-eight hours to vacate the house, and if they did not do so, they should storm it with 'stones, tyres and tomatoes', spit on the house-owner when he walked out of the house, and put up a Bajrang Dal board in front of the residence.[39]

Modi himself allowed this thin mask of moderation to slip whenever he felt the need to personally stoke majoritarian sentiment. In his own unique fashion, he spoke, in the heartland of Bihar, of the 'pink revolution', alluding to the UPA government's alleged support for beef export by subsidizing slaughter houses.[40] In Vadodara, he charged that secular opinion was in fact, divisive, and he declared that he would rather lose the election than fall to these strategies, trying to turn on its head the moral case for secularism.[41]

But even more damagingly, he stormed Assam with exhortations against Bengali Muslims, describing them as illegal immigrant Bangladeshis, ignoring the fact that more than nine out of ten Bengali Muslims in the state are legitimate Indian citizens.[42] He advised them to pack their bags after 16 May! On 1 May Assam witnessed one of the most brutal massacres since Nellie, targeting mostly Muslim women and children. Yet, a day after this massacre in the Baksa district, Modi thought nothing of reiterating his threats against Bengali Muslims in Bengal, declaring that those who did not worship the goddess Durga were not welcome in the state. Like every other statement in the campaign, this too received wide media notice, including *The Hindu* and *India Today*.

~

Bullets rained from all sides. Men armed with automatic weapons chased after a crowd of terrified, fleeing women and children. Romila Khatoon ran behind her mother and leaped with her into the currents of the Beki River which ran along the village. As she dived into the water, her mother carried her four-month-old baby in one arm and her three-year-old son in the other. She tried desperately to swim with them to safety, but a bullet hit her and she drowned. Her baby was swept away by the current. Romila's three-year-old brother tried to swim, but was soon also pierced by a bullet. Romila swam underwater as far as she could. That was how she survived.

We met Romila with her bereaved father a few days later in a camp across the river from her village, haunted by her memories. I was part of a fact-finding team assembled by Seema Mustafa of the Centre for Policy Analysis, along with journalists Anand Sahay and Satish Jacob and academic Anuradha Chenoy. We crossed the river in a leaking boat, trekked through long stretches of low waters, and finally arrived at Narayanguri, the last village in the Baksa district of Assam bordering Bhutan. This settlement of Bengali Muslims borders a thick forest which stretches into Bhutan. The village had been razed to the ground, all seventy-two hutments charred, and emptied fully of its residents.

Women and children we met at the camp described to us the events of 1 May 2014. Most men of their village had crossed the river to shop at the village market, as was their practice. At around 3 in the afternoon, a group of armed men entered the village and began to shoot indiscriminately. Ten-year-old Mohammed Islam said that they shot dead his mother and seven-year-old sister in their home. As he ran, bullets flew from both sides. He still managed to flee to the forests and hid behind trees. From there he watched as his loved ones and neighbours fell one by one; many shot as they tried to swim away.

After all the residents of the village were either dead or had gone into hiding, the attackers set their homes on fire. They then disappeared into the forests as suddenly as they had appeared. Hours later, when darkness fell and security forces came in by boats, they announced on the loudspeaker in the mosque that all was safe, and any survivors should emerge from where they were hiding.

The children mentioned the names of forest guards of their village among their attackers. The Bodo Territorial Council had appointed surrendered Bodo militants as forest guards, and armed them with rifles. The surrendered militants had never been seriously disarmed by the state government. Many were known to hide in the forests between the village and Bhutan, and they joined the guards with automatic weapons. Yet people complained that they were being pressurized to erase the names of the forest personnel they recognized among their attackers. In the many cycles of violence which have racked Assam since the late 1970s, virtually no one has been punished, which is why the attacks recur with impunity.

It is remarkable that this same village had witnessed a slaughter of the same scale almost exactly twenty years ago, in 1994. Armed Bodo militants had at that time attacked Bengali Muslims, and the survivors had taken refuge in a village school. The school was set on fire and close to fifty people—many of them again women and children—were charred to death. Then, as now, people recognized many of their attackers. But no one has been punished for these crimes against humanity.

The autonomous Bodo Territorial Council has forty-six members, of which thirty are reserved for Bodos, and only five for non-Bodos. But Bodos are less than a third of the population of the area, matched in numbers by Bengali Muslims and the 'tea-tribes' who were brought in as tea-garden labour from central India 200 years ago. These histories cannot be erased. Areas cannot be 'cleansed' of non-Bodo populations by brutal massacres of the kind that Narayanguri witnessed. These ethnically diverse peoples cannot be barred from participation in governance, and reduced to second-class citizenship.

When the dead were counted in Narayanguri in 2014, they numbered forty-five, and another ten people were missing. Their only crimes were that they were Muslim and spoke Bengali. Just a month earlier, the BJP prime ministerial candidate, Narendra Modi, addressing an election rally in Dhemaji, Assam, had been quoted by the Press Trust of India as saying, 'Aren't rhinos the pride of Assam?

These days there is a conspiracy to kill them. I am making the allegation very seriously. People sitting in the government...are doing this conspiracy to kill rhinos so that the area becomes empty and Bangladeshis can be settled there.'[43] He also deplored what he called 'intrusions' from people in Bangladesh who he alleged were taking up jobs in India. He said it was time that these 'intrusions' stopped.

It is debatable if Modi's exclusionary election speech directly spurred the violence in Baksa. But in my many visits to Assam, I observed how Modi's rhetoric found many answering echoes in the deeply divided Assamese society. There is no doubt that indigenous groups like the Bodos have legitimate anxieties about the preservation of their land, forests and way of life, all of which must be addressed. But Bengalis have been lawfully migrating into the area from the nineteenth century, and scholars have established that not more than 10 per cent of Bengali Muslim residents in Assam could be illegal immigrants. And to the extent that India does indeed have an influx of economic refugees escaping hopeless poverty in their own countries, the country needs to debate if they should be purged and demonised, or whether it should keep its doors open for the needy of the world, as it has for centuries.

~

India's sharp swing Rightward is not unique in the world. The elections to the European Council were held around the same time as India's in 2014. In country after country, ultra-nationalist, xenophobic parties captured significant segments of the vote share. Editor Samar Halarnkar observes a global trend of 'the rise of nationalist strongmen and Right-wing parties, mirroring the emergence of the BJP and Modi in India in the 2014 elections. These are usually—but not always—darkly impatient leaders with poor or blue-collar origins, tapping into the insecurities and aspirations of a formerly (in western nations) or eager-to-be prosperous (in the emerging world) working class'.[44]

He gives many examples. In France, Marine Le Pen's National Party, with its strident anti-immigration, anti-Euro position, won the highest number of votes in the deeply divided country and pushed the ruling socialists to a humiliating third position. Le Pen's party could once command only 1 per cent of the French vote, but now has the support of one in four voters (comparable to BJP's one in three). Harlankar finds many similarities with Modi in strongman Recep Tayyip Erdogan of Turkey, who strengthened the country's economy and dismantled the legacy of its secular founder, Kemal Ataturk, steering its transformation into an Islamic nation. The ultra-Right Austria Freedom Party won one in five seats, and the near-Nazi ultra-Right Golden Dawn in Greece rose to become the country's third most popular party. The story was repeated in Denmark, where the far-Right People's Party, which is opposed to immigration, won the highest number of votes, and the second winner was another far-Right, racist and anti-Semitic party Jobbik. He observes similar trends in Britain, Hungary, Holland, Norway and Slovakia. In Russia, too, Vladimir Putin's political style resembles that of Modi's. Japan's prime minister, Shinzo Abe, reveres the war criminals of World War II. Significantly, the only countries which defy this current global trend are low-income countries.

According to Harlankar, what is common in all of these leaders of wealthy or emerging economies is that, like the BJP, they focus hard on economic revival after coming to power. They 'tend to be populist, even xenophobic, in their rhetoric but capitalist in their approach, encouraging investment from big companies, tycoons...and foreign investors. They express an often abusive hate of liberals and minorities...evoke an era of masculinity, traditional roles for women and an intolerance (except in western Europe) of homosexuality. Television and social media are the tools of choice for the aggressive, insecure middle classes that propel the rise of the new Right and are adroitly used by parties that tap into the discontent and impatience'.[45]

Novelist and scholar Amitav Ghosh tracks the remarkable parallel journeys of India and Turkey. Both, he notes, are 'multi-ethnic and multi-religious, with very marked differences between regions...Both republics were born amidst civil conflict, war and massive exchanges of population. In no small part was it due to these experiences that secularism came to attain an unusual salience in the two countries: it was considered indispensable for the maintenance of peace and equity within diverse populations...But since religion plays an important role in the lives of the vast majority of Indians and Turks, secularism was always an embattled aspiration, in both countries. Yet, through the latter decades of the 20th century, even as the banners of secular-nationalism were beginning to look increasingly tattered, their bearers somehow managed to retain their hold on power in both Turkey and India.' He tracks the remarkable parallels in the political careers of Erdogan and Modi; both, he notes 'are men of their time and have both come to power by riding a wave of neo-liberal globalization: their rise is proof that an economic ideology, when wrapped in a packaging of religious symbols and gestures, can have a tremendous electoral allure.'[46]

Half a decade is a long time for Modi's government to demonstrate and operationalize its worldviews and priorities and the direction it seeks to take the country. But these global trends suggest that his leadership will be marked by hard market economics, populism and a changed relationship with India's minorities, especially the Muslims. Editor Prem Shankar Jha warns, 'In India, extremists in the Sangh Parivar have elected Muslims to be the scapegoats. If Modi does not rein them in, India will, literally, have no future. For India is a world of minorities, in which the Muslims are only the largest. An attempt to impose cultural homogeneity upon them will lead to its disintegration.'[47] But the early indications are not encouraging for the minorities. Modi's minister of minority affairs, Najma Heptulla, shortly after assuming office denied that Muslims are even a minority, implying that they are not entitled to special protections.[48] A man accused in the Muzaffarnagar riots for inciting enmity between groups, Sanjeev Baliyan, was appointed a minister in Modi's cabinet. A police officer charged with the extra-judicial killing of a young

Muslim teenager, Ishrat Jahan, in a staged 'encounter' was reinstated, another released on bail.

Some fear that the secular Constitution of the country will be formally altered on Modi's watch. But I feel it is unlikely that the word 'secular' will be formally excised, or that Section 25 of the Constitution which guarantees freedom of religion, will be amended. But, as historian Mukul Kesavan observes, the BJP's claim that it will ensure development for all but appeasement to none is not reassuring, because, in the BJP's lexicon, appeasement means special protections for Muslims.[49] It is to be seen if Modi will pull back on scholarships for Muslim children and development funds for Muslim settlements in the country, as he has done in Gujarat earlier. If he ends the subsidy for Haj travellers, I will not shed any tears; the subsidy does nothing to address the real material concerns of the ordinary Indian Muslim. My fears are graver—that his tough talk on terror will translate into even greater profiling of Muslims as terrorists and increase the soft-peddling of terror perpetrated by Hindutva organizations. But my deepest fear is that, in practice, the minorities of India will be made to accept second-class citizenship, and that this practice will be cumulatively embedded in new social, economic and political relationships between India's religious communities. The chief patron of the Vishva Hindu Parishad (VHP) and senior RSS leader, Ashok Singhal—who, as noted by Prashant Jha of the *Hindustan Times*, had a front-row seat at Modi's swearing-in—declared ominously after the elections that the 'tables had turned' and the polls were a 'setback to Muslim politics' used by 'foreign and divisive forces to destroy our identity'.[50] The recent Lok Sabha polls had shown that an election could be won 'without Muslim support'. It was time for them to learn their lessons. 'Muslims will be treated as common citizens—nothing more, nothing less. And, they must learn to respect Hindu sentiments. If they keep opposing Hindus, how long can they survive?' Singhal elaborated that Muslims should give up claims over Ayodhya, Kashi and Mathura and also accept a uniform civil code. 'We'll then give them love, and not claim any other mosque sites even though there are thousands built on the ruins of temples. But if they don't accept it, they should be prepared for further Hindu consolidation. It has happened at the Centre, it will happen in other states.'[51]

Gopalkrishna Gandhi, in an avuncular open letter to Modi, reminded him about his duties to India's minorities. 'In the olden days,' he wrote to India's new prime minister, 'headmasters used to keep a salted cane in one corner of the classroom, visible and scary, as a reminder of his ability to lash the chosen skin. Memories, no more than a few months old, of the riots in Muzaffarnagar which left at least 42 Muslims and 20 Hindus dead and displaced over 50,000 persons, are that salted cane. "Beware, this is what will be done to you!" is not a threat that anyone in a democracy should fear. But that is the message that has entered the day's fears and night's terrors of millions.' He continues, 'No one should have the impudence to speak the monarchist language of uniformism to a republic of pluralism, the vocabulary of "oneness" to an imagination of many-nesses, the grammar of consolidation to a sensibility that thrives in and on its variations. India is a diverse forest. It wants you to nurture the humus that sustains its great variety, not place before it the monochromatic monoculturalism of a political monotheism.'[52]

But, 'If there is a message from Elections 2014 it is that India has been changing,' Raghav Bawa observed in a perceptive commentary on the elections in the *Economic and Political Weekly*. 'It is becoming a society where those with a voice are becoming less tolerant, less compassionate and more aggressive towards those without a voice. This is just the atmosphere for an aggressive mix of religion and nationalism to find expression.'[53]

It is this changing society which this book chiefly addresses, not just its expression in the political choices in election booths.

The Myth of Violence

The most widely held bias against Muslims is that they are religiously and culturally socialized in ways which creates in them a huge tolerance for violence. For a long time in India, this belief was nurtured through a chauvinistic retelling of history, in which Muslims through the medieval age were portrayed as invaders and marauders who looted the country, subjugated its Hindu populations, desecrated and demolished Hindu places of worship, and forcefully converted millions of hapless Hindus to Islam at the point of the sword. Prime Minister Modi, in his first address to India's Parliament, chose to reinforce this reading of India's history by speaking of 1,200 and not 200 years of India's slavery, thereby extending the period of India's bondage not just to the years of colonization, but to the millennium in which the majority of rulers were Muslim.

Contrast this with Maulana Abul Kalam Azad's words, 'Eleven hundred years of common history have enriched India with our common achievements. Our languages, our poetry, our literature, our culture, our art, our dress, our manners and customs, the innumerable longings of our daily life, everything bears the stamp of our joint endeavour.' He goes on, 'This joint wealth is the heritage of our common nationality and we do not want to leave it and go back to the time when this joint life had not begun.'[54] This could be the voice of every Muslim who chose secular India over a Muslim Pakistan.

Mridula Mukherjee, noted professor of history, describes Modi's interpretation as the 'standard Hindu communal view of history'.[55] This highly coloured and partisan recasting was part of the colonial project so that the colonial rulers could present themselves as sources of enlightenment instead of plunder and pauperization; and this project suited the designs of both Muslim and Hindu fundamentalists.[56] It is common for middle-class Indians today to ignore the actual facts of history—that there were both enlightened and oppressive Muslim and Hindu rulers; that Muslim rulers may originally have come from other countries but made this land their home; that conversion happened mostly voluntarily because people from the lower castes were drawn to the egalitarian teachings of Islam; and that in most phases of medieval history, Hindu sects were unmolested in pursuing their own faith and modes of worship.

The belief in the special and unique legacies of a violent history of Muslims are aggravated across north India by received, partial memories of Partition, which recount Muslims as killers and rapists, forgetting that the same violence occurred against Muslims at the hands of Hindus and Sikhs on this side of the border, and that many Muslims also saved Hindu and Sikh lives.

The preconception uniquely linking Muslims with violence gained a great fillip with the Global War on Terror. How many of us have not received a text message or Internet posting remarking that whereas all Muslims are not terrorists, all terrorists are Muslims? Most of us accept this to be a sad but undisputed fact. It is telling that we do so uncritically, especially in India, a country which lost the Father of the Nation, Mahatma Gandhi, and two prime ministers, Indira Gandhi and Rajiv Gandhi, to terror perpetrated by non-Muslims.[57] Both central and northeastern India have also been aflame for decades, but again, almost none of the chief actors in these regions are Muslim.

Firstly, we have accepted the uncritically selective understanding of which acts of mass killing qualify as terrorism and which do not. Nivedita Menon, noted feminist writer and professor of political thought at Jawaharlal Nehru University (JNU), rightly contests the official definition of 'terrorism'. 'Killing twenty people by a bomb blast is considered terrorism,' she points out, 'but the killing of thousands of people in 1984 or more than a thousand people in Gujarat in 2002 (or, for that matter, the killing of 40 people in Muzaffarnagar, 68 people in Orissa in 2008, etc. etc.) are not. All riots involve planning, stockpiling of weapons and systematic attacks. Why then are they not considered terrorism?'[58] This influences the judiciary as well, which awards the death penalty for crimes of 'terror' but not for hate-spurred crimes during instances of communal violence.

I am firmly against the death penalty for any crime, but I find these double standards popular in the middle class as well as the judiciary intriguing and morally repugnant.

But even accepting the government's definition of who a terrorist in India is, Menon points out that 'less than a third of the organisations banned as "terrorist" under the Unlawful Activities (Prevention) Act are Muslim organisations. Internationally, the group that engaged in the most suicide bombings in the world was the LTTE in Sri Lanka—a militantly atheist group whose members are mostly of Hindu and Christian origin.' She also points to data put out by the South Asia Terrorism Portal which shows that between 2005 and 2014, twice the number of people were killed by Northeastern and Left-wing groups, which are all non-Muslim organizations, and the largest Northeastern terrorist organization in this period (ULFA) has a 'mostly Hindu, upper caste leadership'.[59, 60]

In an article for the *Frontline*, journalist Praveen Swami also points to data from the South Asia Terrorism Portal, according to which, deaths caused by Muslim attackers accounted for just one-fifth of the total civilian and security force fatalities between 2008 and 2013.[61] In this period, terrorists in Jammu and Kashmir, and Islamist terror groups such as the Lashkar-e-Taiba and the Indian Mujahideen killed 934 civilians and personnel of the security forces. Maoists and terrorist groups in the Northeast killed 4,163 people during the same period. He further documents that, barring the year 2008, Islamist terror groups accounted for 10 per cent or less of terrorism-related civilian and security force fatalities. This, he points out, is less than the community's share in India's population. 'Even in 2008, which saw a peak in Islamist violence—four major urban bombings, as well as the 26/11 attacks—killings by Muslim terrorists accounted for well under half of all civilian and security force fatalities. The insurgencies in the states of Assam, Manipur, Meghalaya, Mizoram and Tripura involve myriad Hindu, Christian and tribal groups; none of the major armed actors is Muslim. The Maoist insurgency also involves Adivasis and caste Hindus, not Muslims.'

Every major bomb explosion is followed almost immediately by a government statement claiming that one or more Islamist terror groups were responsible, and this is uncritically relayed by the press—without even a disclaimer, or the word 'alleged'—and accepted as truth by popular public opinion. No one asks how the government is so certain who set off the blasts within minutes of the detonation. If it knew in advance, why did it not prevent it? And if it did not know earlier, how was it so sure within minutes of the blast? This obvious official disingenuousness is possible because it falls on the fertile soil of popular prejudice against Muslims for their alleged allegiance to terror. Some courageous and impartial investigation by some of the country's finest policepersons, such as Hemant Karkare, have revealed that many of the terror cases earlier attributed to Islamist organizations were actually the handiwork of shadowy outfits with allegiance to Hindutva thought.[62] However, this has barely entered middle-class consciousness—and certainly not drawing-room conversations on terror. It is thus that middle-class Indians are able to block out the idea that many terror attacks are established to be conspiracies by people who owe no allegiance to any faith, including their own.

This same assumption that terrorist attacks must be the handiwork of Muslims is found elsewhere in the world as well. When bombs were detonated in Oslo on 22 July 2011, most people assumed—and the *New York Times* even reported—that this was an attack conducted by Muslim terrorists. Although this was redacted soon, the paper justified the assumption, stating that Norway had been threatened by Al Qaeda and could be targeted for sending Norwegian troops to Afghanistan.[63] It was proved, later, that the bombing had been planned meticulously by a young white supremacist, Anders Behring Breivik, who also shot down sixty-nine young people at a youth camp organized by the Norwegian Labour Party.

Even more generally, very few terrorist attacks in Europe are carried out by Muslim groups. 'In 2007, two out of a total of 581 terrorist attacks in Europe were carried out by Muslims; in 2008, not one of the 441 documented terrorist attacks was by a Muslim. In 2009, there were 294 terrorist attacks, out of which one was committed by a Muslim. The vast majority of terrorist attacks (237 out of 297) were perpetrated by White, non-Muslim separatist groups mainly in Spain and France.'[64] Data gathered by sociologist Charles Kurzman showed that while thirty-three people in the US died of terrorism perpetrated by Islamists after 9/11, over 300 died in mass shootings by people from other religious identities.[65] The Centre for Research on Globalisation went back further to find that only 2.5 per cent of the terrorist attacks in the US from 1970 to 2012 were carried out by Muslims.[66]

The belief that Muslims as a rule subscribe to violence becomes the rationale among many to justify even massacres as heinous as the one that happened in 2002 in Gujarat.

I recall a particularly dear friend from my boyhood days in boarding school, who is otherwise affable, gentle and liberal. When he crafted the same rationalization, that the massacre had happened in response to the burning of the Sabarmati Express in Godhra, I first contested the version that the train had indeed been set aflame as part of a conspiracy by Muslims—the forensic evidence suggested a fire accident.[67] But even if indeed some Muslims had actually committed this horrendous crime, I continued, how did it justify the killing of even one other Muslim? By this principle of vicarious responsibility, I told him—since he belongs to a community notorious for exploiting people with usury and unfair trade—he should be fine with people killing him in retribution. Indeed, by this measure, no upper-caste Hindu should remain alive, because of how they have oppressed generations of Dalits. And, indeed, no man should remain alive anywhere in the world, for what they have done, in every country, in every phase of history, to women. My friend found it hard to forgive me for this outburst, and we lost touch for many years. More recently we have again picked up the strings of our old friendship—this is one case where affection did finally overcome politics—but we always tread carefully in our conversations when we meet, to avoid the thin ice of the questions regarding collective Muslim culpability for violence or, indeed, of Modi's leadership.

~

Despite overwhelming evidence, supported by virtually every commission of enquiry established after every major communal riot, and many independent, scholarly studies, that the large majority of victims in almost every communal riot are Muslims, the middle class remains convinced that during riots, Muslims are always the aggressors. This is what that indefatigable warrior against prejudice, Ram Puniyani, calls the 'social common sense', which remains unshaken with its preconceptions and prejudices despite all evidence to the contrary.[68]

In a 2006 article in *Frontline*, Praveen Swami refers to the work of senior police officer V. N. Rai who has carefully researched communal riots and police bias and calculated that between 1968 and 1980, 1,598 Muslim people were killed in communal riots compared to 530 Hindus.[69] This means that in this period, three out of four persons killed in communal violence were Muslim, yet we persist in regarding them as the primary aggressors. I have been carefully studying major episodes of mass communal violence since the 1980s and observe a clear change in the pattern of this violence. Earlier, many 'riots' involved significant levels of violence from both sides of the religious divide, although minorities faced the heaviest loss of property and life, as well as sexual violence. However, since 1983, when one of independent India's most gruesome and most ignored massacres happened in Nellie, Assam; 1984, when Sikhs were targeted in Delhi; 1986, when Hindu-Muslim clashes took place in Hashimpura; 1989, when sectarian violence raged for two months in Bhagalpur, Bihar; 1992-93, Mumbai; 2002, Gujarat; 2006, when Christian tribals were killed in Kandhamal, Odisha; and 2013, Muzaffarnagar, I have seen that this violence is almost always overwhelmingly one-sided, with most losses lying with the minority community, and openly enabled by partisan states. These are not riots but pogroms. (One major exception are the Bodo-Muslim clashes in Lower Assam in 2012, in which Bodos suffered almost identical violence in areas where Bengali Muslims were in the majority as Bengali Muslims suffered in Bodo-majority areas.) But still, popular middle-class discourse continues to regard Muslims as indisputably the principal aggressor even in all cases in which they were almost the exclusive target.

On the flipside, there is also a continuous attempt to play down the numbers of lives lost, and to suggest that a significant proportion of people killed were actually Hindus. Minister of defence for the National Democratic Alliance, George Fernandes, infamously declared in Parliament in a debate about the 2002 carnage: 'There is nothing new in the mayhem let loose in Gujarat...A pregnant woman's stomach being slit, a daughter being raped in front of a mother aren't a new thing,' adding that 'such things have been happening for 54 years in India...'[70] In Muzaffarnagar, which I visited soon after the riots, people kept asking me about the 'Hindu' camps, and why we, the Muslim-loving Lefties, were not worried about conditions there. The district magistrate of Muzaffarnagar told me, when I met him as part of a fact-finding team, that of around 50,000 people displaced and kept in camps when the violence was at its peak, just 800 were Hindu Dalits (no Jats), who had fled briefly from Muslim-majority villages as a precaution, but returned soon after. But people were aggrieved that we were not helping survivors in Hindu camps which, actually, did not exist!

The conviction that Muslims are aggressors even when they are manifestly and overwhelmingly the victims plays out in the prejudiced mind in ingenuous ways. During my year of self-imposed exile to Ahmedabad after the carnage, I developed unbearable backache. A friend insisted on taking me to a group of doctors working in a leading private hospital. When the doctors learned what I was doing in Gujarat, their conversation unsurprisingly turned to the communal riots they had seen in Ahmedabad over the years. One doctor said, 'When Muslim persons injured in riots would come into the government hospital in which I worked, I found they usually had simple shallow injuries. But when Hindus were brought in, the knife injuries would be deep and complicated, because Muslims are taught how to injure and kill with a thoroughness and cruelty which

Hindus are incapable of.' Their conviction, that Muslims are particularly skilled at aggression, despite witnessing the unimaginable cruelty that had been visited upon the victims, mostly Muslim, remained unshaken. I was particularly shocked when one of the doctors added, 'It is for this reason we had an unwritten policy during the riots in all our government hospitals. If Muslims who were injured were brought in, we would always treat them without anaesthesia. Anaesthesia was reserved only for Hindu victims.'

This 'blaming the victim' plays out in many other ways during communal riots, to breach the natural flow of human sympathy with the survivors. In Muzaffarnagar, within three months of the violence, the state government forcefully shut down all relief camps at the height of winter, even though people were too terrified to return home in a continuing climate of hate.[71] As a result, hapless survivors were left unprotected in the open, and at least fifty children were reported to have died in the winter chill.[72] The insensitivity and lack of elementary compassion on the part of the state administration appalled me.

But I heard many officials—and even some journalists—observe privately that the government had to shut down the camps because Muslims otherwise were getting habituated to eating 'free food' for no work in the camps. This, again, is something I have heard in the aftermath of riots I have managed as a district officer over the years, and also in Gujarat when camps were again shut down within six months to give an impression of normalcy before the state elections. I wish anyone who believes that a human being would voluntarily choose to live with his or her loved ones in a relief camp in India—in humiliating, unsanitary, under-served and highly cramped conditions—would himself spend a night, along with his loved ones, in one of these camps and then decide if any human being could choose this life of 'free food' out of laziness and greed.

As a small offering of solidarity, I spent one night in the Shah Alam Camp in Ahmedabad in 2002 among ten thousand others, and it is a memory which I will carry until my death. Ten thousand people—body pressed against body—slept within the narrow confines of the medieval mazaar amidst graveyards. People were stoic in their memories of suffering, betrayal and loss, and busied themselves in the everyday tasks of daily survival. A child needed milk, a baby was being born, a sick old man needed care. There were barely a score of toilets for ten thousand people, and a person could bathe only once in nine days. I recall the stench of unclean toilets and crowds of bodies packed together, the absence of privacy, the shame of pushing among the crowds for food, the broken childhoods of children, women delivering babies in the camp, and so many other indignities. My stomach was violently infected for a month after my stay in the camp. Musthaq, a young resident of the camp who went on to join us as a peace worker, said to me, 'I was the youngest in my family, and everyone spoilt me. The killings broke out in our colony Naroda. I saw children and women being burnt alive. I saw our neighbours loot and burn our home. I still did not cry. We were transported in trucks to Shah Alam Camp a day later. I still did not cry. Volunteers had cooked rotis for thousands of people streaming into the camps. There were no plates; the rotis were strewn on the dirt floor. My family was famished, and I saw them push other people to grab the rotis from the bare dirt. It was then that I began to weep for the first time.'

I also recall a young American friend, Jan Mohammed. Originally a Gujarati Muslim, his family emigrated to Uganda but was exiled during Idi Amin's regime. They rebuilt their lives in California, but his father, a staunch Gandhian, dreamt of sending his son as an adult to Gujarat to rediscover Gandhi. As chance would decree, he was in Gujarat volunteering with an NGO when the carnage broke out, and suddenly he discovered that *he* was the 'other', the 'enemy'. He began to spend long days in the relief camps, and would return wearied and saddened each night. His hostess was an otherwise kindly, elderly, Hindu Gujarati woman. Genuinely concerned by her young guest's daily and deepening dejection, she said to him, 'Don't take it so much to heart, son. These poor

Muslims stay in camps because they like to eat free food.' Jan Mohammed tells me that when she said that, he remembered the stench of packed, unwashed bodies, the clogged bathrooms and stale food to which he was witness day after day. For anyone to suggest that people *chose* this life made him feel that as a Muslim, he did not belong in that home. Something broke within him and he decided to return to California, exiled once again.

I also recall an incident in the Khargone district when, as the district magistrate, I was immersed in trying to help the survivors of a small local riot connected with the build-up to the Babri Masjid movement in 1989. An RSS activist with a red tika on his forehead walked into my office one day and said, 'Collector saab. We all can see how much you have taken this riot to heart. But you should not. These Muslims set fire to their own homes only so that they can get compensation.' At that time, the compensation was the princely sum of ₹2,000. I was overwrought, perhaps, and could not hold myself back. I got up and pulled the startled man by the hand to the door of my office, saying, 'You have to come with me now and set fire to your own house. I will give you ₹2,000 from my personal bank account right away. But first, you must set fire to your house in my presence,' and continued to drag him out until he freed himself from my grip and fled.

The Alleged Fifth Column

Blaming the Muslim victim is also tied up with the middle-class conviction that Muslims are anti-national, a fifth column who live out their lives on the largesse of Indian resources but whose hearts beat for Pakistan. Scholar administrator N. C. Saxena, who served for many years in the Uttar Pradesh administration, tells me of a textbook he saw in Uttar Pradesh schools years ago which lauded the patriotism of Abdul Hameed, a heroic soldier killed in the 1965

India-Pakistan war and was awarded India's highest bravery award, the Param Veer Chakra. The text ended with the line, 'He was Muslim; *even so* he was a patriot.' (My italics. This text has subsequently been amended.)

Since my father-in-law served in many senior positions in the armed forces, several of his friends who visit our home are senior defence officers. Without over-generalizing—and there are, indeed, thankfully, some wonderful exceptions—I find among them a high degree of anti-Muslim prejudice, converging seamlessly in their minds and hearts with a nationalist-militarist hostility towards Pakistan. I recall one particular discussion with a senior naval officer. 'All Muslims are anti-national, you have to accept this,' he declared with conviction. I had to ask, 'Sir, what is the empirical basis of your belief?' 'They created Pakistan,' he thundered, 'what more proof do you require?' For a while, I was stunned into silence.

There are, incidentally, only 29,000 Muslims in India's 1.3 million-strong military, or just 3 per cent—as against their share in the population of around 14 per cent.[73] Among the 449 soldiers who lost their lives in the most recent war against Pakistan in Kargil, twenty-three, or 5.12 per cent, were Muslims. Says journalist Ajaz Ashraf, 'This shows, first, that the fatalities among Muslim soldiers were marginally higher than their presence in the army. Second, it proves false the Hindutva brigade's propaganda that Muslims can't be loyal to their country. This is because...in the Kargil war against the Pakistanis, Muslim soldiers battled as ferociously as any, regardless of the religious identity of their foes.'[74]

The belief of the admiral that 'Muslims' created Pakistan derives from the same tendency to regard all Muslims as a homogenous community with a unified consciousness and uniform social and political choices. The role of the Muslim League in the creation of Pakistan does not in any way make every Muslim culpable. It was largely elite Muslims from stretches of north India who chose to migrate to Pakistan. India today has more Muslim residents than both Pakistan and Bangladesh, and their ancestors voluntarily *chose* to live in secular India over Muslim Pakistan. The patriotism of a Hindu who chooses to migrate to the US is not questioned. On the other hand, the large majority of Muslims I encounter are grateful that their parents or grandparents chose to continue to live in India. Senior journalist Saeed Naqvi remarked after a visit to Pakistan to meet relatives that he was relieved to return to India. He joked that the problem with Pakistan was that there were too many Muslims! He was happy that he had been raised in a much more pluralist and diverse society. Indian Muslims across class, caste and gender, are troubled by the persisting ethnic and terrorist violence in Pakistan, and its intolerance of minorities.

It is important to recall Maulana Azad's passionate opposition to the idea of Pakistan, and his sadly prophetic words as president of the Indian National Congress on 15 April 1946. The idea of Pakistan, he said, 'is harmful not only for India as a whole but for Muslims in particular. And in fact it creates more problems than it solves. I must confess that the very term Pakistan goes against my grain. It suggests that some portions of the world are pure while others are impure…Islam recognises no such division and the Prophet says, God has made the whole world a mosque for me. As a Muslim, I for one am not prepared for a moment to give up my right to treat the whole of India as my domain and to share in the shaping of its political and economic life…They (Muslims) will awaken overnight and discover that they have become aliens and foreigners…Two states confronting one another offer no solution of the problem of one another's minorities, but only lead to retribution and reprisals by introducing a system of mutual hostages. The scheme of Pakistan therefore solves no problem for the Muslims.'[75]

There is also remarkably little radicalization among Indian Muslims. A large number of Sikh Khalistani militants in the 1980s traced their alienation specifically to the anti-Sikh violence of 1984. But, despite similar anguish after the carnage of 2002 in Gujarat, there are very few credible reports of survivors taking up arms against the state. It is not that they have submitted passively to injustice.

The Legitimization of Prejudice 199

They have relied mainly on the instruments of democracy and law to fight the grievous wrongs they suffered, and they have organized this resistance in solidarity with large numbers of non-Muslims. Indeed, although most victims of the carnage in Gujarat were Muslim, many more than 90 per cent of those who fought this injustice—often at great personal costs—are non-Muslims: justice workers, human rights activists, journalists, writers, film-makers and police officers, among many others.

It is this shared sense of solidarities across faith and identity which endures—although under great stress—in India. The majority of Indians, both Hindu and Muslim, continue to demonstrate in the ways they live their lives, and in the choices they make even while facing injustice and inequity, their shared and equal commitment to India's secular democracy. It is not the nationalism of Right-wing Hindutva groups—which indeed mirror the exclusivist nationalism of the military and religious fundamentalist elite of Pakistan—but one which is much more inclusive and which is essential to India's civilizational ethos.

~

In the emotionally charged aftermath of the 26/11 Mumbai terror attack, senior film actress Simi Garewal bemoaned on prime-time television the pro-Pakistani sentiment she alleged was graphically rampant in slums and ghettoes in Mumbai. She said that when she looks on to these slums from the window of a restaurant she often frequents, all she sees are Pakistani flags.[76] She did not know the difference between the green flag, which is a marker of Islam, and the national flag of Pakistan. (My friends teased me about my special discomfiture at her public display of bigotry, because after Meena Kumari, Waheeda Rehman and Nutan, Simi Garewal used to be my favourite actress.

There is also the sensitive question of taking sides in cricket matches when India plays against Pakistan. The allegation is that 'all' or 'most' Muslims in India celebrate when Pakistan wins against India. This is certainly not true. It is correct that some Muslim young men do cheer when Pakistan wins, but they are certainly not the majority. The fact that they do so is problematic, and it is important to understand the reasons for their alienation rather than merely condemn their lack of patriotic fervour. And when people in authority respond with extreme reactions to these displays of support, positions harden. Sixty-seven Kashmiri students in a private university in Meerut were suspended and forced to return to their homes after they cheered for Pakistan in an Asia Cup match against India in early 2014. The police went further, accusing them—incredibly—of sedition, charges which were subsequently withdrawn after opposition on a national scale but, by then, damage to the psyche of multitudes of Kashmiris, not to speak of the students, had already been inflicted.

My favourite cricket story is one related to me by a nyaya pathik colleague in Gujarat. It sounds apocryphal, but he insists it actually happened. He was visiting a village on work, and found a large number of people gathered in a tea-shop, listening tensely to radio commentary on the last overs in a cliff-hanging finale of an Indo-Pakistan cricket match. It looked like Pakistan was set to win, and the tea-stall owner dourly predicted that if Pakistan indeed won, fireworks would resound from the Muslim enclave in the village. The nyaya pathik refuted his prophesy, and the tea owner invited him to wait at the tea stall for the end of the match. Pakistan did indeed win, and there was a deathly silence from the Muslim quarter of the village. The nyaya pathik was triumphant.

However, the tea-stall owner replied, 'See, *this* is what Narendra Modi has been able to accomplish!'

Being Muslim in India Today

'In so many ways, I feel reduced to a second-class citizen in my own country, only because of my Muslim identity. I fear we are losing every day the India we love.'

The Legitimization of Prejudice   201

These words of anguish and loss, with small variations, echoed in many diverse voices of women and men from far corners of the country in a national meet on the status of Muslims in India today, organized by Act Now for Harmony and Democracy (Anhad) in Delhi from 3 to 5 October 2009.[77] Many individuals and representatives of organizations gathered from several parts of India to testify in the meeting. In a climate of discrimination and bias, both by the state and society, they described how hard it is for working-class Muslims to live with dignity in new India. The predominant mood in these conversations was of sadness and disappointment, and of ever-mounting despair. Muslim citizens shared their growing disillusionment with all institutions of governance, particularly the police and the judiciary, as well as with political parties and, to some extent, the media, and of an unspoken sense of fear that never goes away.

In the hearing, Bilal Shiekh, a young lawyer from Gujarat, spoke with bitter irony about his arrest by the Anti-Terrorist Squad (ATS), Pune, on charges of terror, for which he was ultimately acquitted. 'I was born in a Muslim family, given a Muslim name and grew up and started studying law. It was the IB [Intelligence Bureau] who told me what jihad was. I did not know either Urdu or Arabic. I only knew how to offer Namaz.' He goes on, 'The Mumbai ATS has great stamina, they can give 50 slaps in one go. I had to gather my strength to stand under that volley of slaps…It is Allah's grace that I am standing before you today. Or you might have heard of another false encounter in which I would have been killed and my parents would have been standing here in my place. All those Muslims whose numbers were stored in my mobile phone were thoroughly questioned by the police. Even today my friends' parents curse me and ask them why they made friends with me…When I studied Master of Human Rights and International Law, I learnt that there are so many international conventions and treaties that India is a signatory of. But these are not upheld at all. When I read the fundamental rights and the Prisoners' Manual I thought that the accused enjoy many rights, but when I was in prison the jail staff and the media treated me like a "mastermind" of terrorists. My case was eventually discharged. I don't believe that there is democracy here.'

Nihal Ahmed Ansari testified for a power loom worker, Noorul Hooda, from Malegaon in Maharashtra. Noorul was arrested from his house at about 11 a.m. on 8 October 2006. That night the police brought him back and proceeded, without a warrant, to search his house. The next day, the police booked him under Sections 10 and 13 of the Unlawful Activities Prevention Act (UAPA) in connection with the Malegaon bomb blasts, which had taken place on the same day, and presented him before the judicial magistrate of Malegaon. He was first taken to the Azadnagar Police Station in Malegaon, but transferred a few days later to Arthur Road Jail in Mumbai. Twenty-one people died in Malegaon in those bomb blasts, all Muslim. The thirteen who were held by the ATS in that case were also all Muslim. Noorul was charged with having aided and abetted the incident by transporting bombs on his bicycle. He was, however, at the local mosque until 1 p.m. on that day.

The Maharashtra Control of Organized Crimes Act (MCOCA) is an instrument, in which—in the manner of many other such draconian acts—a confession made by an accused in police custody can stand as evidence for his trial and conviction in court. Many lives have been ruined this way, because the police usually extracts a confession under torture, which then serves as evidence. The injustice is of such a great degree that the accused is not even given a copy of the confession he has made. The same happened with Noorul Hooda. Electric shocks were administered, and he was beaten on his forehead and ears. His ribs were battered. Even the attending doctor, Maitli, asked him to confess to avoid further injuries. He refused to do so and was therefore given more electric shocks. He had been picked up during the month of Ramzan, he was fasting, and he was beaten so badly that he fainted. The officers committing the torture threatened Noorul that if he did not confess, they would bring his sisters to the police station, strip them naked and take their photographs. They also threatened to put his brother in jail. When he finally succumbed to these threats, they took his signature on a blank piece of paper. This was used by the police to draft a fake confession.

It was later proved that the Malegoan blast was the handiwork of terrorists with Hindutva affiliations.[78]

Almost no one who bears a Muslim identity is exempt from the fear that they, or members of their families, can be subjected to the allegations of links with terrorist organizations; and to detention, torture, encounter killings, or prolonged, multiple and biased trials. Even when the victims are acquitted or discharged on being found innocent, they are not compensated for the destruction of their lives and reputations. Although the charges against the victims are, in most cases, found ultimately to be totally cooked up, no action is taken against the police officials. This has resulted in a sense of impunity among the police, because of which they casually and callously pick up and victimize innocent Muslims, sometimes to extort money from them, but mostly to demonstrate how effectively they have nipped terrorism in the bud.

The testimonies also showed the pervasive communalization of the criminal justice system across states in the country. When the police charge-sheets victims for terror crimes, the trials go on almost interminably, during which people who are not well off are virtually defenceless. And, in some cases, bar associations prevent lawyers from appearing for persons accused by the police of such offences, and harangue, stigmatize and boycott the few who do. Many men are charged with multiple crimes—sometimes twenty, or even fifty—in different states, making it impossible for people to defend themselves. Even if the legal justice system worked efficiently, it would take many years, sometimes decades, for all these cases to be heard and concluded against each of the individuals. For all these years, the accused would continue to be held in detention. Nothing could possibly compensate for the lost years, and for the suffering of people's loved ones.

A regular pattern, recurring after every terror attack, emerged from testimonies by people from across the country—including Maharashtra, Gujarat, Karnataka, Andhra Pradesh, Madhya Pradesh, Uttar Pradesh, Jammu and Kashmir, and Rajasthan. Muslim, mostly male youth, usually working class, and often with no criminal records, are illegally picked up by policemen in plain clothes and taken blindfolded in unmarked vehicles to locations like farmhouses. There, confessions are coerced out of them.

No profession, no part of the country, is safe if you are Muslim. It is almost as if being Muslim and—usually—male makes you an automatic suspect of terrorism, and it is not the burden of the state to prove your guilt but your own responsibility to prove your innocence.

~

However, at the meet organized by Anhad, the anguish of Muslim citizens was not restricted to being targeted in the name of terror. People also underlined their many unrealized aspirations. Many spoke of the importance they attached to modern and high-quality schooling and higher education, for both boys and girls, and sought much higher levels of public investment in modern mainstream schools and institutions of higher learning. There was the dread of criminal profiling, and there was also the lived experience of day-to-day discrimination; in education, employment, housing and public services, which entrap the community in hopeless conditions of poverty and want. This is fostered in situations of pervasive communal prejudice in all institutions of the state, especially the police, civil administration and judiciary; the political leadership of almost all parties; large segments of the print and visual media; and the middle classes, and the systematic manufacture of hate and divisions by communal organizations.

In the meeting, many people carefully and thoughtfully analysed the flaws in the schemes rolled out by the UPA government to address the low social and economic indicators documented by the Sachar Committee. The Central government launched a programme for greater investments in districts with high minority populations, and a scholarship scheme for minority children. It was pointed out that the per capita levels of investment for the community are still abysmally low. The new schemes for investment in districts with high minority populations, cover, at best, 30 per cent of the total population.[79] These programmes, which represent the UPA government's major initiative to address the socio-economic backwardness of the community, are for overall development of districts with higher minority populations rather than targeted programmes focused precisely on the minorities; therefore they proved blunt instruments as much of the expenditure is on general infrastructure and little to directly benefit deprived people of the community. The scholarship programme for girls and boys from minorities was encouraging, but this scheme also suffered from infirmities of procedure and targets which limited its impact. Financial institutions, including nationalized banks, were reluctant to extend credit to Muslims.[80]

There were many testimonies about the open prejudice and bias within public institutions towards Muslims. There were also reports of profiling against Muslims by the criminal justice system even beyond terror crimes, reflected in the disproportionately high number of Muslims in jails. It was claimed that many sensitive and senior positions in both Central and state government institutions, including in the home, education, social welfare and information departments, continue to be held by officials who have sympathy for communal ideologies and organizations, and the UPA government had done little to identify and replace them.

But it was confirmed that these prejudices are equally evident outside government as well; in particular, in sections of the media. Textbooks often showed similar bias, and this is particularly dangerous because for millions of poor and especially rural children, the textbook is the only accessible source of the printed word. People also reported bias in recruitment to jobs in the private sector.

Muslim men and women from many parts of India confirmed difficulties in getting homes on rent or on sale in non-Muslim localities, or admissions in schools and institutions of higher education. People spoke of systematic efforts in many corners of the country to destroy and boycott the livelihoods of Muslims. Sustained decentralized hate campaigns were organized which portrayed Muslim men as predators who target Hindu girls; as people who slaughter cows which are sacred to the Hindu community; and vigilante groups—supported tacitly by the police—targeted Muslims violently for these alleged social violations. Incidentally, both these hate myths were deployed with lethal impact by the BJP in 2104.

These voices in the Anhad gathering were not simply of victimhood or of injustice to a particular community. They testified to the massive and varied challenges that have been mounted to the basic values of the Indian Constitution, including democracy, secularism, fraternity and the rule of law, even more gravely magnified with the voting in of a government with a majoritarian ideology and record. It is not just the future and well-being of a community which is under threat. What is under grave assault is the idea of India itself.

Prejudice and the Middle-Class Muslim

In the prevailing climate of anti-Muslim 'social common sense' in the middle class and the state, life is hard not just for working-class Muslims but also for Muslims who are otherwise protected by being embedded in the middle classes.

In Aman Biradari, where I work, we have tried hard to create pluralist work spaces in which everyone feels welcome. I am proud that many of our staff are Muslim, not by any conscious reservation, but by striving for an environment where they feel as safe and welcomed as any other person. There is also a great mixing of classes, as many staff members are working-class people who have had fewer chances at formal education, who work with full equality with more conventionally educated middle-class social workers and lawyers.

This was important also because a lot of our work is among survivors of communal conflict, the majority of who are Muslim, and with street children and homeless people of whom—as it happens in places like Delhi—around half are Muslim. In one of our children's homes, the majority of children were recruited from a colony of disabled beggars called Viklang Basti. It turned out that the majority of the families who made a living by begging happened to be Muslim. When visitors and donors remarked disparagingly to me that 90 per cent of the children were Muslim, I replied that the children they saw were Muslim *and* Hindu. I was proud that my colleagues who recruited these children—who happened to be Hindu—did not see Muslim or Hindu children; only children living on the streets who would be forced to beg like their parents if they did not find a residential school to take them in.

I like to observe how the consciousness of the differences of faith has dissolved in our pluralist work spaces, and people are evaluated and friendships and alliances made based on qualities of character rather than identity or class. Festivals are also effortlessly shared. The only time I find my Muslim colleagues suddenly reminded of their 'separate' identity when news filters in of terror attacks, especially within India. I find, all at once, that their bodies are taut, their eyes downcast, their voices subdued, and their faces pensive. A few months after the bomb explosion in Sarojini Nagar Market in Delhi in October 2005, I was told that a young man who serves tea in the office asked the Muslim staff, 'Is there a Muslim festival these days?' They said no, and asked him why he thought there was one. 'Oh, because you all are blasting bombs, I thought this was your way of celebrating a festival.' No one complained, but I felt saddened that we were still unable to shield my colleagues from the bigotry of the wider world even in our offices.

But I probably should not have been surprised. How could they be protected from the growing intolerance and bigotry of urban middle-class spaces? In fact, all of them without exception confide about problems they face in renting houses outside Muslim ghettoes like Jamia and Chandni Chowk. The pattern is familiar. The house-owner, on the verge of sealing the deal, asks for their names and then never gets back. (If things are bad for Muslim families, they are worse for single Muslim women. The worst off are Kashmiris.) While some house-owners blithely state that they will not rent their spaces out to 'meat-eaters', others are still more direct; they state, frankly, that Muslims may have 'terror links', and are unsuitable as tenants.

The Hindu published a report in 2012 describing this 'housing apartheid'. It stated how a property agent representing a homeowner in the New Friends Colony firmly told the reporters, 'The landlords want only Indians, not Muslims.' Yet another broker in New Friends Colony said to these reporters, who were posing as a Muslim couple, 'Another Muslim wanted to take the flat on rent but he was also refused by the owners. Even though it suits your budget and needs, there is no point in showing you the flat. The flat has been vacant for a long time but they will not give it to a Muslim.'[81] Yet another report states that the Muslim staff members as well as the old generation of teachers of JNU have mostly returned to Muslim-dominated areas after retirement, because they could not find houses in mixed middle-class colonies of Delhi.[82] *The Hindu* also reports that even in Mumbai, areas are unofficially demarcated as 'Sena type' in which Muslims find accommodation hard to find. In Walkeshwar in Mumbai, 95 per cent of landlords refuse housing to Muslims, suggesting either spontaneous bias of the house-owners or unofficial fatwas of extremist Hindu organizations.[83] In Ahmedabad, the divide is near total. I have described in my book, *Fear and Forgiveness*, of how people speak of 'borders' in a matter-of-fact way as an acknowledged and unproblematic feature of their city's social geography, between the upmarket, new, Hindu areas and the down-market old Muslim parts of the city.[84]

Basharat Peer writes in the *New York Times* of a visit to Juhapara in Ahmedabad, on the 'other' side of the 'border'. 'Ahmedabad ceases to swagger in Juhapura, a southwestern neighborhood and the city's largest Muslim ghetto, with about 400,000 people,' he says,

The Legitimization of Prejudice

observing during his visit there its narrow streets, shabby buildings and dense crowds. 'The edge of the ghetto came abruptly. Just behind us was a row of tiny, single-story houses with peeling paint. Up ahead, in an empty space the size of a soccer field, children chased one another, jumping over heaps of broken bricks. "This is The Border," my friend said. Beyond the field was a massive concrete wall topped with barbed wire and oval surveillance cameras. On the other side, we could see a neat row of beige apartment blocks with air conditioners securely attached to the windows—housing for middle-class Hindu families.'[85] Asif Pathan, a forty-one-year-old resident, says to Peer with sarcasm, '"The sun is allowed into Juhapura. The rain is allowed into Juhapura. The wind is allowed into Juhapura. I get a bill for water tax and pay it, but we don't get piped water here."'[86]

Ather Farouqi, reporting on the ghettoization of Muslims, states that no multinational bank provides the inhabitants of Muslim colonies with credit cards; multinational pizza and burger outlets based in upmarket areas close to 'Muslim ghettoes' refuse to deliver in these areas. Even housing loans are not extended by most nationalized banks in 'Muslim' areas like Jamia Nagar in Delhi and New Delhi.[87] The Sachar Committee confirms that some banks have identified a number of areas with a high Muslim population as 'negative geographical zones' where bank credit and other facilities are not easily provided.[88]

The Sachar Committee also highlights the very low representation of Muslims in both public and private employment. This is well known, and reflects an undercurrent of discrimination in work places. Muslims constitute 6.3 per cent of the workforce in the Railways, 4.5 per cent in banks, 2.2 per cent in the Reserve Bank of India, 3.2 per cent in security agencies, 3 per cent in the IAS, 1.8 per cent in the Indian Foreign Service, and 4 per cent in the Indian Police Service.[89] S. L. Rao, in an article in *The Telegraph*, similarly confirms that Muslims occupy far fewer positions in government employment in relation to their population. In key states, Muslims had 6.3 per cent share in state government employment, 7.8 per cent in the judiciary and 7.4 per cent in public enterprises, all less than half their total representation in the population.[90] Journalist S. A. Rahman reports that in West Bengal, where Muslims constitute 27 per cent of the population, their representation in government jobs is as low as 4 per cent, despite more than three decades of Left rule. He also finds that Muslim participation is also strikingly low in the private sector.[91]

Academics Sukhadeo Thorat and Paul Attewell report the findings of an interesting study to determine whether the likelihood of receiving a positive response from an employer differed according to whether the application was made by someone with a high-caste, a Muslim or a Dalit name.[92] The results showed that on average, college-educated lower-caste and Muslim job applicants fare less well than equivalently qualified applicants with high-caste Hindu names, when applying by mail for employment in the modern private-enterprise sector. These discriminatory outcomes occurred at the very first stage of the process that Indian university graduates go through while applying for a job. Nivedita Menon similarly reports a study, published in the *Economic and Political Weekly* in 2007. The authors of the study responded to 548 job advertisements from private sector companies with three identical applications—one with a high-caste Hindu name, one with a Dalit name and one with a Muslim name. Even though the applications were otherwise identical, the Dalit name was approximately one-third less likely to get called for an interview, and the Muslim name was two-thirds less likely.[93]

Both in mixed employment and housing spaces, to the extent that they exist, there tends to be a bias against Muslim persons who are religious or wear cultural markers like beards or head-scarves. They are seen as 'fundamentalist' whereas a temple-going Hindu man with his forehead conspicuously strewn with ash, rice-grain and vermilion is merely god-fearing. But even those who are more cosmopolitan in dress and demonstrate no perceptible religious fervour are still frequently stereotyped, on the presumption that they carry regressive

'Muslim' positions on issues. On television, if the 'Muslim viewpoint' on an issue is solicited—as though there is any such homogenized Muslim position on any issue—then a maulvi is summoned, and he will never disappoint the reporter by airing the most anti-women and regressive views possible. Concurrently, a 'Hindu' position on issues is rarely presumed. Pluralist views are sought and presented from a diversity of 'Hindu' opinions. If a Hindu godman is interviewed there is no doubt that he does not speak for the rest of us. A middle-class Muslim still has to carry the burdens of the misogynist maulvi, whatever her personal positions on the matters at hand may be.

People sometimes object to employing Muslim domestic help as well. In the cosmopolitan colony in Delhi in which I live, I still find that Muslim part-time domestic help initially adopt non-Muslim names. Only after they are comfortable with you, do they share their Muslim identities. Barin Ghosh, who ran a domestic help agency in Kolkata until recently, affirmed that many recruitment agencies help Muslims find jobs by introducing them as Hindu. 'Almost 95 per cent of the clients in my agency were Hindu and while seeking domestic helps, as much as 80 per cent of the Hindu clients informed us that they would not employ any Muslims,' Ghosh said.[94] When responding to taxi bookings, agencies sometimes ask, 'Driver Muslim hai. Chalega? (The driver is Muslim. Will that work for you?)'

Incidentally, I have found Muslim street children also deploying the same defence mechanism. They give religiously neutral names, like Munna or Raju. It is only when they know you well that they disclose their real names. They report that the police are likely to deal much more harshly and violently with them if they state a Muslim name.

But the most disappointing finding for me is the experience of middle-class Muslim children in elite schools. Many Muslim friends report commonplace stories of their small children returning from school in tears, because they were called 'Osama' or a terrorist, or advised to 'return' to Pakistan. A friend told me that her daughter's teacher, after Narendra Modi's massive election rally in Delhi in 2014, spoke glowingly in her class about the possibility of Modi becoming India's prime minister. My friend's daughter, because of her Muslim surname, thought it discreet to maintain silence. But the teacher picked her out and pointedly asked for her opinion. She was still non-committal, but the teacher said that 'of course' she would be against Modi because she was Muslim. My feisty friend, her mother, did not take things lying down, and complained to the school management, ensuring that the teacher was held accountable. But how many parents can ensure this?

In 2012, of ninety-two schools in Delhi (mostly elite private schools) which provided some sort of information on their websites, as many as twenty (or their branches) admitted no Muslim child, while seventeen admitted only one Muslim child each. Although Muslims comprise about 15 per cent of Delhi's population, less than 0.5 per cent of those admitted were Muslim children.[95, 96] The unwritten embargo on all but a tiny fraction of Muslim children in elite schools is an open secret which, sadly, evokes little outrage. My daughter, who completed her schooling in an elite Delhi school, had at least some Muslim classmates. Her cousin in the same school a decade later had none. While data on the numbers of applications of Muslim children is hard to access, the Muslim middle class is not small—and all of them would want their children to study in these elite cosmopolitan schools. It would be safe to assume that a middle-class Muslim child is much less likely to find admission than non-Muslim children. (Children from Christian, Sikh, Parsi, Jew or other minority groups seem to face no problems in getting admission.)

In a study conducted as part of the National CRY Fellowship Programme in 2009-10, it was found that Muslim parents unanimously regarded modern mainstream education as the single most important factor which could safeguard their children's future and all clearly articulated a preference for reputed private schools.[97] However, Muslim parents said they often face overt discrimination from school authorities. They reported that authorities lack civility, question them rudely and display suspicion and hostility. Many talked about consciously opting for Christian schools rather than the Hinduized 'regular' public schools as, at some level, they felt that Christian schools were not only 'good', they also respected minority sentiments. On the part of the students, the report stated that Muslim children face discrimination in school in the form of communalized course content, getting unnecessarily picked on by teachers and peers, being classified as Muslims in front of peers and being harassed by teachers.[98]

One Muslim mother interviewed in Jamia Nagar, Delhi, said, 'On the basis of criterion, I feel that we would have scored at a higher end in the points scheme, yet in not one school did my child gain admission. Only after recommendation from an MP could I get my child admission. That's what's scary, I could maybe circumvent the situation, but can any "*aam*" Muslim do that.' She added. 'One of the teachers termed Muslims as "non-Indian" and pointing to my daughter said that these Muslims are always involved in these terrorist activities.'[99]

I assumed that one perennial danger faced by working-class Muslim men from which middle-class Muslims are protected would be from arbitrary arrests based on allegations that they are terrorists. But even this is not always the case. This was illustrated dramatically to me some years ago. A young man worked in an IT company in Gurgaon and, one day, wrote a very short post, rudely dismissive of Narendra Modi, then chief minister of Gujarat, on some social networking site. The next thing he knew, he was arrested on terror charges and flown to Ahmedabad. His family was distraught. A friend of his family knew me and was aware that I and my colleagues were working for legal justice among the survivors of the 2002 carnage in Gujarat. She asked if we could assist them in any way. The family was terrified, and they knew no one in Gujarat. I assured her that we would treat them like our own family. We picked them up at the airport and they stayed with us for a day while we tried to help them find a lawyer. Then they suddenly disappeared, abruptly cutting us off completely. I think they had been warned that being associated with us would be dangerous in Modi's Gujarat, because I was seen to be one of his public critics. I don't blame them at all for letting us go after that. Negotiations were undertaken, the details of which I do not know or care to know. I think the young man apologized. A small news report appeared that the chief minister had pardoned him for his misdemeanour and he was finally released, greatly sobered after being pulled back from the brink.

The Mosque in Ayodhya

Some events leave a permanent mark on the history of a people. For many in my generation, one such moment was the felling of the Babri Masjid in Ayodhya on 6 December 1992. The three domes of the historic mosque came crashing down after triumphant crowds of exultant young men—mobilized and cheered by political leaders who were destined only a few years later to lead the nation—scaled its walls and planted saffron flags on the pinnacles of the shrine. I wept then, as did large numbers of my countrymen and women.

This event marked the climax of anti-Muslim sentiment in independent India. Therefore, any account of anti-Muslim prejudice would be incomplete without briefly recounting that traumatic phase in India's public life, which may have passed but which could easily be rekindled now. Either way, its long and dark shadows still fall on the public conscience, and still powerfully fuel the demonized construction of the Indian Muslim.

For more than a decade in the brief history of post-colonial India, the fate of a small piece of land not much larger than a football field, in a dusty north Indian town called Ayodhya, dominated national politics in India. Governments rose and fell, blood flowed periodically on the streets, thousands of lives were lost and homes gutted around a single bitter dispute. Should a mosque built in 1528 on that site during the reign of the first Mughal emperor Babar be allowed to stand, or should a grand temple be built in its place? A large segment of Right-wing Hindu nationalist opinion claimed that Babar had demolished a Ram temple to build the mosque at that site, and 'national' pride—which, of course, excluded the pride or otherwise of Muslim citizens—required that the mosque be pulled down and replaced by a grand Ram temple.

The Babri Masjid evolved into a virile, powerful symbol used by Hindu nationalist organizations to revive a battle whose lines had been drawn much earlier, during India's struggle for freedom. The combat was not about competing claims of the followers of Ram and Allah to a disputed site. It was about the character of free India. Would India be a nation which guarantees all citizens the freedom to practice and propagate their faiths, and assures them equal rights and protection under the law? Or would it be a state in which people of minority faiths would live as second-class citizens, in perpetual cultural and legal subordination?

India won freedom in a frenzy of blood-letting and separation. Riots which took place during the Partition left a million dead and more than ten times that number uprooted from the lands of their ancestors. The Constituent Assembly of the newly independent Indian republic voted for a secular democratic Constitution, drafted by a leader from one of India's most oppressed castes, Babasaheb Ambedkar. Mahatma Gandhi's last battle was to secure a fair deal for the Muslims who had migrated to Pakistan. This enraged some members of extremist Hindutva formations and they took his life.

It was Gandhi's death which stunned the people of diverse faiths in India and it was mainly because of his death that communal peace held for a decade and a half. The RSS, and its political front the Jan Sangh, tainted by allegations of complicity in Gandhi's assassination, remained for the most part on the relative margins of India's political and social life in these early years of nation-building. It regained initial political respectability when it was permitted to join the struggle against the Emergency in the mid-1970s led by Jayaprakash

Narayan. In the 1984 general elections, the BJP won just two parliamentary seats.[100] It sought a cause and a symbol to rally majority Hindu sentiment and found it in the Babri Masjid dispute.

For 500 years, Muslim people had routinely worshipped in the Babri Masjid, said to have been built in 1528 by Mir Baqi, a general in the service of Babar. Hindus worshipped at the Ram Chabootra in the open area adjacent to the mosque, in a spirit of mutual communal goodwill. The disputed claim of Hindus to the land on which the mosque stood is based starkly on two acts—one of stealth and the other of naked aggression—and on the alleged 'faith' of the majority. In 1949, overnight, statues of the deity Ram were placed surreptitiously in the mosque under its central dome. A furious Nehru directed the district magistrate, K. K. Nayyar, and chief minister, G. B. Pant, to have these removed but they didn't comply. (Nayyar later resigned from the ICS and became an MP of the Jan Sangh, which was a predecessor of the BJP.)[101] Muslims stopped offering namaaz, but Hindus were granted limited rights of worship. In 1986, another partisan court ruling and the tacit support of the Central Congress government led to the temple doors being opened fully for the Hindus.[102]

In 1989, the RSS launched a countrywide Ram Shila programme, in which bricks were collected from villages and towns to be sent to Ayodhya to build the temple.[103] There was a surge of popular support for this campaign. I was then serving in a small district, Khargone, in Madhya Pradesh—classified as 'communally sensitive'—at that time, and witnessed first-hand the sudden and precipitous decline in communal relations that this movement rapidly accomplished. In a few brief months, the movement captured the popular Hindu imagination with hate for the 'other' 'foreign' 'aggressing' community of Muslims, symbolized by the offending mosque. In many towns, aggressive mobs openly brandishing weapons marched with the bricks that people had donated, shouting aggressive and offensive slogans against Muslims, and riots broke out, targeting lives, gutting homes, livelihoods and shrines. I recall that some 108 towns and cities in the country were simultaneously under curfew in those dark days.

The communal divide widened further with BJP leader Lal Krishna Advani going on a Rath Yatra in September 1990.[104] As his air-conditioned vehicle advanced nearly 10,000 kilometres from Somnath—chosen for its communally emotive history, as this was where a temple had been razed in 1026 by Mahmud of Ghazni—towards Ayodhya, it left a sombre trail of bloodshed and fear in the hearts of Muslim citizens across the country.

The slogans raised in those years were chilling. Indian Muslims were told:

Musalman ke do hi sthaan
Pakistan ya kabristan

(There are only two places for a Muslim
Pakistan or the cemetery)

There were also open calls for insurrection to the police:

Hindu-Hindu bhai bhai
Beech mein vardi kahan se aai?

(All Hindus are brothers
Then how can the uniform come between us?)

The anthem of the movement was 'Mandir wahin banayenge!', 'We'll build the temple at the very spot where the mosque stood!' For fifteen years, India was transformed into a country divided by religion-fuelled hate. The movement climaxed in the demolition of the mosque in 1992 by a rampaging mob, applauded by leaders of the BJP who were swept to power in state and Central governments; and in gruesome communal blood-letting, including in Bombay and Gujarat.

For the leaders of the movement, the fact that it is impossible to confirm the exact piece of land on which Ram was actually born, or even whether he was a historical figure, was irrelevant. They declared that this belief was a matter of faith for the Hindus, who constitute the nation's majority population, and therefore their faith should be respected by Indian Muslims, by the courts and the legislature, as well as by secular democrats. They believed that Ram was indeed born exactly below where the central dome of the Babri Masjid then stood. The removal of the mosque and the restoration of the Ram temple would avenge and correct the historical subjugation and humiliation of the Hindu people by Muslim invaders.

It mattered little to them that their claims were weak in both history and law. Independent scholars mostly agree that there is no convincing archaeological or historic evidence to show that Babar actually pulled down a Ram temple to build the mosque. The matter was referred to the highest court of the land, but the Hindutva leadership refused to be bound by the mediation of the courts in the event that they ruled against their claims, because they believed—in defiance of the fundamental premises of secular democracy—that even law must subordinate itself to the faith of the majority. There is also no consensus even of faith among practising Hindus about the birthplace of Ram. In Ayodhya itself, there are thousands of temples which claim to be the deity's birthplace. The majority of residents of Ayodhya opposed the Ram temple movement from the start, not least of all because they believed that Ram was a symbol of righteousness and compassion, and not of rule by violence, partisanship and fear.

The majority of Hindus also opposed the basic premise of the Hindu nationalists, that it is legitimate to avenge and correct the alleged wrongs of history. Why should people have to carry the burdens of their respective histories, and to atone for them? And if indeed they must, why then should the responsibilities of these burdens be so selective? History bears witness, for instance, that Buddhism was violently crushed and wiped out from large swathes of India by Brahminical Hinduism; in that case, what prevents someone from demanding that Hindu temples be pulled down and replaced by Buddhist stupas?[105] And why should all of these not give way to animist tribal shrines, because they dotted the landscape of what is today called India before any newer forms of worship came about?

Seventeen years after the demolition, a judicial commission headed by Justice Manmohan Singh Liberhan indicted the entire leadership of the BJP and RSS, saying that it had 'entered into a Joint Common Enterprise for the demolition of the disputed structure and the construction of the temple in its place'.[106] The Central government, led by Congress prime minister Narasimha Rao, unconscionably watched passively not just the razing of the mosque, but also the construction of a makeshift temple at the site over thirty-six hours. This was consistent with the Congress's policy of appeasing extremist Hindu nationalists rather than defending the Constitution and the law of the land. The country broke out in its worst frenzy of communal violence after Partition, which continued sporadically until the carnage in Gujarat in 2002.

The BJP reaped a rich political harvest from its campaign of hate and it joined the Central government for the first time in the late 1990s, in alliance with a number of opportunistic 'secular' parties. Every institution of Indian democracy let down the Indian people in these critical and dangerous years. The local newspapers glorified the rioters as Ram bhakts or devotees of Ram, and the national media helped in the re-invention of leaders like Advani as moderates, whitewashing their central role in fomenting communal violence and planning and leading a campaign that defied India's secular democracy. Courts have not punished any of those guilty for the crimes of 1992 or the riots that followed in their wake. The Liberhan Judicial Commission confirmed the criminal role of leaders of the BJP and the RSS, but recommended no criminal action against them.[107] When the report was finally submitted in 2009, the UPA, led by the Congress, was in power at the time. It lost no time accepting these recommendations. This was in keeping with the traditions of impunity that surround political hate crimes in this country. The Supreme Court to date prevaricates and refuses to pass rulings about the legal claims to the disputed land, and to restore the primacy of the law in resolving differences.

The dust raised by the demolition heralded, for over a decade, the triumph of politics founded on hate and difference over ancient traditions of tolerance and pluralism. It marked the victory of frenzied mob violence over the restraints imposed by modern systems of law and the secular democratic Constitution which the people of India gave themselves after India became free. It denoted the betrayal of the pledge that the people of India made to each other that this would be a land in which it would not matter which god you chose to worship, or if you chose to worship none; it would not count if you were of this caste or that, if you were a man or a woman, if you were wealthy or destitute. You would be a fully equal human being and citizen, assured of equal protection by the law of the land.[108]

Under the rubble of the fallen mosque lay the idea of India itself, critically stricken but not dead.

~

Eighteen years after the tragedy, the three judges of the Special Full Bench of the Allahabad High Court, S. U. Khan, Sudhir Sharma and D. V. Agarwal, hearing a sixty-year-old title suit filed by one Gopal Singh Visharad over offering worship at this bitterly contested property, could have corrected these immense wrongs and restored to public life principles of justice, secular democracy and rationality. But they again failed us comprehensively. I felt dismayed and betrayed. And, again, I was not alone.

The court ruled that the disputed land be divided into three parts, with the Ram Janmbhoomi Nyas, Nirmohi Akhara and the Sunni Waqf getting a third each. However, it also concluded that the mosque was indeed located at the site of Ram's birth, and that it was built at the site of a temple which preceded it. Justice Agarwal ruled that the 'area covered under the central dome of the disputed structure is the birthplace of Lord Rama as per faith and belief of Hindus'. Justice Sharma was even more categorical that 'the disputed site is the birthplace of Lord Ram'.[109]

It is utterly extraordinary that the Court passed judgement not on the basis of material fact and evidence, but on the questionable belief of faith. What is more, as already observed, even this 'belief' is not held universally by all Hindus. Tulsidas, the author of *Ramcharit Manas*, was an adult at the time when the Babri Masjid was built, and he never mentioned that this was the site where Ram was born. The 'faith and belief' referred to by the judges was not that of Hindus but of Hindutva organizations which subscribe to an alternate political ideology of a theologically Hindu India, one that contravenes the Indian Constitution.

The judges relied on questionable archaeological evidence collected when the BJP was in power in 2003, which was contradicted by most independent historians. But the issue of whether a temple existed in ancient times at the site was irrelevant while adjudicating a title suit according to modern law, and not medieval sentiment.

I was amazed by commentators who endorsed the judgement as balanced and just. They recommended 'moving on', and did not acknowledge that closure is impossible until justice is seen to be done by all parties to a dispute. It is true that this case was not for fixing criminal liability, but its rulings endorsed ideologically all the major premises of the Ram Temple movement. On grounds of dubious history and 'faith', and adverse possession derived by deceit and aggression, the judges awarded title of the land under the central dome of the demolished mosque to Hindus to construct a Ram temple. With this judgement, a movement which challenged India's secular Constitution, took hundreds of lives, and fostered fear and hate, enjoyed another moment of triumph.

I took heart, when the judgement was announced, that middle-class youth who then were not yet born, or were children when the movement was at its peak, refused at that moment to be mobilized in hate campaigns. But I wonder today if I was right in my optimism that those young people were at least apolitical. In Modi's momentous rise, the symbols today may be different and ostensibly more cosmopolitan. But the core issue remains unresolved. Is India, will India, should India, and must India remain—equally—a nation for all its citizens? I don't think India's poor, even today after BJP's triumph in 2014, seriously dispute the right of all who live here to this land. It is the middle class I am unsure about.

Hindutva Demographics

In the aftermath of the 2002 carnage, Narendra Modi often mocked Muslims with the slogan: 'Hum do, hamare do; Woh paanch, unke pachchees! (We are two, and we have two children; they are five, and they have twenty-five children!)'[110] In this he was only recirculating another favourite myth of Hindu nationalists, that Muslims are deliberately breeding many children and will one day outnumber Hindus in their 'own' land. He was also underlining with his discourse of 'we' and 'they', the 'otherness' of Muslims. He followed this up with what I believe is probably the single most offensive statement made by a head of government in independent India against a segment of his own people. Asked why the government was not establishing relief camps for the two hundred thousand people displaced by the carnage, he replied, 'I don't want to set up baby-producing factories.'[111] Seven months after Narendra Modi became prime minister, BJP MP from Unnao, Sakshi Maharaj, similarly made a call—widely reported in the national press—to Hindus to correct the alleged reproductive excesses of Muslims by producing four babies each.

I once met a local VHP leader in Ahmedabad who did not know who I was. 'How can we live with these people?' he asked me. 'If you go to a typical Muslim home early in the morning, what will you see? The door of a tiny one-room kutcha house will open. First, the man will emerge in his blue lungi. Then his four wives will walk out, followed by fifteen-twenty children. Then there will be a herd of goats. And after that come a squawking brood of chickens. I don't know how they live. But we *cannot* live with them.'

I doubt whether he actually ever saw this 'typical' Muslim household but he is not only convinced that it exists but that it abounds, that it is the rule rather than the exception. Ram Puniyani points out in his *Communal Politics: Facts versus Myths* to all who are willing to hear his words of reason that 'the male-female ratio cannot permit the "luxury" of four wives to the Muslim males unless three-fourths (75 per cent) of them go without marriage'.[112] He shows from the 1981 census, that for every 1,000 Muslim females there are 1,068 Muslim males. 'One has to conceive of gigantic mental acrobatics…to believe that all Muslim males can have four wives.'[113] He also points to an earlier (1961 census) report which showed that the incidence of polygamy was slightly *lower* among Muslims (5.7) as compared to Hindus (5.8)!

Nivedita Menon also points to data from the National Family Health Survey showing that Muslim and Hindu women have the same fertility rate for the same age and economic level. She shows that the fertility rate of Muslims in states like Tamil Nadu and Kerala is far below that of Hindus in Uttar Pradesh, Bihar or Rajasthan, for instance. Fertility rates are higher in poorer communities, and it is only this which explains the slightly higher growth rate for Muslims overall because, on average, Muslims are poorer than Hindus. Common sense would also indicate this. 'Poverty and lack of facilities are far more important than religion in deciding how many children you have.'[114]

Social scientist Mohan Rao and historian Tanika Sarkar also remind us that the alarmist saffron demographics have an old vintage, whipping up anxieties over generations about galloping 'Muslim fertility rates', their uncontrolled breeding and the dying of 'the Hindu nation'.[115] Rao points to a book written in 1909 by U. N. Mukherji called *Hindus: A Dying Race*, which deeply influenced the Hindu Mahasabha and the RSS.[116]

Hindutva websites typically claim, shrilly, that 'Islam is gradually gobbling up India by demographic aggressions or increasing their population. They are increasing their number through (1) polygamy,

(2) deliberate rejection of the family-planning measures (3) illegal infiltration of Muslims from Bangladesh and (4) conversion of Hindus to Islam.'[117] To illustrate what 'saffron demographics' entails, Rao points to a speech in 2004 by VHP president Ashok Singhal that Hindus should give up family planning so that their population does not decrease. Singhal claimed that the population of minorities, especially Muslims, had been rising at 'such a fast pace' that it would be 25 to 30 per cent of the total population in fifty years. Singhal also said that it would be 'suicidal' for Hindus if they did not raise their population.[118] Likewise, Rao quotes a report from *The Hindu* about a massive public meeting in 2005, attended by the chief minister of Madhya Pradesh, where the leader of the Madhya Pradesh unit of the RSS claimed that the Muslim population was increasing at a rapid rate, and that this, combined with 'infiltration' of Muslims from Bangladesh, portended doom for India. The VHP, he says, also opposes abortion because they allege that a disproportionate number of Hindu women utilize abortion facilities.[119]

Similar alarmist fears of being demographically submerged by large-scale immigration of Muslim people, and the mythical hyper-masculine Muslim male and the suppressed but highly fertile Muslim female, suggest a much wider appeal of anti-Muslim demographics. Mohan Rao describes the curious and chilling case of the 2011 Norwegian mass murderer Anders Behring Breivik, who claimed that Norway would become a Muslim-majority country by 2050 (although current trends would take the Muslim population only to 7 per cent by that year). Breivik felt a close affinity with Hindutva ideologies; they share a common dread of being submerged by swelling populations of Muslim people. In the manifesto he left behind, Breivik describes the slaughter of Hindus in the Hindu Kush by Muslim invaders, and the appeasement of these aggressors and the victimization of Hindus by 'cultural Marxists' who control the Indian government.[120]

The Improbable Story of 'Love Jihad'

I had assumed that the hate mythology of love jihad was a new innovation wrought by communal organizations. But, according to historian Mridula Mukherjee, its roots go as far back as the Partition, with the demonization of the meat-eating Muslim male as a sexual predator, contrasted with the effete, vegetarian Hindu. Rumours were deliberately engineered by communal Right-wing Hindutva organizations about Muslim men abducting Hindu women resulting in what historian Tanika Sarkar describes as 'a kind of penis envy and anxiety about emasculation that can only be overcome by violence'.[121]

In recent years, it is this disturbing phenomenon which has evolved into the 'love jihad', a myth so implausible and fanciful that it would be laughable were it not so deadly. Love jihad has resulted in prolonged, low-intensity communal mobilization and violence against Muslims over the last few years in the coastal areas of Karnataka; contributed to communal tension between Muslims, Hindus and Christians in Kerala; and is the main basis on which hate was 'created' for a high-intensity attack against local Muslims in Muzaffarnagar in 2013, leading, ultimately, to the state-wide polarization of Hindu voters across Uttar Pradesh against their Muslim neighbours, and the ascension of BJP to power in the state.[122, 123]

In the conception of 'love jihad', good-looking Muslim boys are trained in madrassas to lure Hindu girls into fake love affairs. They are equipped with the necessary instruments for romantic entrapment—attractive clothes, trendy gadgets and motorcycles—all to lure unsuspecting Hindu girls into marriage. The girls are then converted into Islam, married and used to produce large numbers of Muslim progeny.[124] There are other even more fanciful versions as well, that the love jihadi later uses the Hindu girl as a sex slave, or trafficks her.[125] The assumption is not just that Muslim boys are trained to 'lure' Hindu girls, but also that young Hindu women are empty-headed, lack any agency or discernment, and are unable to protect themselves without the vigilant intervention of their male co-religionists.

Writing for *The Hindu*, Mohan Rao reproduces the pamphlet below, and reports that the Akhil Bharatiya Vidyarthi Parishad (ABVP)—the student wing of the BJP—is distributing these circulars warning Hindu students against the designs of their Muslim classmates in as enlightened, pluralist and cosmopolitan a university as JNU, Delhi.[126]

This poster, attributed to the 'Anti Love Jihad Front' appeals to Hindu brothers to awaken and become vigilant.[127] The pamphlet shows a bearded Muslim boy on a motorcycle, with a love-struck Hindu girl riding pillion. It claims that Muslim boys assume Hindu names, even wear a saffron string on their wrist and red tika on their foreheads, trap Hindu girls in the web of love, convert them to Islam, produce children with them, torture, and ultimately abandon them. It cites the examples of 'Bollywood' actors Aamir Khan and Saif Ali Khan, who they allege married Hindu girls, had children from them and then abandoned them. (It is true that they separated from their

first wives, but then so has actor Hrithik Roshan, a Hindu, who has separated from his Muslim wife.) Even a helpline number has been provided.

~

It was in Mangalore in coastal Karnataka that I first encountered the mythology of love jihad and witnessed the potency of its poison. I had been invited there in 2010 by my friend Arvind Narrain of the Alternate Law Forum, and a remarkable collective of local progressive journalists, teachers, students, engineers, businessmen, actors and writers who were alarmed about the social schisms being engineered in their society.

I found that in the picturesque coastal regions of Karnataka, fear had become a dominant motif of everyday life for its Muslim residents. A range of self-styled vigilante groups, with tacit support from the police and the state administration, dominated social life in the region, as they peremptorily dictated and enforced what they regarded to be permissible social conduct. They opposed, often with open violence, the meeting of young people of different religious identities. They combatted women who drank, danced or entered beauty pageants, but were also incensed by the burqa and the hijab. They assaulted Christian places of worship, priests and nuns, to 'save' the Hindu faith from conversions. Teams of young men 'rescued' cows on sale for slaughter.

Local newspapers regularly carried glowing reports of how the alert intervention of these vigilante groups—which included the Sri Ram Sena, the Bajrang Dal, the Hindu Rashtra Sena and the Hindu Jagaran Vedike—had succeeded in preventing young Muslim men from enticing and 'trapping' Hindu girls.

I found that across coastal Karnataka, these vigilante groups had recruited an impressive army of volunteers, which included bus conductors, waiters in way-side eateries and cinema ushers. If a Hindu girl met with or talked to a Muslim boy—in a cinema auditorium, tea-stall or bus—the usher, waiter or bus conductor would inform the nearest local unit of one of these Hindutva groups. Typically, even before the film would end, or the bill would be paid in the restaurant or the bus would reach its destination, activists would arrive, armed with sticks and rods. They would thrash the young Muslim men, slap the women, and drag the couples to the nearest police station. The district head of the Bajrang Dal, Sudarshan Moodabidri, boasted that 'his boys' had 'solved' over 200 such 'cases' in just two months: 'Sometimes it becomes necessary to use force. Fear of such action should deter such misadventures. Girls reform themselves once they are thrashed and humiliated in public, but boys are tougher to control.'[128]

The police were usually supportive of their exertions, and they detained and beat up the Muslim men, and also summoned the parents of the Hindu girls to the police stations. Police further humiliated and chastised the parents, and warned them to keep their girls 'in check'. Sudipto Mondal reported in *The Hindu* that a fifteen-year-old girl sat next to the brother of a Muslim girl-friend whom she encountered by chance in a bus, and the boy was thrashed by the vigilantes and her father summoned to the police station. The humiliated girl hung herself. The police registered a case of abetment of suicide against the Muslim boy.[129] Vigilantes prevented Hindu friends, both boys and girls, from going for a Ramzaan lunch to the home of a Muslim friend. Groups of young friends of mixed religions were attacked for going for picnics or films, organizing parties in their homes, travelling collectively to college, or eating and drinking in each other's company. Both police and local news reports often referred darkly to the 'crime' of these young people of 'having fun' together. Matters would be, of course, far grimmer if anybody wished to marry across religious boundaries. The People's Union of Civil Liberties, Karnataka, in a report 'Cultural Policing in Dakshina Kannada: Vigilante Attacks on Women and Minorities', compiled tens of such reported incidents in just a single year. The authors, Ramdas Rao, Shakun Mohini, B. N. Usha and Arvind Narrain, warned against this frightening level of social surveillance and daily vigilantism, by which 'everyday acts of living in a multi-religious society' were being 'rigorously policed and ordered by vigilante Hindu groups'.[130] The aim was 'social apartheid where the various communities become self-enclosed structures with inter-community social interaction being actively discouraged'.[131]

Matters deteriorated further after the BJP government came to power in 2006. The police refused to take action against vigilante groups who beat up and insulted young people with impunity. Instead, they assisted and collaborated in this extra-legal, criminal intimidation. Both the chief minister and the home minister, by implication, also justified planned attacks on churches by referring to 'the spontaneous anger' of the people against conversions, echoing Vajpayee's implicit rationalization of anti-Christian attacks. (It may be recalled that when missionary Graham Staines was burned alive in rural Odisha along with his two small sons, Prime Minister Vajpayee had called for a national debate on conversions, a subject I will return to in a later chapter.) Activists have tirelessly collected evidence of hundreds of incidents in which vigilantes have banned—usually with tacit police support and widespread social sanction—all relationships, even just friendships, between Hindu girls and Muslim boys.

Mohan Rao quotes the Hindu Janajagriti Samiti's claim that 30,000 young women have been duped by 'Love Romeos' in the state. He also points to disturbing judicial support for the campaign. 'The Kerala High Court ordered an enquiry in 2010, while the Karnataka High Court, in the same year, stated that a case involving a 23 year old woman who had converted to Islam to marry a Muslim man had "national ramifications concerning security, besides the question of unlawful trafficking of women"...and ordered the woman be "restored" to her parents while the police investigated the case.' The silver lining was that the Kerala Police reported finding no evidence of love jihad, and the Karnataka Police clarified that 404 girls were in fact missing during the period and that they had been able to trace 332 of them. The majority of them were Hindu girls who had eloped to marry Hindu men.

~

People of diverse faiths who live together do not spontaneously turn upon each other. There are three essential requisites for the fomenting of mass communal violence. The first is the deliberate manufacturing of hatred. The second is the manufacturing of a 'riot'. The third is a complicit state—no riot can continue beyond a few hours unless the state actively wishes it.

Communal organizations have long perfected the art of manufacturing hatred against the 'other' community by cynically deploying rumour, innuendo and falsehood. The issue chosen to demonize the 'other' varies based on what resonates and enrages most.

In Muzzafarnagar, in the patriarchal Jat community, the issue chosen to foment hatred was women's 'honour'.

Three young men, one Muslim and two Jat, were killed in a violent clash on 27 August 2013 in Kawal village in the Muzzafarnagar district. This incident was paraded as an example of 'love jihad'. The claim was that the Muslim youth, Shahnawaz Qureshi, had been killed by the brothers of a Jat girl, whom he had allegedly been stalking, in a socially justified act of 'honour killing', and that these cousins, Sachin Singh and Gaurav Singh, were killed in revenge by a violent Muslim mob. Soon after the incident, Member of Legislative Assembly for the BJP, Sangeet Som uploaded a video of two young men being attacked and brutally lynched to death by a mob in Sialkot, Pakistan, claiming that the footage was of the Jat boys Sachin and Gaurav being killed by a crazed Muslim mob.[132] This video was circulated widely through mobile phones, and fuelled rage against local Muslims. The BJP MLA was arrested but released after nineteen days.[133]

Later investigations revealed a very different story. The motorcycle which one of the young men was riding had accidentally touched the bicycle of the other. This led to a heated exchange of words. Thereafter, Shahnawaz went to the Muslim enclave for afternoon prayers. Meanwhile, Sachin, Gaurav and seven other men gathered to avenge the perceived insult Shahnawaz had heaped on them. They surrounded and stabbed him, and then tried to flee. The others escaped but

Sachin and Gaurav were caught. People rushed Shahnawaz to the hospital, and when he died, the cousins' captors murdered them in vengeance.

This story did not serve the political objectives of those who seek to profit from popular anger against Muslims. An emotive alternative narrative, of sexual predation and honour, was constructed. It served its purpose of generating mass hatred among Hindus, not just in Muzaffarnagar but across the state of Uttar Pradesh, against their Muslim neighbours. The murderous attacks, arson, rapes and the mass exodus which followed were the harvest of the falsehoods deliberately propagated. Thousands spent a bleak winter under tents and continue to live in abject fear of returning to their homes.

In an interesting aside, Mohan Rao, who was returning from a fact-finding visit to Muzaffarnagar, related to me the strange ways in which saffron demographics play out in a riot-torn area to justify violence. In the discussions Rao and his colleagues held with the Jat leaders of the area, they claimed that Shahnawaz was one of nine children, whereas both Sachin and Gaurav were the only sons. This was factually inaccurate, but that did not matter. The point they made was that the Muslims can afford to stoke violence because they have so many children, so that the loss of one or the other is tolerable for them. But since Hindus resort—in the national interest—to family planning, the loss of Hindu boys in such violence is much more tragic and intolerable.[134]

Many political commentators agree that the Jat community in western Uttar Pradesh, and probably Hindus across caste lines in the state, voted for the BJP because they believed that this is the only party which can 'tame' the Muslims. The fact that Muslims are not guilty of the crimes which generate so much majoritarian anger against them is strangely irrelevant after hatred takes roots in people's hearts. Even if a person from a community commits a crime, does this justify the reprisal killing of even one other person of the same community? Why does popular hatred persist even after criminally propagated falsehoods are exposed? And when the initial story turns out to be a fabrication, why is there no public remorse from people who justified the attack? These are ethical issues in our public life which we have sidestepped for too long.

The second requirement for communal violence to occur is the manufacture of the riot itself. Building on the groundswell of local Hindu fury against their Muslim neighbours, a mahapanchayat was convened on 7 September 2013 with the explosive theme 'Beti bachao, bahu bachao!' ('Save your daughters, save your daughters-in-law'). Fiery speeches were made against Muslims and, after the frenzied crowd dispersed, they attacked Muslim settlements. In the majority of villages, Muslims were labourers on the sugarcane fields of Jat landowners. Their houses were set aflame and looted, some were killed, and terrified people fled to the safety of numbers in Muslim-majority villages.

The third prerequisite for a manufactured riot is a complicit state administration, which fails in prevention, control, rescue and relief. The administration took no steps to quell the rumours, arrest those stoking hatred, or prohibit the mahapanchayat. Once violence broke out, the police forces mostly stood by, watching, as the crowds attacked Muslim settlements, without using force or firing to disperse the furious mobs. They did not rescue the escaping people; instead, survivors depended on wealthy Muslim landowners to protect them as they fled. The administration did not establish relief camps; instead, these were organized by the victimized community in Muslim-majority villages. We found little presence of the state in these camps: it did not organize sanitation, healthcare, childcare or police outposts to record people's complaints.

I had hoped that the Gujarat carnage of 2002 would be the last in which cynical politics would succeed in fomenting hatred and organizing communal massacre, and the last in which the state would abdicate its duties for relief, rehabilitation and justice. But now events in western Uttar Pradesh demonstrate how easily, even today, communal organizations and parties can manufacture both hatred and a riot, even between communities which have no history of violence or animosities, based on the most bizarre hate folklore like love jihad. And reap a rich political harvest as the outcome.

Profiling 'Criminals' and 'Terrorists'

Discrimination and prejudice, legitimized in the middle classes and, by extension, the state over which it has greatest influence, takes an enormous toll on stigmatized people, in this case Muslim minorities in India. The vast majority lives in poverty in under-served, crowded ghettoes, battling the everyday reality of discrimination in schools, work and public spaces. Even middle-class Muslims, as we have observed, are not protected from discrimination despite better economic conditions and greater social capital.

But perhaps the gravest suffering imposed by the legitimization of prejudice among Muslims—and, indeed, societal indifference—is the ever-looming threat and actual profiling of Muslim men in regular crimes and, especially, in terror crimes, to which so many of the participants in the Anhad conference had alluded. The National Crime Records Bureau reports that at the end of 2012, Muslims constituted about 17.8 per cent of the convicts in jails, 21 per cent of undertrials, 28.3 per cent of detainees and 39.9 per cent in other cases, although they constitute 14 per cent of the total Indian population.[135] In Rajasthan, 18 per cent of Muslims are in jails against a population share of 8 per cent; in West Bengal, at 45 per cent, they are nearly double their population share of 25 per cent. In Maharashtra, Muslims are a third of jail inmates, and a fourth in Uttar Pradesh. Except Jammu and Kashmir, Puducherry and Sikkim, there are disproportionate numbers of Muslims behind bars in almost all other states.[136]

The silver lining is that because the percentage convicted is less than the undertrials, it can be assumed that large numbers of arrested Muslims were released by the courts, especially when the inverse is true of all other communities.[137] But criminal lawyer Majeed Memon also concludes that 'the revelation that the number of Muslim undertrials is higher than the number of Muslim convicts shows members of the community are more vulnerable to false arrest. This strengthens the belief that communal prejudices, to some extent, exist in the police force. This needs to be carefully examined and effectively remedied.'[138]

A study conducted by the Tata Institute of Social Sciences confirms bias against Muslims by the police, the administration and the judiciary in Mumbai.[139] It found that most Muslims are jailed on petty charges like liquor trade, theft, loot, etcetera and they don't get any legal assistance or advice; nor are they aware that they are entitled to free legal assistance. They lack political power or backing. The study revealed that 43.6 per cent of prisoners were not in a position to hire a lawyer on their own and 61 per cent were not aware that there was an NGO in the jail from which they could seek assistance.[140] It found that 58 per cent of Muslims were either illiterate or had received only elementary education—the 2011 census had found the overall illiterate population to be 18 per cent.[141]

But the situation is even graver for people charged under terror laws. In a study for the 'India Exclusion Report', Warisha Farasat observes that 'no other word has been misused more often in the 21st century than "terrorism". Across continents, countries have redefined many fundamental human freedoms and substituted them with extraordinary legislations that subvert these basic guarantees and each time, the so-called fight against terrorism has been the alibi. India, in its own "war against terrorism", has been no different'. She continues that there is 'extensive misuse and misapplication of terror laws, particularly in terms of their selective targeting of religious minorities, Dalits, adivasis, activists and political opponents'. She finds that 'terror laws suspend certain legal and constitutional protections, such as those related to arbitrary detention and due process, making it easier to detain, harass or convict people charged under these laws. As a result, terror laws have often been used to target innocent persons or organisations under the guise of tackling terrorism'. She also finds that 'the wrongful arrests and detentions are based on the following factors: the pressure on the investigating agencies to produce instant results after a terror attack or a bomb blast; criminalising of all forms of dissent, and the communalisation of the police forces, bureaucracy and judiciary, especially the lower courts'.[142]

Untold human costs are paid by innocent men wrongly detained in jails for years without bail or trial, costs which aren't mitigated even by their release. There is nothing that can restore the lost years of life; the stigma, penury and suffering of loved ones left outside. I have worked closely with men wrongly jailed on terror charges in two big cases—the Godhra train-burning case of 2002, in which they were acquitted and released after nine years, and the Mecca Masjid bombing case in Hyderabad in 2006. I will recount here two stories to illustrate the enormity of human suffering which are ultimately the wages paid for prejudice condoned by society.

~

Bibi Khatoon's three grown sons, Shamsher, Sultan and Sadiq completed nine long years in jail before they were finally acquitted at the end of a protracted, meandering trial for their purported involvement in the alleged arson on the Sabarmati Express. Their crime was not proved, and both the Gujarat High Court and the Supreme Court concluded that there was no evidence of any terrorist plot to attack the train, despite the Gujarat government's strenuous claims that such a conspiracy had been hatched.

On the evening of 27 February 2002, when the incident took place, a large contingent of policemen in plain clothes arrived in Rehmat Nagar in Godhra. In this slum, a few kilometres from the railway station, live mainly working-class Muslim people: car mechanics, drivers and casual labourers. Bibi Khatoon's sons had just returned home from work and were drinking tea. Policemen, their faces covered with scarves, arrested her boys along with eleven other young men from the colony. The women raised an alarm and ran after the vehicles into which their men had been bundled. One policeman reassured Bibi that her sons would return home after they met their bade sahib (senior officer). Bibi repeated sadly years later,

'It seems that their bade sahib has still not arrived after all these years.'

When none of the men, some still teenagers, returned that night, their families panicked further. They spotted them in the railway police station, but were not allowed to meet them, or give them food and clothes. The men soon disappeared and no policeman in Godhra or Ahmedabad was willing to tell the distraught families where their loved ones were.

Three months later, Bibi's husband received a letter from their sons, informing them that they were lodged in Sabarmati Central Jail in Ahmedabad. They were among the 131 people charged with a terrorist conspiracy to burn the train in Godhra. The law under which they were charged was the dreaded POTA, or the Prevention of Terrorism Act, which provided for detention without bail for people accused of terror crimes. (Incidentally, the state government has not charged a single person under this severe law for the massacre of Muslims which followed the fire on the train.)

Bibi was heartbroken when she met her sons for the first time inside the formidable prison. They were thin and their eyes were haunted. They whispered about torture and beatings, in low voices so that the jail staff who stood by could not overhear. They said they were forced to drink water from the same bucket in which they urinated. Bibi's husband assured their sons that he would do everything that was possible to get them out of jail. He urged the boys to not lose hope.

Back home, the challenge was to keep the kitchen fires burning, since there were now no sons to earn money. Bibi's eldest son had two boys in school. Their second son had married just months before his arrest. His wife delivered a girl while he was in prison. He became a stranger to his own daughter. Their youngest was still in his teens. The old father looked for casual employment, and Bibi and her two daughters-in-law tried to find work, cleaning dishes and sweeping floors in people's homes in Godhra. Work was harder to find because they were tainted 'POTA families'.

In September 2004, the newly elected UPA government in Delhi repealed POTA, because its provisions deprived the accused of their elementary democratic rights of fair trial. But, paradoxically, it did not repeal the law retrospectively, therefore those who were already detained under its provisions, like Bibi's sons, continued to be held and tried under the discredited law. Some organizations helped the families of the accused fight their cases in court. Nitya Ramakrishnan, leading criminal lawyer from Delhi, and advocate Hassan were among those who represented the accused. The charge of the state government was that the mob launched a murderous pre-planned attack on the train, and threw petrol into the compartment from outside. But forensic reports established that it was humanly impossible for petrol to be poured in. It found no evidence of hydrocarbons inside the compartment. The lawyers also pointed to many other holes in the case made out by the state police.

In the tortuous nine years that the case lasted, there were many rulings in favour of the accused. Each time Bibi and other families hoped for the release of their loved ones. But these hopes were always betrayed. In 2005, the Review Committee appointed under POTA held that there was no evidence of a terrorist conspiracy, and even less one which threatened the unity of India, therefore no case could be made out under POTA. But the state government was unwilling to accept this finding. It appealed instead to the High Court which, in February 2009, upheld the conclusions of the Review Committee. This was further endorsed by the Supreme Court. Even so, the state government did not release the accused. Instead, it charged them afresh, this time not under POTA, but the Indian Penal Code. However, the accused were not granted bail even under the ordinary criminal law of the land, although many like Bibi's three sons had spent five years in jail.

Meanwhile, four years after his sons went to jail, Bibi's husband was diagnosed with throat cancer. His sons were granted one day's parole each to meet their father one last time before he died. After his death, the burden of supporting the large family fell on ageing Bibi's shoulders. Crippled by an accident and old age, she was unable to work. Instead, she was reduced to begging. She hobbled from house to house in Godhra, begging all day for a few rupees or some food. Her older grandson was in Class 10. He needed money for books, uniform and examination fees, which she raised by begging. But he failed his examination and she pulled him out of school. She withdrew her younger grandson from school even sooner, after Class 8. Both then earned ₹50 a day working in a garage.

The visits of the family to see them in jail tapered to once every six months. The bus fares cost what they earned in a full month. And all for a meeting which would barely last five minutes, through two screens. The boys were emaciated, and had contracted diseases like tuberculosis. Safiq, Bibi's youngest, had lost his mind in jail. He spent his days in jail compulsively collecting and eating paper and scraps, and sometimes assaulting other prisoners and even the jail staff. He did not recognize his family any more. Bibi mourned, 'His milk teeth had barely fallen out when they took him away. What have they done to my little boy?' Their lawyers' applications for his parole, so that he could be treated, were rejected.

Bibi was mortified that she was forced to beg to keep her family alive. She was ashamed, also, that her sons had been charged with such a heinous crime. 'I am an unlettered woman, my son,' she said to me. 'I do not understand the law. But explain to me why my sons continued in jail all these years when they were innocent.' Her three sons, now broken men, were returned to her after nine years, by a state which was unable to prove their guilt in any crime.

~

I met Ibrahim Junaid in his hometown, Hyderabad, for the first time when, stigmatized as a terrorist, the young man, merely twenty-five years old, was out on bail after five months in prison, trying desperately to prove his innocence and to complete his medical studies. He found himself barred from rejoining his college of traditional medicine in the old city of Hyderabad, and from giving his final examination.

He was finally acquitted of all charges two years later and rejoined medical school. Today, scarred for life by his torture and years in jail, he still tries to live a normal life.

This is his testimony.

As was his practice every Friday, Ibrahim walked on a hot summer afternoon with his friends from the unani medical college to the Mecca Masjid nearby. The prayers and the weekly sermon had ended, and the crowds of worshippers were drifting to the exit. Ibrahim heard a massive explosion behind him, and turned to find the mosque choked with thick smoke and was deafened by the screams of men running in every direction. Ibrahim saw a man with his skull half open, and many scattered limbs. People panicked further with rumours that more bombs would explode. As he was running out, he found one of their college professors lying unconscious, his limbs fractured. He called out to his friends in the mayhem, and they rushed him to hospital in their principal's car. Ibrahim heard later that the city police had announced, within hours, that the attack had been planned by an Islamic terrorist group, and it fired upon a crowd of Muslim protesters who were enraged by what they perceived to be the police's failure to prevent the terror attack on the mosque.

For days after the bombing, Ibrahim just slept in his home, haunted by images of the dead and twisted bodies in the mosque. On the eighth day after the explosion, he was summoned by the Special Investigation Cell of the Hyderabad Police. The officer questioned him about who was responsible for the attack. Ibrahim said he did not know, but countered to ask how the police were so convinced that the terrorists might not have been of another community. He was grilled the whole day, and for next three consecutive days, and then from time to time. They then began to ask him whether he had himself not planted the bombs.

His brush with the police had begun some years earlier, when he was twenty-one, during his first year in medical college. Ever since he was a child, Ibrahim Junaid had wanted to become a doctor. His father, a welder in the old city of Hyderabad, was convinced about the worth of education and Junaid had no difficulty in persuading him to support his studies, as he had provided well beyond his means for his other children too. It was in a college of traditional unani medicine that he was able to find admission, not far from the historical Mecca Masjid in the old city.

A dispute had broken out at a neighbouring Muslim cemetery when Ibrahim was in his first year of college. Some local activists of the VHP had secretly installed an idol of Ganesh at the Musaram Bagh cemetery, and worshipped the deity during the annual Ganesh festival. They had begun this practice a few years earlier but, instead of heeding the protests of the local Muslim residents, the scale of the celebrations and worship of the idol had only grown with every passing year. That year, in 2003, Ibrahim had joined a delegation of around seventy local people to lodge a formal protest at the police station and seek the removal of the idol. They feared that the Hindutva activists were planning to occupy the entire graveyard and build a temple over it. Their efforts were supported openly by the local BJP MLA, and tacitly by the local Congress leaders as well. The police stonewalled their protests, and tempers rose further when the BJP MLA began to argue with the hot-blooded protesters, led prominently by Ibrahim, outside the police station. The police authorities followed this with a cane charge to disperse the angry crowd.

Shortly after, the police registered a case against Ibrahim and four of his friends, accusing them of a conspiracy to kill the BJP MLA. He was twenty-one years old then. They were picked up by the police and held in an unknown location, boxed, kicked, slapped and beaten repeatedly on the soles of their feet with belts made from worn-out truck tyres. When their feet swelled painfully, they would be forced to walk until the swellings subsided, and then the beatings would start again. Ibrahim's parents were not informed of his arrest, and they sent telegrams to the chief justice of the High Court and the police commissioner. On the third day, they were presented before the magistrate, who remanded them to jail.

It was the first time that Ibrahim had seen the inside of a prison. The men were each issued a blanket and a mat, and Ibrahim shared a barrack with close to eighty petty criminals. Ibrahim spent much of the day reading the Quran. They would be released into the jail courtyard at 6 every morning, and be given three simple meals at 7 and 11 in the morning, and 4 in the evening. At sundown, around 6, they would be returned to their barracks. Ibrahim looked forward to the meetings with his parents twice a week, even though his mother wept a lot. They assured him that they had engaged a good lawyer and had raised money for his bail. After three months of incarceration, he was granted bail. His college accepted him back after his first arrest, and although the police summoned him regularly, and there were many court hearings, he persevered with his studies and managed a first division in both his first and second professional examinations.

Maybe it was because of this early skirmish with the law that the police rounded him up after the series of bomb explosions in Hyderabad in 2007. Maybe it was because he kept a beard and was deeply religious. Maybe it was because his parents chose, when he was twelve, to interrupt his studies in a Christian missionary school, and send him instead for four years as a day scholar to study at a local madrassa. They wanted at least one son to become a Hafiz, or one who memorizes the entire Quran. They were not disappointed, because Ibrahim successfully graduated in four years from the madrassa. But he still wanted to be a doctor, and struggled to join another private school and pass his high school examination.

But Ibrahim is convinced that the police specially targeted him, most of all, because he had joined a human rights group six months after his first release from jail. He was attracted to the Civil Liberties Monitoring Committee because of its brave and outspoken stand against police excesses. Months before his arrest, he had been prominent in protesting the extra-judicial murder of Sohrabuddin and his wife Kausar Bi by the Gujarat Police, with active connivance of the Hyderabad forces. The police official argued that Sohrabuddin was a petty criminal and deserved his death. Ibrahim persisted, 'Even if he was a criminal, you should have charged him and let him face the courts. And what about his wife? Was she also a criminal?' The policeman was irritated, and asked him, 'Are you trying to be a leader?'

Shortly after the second round of terrorist bomb attacks in Hyderabad in 2007, Ibrahim went on a study tour with his teacher and colleagues to Delhi and Mussoorie. He had barely alighted from the train on his return when three men grabbed him by the waist and dragged him to a waiting vehicle. They threatened him to remain silent, or else he would be killed. They drove to Purana Pul, and then they blindfolded him and tied his hands behind him. The vehicle drove for around two hours before they finally alighted at a building. It was a location far from the noise of city traffic.

Inside the building, they took away his mobile and money. Near midnight, they stripped him down to his underwear. Two men pulled his legs wide apart, another held him down by the shoulders and pounded him. They administered electric shocks by turn on his genitals, ears, lips, nipples, temple and joints until he passed out. They would revive him and start again, beating him on his soles with a rubber belt. Between communal taunts, they asked him again and again who was responsible for the blasts. He pleaded that he did not know, and had nothing to do with the terrorist attacks in the city. Early morning, when he fell unconscious one more time, a man walked all over him with his boots, then dragged him still naked into an air-conditioned room where, shivering and in unbearable pain, he tried to fitfully sleep.

The same routine continued as day passed into night and then became day again, until he lost count of time in a haze of torment and dread. He began to pass blood in his urine. Outside, unknown to him, the human rights organization of which he was a member convened other human rights groups and members of his family, as well of those of more than twenty other young people who had been similarly abducted and detained. They filed habeas corpus petitions in the High Court, petitioned national and state human rights and minorities commissions, and convened high-profile protest meets and press conferences. Ibrahim's parents were prominent in all these protests and appeals.

The police finally succumbed to the pressure and produced the young men before the Secunderabad metropolitan magistrate at his official residence, claiming that they had just been arrested a few hours earlier because of their subversive attempts to incite Muslim youth against the state. The magistrate emerged briefly from his house, counted the men, and said, 'Send them to jail.' He did not give the detained men a chance to speak, or even glance at their injuries.

In jail, the routine followed in Ibrahim's first incarceration was repeated, with one important difference. The prison officials, and even some of the jail inmates began to taunt them as 'traitors', 'terrorists' and 'ISI agents'. They were segregated under high security and stigmatized. Human rights organizations collaborated with the state human rights commission to investigate the allegations against the police made by Ibrahim and others, and encountered sufficient collaborative evidence to find them credible. The jail officials had also recorded the many bodily injuries suggestive of torture, at the time when the men were incarcerated, because they did not want to be charged with torturing them after they were imprisoned.

One by one, the jailed youth got bail. For Ibrahim, it took five months, with the police strenuously in opposition. He was taken while in custody to the FSL Laboratory in Bangalore for a 'narco-test', in which he recalls being injected with a drug popularly known as truth serum, after which he was questioned. He has no memory of what transpired there. In the end, a bail of ₹50,000 was granted. His mother sold her jewellery to make his bail.

It is remarkable that the charge sheet that was finally produced by the Hyderabad Police could make no allegation linking Ibrahim or any other young men abducted at that time to the terrorist attacks in the city. Instead the charges were far more general, claiming his sympathy with jihadi ideology, which resorts to terror 'so that they can rule India as they are ruling Pakistan (sic)'. He was said to have been arrested from a meeting at the railway station, and found to be in possession of seditious literature and VCDs 'showing the clippings of Gujarat communal riots and beheading of western forces by the Jihadi elements, thereby provoking Muslim youth to take revenge against non-Muslim communities...'[143]

After his release on bail, he tried hard to re-enter his medical college and appear for his examinations. But although his classmates, both Hindu and Muslim, welcomed him back, the dark taint of charges of treason and support to terrorism made his college authorities wary. They could not afford trouble with the law. He wondered when, if ever, he would be able to complete his medical education. He took the matter to the High Court, which ordered his college to re-admit hm. He finally picked up his studies again and completed them.

Ibrahim, like all the young men who were abducted and tortured by the Hyderabad Police, faced a terrible dilemma when he first met me. If he spoke out publicly against the atrocities he had suffered, he feared retribution from the police. He could be framed further for crimes of sedition and terror, tortured, or even killed. But if he continued with his silence, in dread of punitive action, he still remained in danger of suffering the same outcomes that they fear from a force that has become accustomed to impunity in its battles against both alleged Maoists and terrorists. Ibrahim was clear about his choice; that he would fight injustice head on, and face the consequences. That is why he insisted on speaking with me, and that I should write his story. I did, and published it in *The Hindu*.[144]

He was ultimately acquitted after two years, as was every single young man who had been charged. It now turns out, with the confession of Hindutva leader Aseemanand, that the bomb blast during Friday prayers in the Mecca Masjid in Hyderabad was a conspiracy hatched by Hindutva organizations.[145] Junaid today runs a small unani practice in old Hyderabad. But he was determined after his release that we should file a petition demanding that the police be made to pay a compensation for his years of torture and unjust incarceration, and that of the other young men who were arrested with him. I willingly agreed to be party to a petition demanding this compensation, as a symbol of public atonement for a public crime which is almost beyond forgiveness. The court has yet to decide on this plea.

Junaid tells me his small unani medical practice is doing well. He is still haunted by memories of torture and unjust incarceration, but is grateful that he was freed ultimately, both from jail and the taint of supporting terror. He is able to laugh, but the pain never completely leaves him. His wounds may heal, he says, if the policemen who framed and tortured him are punished one day.

Competitive Conversion

The winds of hatred systematically manufactured against demonized communities have frequently scorched India. The large majority of these campaigns of hate target the populous Muslim community but, in the 1980s, the Sikhs were targeted, and from the turn of the century, violence has been mounted against the tiny Christian minority who peacefully inhabit most corners of this diverse land.

The attacks on Christians take mainly three forms. The first is of violent assaults on Christian priests, the rape of nuns, the destruction and desecration of churches and chapels, and the burning of the Bible. These have recurred with growing frenzy since 1997-98, when a priest was paraded naked in the Dumka district of Jharkhand, and nuns were raped in the Jhabua district of Madhya Pradesh and the Mayurbhanj district of Odisha.[146] In the same district, a priest was murdered in 1999. Churches were destroyed in the Dangs district in Gujarat in 1998. The situation was so severe that India's home minister, L. K. Advani, admitted in Parliament that there had been 400 attacks on Christian priests, nuns and churches between 1998 and 2000.[147]

These attacks continued unabated in the new century and spread to cities. Physical attacks on priests and churches have been reported from locations in Jharkhand, Madhya Pradesh, Karnataka, Tamil Nadu, Rajasthan, Kerala, Odisha, Maharashtra, Chhattisgarh, Andhra Pradesh, Uttar Pradesh and sadly, in the run-up to the state elections in early 2015, from the national capital. There is a common pattern, firstly of the surreptitious or the open burning down of Christian places of worship, and of armed mobs of Hindutva activists thrashing the priests, often in front of their families, sometimes proudly before the cameras of television channels, conveniently invited to broadcast the assault, accusing them of propagating a 'foreign' religion by fraud and insulting the Hindu faith, and demanding that they be permanently expelled. The police accompanied the mobs on occasion, but rarely restrained the attackers or registered complaints against them. Instead, at times, it arrested the priests.[148]

A second form of intimidation is when converts are themselves attacked. A people's tribunal convened by Angana Chatterji and Mihir Desai painstakingly tracked the frightening sequence of such attacks in the state of Odisha. Their long and chilling list included: in 1999, 157 Christian homes were set ablaze in Ranalai village, and three people suffered gunshot wounds; in 2003, seven women converts and a pastor were forcibly tonsured in Kilipal village, and a socio-economic boycott was imposed on them; fifteen homes were burnt down in 2005 in Gandhavati village, and so on.[149] The worst attacks happened in Jhabua, Madhya Pradesh, in 2004, and in Kandhamal, Odisha, in 2007-08, both of which I describe in some detail in later sections.

The third strategy for intimidation is the mobilizing of large masses for 're-conversion', ghar wapsi, ceremonies, mainly in tribal regions, in which thousands of alleged Christian converts are welcomed 'home' to Hinduism. Dilip Singh Judeo, the BJP leader who led the ghar wapsi campaign with vicious speeches goading violence against converts, claimed in 1999 that by then 165,000 persons had been reconverted.[150] But all such claims are highly exaggerated, because independent investigations confirm that the majority of those who are taken to these rallies are not converts to start with. Also, most tribal people were not Hindus in the first place, but animists. There has been a fresh resurgence of this form of intimidation since the ascendancy of the Modi-led Central government in 2014.

These attacks are justified by the RSS and its supporters as righteous expressions of mass popular resistance by an enraged Hindu majority against the allegedly anti-national machinations of Christian missionaries. They claim that these missionaries coerce and bribe hapless dispossessed tribal and Dalit people with their foreign-funded educational and health services into the 'foreign' Christian faith. At its most extravagant, the missionaries are depicted as instruments of the CIA and the Pope who are on a mission to evangelize all of India and reduce Hindus to a minority. Sangh propaganda graphically depicts this alleged clash of patriots with traitors in pamphlets, posters and, more recently, compact discs, through emotive images such as of the cross being triumphantly pierced by a trident, and dripping with blood, or comparing the destruction of churches with Ram's final assault on the demon Ravana.

These claims find a sympathetic echo in many people belonging to the middle class. Arun Shourie wrote a whole book about his anguish at this sinister 'harvesting of souls'.[151] And, as already noted, when there was international outrage following the burning alive of missionary Graham Staines—and his two small sons—who was working in hinterland Orissa with leprosy patients, the former prime minister A. B. Vajpayee responded with a call for a national debate on conversions. Even Congress governments in states like Himachal Pradesh thought it fit to bring in anti-conversion legislation.

In this clouded climate, prejudice refuses to be illuminated or chastened by voices of reason. In the first place, as John Dayal, journalist and human rights worker, argues in his impassioned book, *A Matter of Equity: Freedom of Faith in Secular India*, Christianity was not a British colonial import.[152] This is another falsehood propagated by the Sangh. India has always been uniquely welcoming of the world's diverse persecuted populations; and Christianity struck deep roots in the country one millennium before it gathered millions of followers in Europe. Although there is no evidence to confirm the legend that Thomas the apostle, a disciple of Jesus, himself preached the message of the Christian faith on Indian soil, it is historically confirmed that the Indian Christian community had established itself in India's southern peninsula by the second century AD.[153] Dayal celebrates this as one more contribution to the diversity of this 'wondrous and great' land of as many as 4,635 communities, only 3 per cent of which derive their names from their religious faith.

In many districts that I served, missionaries have reached love and hope to the most wretched of India—its leprosy patients, orphans, the disabled and the infirm—rarely with conversions, and in ways that few other Indians have even tried to achieve. But it is also true that missionary conversions of the past have tended to de-tribalize proud tribal people, in ways akin to the impact of the exemplary Hindu missionary organization, the Ramakrishna Mission. There have no doubt also been problems with the missionaries who acted as an adjunct of colonial rule, as Dayal himself admits.[154]

But Ram Puniyani points out that even after nearly 2,000 years since it first came to India; 200 years of British colonial rule; as well as the constitutional protection provided in free India of the right to pursue and propagate one's religious faith, the percentage of Christians was reported in the 1971 census to be a tiny 2.6 per cent of the Indian population.[155] Their share in the population fell to 2.3 per cent in 2011.[156] If numerous new souls were indeed being harvested, the ratio would not have so obviously dropped.

The orchestrated battery of assaults mounted on Christians over the past decade is actually calculated to reduce the entire diverse Christian population of India to fear and subjugation. Rich political harvests have ensued from this hate in all tribal regions of India and the focus of the campaign is now gradually shifting to cities. This new agenda of the Sangh was probably crafted because the objective of breaking the spirit of Muslims, to live with fear in ghettoes, has already been substantially achieved after the demolition of the Babri Masjid and the massacre in Gujarat in 2002. A new minority is to be now 'domesticated' into living with fear.

~

Although attacks on Christian priests, nuns and places of worship have occurred from time to time, one of the first major anti-Christian riots was one that occurred in the district of Jhabua, which is home to a large population of Bhils.[157] I spent the early years of my service as a sub-divisional magistrate and, later, as Collector in the 1980s in the neighbouring tribal district of Barwani. I could never then have foretold that this arid Bhil heartland in western Madhya Pradesh would yield, in 2004, a harvest of hate. For the first time in the history of the district, homes and properties, mainly belonging to tribal converts, were targeted and destroyed in many locations.

As I walked through the torched and looted homes in the city of Alirajpur, it brought back painful memories of the many riots that I have been witness to. Except that this time, the victims, the manufactured enemies, were new, and the winds of violence had traversed virgin territory, sweeping through a remote tribal region—inhabited by a proud and colourful people—which had never witnessed sectarian violence in its entire history. I wondered, then, how many new frontiers the warriors of hate would open in our land.

~

On a quiet Sunday evening on 11 January 2004, a nine-year-old girl was brutally raped and strangled in a public toilet within a church compound in the town of Jhabua.[158] Her bloodied and savaged little body was discovered the next morning. It did not take the organizations of the Sangh Parivar long to allege from the rooftops that the priests in the church had raped and killed the child. Calumnies were heaped on the church in meetings and rallies organized across the district. It was even alleged that churches are bastions not only of anti-national activities, but even of rape.[159]

The superintendent of police, Mayank Jain, responded with exemplary impartiality and professionalism. Within four days, he arrested a young man, Mahesh, who confessed to the crime. Jain was immediately transferred.

What the police investigation revealed was that Mahesh, who worked as a peon in an insurance office, lived close to the church. The little girl sold vegetables along with her twelve-year-old brother on a pavement outside the church. On the fateful evening, Mahesh bought vegetables from the children but said he needed to borrow money from the nuns in the church. It was on this pretext that he took the little girl into the church, where he allegedly raped and killed her.

The Sangh Parivar was furious with what they saw as the 'unseemly haste' of the police to solve the case. The following morning, 16 January, a sadhvi from Gujarat, Krishna Behen, arrived with a clutch of her women followers at Aamkhut, a predominantly Christian tribal village. There is an old church campus, where a white missionary ran an orphanage, dispensary and school hostel for nearly half a century. After her departure, the orphanage closed down but the school and dispensary continue.[160]

The sadhvi and her followers gathered together some of the non-Christian tribal residents of the village and reached the school, where a board examination was in progress. The sadhvi entered the classes and distributed incendiary pamphlets to the children, describing Christianity as an anti-national conspiracy to destroy the Hindu faith. She exhorted the Christian students to abandon Christianity, a religion which, she alleged, promotes rape and treachery. Her followers pulled off the crosses which the children were wearing around their necks and tore up their examination sheets. The teachers pleaded helplessly with their attackers, then finally abandoned the examination and shut the school down.

After the sadhvi was finally persuaded to leave with her followers, crowds gathered at the police outpost to register their complaint. As the head constable insisted on awaiting the orders of his seniors, the newly elected MLA from Alirajpur, Nagar Singh Chauhan, arrived with an enraged, armed mob. The local residents also brought out their weapons. Bullets and arrows flew, and vehicles were set on fire.

The sub-divisional magistrate rescued the MLA and took him in his jeep to Alirajpur. There the politico gathered a large mob, as his followers exhorted revenge against the Christians on loudspeakers mounted on jeeps. The mobs then looted and burnt down a number of Christian homes, mainly owned by government servants.

The subsequent actions of the police followed the pattern usually seen in anti-Muslim communal violence. Large numbers of Christian men, and even some women, including priests, were rounded up. The Hindu mob leaders, including the MLA who was a history-sheeter, walked free. The minorities were just beginning to learn the lessons of how to live with fear in an openly partisan state.

~

Of a total population of close to 1,200,000, as many as 85 per cent of people in Jhabua belong to tribes. The church which was vandalized was established more than a century ago, but the percentage of Christians in the district is not more than 4 per cent.[161] The manufacture of fear and hatred against this tiny minority is the result of long years of effort by several front organizations of the Sangh Parivar, especially Seva Bharati. Their efforts were further galvanized a few years earlier with the massive mobilization and recruitment of educated tribal youth as RSS workers in virtually every village. They were drawn mainly from the Bhagats, tribal families converted by the All World Gayatri Parivar over the past two decades to vegetarianism and abstinence. The Bhagats had adopted Hindu gods and forms of worship, like the havan.[162]

In a massive mobilization, tens of thousands of pictures of Hanuman were distributed in every tribal home, and he was re-invented as a tribal king. Triangular saffron flags were hoisted in hutments in every remote tribal hamlet. Single-teacher Ekal Vidyalayas were set up by the Seva Bharati, and the local teachers indoctrinated into the ideology of the Sangh Parivar through a series of camps.

Typically, both the Congress and the wide network of local 'secular' NGOs watched on helplessly. Even more typically, Congress leaders belatedly tried to join the bandwagon. As the Sangh Parivar organized huge Ganesh celebrations, in which thousands of tribal people participated, local Congress leaders responded by establishing their own rival Ganesh festivals!

In a wayside market, populated mainly by tribals and discordantly festooned with aggressive saffron banners and flags, we stopped for tea at a small stall. The owner had pasted on his window a slogan very different from his neighbours:

Har dharam ka gulistan
Hai Hindustan hamara

(Our India is a garden
In which every religion flourishes)

Amidst the swirling, steadily building storm of hate that was sweeping this remote tribal outpost, I wanted to hold the tea-stall owner in an embrace.

~

The gravest communal attack mounted on Christians happened one terrifying Christmas in 2007, against tribal and Dalit Christians who inhabited the second-poorest district of Odisha, Kandhamal. That year, targeted violence which had long been smouldering exploded, and continued to rage for another full year. During this time, 600 villages were ransacked, 5,600 houses were looted and burnt, 54,000 persons rendered homeless, 295 churches and places of worship destroyed, and thirteen schools, colleges and orphanages were damaged. The official death toll was thirty-nine although, unofficially, the figure is claimed to be closer to one hundred. Thirty thousand people were forced to live in relief camps, and it is estimated that nearly half are still unable to return home.[163]

Four years later, many of the survivors gathered in Bhubaneshwar to remember and to mourn. In an exhibition organized by Anhad, some of the vandalized remains of churches and homes were displayed. In one corner, blurred, blown-up, passport-sized pictures of men and women who had been killed were pasted on bamboo sticks. Many stood there and wept quietly. The occasion was the release of the report published by the National People's Tribunal on Kandhamal, aptly titled, 'Waiting for Justice'. The tribunal was chaired by Justice A. P. Shah, and included among its members Syeda Hameed, Ruth Manorama, Mahesh Bhatt, Vinod Raina, Vrinda Grover, Miloon Kothari, P. S. Krishnan and Sukumar Muralidharan. I, too, was a member.

Although the states of Odisha and Gujarat are located at the furthest eastern and western corners of India the violence—of 2007-08 in Odisha targeting Christians, and of 2002 in Gujarat targeting Muslims—had many striking and deeply troubling similarities. Each was characterized by a long build-up of hatred against religious minorities; there was evidence of systematic advance preparation; state authorities were openly complicit in enabling the violence to persist for weeks and months; the attacks were unusually brutal, especially when targeting women; thousands were displaced and discouraged from returning to their homes and faced organized social and economic boycott. And in both, compensation was tight-fisted and justice systematically subverted.

There was evidence, in both Gujarat and Odisha, of systematic planning and organization prior to and during the attacks, as though perpetrators were only waiting for a flashpoint to let loose. These were not spontaneous outbursts of mass anger; they were planned attacks cynically facilitated and criminally abetted by the administration in the two states. The report on Kandhamal published by the tribunal noted: 'Victim-survivors testimonials repeatedly referred to the perpetrators wearing red head bands, carrying numerous weapons such as axes, daggers, swords, guns, crowbars, pickaxes, lathis, bows and arrows, lighted torches, bombs, petrol and kerosene barrels, trishuls, tangia, pharsa bhujali and bars.'[164] They could have been speaking of Gujarat where I heard literally hundreds of similar testimonials.

One survivor, Keshamati, recalled: 'It is "Sahukars" from the towns of different parts of Kandhamal who took the leadership in creating the violence, supplying weapons, arms and explosives like petrol and diesel to some of our people.'[165] Another added, 'The rioters brought trucks from other villages and they carried away valuables from our villages.'[166] Many spoke of preparatory meetings in villages the night prior to attacks.

In Odisha, like in Gujarat, attacks were marked by exceptional cruelty. Kanaka Nayak recalled the horrific slaughter of her husband when he refused to reconvert to Hinduism. 'They spat on him and started to sing and dance around him; they paraded him, and dragged him. They told him "you sing your songs and let Jesus come and save you". And they started attacking and cut his body into three pieces.'[167] Many women were attacked. Christodas recounts, 'When we were fleeing to the relief camp, my wife was attacked with a sword by a violent mob...I saw her palms being cut; she had a cut on her skull and her backbone.'[168] An orphanage was destroyed. While the warden's body was being set on fire, special care was taken to ensure that the lower parts were completely burnt to destroy all evidence of gangrape.[169]

Women who suffered sexual violence in both massacres continued to live with the twin agonies inflicted on them by memory and shame. One said in confidence to the tribunal, 'The attackers removed their mask before they raped me. Earlier, they would respect me. I was shocked that they took revenge on me for my uncle's refusal not to convert to Hinduism...Lots of things have changed in my life after that incident. I have been in hiding. I am traumatised, sad, depressed and struggling. I feel ashamed. I am unable to forget about the incident and carry on with life. But I feel I should be strong to get justice.'[170]

Another surprisingly common feature in the two mass slaughters was the role played by women's organizations such as the Durga Vahini. The tribunal records evidence of the mass mobilization of women who formed violent mobs and perpetrated attacks.

The two massacres were also linked by the state's open support of the violence. The National Campaign on Dalit Human Rights reported: 'The local government by and large not only stood by and silently watched, as the horrendous events were unfolding, but in several ways, according to the eye-witnesses, facilitated the gangs indulging destruction of human life and valuable property. What followed by way of administrative action—controlling the situation, relief measures for the afflicted and punishing the guilty—could only be described as formal—ritual motions to satisfy the letter of the law.'[171]

Survivor Premashila testified to the tribunal, 'The police and the district administration were aware of strategies of the rioters before the incident took place, because these rioters were organising meetings, rallies in the presence of the police and district administration in many places.' Father Kullu described their role in the destruction of the Madhupur Church: '…in front of the police and the deputed magistrate the rioters destroyed, burnt and ransacked everything whatever they could in two hours. Many valuables were stolen. They completely destroyed the church, priest residence, hostels, convent, dispensary and Maria grottos.'[172]

In both carnages, people were attacked because of their adherence to 'foreign religions', in one case Islam and the other Christianity. The tribunal noted, 'Thousands of Christians being chased and herded in groups into Hindu temples and forced to undergo "reconversion" ceremonies with their heads tonsured. They were made to drink cow-dung water as a mark of "purification" and some of them forced to burn bibles or damage churches to prove that they had forsaken the Christian faith. The "reconverted" Christians were forced to sign "voluntary declarations" stating that they were becoming Hindus voluntarily—a condition required by the anti-conversion law in Orissa.'[173]

VHP leader Pravin Togadia enjoyed free passage across the state in the build-up to the protracted violence. He thundered, 'There is no place for Christians. If Christians don't become Hindus, they have to go. We don't care where they go. They must leave Orissa.'[174] The purpose of the violence was to punish and terrorize those Dalits who had converted to Christianity a few generations earlier.

In the wake of the violence, as tens of thousands were driven out of their homes, the Odisha government established elementary relief camps which were incompatible with human dignity; overcrowded, under-served and particularly insensitive to women and children. The National People's Tribunal on Kandhamal recorded: 'A common living space for both men and women in the relief camps, some places having just two bathrooms without roofs for 5000 people and no toilets facilities...insufficient or no place to sleep, difficulties in staying and also no privacy for women. Inadequate sanitary supplies caused women difficulties during their menstruation.' In addition, 'women were reportedly given 30 minutes to go out of the relief camps for toilet, and if they failed to return within the stipulated time, they were reportedly punished by the CRPF personnel who were guarding the camps'.[175]

Another similarity between the two carnages is that even long after the violence finally abated, the persons evicted from their homes were not welcomed back. In order to return, stringent and humiliating conditions were laid down. In Gujarat, Muslims could not pursue legal recourse against their tormentors and had to live separately from Hindus, in perpetual economic and cultural subordination. In Odisha, the requirement was a 'reconversion' to Hinduism—even though many were animists and not of the Hindu faith in the first place. As Deobhanja testified, 'We are not allowed to enter into our native village and stay there in our patta land, unless we embrace Hinduism. We have no access to forest to get fire wood and minor forest produce for daily use and drinking water, tube wells and wells for water. We are socially boycotted by them.'[176] If they still chose to return, they faced social and economic boycott, and the constant possibility of recurrent attacks.

The objective of such boycott in both states was to ensure that the victims were damaged not just during the attacks, but were actively prevented from rebuilding their livelihoods, and therefore continued to languish in extreme poverty. This aim was fulfilled substantially in Gujarat, but was further damaging in Kandhamal, where the victims were in extreme poverty to start with. As the tribunal noted, more than half the victim-survivor population worked as daily wage labourers, which made them dependent on other communities to employ them. Following the violence in Kandhamal, and the subsequent and ongoing socio-economic boycott, many of them were compelled to migrate to other parts of the state and country.[177]

The small farmers were the next largest group targeted during the violence. Some lost their land to forced migration; others their livestock and their stocks of fertilizer. Even small traders were devastated. A woman testified that she lost her business of selling dry fish etcetera, and her husband was no longer appointed as the ration seller at the gram panchayat because the Hindus refused to buy things from him.[178]

In this climate of organized social boycott, efforts of survivors were further hampered by the meagre and reluctant reparations offered by the state. In Odisha, as in Gujarat, owners of fully damaged homes were paid a maximum of just ₹50,000, even though the cost of damaged property sometimes ran into several lakhs. Even these were routinely undervalued. The state had no standard procedures for assessment and appeal. There was also no programme to restore damaged livelihoods. Further, no support was given to damaged schools, hostels, clinics, hospitals and orphanages.

The grimmest parallel between the two carnages was in the systematic subversion of justice. Testimonies presented before the tribunal repeatedly stated that the police refused to register FIRs. The tribunal was informed that, of the 3,232 complaints filed by victims, only 832 were actually registered by the police. Between seventy-five and 123 people were killed in the violence, yet only twenty-six murder cases were registered as of February 2010.[179] For instance, Sister Meena was first dissuaded by the police from registering an FIR with regard to the gangrape and sexual assault on her, and when she insisted, she was prevented from writing details of the crime including the complicity of certain police officials.[180] Many spoke to the tribunal of the failure of the police to arrest perpetrators, even though they were named in the complaints. They also clarified that the police's refusal to take action against the perpetrators was a result of the police actively protecting the perpetrators. They were harassed through the lodging of false and baseless allegations against them, or threatened that they would be arrested on false charges if they demanded accountability and continued pursuing justice.

The report published by Multiple Action Research Group (MARG) noted that the police, which was itself complicit in the violence through myriad acts of omission and commission, had been conducting the investigations.[181] Investigations were conducted in a biased and shoddy manner. Some spoke to the tribunal of how they were being forced to live in hiding while pursuing the cases in courts. Others spoke about their inability to testify in court if they were not given adequate protection. Some of them spoke about how they had complained to the judge and the police about the threats and intimidation, yet had not received any assistance.

In Kandhamal, as in Gujarat, brutal violence against religious minorities was enabled primarily by communal mobilization and a complicit state, and survivors were denied reparations and justice by sustained social boycott and bias within state institutions as well as the judiciary. This is the story of other massacres as well, including that of Sikhs in Delhi in 1984.

~

Free India was born in a tumult of religious hatred. This fact, and that this country is home to followers of almost every major world religion, persuaded members of the Constituent Assembly to exercise great care to protect the freedom of religious belief in India's Constitution. After extended debate, it decided that this freedom should not just be to practise and profess one's faith, but also to propagate it. K. M. Munshi declared that 'under freedom of speech which the Constitution guarantees, it will be open to any religious community to persuade other people to join their faith'.[182]

However, Hindu nationalist organizations have never reconciled to this fundamental guarantee of the Constitution. They resist it because they believe that the Hindu majority is being persecuted in 'their own country', and enduring incursions by its minorities.

The premise of the campaign to reconvert those who left Hinduism for Christianity and Islam—described as ghar wapsi or homecoming—is that the Hindu faith is home, and conversions to 'foreign' religions constitute betrayals. I recall that when Gandhi was asked if he agreed that only Indian faiths should have place in India, he replied affirmatively. Indian faiths, he explained, such as Hinduism, Islam and Christianity.

In tribal regions in particular, propaganda has long been mounted against the 'menace' of Christian conversions. The facts don't bear out claims of mass conversions. Christians constituted 2.5 per cent of India's population in 1981, and 2.3 in 1991, 2001 and 2011.[183] If large-scale conversions were indeed occurring, their numbers would have swelled. But when have hate propagandists been deterred by truth? This sustained misinformation has resulted in profound and sometimes violent schisms between Christian and other tribal people, and rich electoral harvests for the BJP.

The contention put forth by the propagandists is that Hinduism is denied a level playing field for conversions because enormous funds coming in from overseas support the work of Christian missionaries. But the truth is that, today, there is no shortage of Indian diaspora who fund the work of Hindu nationalists in tribal India. A massive network of educational institutions, sponsored by the RSS family, has grown in central India, and the Northeast is fast being penetrated too. However, in the competition between proselytizers and evangelists, few can match the selfless quality of educational and health services which Christian missionaries offer, even to the most despised and excluded sections of society, such as the leprosy-stricken. At the same time, there is no doubt that some fundamentalist Christian evangelists do promote hatred of both tribal faiths and Hinduism. Christian fundamentalism is also a problem for non-Christian minorities in Christian-majority Mizoram.

An even greater problem is the ritualized and religiously sanctioned inequality of caste inherent to the Hindu faith, which renders egalitarian faiths like Islam, Christianity and Buddhism attractive to those enduring caste violence and discrimination at the lowest rungs of the Hindu social hierarchy. T. T. Krishnamachari, member of the Constituent Assembly, noted that conversion 'depends on the way certain religionists and certain communities treat their less fortunate brethren'.[184] The large majority of converts to egalitarian faiths are, not surprisingly, from the lowest Hindu castes, who are moved by the hope that they will achieve greater social dignity and gain opportunities to study and escape the socially humiliating livelihoods forced upon them by caste compulsions. It is their ongoing, collective tragedy that even Islam and Christianity in India have absorbed ideas of caste, therefore their journey to social equality continues to be hamstrung by old barriers.

But the barriers remain highest in traditional Hinduism. A story is told of the Shankaracharya of Puri who was presiding over a reconversion programme and was asked by a pesky journalist, 'Now that you have welcomed them back into the Hindu faith, I am sure you will welcome them into your temples?' The Shankaracharya clarified that the converts would be allowed only to enter separate temples, and marry specifically within their castes or tribes.

The anxieties that the Hindu fold will lose its lower castes and the tribes to Christianity and Islam led legislatures in eight states to pass laws to regulate religious conversions—Madhya Pradesh, Odisha, Arunachal Pradesh, Tamil Nadu, Gujarat, Chhattisgarh and Rajasthan. And now that the BJP is installed with a majority in Parliament, the clamour is rising for a national anti-conversion law. These laws criminalize religious conversions by what is described as force, inducement or fraud. The peril is that these terms can be expansively interpreted. Force could, for instance, include the threat of divine retribution; fraud, the promise of rewards in an afterlife; and, inducement, free services in school or hospital. Impoverished new converts and priests have actually been jailed under these clauses, and punishment can extend from three to five years in jail. Prior permission of the district magistrate is also required in some states; and while applications for conversion out of Hinduism are withheld for years, they are promptly sanctioned for conversions into Hinduism.

Criminalizing religious faith carries grave dangers, both for religious freedoms and minorities, especially in the aggressively majoritarian climate which prevails today. It can bludgeon minorities into fear and submission in the way blasphemy laws have done in Pakistan. It can also result in the cynical manipulation of very poor people by communal formations, such as the Bengali Muslims in Agra who were asked to choose between deportation and ration cards—which are proxies of citizenship certification—and the job reservations offered as inducement to Christian and Muslim Dalits in Kerala.

In this divisive competition for the religious allegiance of India's poorest and most vulnerable people it is important to recall the gentle counsel of one of the world's tallest public figures, the Dalai Lama. 'It does not matter which God you worship,' he declares, 'or even if you worship no God. What is important is to be a compassionate human being.'

Remembering and Forgetting 1984

On 31 October 2014, the thirtieth anniversary passed by—almost unnoticed—of the days when Delhi was engulfed in the bloodiest frenzy of communal slaughter since the Partition riots of 1947, extinguishing over 3,000 lives. Ganga Kaur, who lost her husband, brother-in-law and four nephews in the carnage sighs, 'Every time

November returns, we remember. This history will only die with us.' Yet 'the official memory of 1984 is a blank, erased slate', rages journalist Nilanjana Roy, 'wiped tapes where no voices speak...commission reports that nobody was to blame, nobody would be blamed'.[186] 'The important thing,' writer Pradip Krishen adds, 'surely, is to remember'; it is immoral to just 'move on', 'to gloss over the terror and coordinated cruelty'.[187] In her personal battle against our collective forgetting, Gauri Gill has compiled a luminous, heart-breaking booklet of her photographs of the widows' colony in Tilak Vihar, Delhi, with testimonies, narratives and poetry.[188]

We gathered in Delhi to collectively remember the anti-Sikh pogrom of 1984, as ageing widows wept, with dignity but with fury. The spectacular failures of the country's criminal justice system to prosecute the leaders of the carnage has left their wounds raw and unhealed, even after decades. Many courageously and tenaciously offered to become witnesses in open court, but none of the leaders of the massacre were punished. Darshan Kaur, who testified against Congress leader Hari Krishan Lal Bhagat, recalls being offered ₹2,500,000 to retract her statement in court. She refused with the words, 'Bring back one of the twelve family members I have lost and I will consider your offer.'[189]

Their unassuaged wrath stems also from the organized nature of the massacre that felled their loved ones. Roy recalls, 'They had time to create their organised massacre. Time to buy chalk [to mark Sikh homes], to cyclostyle voters' lists, to organise the necessary supplies...The end product of this organisation, this careful, unspontaneous massacre, was bodies and blood and then, decades of amnesia and an unspooling list of things undone. FIRs that the police had not filed. Cases against politicians that never went through the courts. Eyewitness accounts blanked out and erased.'[190]

Gauri's little book contains numerous testimonies of the widows and their children. Darshan Kaur recounts, 'I have seen nothing of life. I have only cried. But still, you may have noticed, none of us is a beggar. I trekked 35 kilometres to work every day, but I have not begged.'[191] Nothing had prepared these mostly unlettered working-class women to face the world alone. But they fought valiantly, often heroically, to raise their children and grandchildren, battling profound loss, memory and penury. Gopi Kaur was given a job as a water woman in Kailash Nagar. But 'I never knew how to take a bus, had never stepped out of the house...I would first be dropped by my brother, then my son. In the bus I would go crazy, crying right up until Darya Ganj.'[192]

Pappi Kaur was only fifteen when eleven members of her family were killed, and she hid under a heap of corpses to escape the rampaging mobs. Today she makes a living making electrical sockets. Manjit was just a month old when his father, grandfather and three uncles were all burned to death. His mother died of cancer, and he dropped out of school to work as a driver. Auto-rickshaw driver Gurdayal says, 'My father and two brothers were both killed in the '84 riots, and here I am, uneducated, trying my best to make ends meet.'[193]

Many of their children, especially sons, now middle-aged men, could not cope with gruesome memories of the brutal ways their fathers were killed, and fell prey to mental illness and drug addiction. Bhaggi Kaur who lost her husband in 1984, now mourns her son who took an overdose of painkillers eight years earlier. The widows lamented, 'Our lives lie in ruins, as do those of our children. If we can see any hope in the far distance, it is that maybe our grandchildren will one day be able to see a little happiness.'[194]

Few could believe that the great sprawling metropolis of Delhi in free India was capable of such unbounded cruelty. Artist Shuddhabrata Sengupta is not alone when he says he has never forgiven this city.[195]

And yet, alongside this, what is often forgotten is that 1984 witnessed not just the lowest depths of cruelty to which this city has fallen, it also marked its finest moment of collective compassion. Students, homemakers, teachers, journalists, lawyers, doctors and many others joined hands to constitute the Nagrik Ekta Manch, which saved many lives, ran relief camps, offered empathy and healing to bereaved widows and children, helped file police complaints, testified and compiled citizens' fact-finding reports, formed peace committees and fought hatred in the streets and in their homes.

Sengupta was a schoolboy of sixteen when he saw Sikh men being burnt alive; he recalls that he suddenly grew into a man. He volunteered for many months with traumatized children. Uma Chakravarti and Nandita Haksar prepared what remains the most truthful, unflinching account of this shameful, organized massacre.[196] Teachers like Mita Bose and homemakers like Jaya Shrivastava and Lalita Ramdas stepped out of their homes and colleges to run relief camps and document the massacre. They recall running from house to house, seeking donations of clothes and medicines. Some people opened their purses, other slammed the doors, declaring, 'They deserved this.'

It was Delhi's deliberate amnesia and indifference to the lives mangled by that great frenzy of collective hate which paved the way for other massacres in other cities. If hope still endures, it is only because of the wonderful collective compassion which this city demonstrated twice, once to offer homes and solace to survivors of the Partition, and once for those broken by the 1984 carnage. Maybe if we find that compassion again, we can rediscover the lost soul of this uncaring city.

~

India witnessed two towering calamities in 1984. Both were human-made, and both were marked by unconscionable betrayals by the state. A month after the slaughter of 3,000 Sikhs in the worst single episode of targeted communal violence in Delhi, a poisonous gas leak from a Bhopal factory into a sleeping city killed, according to one official estimate, 15,000 people over the years, and left a bitter legacy of chronic ailments among half a million people.

Just as the pogrom against Sikhs in 1984 was cynically created, the casualties in Bhopal arose from a different source of human malfeasance: the criminally careless leakage of close to 26 million tonnes of the highly poisonous gas, methyl isocyanate (MIC), from a pesticide factory owned by Union Carbide.

The high numbers of fatalities in both these calamities could have been averted had governments acted fairly and promptly. A number of commissions and committees have confirmed that state functionaries became willing accomplices in the pogrom. In Bhopal, the state administration was initially largely absent, bent instead on saving their own lives. As public health experts Jayaprakash and Sathyamala recount, Union Carbide officials kept insisting that MIC was only an irritant and not lethal, and with the concurrence of state officials opposed the administration of sodium thiosulphate, which was the only known antidote to cyanide poisoning, and which if applied could have saved many lives and prevented the aggravation of injuries.[197]

States too failed dismally, over the decades which followed, to provide assistance to the survivors to heal and rebuild their lives. The riot survivors were initially granted a small monetary 'compensation', which was enhanced later by court interventions. But governments did too little to help survivors rebuild their livelihoods, and even less to mitigate the grave psycho-social burdens which the survivors—especially widows and young children—carried of the massacre.

The Bhopal story is even more dismal. Jayaprakash and Sathyamala record that while every attempt was made to officially underplay the magnitude of the disaster, very little effort was made to provide proper medical care to the victims or to ensure that adequate compensation was paid to them, based on the actual degree of injury suffered. The shocking conclusion of an earlier report—Against All Odds—by independent public health experts was that 'the Directorate of Claims, Bhopal, has "defined" away the injuries of more than 90% of the victims as "no injury" or "temporary injury".'[198]

Interventions by courts provided some limited succour to survivors in both instances. After prolonged litigation, the Supreme Court held that the survivors of the anti-Sikh carnage should be compensated on the same norms as the Motor Vehicles Act, which led to a steep increase in compensation. In Bhopal, the Supreme Court directed that independent epidemiological surveillance systems of gas victims be established to determine compensation levels and health responses. But the government and Indian Council for Medical Research (ICMR) made little effort over the years to identify all gas victims, monitor their health status or provide them adequate care.

The court also ordered in Bhopal that lifelong health cards be given to all, but thirty years after the disaster, less than 10 per cent have such cards, and most are denied health services for their ever-mounting range of ailments. ICMR took twenty years to admit that it should have administered sodium thiosulphate for treatment of those exposed to MIC, but as a Medico-Friends Circle report points out, none are held accountable for the enormous criminal failure to administer this known therapy to most of the victims, which could have limited deaths and injuries.[199]

The failures of criminal justice to hold those responsible for both these human-made cataclysms is perhaps even more unconscionable. Despite valiant battles against threats and impoverishment, widows of 1984 fought epic battles for legal justice, yet three decades later not a single prominent leader who openly led the mobs of 1984 has been punished; the small numbers convicted were only foot soldiers. Likewise, Indian courts have freed Union Carbide officials from any criminal liability for the crimes of what is the world's largest industrial disaster. Their criminal liability was erased in favour of the civil liability resulting in monetary compensations, and that too at a tiny fraction of what would have been payable had the dead been American citizens. As a result, the suffering of these survivors is unmitigated even with the passage of so many years.

These are the profound multiple miscarriages of justice and reparations for the survivors of both these human-made disasters of three decades past. They remain a permanent dishonour to India's democracy, governance and legal systems.

A Secret Execution

Sometimes the virulence and the insistence of middle-class prejudice can only be appeased with a hanging. The secret execution of terror-accused Afzal Guru on 9 February 2013 in Tihar Jail, Delhi, was one such moment. The Supreme Court almost admitted as much when it had earlier affirmed that 'the collective conscience of the society' would only be satisfied by awarding the death penalty to a man charged with conspiring to destroy India's Parliament. I believe that the only legitimate reason for a court to award any punishment should be the fair application of the law to the evidence placed before it, not the appeasement of alleged majoritarian public opinion.

As a consequence of this pandering, a man in his early forties was marched to the gallows. Bidding a final farewell to his jailors—companions of nearly a decade—he walked calmly, without slogans or calls of recrimination. He was denied the opportunity to meet his wife and teenaged son one last time before he died. Many in the country celebrated his hanging as fitting—but delayed—justice. Others like me were troubled that the man's life had been taken away in their names even though they were not convinced that true justice had been done to him.

Afzal Guru was charged with criminal conspiracy against the state. He was accused of abetting a terrorist attack on India's Parliament on 13 December 2001. He made a written confession of his crime to the police but later retracted it, claiming that he had signed it under duress—he was being subjected to extreme torture; his brother had been placed under detention and his family threatened and harassed; and he had no legal counsel at that time.

The hanging of Afzal Guru raises a thicket of debates—ethical, legal and political—about justice, law, democracy, capital punishment, and a strong state. What is the quality of true justice? Is it enough for it to be lawful, fair and dispassionate, or must it also be tempered with mercy?

For those of us convinced that India should join more than 150 countries of the world today which have abolished the death penalty, Guru's execution only confirms many anxieties about empowering the state to punish those it marks as guilty with death. The first of these worries relates to the possibilities of judicial error. It is true that courts at three levels, including India's Supreme Court, confirmed Afzal Guru's conviction. But doubts about the quality of evidence have also been raised by some of the country's keenest legal minds. The application of terror laws dilutes the standards of evidence required for conviction, and both the trial court and the High Court relied on custodial confessions to police officers in confirming Guru's guilt.

I cannot claim with certainty that the sentence against Guru was unjust. But, equally, I cannot claim with certainty that it was just. Two successive Presidents held back from confirming his death sentence. The death penalty has a finality which cannot be humanly reversed or corrected and its application, in a case where legitimate and strong doubts persist, is a profound ethical problem.

The death penalty also unfairly targets people who are too poor or socially disadvantaged to access high-quality legal representation. It is not surprising that of the thirteen people currently on death row in India, eleven were represented by legal-aid lawyers. It should not be matter of surprise that Justice Krishna Iyer observed that 'capital sentence perhaps has a class bias and colour bar'.[179] Afzal Guru lacked effective legal counsel in the trial court, and this damaged his case irretrievably by the time it journeyed to the higher courts.

Another argument for abolishing the death penalty is the belief that every human being, even those charged with the gravest crimes, should have the chance to reform. By all accounts, Guru was an exemplary prisoner; courteous, considerate and disciplined. In his interviews, he admitted to being drawn in his youth to militancy, but was soon disillusioned and surrendered. The dignity with which he went to his death also shamed a celebrating nation.

The most distressing failure of official compassion and public decency was in denying Afzal Guru's wife and teenaged son the chance to meet him for the last time before his execution. In an interview to *Caravan* in 2006, Guru said, 'This year is the tenth anniversary of our wedding. Over half that period I spent in jail. And prior to that, many a times I was detained and tortured by Indian security forces in Kashmir. Tabassum witnessed both my physical and mental wounds...She gave me hope to live. We did not have a day of peaceful living. It is the story of many Kashmiri couples. Constant fear is the dominant feeling in all Kashmiri households...We were so happy when a child was born. We named our son after the legendary poet Mirza Ghalib. We had a dream to see our son, Ghalib, grow up. I could spend very little time with him. After his second birthday, I was implicated in the case.'[200]

His wife and son were informed about Guru's execution by a letter which reached them after he had been hanged. Jail officials said that he was calm when he was led to the gallows, but asked for a pen and paper to write a final letter to his family. In this letter which he left behind, he wrote, 'I am about to be hanged. Now, near the gallows. I want to tell you that I was not given time to write a proper letter. I am thankful that Allah chose me for this sacrifice. And please, take care of Tabassum and Ghalib.'[201]

The haste and secrecy of the execution also unconscionably denied him his last available legal resource, affirmed by the Supreme Court in the Kehar Singh case, to seek judicial review of the rejection of his mercy petition.[202] The long delay in disposing his mercy petition was strong grounds for judicial consideration of the possible commutation of his sentence to life imprisonment. On the day he was hung, Afzal Guru had completed eleven years, one month and seventeen days in jail, less than three years short of a life term.

The defence of the Congress-led UPA government for this secret hanging, that it would trigger violence in the Kashmir Valley, is untenable. Not just his hanging, but the way he was executed, will long scar the souls of young Kashmiris. After Guru's hanging, many other executions were stayed precisely by giving one final remedy to the victim after the President rejected the clemency petition, but this legal right was deliberately withheld from Guru. Assassins of Indira Gandhi and Rajiv Gandhi accessed full legal remedies available under the law of the land before their final hanging, and were allowed to meet their kin before their deaths, although the dangers of violent unrest by masses of their supporters were no less compelling at that time. A self-assured democracy should be able to find ways to prevent and control violence without sacrificing elementary public compassion. And, indeed, rights under the law which could have saved a life.

Many middle-class Indians believe that the belated execution signalled a strong and decisive state, especially to the 'neighbouring country'. One glance at the daily reality of this neighbouring country will reflect the brutalizing wages of years of 'decisive' politics of militarism and public vengeance. It is not a weak, but a stable, mature and confident democracy which can display compassion even to those whom it believes have most wronged the country.

THE IMPERATIVE FOR PUBLIC COMPASSION

How Will India Change?

Elie Wiesel, Holocaust survivor and a peace worker who lost both his parents and sister in Auschwitz, reminds us that, 'The opposite of love is not hate. The opposite of love is indifference.'[1] And while I am dismayed by reports of Wiesel's fierce opposition to Palestine, it is to these luminous words that I turn while opening this last segment of my book, for an initial, tentative exploration of the possibilities of love, empathy and public compassion being fashioned into instruments of social and political resistance, justice and, indeed, social transformation.

I will reflect briefly on whether love—variously understood as empathy, compassion, caring, solidarity, fraternity, forgiveness and non-violence—contains within it the capacity to dismantle indifference and prejudice. I will try to acknowledge the possibilities, but also the limits to empathy. I will talk of non-violence as resistance, and also of unmapped pathways we can embark upon to claim a more just and caring state, and a more just and humane society. I will also suggest that justice and empathy are closely intertwined, through the mediation of solidarity and fraternity (and because the word fraternity literally refers to a brotherhood, I will speak equally of sisterhood).

In the strange new 'social common sense' cultivated for our times in new India, it is the rich and the privileged who are being led to feel oppressed and short-changed by the poor, rather than the other way round. The dominant narrative is: 'We work hard and earn an honest living, and then we are taxed to supply freebies to the undeserving poor, rather than encouraging them to work hard and pull themselves up by their own efforts.' Likewise, it is the religious majority which feels persecuted by the minority, rather than the reverse: 'Cynical political parties cultivate religious minorities as "vote-banks", and in return they are soft on terror, the mafia, their regressive clerics, religious conversions by fraud and bribery, and on their proclivity to breed large families.' The Preamble to India's Constitution identifies four pillars of constitutional values: liberty, equality, justice and fraternity. Each have been compromised in many ways in India's journey as a republic, but what is often least acknowledged in the dangerous fraying of our fraternity.

~

Amartya Sen, in *The Idea of Justice*, makes an important linkage between human empathy—combined with reason and the love of freedom—and the pursuit of justice. 'We could have been creatures incapable of sympathy,' he says, 'unmoved by the pain and humiliation of others, uncaring of freedom, and—no less significant—unable to reason, argue, disagree and concur. The strong presence of these features in human lives...does indicate that the general pursuit of justice might be hard to eradicate in human society, even though we go about that pursuit in different ways.'[2] The existence of empathy in human nature provides a clue to why, even though injustice has been a feature of all human societies throughout history, every human society has also seen stirrings for greater justice.

Closely related to the idea of empathy is that of compassion. The Dalai Lama—one of the living men in the world I most admire—often stresses the highest value of being a compassionate human being, one who is moved by the suffering of others.

I am most drawn to the idea of what I describe as *egalitarian* compassion, because it does not place the giver on a pedestal above the receiver. The idea is that of two human beings, each equal in dignity and worth, but one in difficult circumstances, to whom the other reaches out with care and—importantly—with respect. Compassion is constructed through feeling the pain of the other as one's own. The related idea of empathy involves both the cognitive act of imagination, of understanding the feelings of another human being; and the emotional, of actually experiencing the feelings of another.

Ideas of love, compassion, empathy and justice recur in most ethical systems, both religious and secular, in diverse language but often with common meanings. Sometimes an explicit linkage is also made, in the way Amartya Sen does, between empathy and justice. Socrates was once asked how long injustice would continue in the world. He replied that it would last as long as those who do not suffer injustice themselves do not feel the same pain and the same humiliation as those who actually endure injustice. In so doing, he underlines the importance of solidarity in struggles for justice. In the Hindu tradition, seeking justice is deemed essential to dharma—a comprehensive idea that includes duty and morality—although this same dharma also prescribes ritual injustice to persons deemed to be of the lower castes and gender, and for this it is a deeply flawed civilizational idea. Liberation theology nurtures the radical potential of Christ's great compassion. In Muslim teachings, it is set down that 'when injustice is law, resistance is duty'. Prophet Mohammed taught that the highest ethical duty of every human being who observes injustice is to resist it. At the very least, he enjoined, when you observe injustice, feel badly in your heart—which is nothing but empathy. The next higher level of duty is to respond not just from the heart but also the mouth, which means speaking out against injustice. The highest duty is to respond with one's hands, to act against that injustice.

But, before I proceed, I must acknowledge a major point of departure from the belief systems of my own past. Wherever I saw inequality, injustice and suffering, I looked for ways to make the democratic state more accountable and effective in correcting these social, economic and political wrongs. Caste and gender oppression needed better, stronger laws and policies for reversal, as did debt bondage, discrimination against minorities, child labour and the denial of education to children, the exploitation of workers, the crisis in farming, displacement, housing shortages, and corrupt governance.

I therefore worked for and celebrated the advancement of the regime of rights legislations, beginning with the right to information as well as the rights to education, wage-work, forest lands and food. I was privileged to be part of both the public campaigns and the actual writing of these laws. To end the injustice of communal pogroms, I sought and helped write a law which makes the dereliction of duty by public officials in preventing and controlling communal violence a criminal offence. This was a law which the out-going UPA government baulked in passing. Most of my work through all my adult life has been to strive in many different capacities for changes in state laws, policies, programmes, processes and institutions, as well as their implementation. I have sought to advance the rights and dignity of oppressed people through advancing the idea and practice of the good state.

Friends have long argued with me that I place too much faith in the state and, indeed, in the law. I have always replied that I cannot conceptualize redistributive justice without a strong state. I know strong states can and do become corrupt and arbitrary. But it is the business of citizens to hold governments accountable, and rights-based laws place powerful instruments in the hands of people for democratic, non-violent resistance. I worry about advocating weak states. A weak state, for instance, would also mean the private provisioning of public goods like education and healthcare. I am convinced that we must make it obligatory for the state to mediate all transfers of land from small farmers and tribal communities to private corporations. I recognize that state administrations will often use these powers for rent-seeking and illegally benefiting private industry. But in the absence of empowered state intervention, powerless landowners will be entirely at the mercy of powerful private corporations. If the state strays, I contain within me and my collectives the power to hold it accountable, however hard this may be in practice. But if the private corporation is oppressive, how can I call it to account?

My faith in the central role of the state for social and economic justice and the protection of the rights of people disadvantaged by class, gender, caste, faith and other social identities remains undimmed. The change within my thinking is my growing recognition that *a just and caring state can only be located ultimately in a just and caring society*. All the inequities and injustice which I have described in this book, without exception, represent profound and culpable failures of the state and its laws, policies and institutions. But these failures of the state are due to the *social* sanction given by the influential middle and upper classes to inequality, prejudice, caste and communal injustice, patriarchy, the differential treatment of children, the oppression of labour, discrimination and violence against minorities and their criminal profiling, and the denials of healthcare, social protection, housing, clean water and sanitation, and a hundred other basic requirements for a decent, healthy life.

This does not mean that progressive laws should not be passed even far ahead of social consensus for these measures. It only means that it is important to be mindful that it is not *enough* for us to agitate for changes in laws and policies. For instance, it is futile to make states more accountable for the protection of women without fighting battles in our own homes for gender equality, for raising men to be kinder and women more assertive, and in schools and work-places for the equality of men and women. It means that it is not enough to fight for stronger laws to end corruption, without recognizing and resisting ways in which the middle and upper classes are not just victims of corruption, but also participants in and beneficiaries of it.

Of course, to achieve greater justice and equity we need better state laws and policies. This is absolutely necessary but this is not enough. We must recognize the ways in which we—people of relative privilege and power—are also acutely culpable in these injustices and inequities, for our failures to fight these more intimate battles, including with our loved ones and colleagues, within the popular discourse, and with ourselves.

Baldly, what I realize today is that India will not change until we—the middle classes—also change.

Limits to Our Empathy

In the winter of 2012, the brutal gangrape of a young paramedical student in Delhi was followed by a rare moment in the public life of the Indian middle class, when public empathy and solidarity were extensively on display. Unaffiliated young people marched the streets of the national capital in anguish and in rage. On the evening when the news of her death came in, I too went to Jantar Mantar with my wife and daughter. In a corner were noisy groups with political affiliations, shouting frenzied slogans before television cameras. But at the protest site, a far larger number of mostly young people sat pensively around lit candles, silently mourning the young woman who had just died. With her ordinary aspirations—to study to become a medical professional, to watch a film with her friend on that particular evening—she could have been my daughter, she could have been your sister or friend. Her savage brutalization and her meaningless loss became our personal tragedies. Many deeply shared the suffering of a woman whose name or face they did not know.

But that brief moment also reminded me of the limits to our empathy. There are a multitude of other brutalized women and girls for whom we do not march on the streets, for whom we do not light candles. They represent the frontiers of our middle-class empathy.

In the cities which we inhabit, the most unsafe human beings are homeless women and girls. In the first women's shelter that we established, I asked the women what had changed most in their lives after they entered the shelter. One woman replied, 'For the first time in seventeen years, when I close my eyes at night, I am assured that no one will molest me.' And then there were the young girls trafficked for domestic or sex work. Many told us that they had run away from violence in their homes, sometimes even incestuous rape by their fathers.

Among those beyond our empathy are also disadvantaged-caste women who suffer routinely rape because men want to exercise power and domination. In 1992, a disadvantaged-caste woman in Rajasthan, Bhanwari Devi, was gangraped and punished because she prevented a child marriage.[3] After the rape, as she fought a protracted and lonely battle for justice, she was repeatedly humiliated and shamed by the police, lawyers and judges. In her village, she and her husband were ostracized for years.

Fourteen years later, women of a Dalit family in Khairlanji, a village in Maharashtra, were violently raped and killed, merely because upper-caste people could not tolerate that the family was modestly prospering.[4] The violence they suffered continued traditions of sexual abuse which rural Dalit women have survived for generations, indeed, for centuries.

The year 2002 saw some of the most brutal sexual assaults on Muslim women in Gujarat. A women's fact-finding team encountered in one camp a young boy who insisted on telling them what rape means. 'Rape is making a woman naked, and then setting her on fire,' he explained.[5] Rape has recurred in many episodes of mass communal violence, including, more recently, against Christian nuns and tribal women in Kandhamal, Odisha, in 2007-08.[6] In 2004, the gangrape, torture and murder of a young woman, Manorama, by security forces in Manipur, caused such grief to women in the valley that in an unprecedented protest, many women stripped naked outside the army installation, demanding that they too be raped.[7] In all sites of armed conflict, rape by men in uniform is not uncommon. The people of the Kashmiri village of Kunan Poshpara are still battling for justice in a case of mass gangrape by soldiers in 1992, more than two decades years after the incident, even after their allegations were confirmed by the state human rights commission.[8]

But the tallest barriers to our capacities for empathy are not related to the victims, but to the perpetrators of these terrible crimes.

Are they also worthy of our compassion, our empathy—or at least a little understanding—even as we condemn their heinous acts? Take the seventeen-year-old boy, who was at that time reported to have inflicted the cruellest violence on the night of 16 December 2012—a charge not borne out by later investigation. He was thirteen when he ran away from home, for reasons we do not know. However, my colleagues and I have taken care of many such boys, and their stories are similar, most often of childhoods of violence and abuse by drunken fathers.[9] On the streets, they grow up abused, beaten and exploited by men in uniform as well as other adults around them. There is no caring and responsible adult who enters their lives, to protect them and believe in them, to show them the way, to teach them right from wrong. Our work has shown us that if you reach out on time, with compassion and conviction, abused adolescent boys of the streets can still be reclaimed.

Take the other men involved in the crime. We have recklessly created a glittering, hyper-consumerist, hyper-sexualized world around them, a world to which they are constantly exposed, but from which they are resolutely barred. These are young men who wish to aspire, but cannot. This leaves them resentful, sullen and angry. We completely disregard the explosive stresses of under-class masculinities and the violence and hopelessness with which impoverished young men live, especially in the inner cities.

None of this is for a moment to justify their gruesome crimes. Nothing can. It is only to also recognize your and my culpability in the crimes of that cold winter night on the streets of Delhi on 16 December 2012, in the violence we foster by our wealth, our unapologetic consumption and our indifference.

~

After the juvenile was arrested by the police for his role in the 16 December rape, a newsmagazine described him as 'India's most hated'.[10] The law at the time of the crime exempted the boy from adult punishment. However, a call went out across the country, and soon gained fever pitch, that no punishment except the gallows was sufficient for him. Not just (understandably) the girls' stricken parents, but television anchors and all hues of commentators demanded hotly that he should be held responsible for his crime like any adult and should suffer the same punishment, the death penalty, for his guilt, as the other men in the bus.

The BJP government, within a few months of assuming power, undertook the alteration of this law. 'Adult punishment for adult crime' became the new mantra. But this raised tangled ethical and legal questions about the nature of childhood, criminal culpability, punishment, reform, justice and, above all, public compassion.

There is firstly the question of the complexion of childhood, and the appropriate adult response to childhood crime. There is incontrovertible scientific evidence about the developmental immaturity of children's brains as they grow, compounded by the confusion of bodily changes and surging hormones, and adolescent struggles to reconcile childish dependence with aspirations of autonomy. Who among us have not traversed this journey of coming of age—of heartbreak, bewilderment, strange longings, anger and fragile hope?

Many of us have been steadied by the caring hand of a parent, teacher, elder sibling or friend. But what about those children who—in these tortuous growing years—have no one they can reach out to?

More than a century ago, in 1909, Julian Mack, a judge from the US advised that juvenile offenders should be treated 'as a wise and merciful father handles his own child'. I would include mothers in this as well, but there is little else that can enhance the wisdom and humanity of Judge Mack's counsel.[11]

In our work with formerly homeless children, my colleagues and I are often confused and we slip close to despair when some—only a few—of our children continue older patterns of behaviour. We agonize over what the most fitting response should be. I offer only this talisman to guide us: 'treat the child as you would treat your own child'. When your own children lose their way, deceive, attack, steal—you correct them, punish them, guide them, but you never stop taking care of them, and never stop believing in them. Then why should it be different for other growing children who lack responsible adult protection in their own families?

Minna Kabir, outstanding child-rights activist, writes of her work with children who enter crime 'because of poverty, because of a drug habit, because of a faulty peer group, because of dysfunctional families, because of an empty stomach, and because of adults who use them…' She affirms that 'every society is responsible for the well-being and care of its children up to the age of eighteen years, especially if they are marginalized, helpless and powerless to do anything for themselves', adding that 'society has to protect its children upto that age, rather than protect itself from its children.'[12]

The assumption that reduced punishment for children would result in an explosion of juvenile crime is unfounded by evidence, globally and in India. In 2011, only 1.1 per cent of all crimes were committed by juveniles.[13] In a country in which nearly half the 1.2 billion people are children, our annual juvenile crime figure of around 30,000 is miniscule, almost negligible. We are not at risk from our children; it is indeed children who have to be protected from adults.

If our aim is to take revenge for grave crimes that some children undertake, like rape and murder, by all means let us imprison, even hang them. But if our aim is to help nurture and reform the child, as we would our own, an adult prison is the least likely site in which a child's intrinsic capacities for goodness can be reclaimed. To deter offences by children in future, the way is not to send them to adult jails or the gallows. Juvenile crime is best prevented by reaching out on time to children deprived of adult protection, with hundreds of open and caring residential schools for them, ensuring food, education and protection. Harsher punishments for juvenile offenders will only brutalize them even more.

I often declare to the street children in our care as they grow into sometimes troubled adulthood: 'Try as you will, I will not lose faith in you.' In our work with children and youth who come from violent backgrounds, we have found that most—but admittedly not all—respond positively to love and to caring adult guidance, and evolve into responsible and often remarkably gentle young people.

A change in the law which criminalizes our children again is a heavy stone we must bear on our collective conscience. Can we remind ourselves that *all* children—yours, mine and those on the streets—need love, trust and guidance, not incarceration and condemnation, to steer them to a path of responsible adulthood.

There is no other way.

Two Sides of a Red Brick Wall

Indifference is primarily born out of the failure and the fatigue of empathy. Empathy requires both a leap of imagination—to imagine how the other feels—and solidarities of feeling—to feel the suffering and humiliation of the other as though they were one's own. In other words, empathy has both a cognitive and affective element: it engages both the mind and the heart. Empathy tends to flow more naturally when the suffering person is someone I can relate to and understand, someone whom I feel is similar to me in some essential, relatable way, because I can then better imagine what the other person is feeling.

Empathy breaks down when I can persuade myself that the 'other' is, in some ways, not like me, not fully human in the way I and the people of my family, my community, my caste, my gender, my race and, indeed, my sexual preferences are. I can do so when I refuse to see or acknowledge that people who are of a different gender, caste, class, religion, sexuality or culture from me are essentially human in the same way as I am, when I am in the sway of normative frameworks and politics which cultivate difference and foster indifference. Pratap Bhanu Mehta speaks of the 'equality paradox'— 'We don't care because we are unequal, and because we don't care inequality will persist.'[14]

Some scientists and philosophers believe that empathy is a uniquely *human* trait, inborn in human beings but also one which can be taught and nurtured. Equally, as we can learn empathy, we find that barriers can be constructed against the natural surge of empathy which would otherwise have arisen had it not been actively blocked. Hierarchies and the politics of difference are two of the most significant walls which can block out empathy from our minds and hearts.

~

Ashish Khetan, then a reporter with newsmagazine *Tehelka*, penetrated the ranks of Hindutva organizations in Gujarat in 2007 posing as a sympathizer and, on his hidden cameras, captured chilling conversations in which activists of the RSS, the VHP and the Bajrang Dal bragged in graphic detail how they slaughtered and raped Muslims in 2002. Even among these conversations, the one that terrifies me most is a conversation with VHP activist Suresh Richard, in which he vividly describes raping and killing a woman even as his wife sits next to him, and nods in approval throughout.

> Richard: Now look, one thing is true...*bhookhe ghuse to koi na koi to phal khayega, na*? [when hungry men go in, they will eat some fruit or the other, no?]...*Aise bhi, phal ko kuchal ke phek denge* [in any case, the fruit is going to be crushed and thrown away]...Look, I'm not telling lies...Mata is before me [gesturing to an image of a deity]...Many Muslim girls were being killed and burnt to death, some men must have helped themselves to the fruit...
>
> Khetan: Must have been a couple of rapes...
>
> Richard: Might even have been more...then there were the rest of our brothers, our Hindu brothers, VHP people and RSS people...Anyone could have helped themselves...who wouldn't, when there's fruit?...The more you harm them, the less it is...I really hate them...don't want to spare them...Look, my wife is sitting here but let me say...the fruit was there so it had to be eaten...I ate too...I ate once.
>
> Khetan: Just once?

> Richard: Just once...then I had to go killing again...[turns to relative Prakash Rathod and talks about the girl he had raped and killed]...the scrap dealer's daughter Naseemo...Naseemo that juicy plump one...I got on top...
>
> Khetan: You got on top of her...
>
> Richard: Yes, properly...
>
> Khetan: She didn't survive, did she?
>
> Richard: No, then I pulped her...Made her into a pickle...[15]

For a woman to endorse the rape and slaughter of another woman—and that too by her husband—shows a profound breach in her capacities for empathy. Innumerable accounts, including television newsclips, are available which show women during the riots spiritedly preparing crude bombs and Molotov cocktails for the men in their homes to use as missiles against the 'enemy'. Not just women but even children suffered unspeakable cruelties, such as that of a boy in Naroda who was made to drink petrol at knifepoint, and then had a lit match thrown into his mouth.[16] Women could approve of such brutality against Muslim women and children only if they were convinced that these Muslim people were not human in the same way as they were. It is the same choking of natural empathy which is successfully accomplished in every communal or caste riot; without this, such mass violence is not possible. And it is because of this suspension of empathy that crowds of people in Delhi, in 1984, watched tyres being thrown around the necks of Sikhs, then set on fire, and laughed at their terrified, desperate 'dance' before they burned to death.

Less dramatically, but no less lethally, empathy dies when one child eats, plays and studies without a care in a middle-class home and another is made to slave twelve hours a day. This happens only because this other child is not perceived to be a child who is like one's own. The same human empathy is breached when the squalor of slums induces rage and their demolition celebration, instead of compassion.

Contrarily, I have also seen, so often through all my life's work, the power of empathy. Most of all while teaching young students, including those of privilege.

A red brick wall encloses the sprawling campus of India's finest business school, the Indian Institute of Management, Ahmedabad. On the pavement just on the other side of this wall lives a large cluster of homeless families—rag-pickers, construction workers and beggars. The chasm that separates life on the two sides of this brick wall seems like the distance between two planets, separated by light years.

I accepted an invitation in 2009 to teach a course every year on poverty and governance to the students studying for an MBA. The challenge of speaking about hunger, homelessness, want and discrimination to a classroom of some of the brightest achievers in the country—who, within months of attending my course, would be recruited to jobs which would easily place them in the top 1 per cent income bracket in the country—was daunting. But I found my students intelligent, engaged and caring, as young people anywhere are.

Instead of an examination at the end of the course, I asked my students every year to each find one impoverished person, in Ahmedabad or elsewhere, and try to learn about her life, write her story, and share it with their classmates. Their first reaction was usually one of understandable panic—how could they cross the formidable distances imposed by history, class, power, language and so much else; they were convinced that these barriers were insurmountable. I assured them that what was required was no more than one human being reaching out to another, and if they could approach the disadvantaged with true respect, the people they were trying to learn from would, in all probability, reciprocate.

For each hesitant young woman and man in my classroom, this became a personal adventure of reaching out, into places of the heart and mind they had never explored, or indeed thought possible. Each came back to recount the wonder of unsuspected lives, of the struggles, dreams, triumphs and the spirit behind every humble, begrimed face. The words of student Pooja Jayaraman, after her moving encounter with Jyoti, a construction worker on the new IIM campus, echoed in many accounts: 'As I walked away that day I asked myself if I had been in the same situation, would I have shown as much courage as she did?' They learnt not pity but authentic fellow-feeling and esteem. Many were also astonished by how hospitable and welcoming these utterly dispossessed persons were.

By the time the students entered my classroom, they had spent nearly two years living on the IIM campus. On the pavements outside the campus, interspersed between the homeless residents—what one student aptly called homeless homes—are innumerable stalls selling street food, cigarettes, DVDs, magazines, newspapers. It is here that students gather long hours most evenings, to 'chill' and 'hang out'. They would have passed their homeless neighbours literally several hundred times during those past two years. But they never before thought of them as *people*, and that too people with worthy stories.

A homeless ragpicker Anand Bhai lived with his family on the pavement adjacent to the walls of IIM Ahmedabad. When one of my students, Manish Verma, met and talked to him, Anand Bhai showed him his part of the footpath, which housed about fifty such families of ragpickers, and said, 'Whatever you see within the enclosure of this part of the footpath is mine.' Later, Manish would describe what he saw on the ten feet of pavement, which 'houses his family, a wooden cart used for collecting scrap, four steel utensils, a couple of jute bags stitched together and a small tent. That is all Anand Bhai can claim to own under the sun.'

A typical day in his life consisted of 'waking up every morning at 6 a.m. and leaving with his fellow ragpickers for a day of work that includes picking up bits of paper, plastic bags, empty mineral water bottles and pretty much anything that can be exchanged for money'. His children are uneducated and beg for money during the day, typically collecting about ₹10 or ₹20 each after a day's hard work.

Describing the uncertainty of what the family can eat at the end of each day, Manish used a metaphor for hunger which only a business student could have thought up: 'The food itself is as unpredictable as the movements of the BSE Sensex. If the day goes well and Anand Bhai is able to pocket a hundred-rupee note, he comes to the part of the footpath he calls home with a piece of chicken, a few tomatoes, onions and coriander to relish what he calls a grand feast. On gloomy days when the earnings are restricted to about fifty rupees, the dinner consists of boiled potatoes and onions with chapattis.'

Before parting, Anand Bhai's unusual visitor asked him one last question: 'What are your ambitions for your children; what do you want them to be when they grow up?' He replied: 'They are the children of a ragpicker and will become ragpickers.'

A similar matter-of-fact absence of hope marked the life of another homeless ragpicker whom Abhishek Gopal and Sougata Basu met. They discovered that Sanjay Bhai was born on the streets of Ahmedabad, and lived the thirty years of his life on the same stretch of road. His family comprised his mother, his wife and two children, a boy and a girl. He would set out with his entire family early every morning with a hired wooden cart to collect refuse, separating them into different categories like iron, bottles, glass and so on, and selling them to a nearby dealer. He too believed that nothing would change in their life, and his son would grow up to be a ragpicker like him.

Megha Jain described the 'home' of another homeless ragpicker: 'On the pavement, Kanti has carved out a small space that he calls home. They have a thin cotton mattress and a couple of old blankets. Some utensils and a large shiny radio-cum-cassette player make up the rest of his movable possessions. The home is defined by a tiny earthen chullah on the edge of the road and a string hung along the wall with some clothes on it. In the mornings they defecate in the open field about 300 meters away. When they leave for work, they roll up all their possessions and dump them behind a wall or some bushes. They aren't really worth stealing, so they have no fear.'

Marly Diallo, an overseas exchange student, wrote about Sabina, a young mother, about thirty years old, who had recently given birth to her fourth boy. 'She lives on a pavement, in front of a road that I take almost every day, without really asking myself how these people live there. Sabina has been living just behind the walls of IIMA for years,' wrote Marly. '[She] keeps their belongings on a ground protected by a fence; all the families can keep their valuables in plastic bags stocked in this area. Otherwise, she keeps her stuff on the pavement. At night or when it rains, the family gathers under a thin plastic tarpaulin, just like everybody does in this street.' Marly ended her account with these words: 'We asked them if they benefited the presence of IIMA in terms of security or help? The answer was clear and sad…there is no interaction with IIMA, just as if these two worlds co-existed without seeing each other.'

In Shared Spaces

If I was India's prime minister for even a day, and there was only one policy change I could execute, it would be to ensure that *all* children— rich and poor, low caste and high caste, Muslim and Hindu, disabled and able-bodied—study *together*. I am convinced that this one single act, more than any other, will change India, because it will create and cultivate spaces which would nurture public solidarity and fraternity.

I remember learning many things from an experiment we first undertook in 2006. For five days we brought together children from the streets who then lived in a residential home we ran, called Ummeed, with children from an elite school in Delhi, the Shri Ram School, in which my daughter spent the last years of her schooling. It taught us a lot, but most of all that inclusion will not benefit just the disadvantaged child. If anything, the child of advantage benefits and learns even more.

A child was talking of how he lost his home and ended up on the streets. He was travelling with his parents in a crowded train when he was very young. He got off the compartment at a station, and the train left with his mother and father. He never found his parents again. For most of his childhood years, he grew up on railway platforms with other homeless children as his only family, earning his food by selling water bottles or ragpicking, battling sexual abuse and police batons, seeking solace in drugs and the comradeship of his friends of the streets.

A teenaged girl his age was listening intently to him. Her parents were wealthy, and she studied in one of the most privileged schools in Delhi. She recounted, as the boy spoke of his life, that she once also got lost and was separated from her parents. She recalled her enormous fear and helplessness at that time. Her good fortune was that her parents found her. As the two children spoke, they wondered what life would have been for both of them had fate dealt with them differently in those short moments—if the boy's parents had found him and the girl's had not. The boy would have been raised in the security and love of his home, and the girl would have faced an even worse destiny on the streets. They closed their eyes for a while to imagine what life would have been had they lived this different existence, and the girl said to her own astonishment, 'I would have been hungry, and one of the first things I would have done would have been to steal food.'

The early responses of both sets of children was expectedly saddled with awkward trepidation. Many of the children from Ummeed—remarkably brave otherwise—initially hid, refusing to join the interactions, worried that they would be treated shabbily and disrespectfully, embarrassed by their faded clothes and their rough manners. The children from the Shri Ram School had their own fears, of how they could possibly relate to the expected coarseness of street-smart children who had grown up without parents and education.

The initial dialogues, in small mixed groups of children, were about their joys and hates; and their dreams. It took only a morning together for many of them to discover how much they had in common—they all loved cricket, films, songs, and were quickly debating their favourite cricketers and actors. They also discovered profound differences, but along unexpected lines. The children from Shri Ram School often included 'studies' among their pet hates but the children from Ummeed almost unanimously chose school education as their most precious acquisition. Many children were unlettered when they joined Ummeed, but they all studied hard and surprised most people by even qualifying for entry into a formal middle school. Reflecting together on this difference, the children from Shri Ram recognized that they took education for granted as it came to them so easily, whereas for the Ummeed teenagers, it was invaluable precisely because they had always been barred from it.

Most children from Ummeed were clear about what they wanted to do when they grew up: several, for instance, saw computer hardware as a profession with a future, as four of their colleagues had already completed a course in hardware engineering from a private polytechnic since they joined Ummeed. A sizeable number chose social work and teaching, because they wanted to save other street children from the lives they had been forced to lead. The Shri Ram children were, in general, more relaxed and less focused about their futures: some saw university education overseas, followed by inheriting their fathers' business as an assured path; some spoke of fashion, jewellery design, architecture or professional golf or football as possible career choices. Many children from Shri Ram admitted that they had not even thought about their futures.

Next, the children were divided into pairs and encouraged to share the details of their lives. The children from Ummeed described to their unbelieving counterparts what life was actually like on the streets. They were stunned by the grit and strength of these children—they would have found it terrifying to sleep a single night alone on the sidewalk of a highway. But there is pain in homes of privilege as well, and some children shared a little of their loneliness and anguish. While some felt that their parents had little time for them, others said that their fathers were too harsh—these were things children had not spoken of to even their closest friends from school. I was touched by a fragment of a conversation in which a former child of the streets was counselling a student of the Shri Ram School. He said, 'Be patient with your father. Try to understand things from his point of view.' Wise for his age, he had seen too many children who had walked out in anger, and had had to live out their childhoods as orphans.

The children living in Ummeed did most of their work themselves—they cooked their own food, cleaned their rooms and toilets, even built additions to their ashram, because we were, at that time, very poorly resourced. The children from Shri Ram School were encouraged to share in this work; help rebuild a fallen boundary wall, plaster it, or plant vegetables. They were delighted at the blisters they got on their hands and the earth that soiled their clothes. The children residents of Ummeed laughed at them. They also trounced them in kabaddi and cricket, and showed off their superior skills in martial arts and wrestling.

The following day, the children discussed the world around them—issues of caste, communalism, gender and class inequalities. Most childen from the Shri Ram School did not know who Dalits were. Many had not heard of the practice of untouchability. A few claimed that caste was a system 'that prevailed only in ancient times'. The children residents of Ummeed hotly contested this, and described how caste discrimination thrived in the villages from which many of them had run away.

I realized once again that the physical distance between the children from Shri Ram School and the children living in Ummeed may have been—sometimes—less than a kilometre, as children sleep on pavements outside the gated colonies of their affluent homes. But this distance is so profound that most people cannot traverse it in a lifetime. Our children were able to briefly span this abyss. Together, they learnt lessons about love and loss, about privilege and denial, about fear and courage, about egalitarian compassion and, above all, our universal shared humanity. And, on parting, some children from the Shri Ram School shared phone numbers, welcomed their newfound friends to their school, or promised to return to Ummeed.

Ways of Giving

The failures of the state to improve the lives and prospects of people born into poverty and social disadvantage coincide with the decline in the traditions of middle-class giving. The Indian urban middle classes and people of privilege today have grown profoundly uncaring about the suffering and injustice which surrounds them. They have forgotten the old ways of giving, and have not yet learnt new ones. Many old forms of giving were rooted in religious beliefs, but some like the langar, which I will describe in more detail, constructed cultural forms of more egalitarian compassion.

In 2010, we undertook a study, in collaboration with homeless people, of religious food charities in Delhi. A major life-need for urban homeless and migrant populations is of nutritious, wholesome and affordable meals. But sizeable numbers among them have no home or opportunities to cook. Instead, they spend around anything between a third and three quarters of what they earn each day—by ragpicking, pulling rickshaws, doing casual daily-wage work, vending or begging—on food bought from carts or wayside eateries. This tends to be oily and dusty, poor in nutrition and hygiene. Soup kitchens are integral to the urban landscape in many modern cities in other parts of the world. Yet, except for states like Tamil Nadu and, on a smaller scale, Chhattisgarh, no government runs large programmes for free or subsidized food for adults. Such food would make destitute and migrant working populations healthier, and enable them to save money to fight their impoverishment. In the Food Bill introduced in Parliament, community kitchens designed after the langar have been eliminated. One reason why states do not invest public resources on subsidized meal programmes is the assumption that this life-need is being attended to by private, and mainly religious, charity. It is for this reason that we decided to investigate religious food charities in Delhi.

We found that only 4 per cent of homeless persons depend completely on these charities for food. These are mainly destitute homeless persons, disabled and elderly men and women, and younger street children with no occupation or income except alms. Working, able-bodied homeless persons also occasionally resort to charity food as a last resort when they have completely exhausted their savings.

The practice of feeding the hungry is deeply valued in all Indian religious traditions—Hindu, Islamic, Christian and Sikh. But we found these traditions eroded, mutated or abandoned in shining, twenty-first century Delhi. We were surprised to find no feeding centres for the destitute run by churches. Other religious establishments ran some feeding programmes in small measures, but few catered to the real need of the homeless—of a sustainable source of wholesome food, offered with dignity.

We were curious about why such small numbers of homeless people depend on food charity, and prefer to spend their scarce resources on purchased food, or even to remain hungry. The first answer that they gave us was that the food is served sporadically, and is not the simple wholesome food that they seek or need. Charity forces persons to be dependent on the timing, menu and availability of food at religious centres, determined by the wishes of the donors rather than the needs of homeless people. Waiting uncertainly for food charity curtails the number of hours homeless persons can work, many of whom are casual job-seekers, and for whom reaching the job market early in the morning is imperative.

Many Hindu temples serve food, but this is usually oily, sweet and served only on fixed days. (There are fine exceptions, like the Hare Krishna temples.) People develop an aversion towards this greasy, sugary food. They crave, instead—the old and disabled as much as working people—simple and easily digestible food, served daily and with dignity. But the giver is not interested in what the receiver needs, only in his divine merit.

However, the most important reason why homeless people and single migrants reject food charities is that these routinely assault their dignity and selfhood. They are compelled to jostle with outstretched, cupped palms, and eat what they receive squatting on a pavement or under a tree. They are often forced to pit themselves against each other in an effort to access the limited food available and the old and infirm invariably fall by the wayside.

We found more dignified forms of charity in the Nizamuddin Dargah and the Sai Baba Temple in Lodhi Road. There, food tokens are purchased by donors from hotels, which have a month's validity, and distributed to the destitute. In Jama Masjid, we found many people patiently waiting for food outside dhabas near the mosque, and for people to pay for their meals. And while this was less dignified, the number of people fed in these narrow lanes was probably the largest in Delhi.

Traditionally, the most wholesome food, served with the greatest dignity, has been in the langars in Sikh gurudwaras. The langar is at the heart of Sikh egalitarian teachings, in which an emperor and a beggar are mandated to be seated side by side and offered the same food, with the same respect. However, we found these egalitarian traditions abandoned in the capital's principal gurudwaras. Sisganj Gurudwara in Chandni Chowk, where the homeless of the city gather in the largest numbers, actively bars the 'dirty poor' from entering the langar. The same attitude is demonstrated by gurudwaras in upmarket areas like Greater Kailash and Vasant Vihar. Bangla Saheb Gurudwara, near Connaught Place, also blocks destitutes from entering the premises and eating at the main langar, but maintains a separate langar for them at the rear. The same food is served in both the langars but, by segregating the needy from middle-class worshippers, the gurudwara fails to live up to the idea of egalitarianism.

I discussed this informally with some managing committes of gurudwaras, arguing that segregation as well as barriers on entry violate, in my understanding, the core teachings of the Sikh faith. They tried to explain to me that the destitute and homeless defile the sanctity of the temple because they are unclean and often drink alcohol and take drugs. I asked them, were the poor different in the times of the gurus? And if the gurus believed that the unwashed masses would not defile the gurudwara, then what had changed? I unsuccessfully reminded the managing committees that the central value of the idea of the langar is not just that the hungry should be fed, but that they must be fed *with dignity*.

This investigation of the religious food charities in Delhi became a fascinating journey, not just into the survival strategies of the poorest of Delhi, but the alarmingly shrinking spaces in the hearts of India's middle class.

~

I take solace that this vibrant, living tradition of giving away food by the community is still alive in rural Punjab; a great example of how love can be a wonderful form of resistance to inequality and difference. In her lyrical documentary, *Gur Prasad: The Grace of Food*, Meera Dewan reminds us that the langar is not merely a generous tradition of the community feeding the hungry.[17] Central to it is the spirit in which people in need are offered food—not ordinary charity, but with egalitarian compassion and solidarity. It requires that people, whether rich or poor, high caste or low, women or men, be seated side by side and offered the same, simple, wholesome vegetarian food. In the Indian context, social differences and hierarchies are expressed by strict barriers and taboos on eating with the 'other'. By requiring that all people eat together, this institution significantly affirms the idea of the intrinsic equal dignity of all human beings.

These ideas of equality, kindness and secularism were brave and revolutionary, especially for India of the thirteenth and the sixteenth centuries, with its deep fractures of caste and religion, and its tradition of oppressing women and people of disadvantage; features of society which, sadly, even continue today. People of disadvantaged castes in many parts of rural India are still culturally barred from sitting shoulder to shoulder with people of higher castes and, even more, from eating together. By challenging these rules, the langar demonstrates how the practice of love can become the most revolutionary of weapons.

Essential to the idea of the langar is also the cheerfulness of service. The hungry and the thirsty are welcomed as honoured guests, and the hosts urge all to eat their full. There is no place in this tradition for piety and sacrifice—you serve in the langar because it gives you joy. The cheerfulness of your service best preserves the dignity of the receiver, who is not a beneficiary of your charity but a comrade.

Underlying the langar are also convictions about the dignity of labour. In a society in which people of some castes were ritually barred from reading and writing, let alone reading the scriptures, Nanak declared that there was as much spiritual merit in reading the sacred books or donating in cash or kind, as in manual labour—sweeping the floors, cooking the langar, or cleaning dishes. The country's labouring castes—and women—discover a new dignity when high-caste men compete for chores to which the lowest castes and women are conventionally condemned.

Dewan's film also evokes the wonderful solidarity which underlies this tradition of rural Punjab. We watch as even very poor people trek long miles to contribute whatever they can to the langar; sometimes just a little flour or a pot of milk. In many villages, in each household, the homemaker sets aside some rotis and vegetables from the food she prepares each day, and teenagers collect the food and take it to the langar. In one of the many carefully chosen, lyrical hymns in the film, the fifth Guru underlines the value of social solidarities: 'Who feeds the new-born birds left behind as they fly across the oceans? Who fends for them? One who joins a supportive community swims across the ocean of life...'

We encounter many volunteers or sewadars of the langar. We meet, for instance, eleven-year-old Navneet, a whole-time volunteer with the gurudwara since he was six. He loved the brotherhood which he encountered in the gurudwara, and decided one day to run away from home, making the langar community his new family. 'I enjoy most forms of service,' the boy says, 'keeping the fire going, rolling bread, serving food and tea.' He adds, with heart-breaking wisdom well beyond his years: 'The heart shows you the way forward. Choose between family and a life of service. I have made my choice.' He is silent about the reasons he left home, but I recognize in his unspoken words stories I have heard from hundreds of boys living on the streets. These other boys had only one choice, but Navneet found in the langar a place of safety, of kindness and giving, and chose it.

The langar is also an alternative sisterhood for many village women. We encounter women who leave their homes at 2 a.m. each night, trudging two hours to reach the langar before dawn. They serve there all day and return home only at 7 p.m., where they labour to complete their domestic chores and catch a few hours of sleep before they set out again. 'Overnight,' they say, 'god releases our exhaustion.' They add: 'Rain or storm, the langar is unending. Through the year, heat or cold, you'll find the food being cooked.'

~

A group of young people employed in corporate jobs and NGOs, with students and homemakers came together in 2009 to organize an annual week-long celebration, a 'festival' of giving, in the week of Gandhiji's birthday. They called it the Joy of Giving Week, but soon renamed it Daan Utsav.

On one occasion, Daan Utsav volunteers met in Bangalore. At the end of the meeting they decided to pool a little money, make sandwiches, and go out and locate people to respectfully share them with. They walked to the railway station, around which numerous homeless people find refuge. They sat down with old men and women they encountered outside the station, chatted with them and offered their sandwiches.

There were still some sandwiches left at the end of the evening, and they wondered if they should offer these to the railway porters. 'But they might throw these back on our faces,' one of them feared. They were still standing around hesitantly when some porters overheard them and walked over, smiling. 'If you want to share your food with us,' they said, 'why don't you?' One of the team members later recalled how grateful they felt that the porters accepted their modest gift so gracefully.

In Hyderabad, Madhulika Sagaram and her colleagues in Adhya Educational Society thought that they would try teaching such lessons in giving to school children. Their plan was simple. Each child in a school would be encouraged to make something to offer to an unknown child as a gift. Many worked with paper and waste products and made birds, animals and flowers out of them; some painted, while children from rural backgrounds brought things they had grown in their fields.

The schools were paired in opposites, high-income schools with government-run schools, urban with rural schools, a madrassa with a convent school, a school for children with special abilities with a school which does not include disabled children, and so on. They called these 'buddy schools'. On the appointed day, children from the schools would visit their buddy school, offer each other gifts, share their lunches, and talk and play together.

In these interactions, the children learnt many life lessons, just as the band of adult volunteers in Bangalore did when they visited the railway station. They learnt about giving and receiving with grace and respect. They learnt that under our apparent differences—of wealth, religion, language and caste—we are all essentially the same human beings. Sagaram's colleagues found that once they were brought together and shared their little gifts, children made friends easily with other children, even though in normal circumstances their worlds would never intersect. They were curious, friendly and open, more than most adults would be in the same circumstances.

A student from an affluent private school observed later that students from his buddy school—a government school with modest infrastructure—were 'more disciplined than us, more helpful, more creative and more down to earth'. Another student from the same school recalled that 'we played, danced and enjoyed the trip. It was fun'. A third was happy to get to know about 'village life, crops and plants'.

Some children became reflective. A student remarked that 'our parents give us everything but still we are very stubborn, whereas the children in the government school hardly have any facilities'. Students from a government school said they 'met new people, learned how to be happy and make others smile' and also learnt 'that small things can make us happy'. One child who participated in the interchange said that it 'inspired me to do some good in the world. We should exchange joys and divide the troubles.'

Volunteers from Daan Utsav have drawn up a list of ways of respectful giving. They include: Go to lunch with your office peon and learn his life story. Have a party with children of domestic helpers in your society. Talk to a homeless person. Gift a meal, or a pair of chappals. Make a pot of chai and serve it to nightwatchmen. Volunteer at an orphanage or a home for the elderly. Help a ragpicker collect and carry waste for an hour…Just some small steps for building empathy.

I often worry about the ways we are raising our children—teaching them by our actions if not our words to be disrespectful of people who are different and less advantaged, and being uncaring about suffering and deprivation. Daan Utsav volunteers are trying to show us small, modest, everyday ways to change this: by changing ourselves a little each time, with tiny, unpretentious actions from the heart, acts of giving, and that forgotten value—solidarity.

Building Solidarities

To a much larger project of striving for a just and humane society, the first contribution which the cultivation and nurturing of empathy can make is by helping build social solidarities. Battles for justice must be fought by people who live with that injustice. To remind us of this, the slogan of many disabled peoples' organizations is salutary: 'Nothing about us without us.'[18] Development scholar Robert

Chambers also reminds us how 'poverty experts' often fail to consult the greatest experts of all: people themselves living in penury.[19]

And yet, I would think that a society would be much poorer if it left sufferers to deal with their problems alone. In a society built around social solidarities, when women are battered, men fight in the forefront for equality with women; when violence decimates the minorities, people from the majority speak out and fight for justice; upper-caste men and women protest and resist caste discrimination; heterosexual men and women join battle against the criminalization of consensual same-sex relations, and so on.

In the aftermath of the Gujarat carnage, I spoke in many gatherings of Muslim people in Gujarat and other parts of India who were devastated by the brutality, of the complicit role of the state and, above all, the fact that Dalits and adivasis were the foot soldiers in much of the violence that was unleashed on them. 'We have lived in peace with our Dalits and adivasi neighbours for generations,' they would recall to me in great sadness. 'How then did they turn against us?'

I would say to them, 'I understand your anguish. But I too have a question for you. When Dalits and adivasis were being oppressed for generations, when did you speak out in their support?' For instance, across Gujarat, Dalits are prohibited from drawing water from the common village well. I asked, 'Is there any village in Gujarat where the Muslims invited their deprived Dalit neighbours to share the well which was used by the Muslim community instead?' And I would explain, 'If the Muslims never reached out in solidarity when Dalits and adivasis were being persecuted, how did you expect that they would stand in your defence when you were under attack?' They could never find a village in which Muslims shared their water sources with Dalits and each time, this set off a great deal of collective introspection.

My conversation with them would continue. I would ask: why do Muslims tend to get agitated mainly when Muslims are attacked? It is exactly the same with Sikhs, Hindus, Christians and people of various identities. Why do we not feel equally aggrieved when people of any faith live with hunger, homelessness, disease and persecution? The Prophet, I am told, said that if one places one's hand on the head of an orphan child, the blessings of Allah would number as many as the hair on the child's head. I point out that he never said 'the head of a *Muslim* orphan child'. Then why is it that Muslim charity contributes to building Muslim orphanages for Muslim children, but not for all children in need?

This applies equally to many charitable interventions by people of all other faiths and persuasions as well—Hindu, Sikh, Jain, Parsi, Christian and Buddhist. I therefore speak of the need for all people who live with injustice and suffering, and all people who share their suffering, to build a new bond between themselves—ek dard ka rishta: a bond of shared pain, born from empathy, solidarity and fraternity. It is this bond which will drive us in the direction of greater justice and caring in our world.

~

In drafting India's Constitution, Ambedkar laid great stress, not just on liberty and equality, but also on fraternity. He said, 'Fraternity means a sense of common brotherhood (and sisterhood) of all Indians—if Indians are seen as being one people. It is the principle which gives unity and solidarity to social life. It is a difficult thing to achieve.'[20] He was convinced that 'without fraternity, equality and liberty will be no deeper than a coat of paint'.[21] Ambedkar dreamed of an India in which divisions of caste and religion would gradually fade away.

However, it is fraternity which has been most forgotten in our Constitution. It is forgotten not just by those chosen to uphold our Constitution, it is lost even in our public and social life, in which the aggressive use of oppositional identities remains for most political parties the most reliable instrument to harvest votes with, and prejudice and inequality are produced and reproduced in our hearts and homes. The idea of fraternity is closely linked to that of social solidarity, which is impossible to accomplish without public empathy; the daily, lived realization that human beings who look different, wear different clothes, worship different gods, speak different languages, have different political persuasions, actually have exactly the same intrinsic human dignity, and experience the same emotions—dreams, hopes, despair, pain, happiness, anger, love, triumphs and defeats—that we do.

~

Noam Chomsky remarked that the idea of social protection is basically the idea, simply, that we should take care of each other. There can be no better encapsulation of the idea of the good state, a state which must be founded on the idea of social solidarity, on the continuous mindfulness of the obligation of the state to care for every person, weak and strong. But Chomsky goes on to say that we live in times when this is considered a profoundly 'subversive' idea. For many today, this idea of social protection—or the duty of social caring—is indeed a dangerous philosophy which must be crushed at all costs.[22]

Those opposed to this idea are either people who believe that markets by themselves are both necessary and sufficient to end poverty, hunger and want, or those who restrict their idea of solidarity to narrow notions of identity, whether of race, ethnicity, community or caste, or any other. These two ideas often converge, as in India's political arena today, which renders the opposition to agendas of social protection and the caring state even more adamant and powerful—and for some, so much more charismatic.

It is not in the nature of markets to care for people who are not useful in a direct utilitarian way as producers or consumers, or to those who do not conform. Popular philosopher Michael Sandel reminds us of the vital difference between a market economy and a market society. 'A market economy is a…valuable and effective tool for organizing productive activity.' A market society is different, he declares. 'A market society is a place; it's a way of life where market relations and market incentives and market values come to dominate all aspects of life. And that's my worry. Without quite realizing it, over the past three decades, we have drifted from having a market economy to becoming a market society, a society where just about everything is up for sale.'[23]

In the age of the hegemony of markets, this is what the India of the middle class has become, a market society. We are easily persuaded when the state tells us that it simply does not have the money to ensure that every child gets nutritious food and good schooling; that old people do not have to sleep hungry; that homeless people do not have to sleep out in the cold; and that children do not have to die only because they cannot afford healthcare. These are people for whom markets can never work. They enter the already crowded zone of our collective amnesia and we are unconcerned that neither markets, nor the state, nor even in most cases non-state public action, are reaching them. We are being convinced that the markets will get to them one day, and until then, they can do nothing better than wait, and suffer patiently, without complaint and without resistance.

As a young person in college, my imagination was captured by a seminal book called *Small Is Beautiful* by British economist Ernst Friedrich Schumacher.[24] I love its subtitle, *A Study of Economics As if People Mattered*, which should be the talisman for all economic theory. He rejects the assumptions that 'growth is good', and that 'bigger is better', and questions the appropriateness of using mass production in developing countries, promoting, instead, labour-intensive 'production by the masses'. He suggests a philosophy of 'enoughness', understanding, in the vein of Mahatma Gandhi and Buddhist thinkers, that human needs can and should be limited; that technology and production should be so organized as to ensure that workplaces are dignified and meaningful first, efficient second; and to recognize that nature and its resources are priceless.

In what I learned from him, and from Gandhian economics, I am driven to question the assumption that the pursuit of the highest possible pace of economic growth should, in itself, be the highest goal of society. Although the question of how much of (priced) goods and services we produce is important (because this creates wealth and sometimes—but often not—jobs), there are other, much more important questions that must be asked in a good society while evaluating state economic policy. These alternate, and in my opinion far higher-order questions are, firstly, *by what means* are these goods and services produced? Are they based on the displacement or the oppression of labour, on the large-scale uprooting of people from their lands, habitats and natural resources, on polluting our rivers and poisoning the air, and on depleting natural resources faster than they can be replenished? Secondly, *what* is being produced: are we spending on weapons and luxury goods—as we observed in the context of India in the first part of this book—when people lack nutritious food, clean water, healthcare and decent homes? And, lastly, *for whom* are these goods and services being produced or, in other words, what is the distribution of income, wealth and consumption?

As society pursues the goal—or mirage—of galloping economic growth, even with all of these caveats, it must care for everyone left out of this growth story. I believe that in a good society, people of every social class and identity should be involved in a huge public debate about what is the floor of human dignity, socially, below which no human being should be allowed to fall.

For me, *this* is the floor of human dignity below which it is morally unacceptable for any human being, *any* human being, to have to live. We should build a new social contract in new and rapidly growing India that we seek a country—and world—in which no child will sleep hungry, no child will sleep under the open sky, no child will be sent to work instead of a school which is as good a school as for any other child her age, no person will be subjected to discrimination or violence because of her identity, no person will be denied free, good-quality healthcare, and no old person will have to work or beg to live with dignity.

We can debate the details, add, delete or refine this list. But it is imperative that we have this public debate to build a social consensus on a minimum agenda of universal social protection. It is this floor of human dignity which should define the poverty line, the amount of resources every household needs in order to achieve this minimum agreed level of human dignity. It will also recognize the principle of differential needs and affirmative action: that if, for instance, there is a disabled person in your household, then you would need two or three times more resources to be in the same place. This floor of human dignity should also become the yardstick against which the performance of every government of any political hue should be evaluated.

It is through such a collective exercise that we will able to build an India and a world which truly, actively cares for all, and which recognizes the intrinsic equal dignity of all persons, regardless of gender, class, race, nationality, caste, faith, sexuality and disability. I am convinced that this is not a utopian set of goals. Far from it, it is both achievable and imperative, within our lifetimes. But for it to be possible, we first need to reclaim the idea which Chomsky spoke of, that we owe it to each other as human beings that we all take care of each other.[25] It requires the kindling of the ideas of solidarity and fraternity, of social caring. The landscapes of our hearts which have been desertified, parched by beliefs that 'greed is good' require the waters of a perennial river of public empathy.

The Legitimacy of Violence

While resistance to injustice is widely endorsed as the highest human duty in most cultures, one debate which has raged through the centuries—and has enormous relevance in contemporary times—is about the legitimacy of deploying *violence* in resisting and combating injustice. This debate has not been settled in most modern societies.

But I, personally, am convinced that not only is resistance to injustice the highest human duty and calling, but that all such resistance must be non-violent.

In all of known human history, and in every society in every corner of the globe, some human beings have always been unjust to others. Those who oppress others variously wield the power of wealth, of ownership of land and capital; of the claims of superiority of a specific gender, race, caste, ethnicity and sexuality over others; of greater physical strength and brute force; of weapons and state authority; and of the claims of superior knowledge and religious sanction. This superior power is deployed against those who have less muscle, resources, social standing or influence, or against those who do not conform to the mores of the majority, to extract submission and fear, cheap or free labour; exercise political, cultural or social domination, and physical and sexual control. The violence of oppression is sometimes naked, brutal and manifest and, in other situations, it is covert and internalized.

Equally, all of human history is also the story of resistance to injustice. Some heroic resistance, epic in scale and solidarity, plays out in open battles against formidable adversaries; other resistance is stealthy and hidden; some resistance is collective, and some individual. A great many of these acts of resistance have failed in their ultimate objectives of eliminating the oppressor or forms and institutions of oppression, but invisibly, even many of these 'failed' efforts, big or small, solitary or cooperative, have contributed ultimately in eroding the hegemonic power of particular forms of oppression. Simultaneously, new and often more lethal forms of exploitation and injustice continuously evolve, and these generate ever-new strivings and forms of resistance.

In the debates around the legitimacy of shedding blood to resist injustice, even those who call for abjuring violence usually nuance their pacifism and prohibitions on violent actions with exceptions for self-defence, or the protection of those who are weaker and in imminent danger. I love the wisdom of a Buddhist fable, which I turn to occasionally when in ethical doubt. A fierce and deadly cobra is converted to the code of non-violence by a Buddhist sage. Some months later, the gentle and learned monk returns to the village where the cobra lives and finds him half dead. Every passer-by kicks him, and children throw stones at him for sport. The sage is alarmed by the plight of his disciple, and asks the cobra why he allowed himself to come to such a pass. 'It was you who taught me to abjure violence,' the cobra says to him. The sage replies: 'I did teach you to not bite people. But I did not tell you to not to hiss!'

As the gentle sage shows us, the right to assertion to protect oneself against violence, and more than this the right to choose violence as a last resort for self-defence, are relatively well-settled ethical and political principles, except with a small minority of wonderful people who advocate pacifism as an absolute fundamentalism. What is much more in debate is the right to use violent means, including taking life, to fight injustice by powerful agents who are usually backed by the state, or *are* the state. This is a paramount ethical and political dilemma in the world as we find it today, because violence—including mass armed resistance, but much more terrorist violence, guerrilla warfare and strategies of individual annihilation—is being used by bands of people who style themselves as representatives of the oppressed to achieve their political ambitions. A much greater number of men and women—thinkers, writers, poets, artists, students and working people—endorse the righteousness of such violence even if they do not actively pick up arms themselves. People also search for the vindication of violence in their interpretations of religious texts, and political doctrines like Marxism and anarchism—although others use the same texts to arrive at diametrically opposite conclusions.

~

In 2011, I found myself fleetingly at the epicentre of the raging Maoist insurgency which has smouldered for decades over large tracts of central India. I had been deputed by the Supreme Court to investigate complaints of starvation in villages of the Dantewada district in south Bastar, resulting from attacks on people's homes and grain stores.

As the state government helicopter descended on to a small clearing amidst the trees, I could see the burnt shells of the homes of the residents. A clutch of people gathered to speak to us. Most were thin, even emaciated; the children showed unmistakable symptoms of malnourishment. Fear and resignation had gouged their eyes out, and stained all their answers to my questions. There were more uniformed soldiers in the village than civilian residents.

The day I visited the village marked the first anniversary of the killing of seventy-six Central Reserve Police Force (CRPF) personnel very near that village. In the village square, Maoists had constructed a red memorial to the eight Maoists who had been killed during that attack. The names of the Maoist 'martyrs' were inscribed in Hindi on the column, amidst triumphant claims of the 'victory' of their successful assault. Officials claimed that the People's Liberation Guerrilla Army was supported by village associations, including that of the village Morpalli where we had landed. They believed that the residents were 'sympathizers' of the Maoist insurgents.

This was perhaps why their homes had been destroyed for the second time in four years. When I visited the burnt-down huts and grain stores of the villagers, and spoke to some of the women there, I could observe that this was not simply a routine, surgically executed attack conducted by the armed forces. There was evidence of vicious personalized hatred of the kind that I have observed only in communal pogroms and anti-Dalit attacks. Metal vessels used in the kitchen had been twisted out of shape and even children's toys had not been spared. The villagers claimed that their homes had been attacked by armed civilian vigilantes of the Salwa Judum, supported by security forces. The Salwa Judum was a civilian militia, comprising rural youth from Chhattisgarh—often surrendered former militants—trained by the state government. Deployed as a part of the state's counter-insurgency strategy, their mode of operations included conducting violent raids on those villages which they considered Naxalite strongholds, often killing and raping its inhabitants.[26] In 2011, the Supreme Court declared the group unconstitutional and illegal. It ordered the government to disarm and disband the Salwa Judum, as well as discontinue the training and deployment of Special Police Officers (also civilians) for combat with insurgents.[27]

The indigent, local tribal communities of the region were trapped in unending cycles of often brutal violence, unleashed consecutively by Maoists, security forces and vigilante armed civilian groups such as the Salwa Judum and its other incarnations. Each group claimed that their attacks were retributive and defensive, and that they had not initiated the violence. But none of the groups could defend such a claim.

The villagers also suffered the consequences of taking sides—or being seen to be taking sides—with each of these warring groups. They were condemned equally if they acted or stayed passive. They were called upon by visiting dalams, or squads, of Maoist militants to supply them food, uniforms and sanctuary. They would frequently comply, whether out of active sympathy for the militants' ideology, or out of fear and helplessness. As a consequence, many ordinary villagers were jailed as Maoist sympathizers under draconian anti-terror and anti-militancy laws by the state and languished for long periods in prison, without the succour of national and international support like that which surged for Binayak Sen, who was sentenced to life imprisonment in 2010 by the Chhattisgarh government on charges of sympathizing with the Maoists. Security forces often camped in the villages, or marched through them, and made similar claims on the impoverished local residents.

The reliance on civilian vigilante groups to fight the Maoists or, more accurately, to terrorize local villagers—and punish them when they are seen to aid the dadas or Maoist dalams—has bitterly torn apart the social fabric of the homogenous tribal communities. It is not unusual, say, for one brother to be a recruit of the Salwa Judum and his sister to have joined one of the Maoist squads, while their parents left in the village struggle to survive the consequences of the violence unleashed by their children. The vigilante groups were, and continue to be, supported actively both by the state government, and, ironically, also by sections of the principal party in opposition. They arm and train them, extend an informal amnesty for all their lawless, violent actions and appoint many as Special Police Officers.

The fragile economic conditions of the residents are aggravated further by the virtual abandonment of the local people by the entire state government machinery, except the security forces. Apart from the then recently resumed public distribution system, almost all other most basic public services were unavailable to the villagers. The Maoists had bombed and razed the school building in 2007, and since then no school had functioned in the village. There was no Integrated Child Development Services (ICDS) centre and I could see highly malnourished children all around me; very few aged persons received pensions. The sub-health centres were also not functioning. This was the only village I had visited anywhere in the country in which the villagers had not even heard of the MGNREGA, let alone possess job cards or receive wage employment in public works.

The elected sarpanch had been absconding from the village for many years. The secretary of the village panchayat had also not visited the village for four years. She had ventured into the village, as had the teacher and the ICDS worker, only because of our visit—although they were presumably drawing their salaries regularly. On enquiry, I found that the panchayat secretary was a non-tribal woman, the wife of the local grain trader and moneylender! She recalled that many years earlier, she would visit the village occasionally with her husband when he went there on business. But since the Maoists had gathered strength, her husband's visits had dried up, and so had hers.

However there were also a few fine and courageous officials at various levels, including, reportedly, the earlier collector of Dantewada, Prasanna, who braved fears of attack and roamed the length and breadth of the district without being blocked or intimidated by Naxalites.

The districts of south Bastar are economically and socially devastated by the conflict, but even otherwise are among the poorest in the country. Equally worrying is data from the 2011 census that the decadal rate of growth of population of these districts is far below that of the rest of the state and the country. In Dantewada, it is as low as 11.90 per cent—and in Bijapur 8 per cent—as compared to 22.59 per cent for the state.[28] This could be because of high deaths because of hunger and illness, displacement, or simply that citizens were not counted by the census officials.

I also spoke to the security forces; all of them uniformed, armed young men from many parts of the country. Some had moved here from other combat locations such as Kashmir. They worked in hostile, unfamiliar and insecure conditions, and could not communicate with the local villagers in their dialect. I tried to remind them that their duty was to protect the local populace rather than to fight them. That these were their own people, caught up in extreme poverty and a prolonged, bloody conflict. They deserved their humane support and protection, not violence and intimidation.

The battle against Maoist violence—and vigilante 'counter-violence'—will be won in the end not by armed commandos and the further shedding of blood, but by schools, health centres, feeding centres and employment. However, this is the one war no one is waging today.

~

In India, the debate about the legitimacy of violence to resist injustice has acquired a special edge of immediacy and topicality, not only because of the state's efforts to quell violence perpetrated by the Maoists, and the bloody acceleration of hostilities by militants in these regions. Other combatants, including those on the far Right of the political spectrum—subscribing to Hindutva or Islamist religious extremist doctrines—have deployed strikingly similar rationales as Left-wing militants to justify the slaughter, plunder and rape of persons based on their identities, or the random killing and maiming of civilian populations. Analogous arguments run through other violent movements, such as through segments of those battling for azaadi, or independence, in the Kashmir Valley; or the Naga, Bodo, ULFA, Manipuri and other identity-based insurgents of India's deeply troubled and divided Northeast.

But I will restrict myself here only to the debates around claims of righteous violence to fight injustice against India's indigenous people in central India, as mustered by Left militants and their supporters. The annihilation of class enemies, an ideology initially propagated by firebrand communist Charu Majumdar, is now formally abandoned, although his words remain a reminder of his violent influence. 'He who has not dipped his hand in the blood of class enemies can hardly be called a communist.'[29] Yet many Maoist factions continue to resort to violence and terror rather than to democratic methods; including, the physical liquidation of people; attacks on police stations and the targeted killing of police personnel; killing so-called informers and 'coverts'; exploding landmines resulting in large-scale deaths; destroying public property; issuing death threats and conducting summary executions; and proclaiming 'bans' on political parties.

In India, the only major sustained civic effort to engage both the state and Maoists in a discussion around violence was organized by a group of concerned citizens in Andhra Pradesh led by the reputed humanist S. R. Sankaran. The Sankaran Committee condemned the arbitrary and violent actions of Naxalite parties which contribute to 'further brutalise the society and lead to the shrinkage of democratic space for mobilisation and direct participation of the people, impairing the very process of transformation that the movements claim to stand for'.[30]

More than forty years of Maoist insurgency in India have not altered the casual acceptance of the inevitability of the loss of life, even of civilians, in such battles. When challenged, spokespersons for the Maoists typically describe these killings as 'mistakes', but such 'mistakes' are considered unavoidable in their righteous war, and continue to recur. It is as though such occasional apologies are sufficient recompense for recurring murders, including those of non-combatants.

Even occasional expressions of 'regret' or 'errors' are typically missing when those killed by Maoists are men in uniform. But I am convinced that the lives of army and paramilitary soldiers are no less precious than those of innocent unarmed citizens who have been killed in the conflict, and indeed the lives of those who have picked up guns against the established order. Human life is precious, and I cannot endorse a hierarchy of more or less legitimate killings. Those who justify the killing of security personnel also ignore the fact that most of these are just poor working-class men, often of peasant stock, who join the police or security forces only as one of the few sources of livelihood available to them.

Frequently, it is argued that opponents of Maoist violence ignore the 'structural violence' of the state and, by implication, equate it with the emancipatory violence of the oppressed. Those who defend violent resistance believe that it is justified because of the unremitting scale and hopelessness of the oppression to which they are subject. There is no doubt that tribal people in India are among its most dispossessed and savagely oppressed. But I find the claim that recourse to arms is the inevitable result of such exploitation, or even moral justification for violence, perilous and erroneous. Less than 25 per cent of India's tribal regions are affected by Maoist violence even today, and even in these districts there is no evidence of mass support of all or most tribal people for the 'dadas' and 'didis' in military fatigues who fight in their name.[31] This also does not mean that those who are not actively waging war against the state are passively submitting to their subjugation. On the contrary, large tracts of these regions are rife with diverse and creative forms of democratic dissent. The binary opposition between violent resistance on the one hand and surrender and complicity on the other, as posited by Maoist ideologues, is spurious and dangerous.

I find it extraordinary that people who oppose the death penalty are willing to support the execution of people by private armies and militant 'people's courts'. In the 'rude justice' of Maoist executions; men and women are eliminated for crimes such as informing the police, joining a rival faction, choosing to opt out of membership of a militant group, or simply belonging to an oppressing category of people. There is not even a pretence of access to any 'due process', except sometimes a public hearing. It is not dissimilar to fake police 'encounters' or extra-judicial killings, in which the police is judge, prosecutor and executioner at the same time—this confluence spawns horrendous injustice. Neither the state nor Maoist militants accept that human beings are fallible and can make errors of judgement, that every human being is entitled to disprove one's guilt, as well as to redeem oneself even after one errs; that the 'mistake' of taking life can never be remedied.

Perhaps the most persuasive argument mustered in support of violence aimed at seeking justice is that violent resistance is the only effective recourse for the defenceless and powerless when pitted against the brutal and unjust might of the state, often backed by corrupt and formidable corporate wealth. Commentators illustrate the futility of non-violent resistance in such profoundly unequal combats. But there are indeed many examples of exceptional success of non-violent struggles. The movement for the right to information, the battles against big dams, and against hate violence are incandescent examples. I have written separately about the extraordinary achievement of the Safai Karmchari Andolan to help bring an end to manual scavenging, one of the most stubborn and degrading practices of untouchability.[32] Gandhi himself battled religious violence, and ultimately lost his life to it. Yet the movements that he led are not failures: Pakistan was created on grounds of religious identity, but the majority of Indians, both Hindu and Muslim, opted for a pluralist democratic state and this idea of India survives continuous assaults by religious fundamentalists.

I believe—and the experience of human history bears me out—that it is violent movements which are much more likely to fail to achieve their initial stated objectives. It is self-evident to me that it is impossible to build a just and humane society by means which are unjust and inhuman. The outcomes of strategies which are built around bloodshed, vengeance, repression and hate will always ultimately be brutal and unjust, even if the violence is undertaken for lofty ideals. During the twentieth century, we witnessed the most ambitious experiments in human history to rebuild ancient, forever unequal societies around principles of equality and justice. But to achieve this, the leadership deemed it necessary to kill, imprison, 'purge' masses of dissenters and 'class enemies' and withhold democratic freedoms. The result was that although millions of people received assured work, fair wages, decent housing, healthcare and quality schooling for their children—to a degree that was impossible for them to even dream of a generation earlier (and sadly often a generation later in these same countries after the collapse of communism)—they rebelled because their spirit felt crushed by omnipresent fear and the bondage of their conscience. It took barely six decades for this experiment to crumble.

This was replaced, regrettably, by a hegemonic world order which generates unprecedented wealth but which still traps millions all over the world in cycles of hunger, disease, unemployment and insecurity; in which governments increasingly abdicate their responsibilities to ensure the dignified survival of all their people; and in which a large population of people are stigmatized only because of their religious identity, and globally live with fear, discrimination, grave human-rights violations and devastating wars.

~

I end this discussion on non-violence by recalling one modest, offbeat, homespun enterprise of alternate non-violent resistance to which I was a close witness. The year was 2003, the location Godhra in Gujarat. On the first anniversary of the fire on the Sabarmati Express, Praveen Togadia scheduled a programme of trishul diksha, in which he proposed to publicly distribute tridents as symbols of continued warfare against the Muslims. The openly sympathetic Right-wing state government refused to prohibit the meeting. The Muslim population of the small town of Godhra once again cowered in their ghettoes and even began to flee.

In this climate of palpable fear, in which a mere matchstick could have set the city ablaze again, a unique idea of resistance was propounded. The plan arose from the ranks of the peace activists of the Aman Biradari whom we had recruited from working-class survivors of the carnage in relief camps. The scheme was not to block the trishul distribution but, instead, to organize an alternate programme the same day. While Togadia would hand out trishuls, the peace activists, in another part of the town, would hand out roses. They called it gulaab diksha. Both sets of organizers strenuously canvassed participation for their respective meetings. In the end, less than 200 young men assembled to receive the trishuls from Togadia. More than a thousand people, both Muslim and Hindu, gathered to collect roses.

Faith and Forgiveness

My personal faith choice is that of agnosticism, the acknowledgement that I do not know if god exists, or if there is life after death. I find this position more scientific than atheism, because even atheism is based on certainty, whereas we truly do not know. But more than scientific rationality, what is more important to me are the social *ethics* of my agnosticism. It is not just that I do not know if there is a god. I do not even want to know, because this knowledge should not be the driving force of my life choices. I love the Sufi story of Raabia in the twelfth century, who feverishly runs up and down the streets of the Iraqi town of Basra with a bucket of water in one hand and a flaming torch in the other. Asked why she carries the bucket of water, she says she wishes to douse the fires of hell. Then why the flaming torch? She wants to set heaven on fire, she says. I should lead the good life neither out of fear of the fires of hell, or the desire for heaven, but only because I am convinced that it is the right thing to do. This knowledge alone should be enough for me.

I recognize more clearly now that our understanding of secularism in this country is not the denial of faith but equal respect for every faith, including the absence of faith. This is the secularism of Ashok, Kabir, Chisti, Nanak, Akbar and Gandhi. Many argue that we should not describe this principle as one of secularism, but find another name for it. I am content to call it secularism, as long as we agree on what it entails. If a person's faith leads them to oppressing women, people of 'lower' castes and sexual minorities, to hating people of other faiths, and into superstition and unreason, then it should be opposed resolutely by all means. But if it leads people to greater compassion, or gives them solace in moments of bereavement, then why should it be negated? Faith may not work for me, but why should I object if it works for someone else? How can I be so convinced that I am right and the other wrong?

The two persons in India's public life who sacrificed the most for the secular idea of India—Mahatma Gandhi and Maulana Azad—were deeply devout, and this is what spurred their politics of unshakeable respect for the faith of others. Gandhi paid for his belief with his life. The two people who, during India's freedom struggle, most influentially led the battles for a state based on religion were Muhammad Ali Jinnah and Vinayak Damodar Savarkar. Jinnah was not a practising Muslim most of his life, and Savarkar was a self-professed atheist. There has to be a moral in this seeming paradox somewhere.

Azad was passionately opposed to the two-nation theory, declaring, 'Religion has never been a binding factor in the formation of nations.' He wrote: 'It is one of the greatest frauds on the people to suggest that religious affinity can unite areas which are geographically, economically, linguistically and culturally different.' He added, 'The basis of the partition was enmity between the Hindus and Muslims. The creation of Pakistan gave it a permanent constitutional form.'[33]

The modern secular state in India has no religion, but is bound by the 'higher morality of the Constitution'. It is also bound to ensure equal protection and equal rights without favour or prejudice to all people regardless of their faith—and their gender, caste, class, language and place of residence. But the democratic state is not simply 'hands-off' religion, as the colonial state was and many Western democracies are. It is not freed from both the right and the duty to reform what is unjust—such as to women, children or disadvantaged sub-groups—under the rubric of accepted religious practice.

I have said in the opening pages of this book that the greatest challenge which all countries will have to face and resolve in the twenty-first century are the ways in which they will deal with the two paramount challenges of inequality and diversity. (Some friends caution that I should add climate change to this list, and they are probably right.) But the understanding of how these challenges are to be dealt with varies widely in different parts of the world. The nation-building project in countries of Europe was sometimes one of coercive—and often violent—homogenization, in which minority languages, faith systems and cultures were forcefully submerged in the hegemony of the majority language, culture and faith. In contrast, India has traditionally dealt with diversity in ways that are respectful of pluralism—although social values attached to the practices of different groups are intensely graded and hierarchical. It is only the Hindu nationalist project which is homogenizing—what Ramachandra Guha once described as an enterprise to create a Hindu Pakistan.[34] It requires conformity with what is deemed to be essentially Indian—upper-caste, male, north Indian, Hindi-speaking, Hindu (and heterosexual). The degrees to which an individual is not any or all of these render that person a lesser Indian. This is why Hindu nationalists have been so implacably opposed to Gandhi's humanist secularism founded on his devotion to the Hindu faith, as much as to the secular democracy enshrined in the Indian Constitution.

~

In early 2013 I was invited to speak about inequality at the Danish Parliament to some parliamentarians, senior intellectuals and activists. Since I had arrived a couple of days early, I decided to look at what Denmark does for its homeless populations, and to learn from it. It was snowing, and temperatures in Copenhagen had plummeted to minus 10 degrees centigrade. I had expected to find the best programmes for the homeless in Denmark. Instead, I was told that the Danish government takes care only of *Danish* homeless people. Since almost every homeless person in the city was non-Danish, I asked who took care of them. I was told it was the church. My local hosts helped me establish contact with the church, and I met a priest, a wonderful, compassionate young woman in jeans about my daughter's age. She said the church was able to provide a roof and food to ninety homeless people. For the remaining—at least a thousand people—there were no arrangements at all. I asked the people assembled to hear me in the Danish Parliament, 'How can you take no responsibility for homeless people at your doorstep, just because they are not Danish? Is this a conversation which you should be having at minus 10 centigrade? And in Scandinavia, the home of the welfare state?'

I realized then how inextricably intertwined are the ways a society deals with inequality and how it deals with difference. India has dealt very badly as a civilization with the challenge of inequality, but has fine historical traditions of religious tolerance and coexistence. In contrast, I found that whereas Scandinavia today sets some of the highest standards on the planet with its welfare state; in dealing with inequality, it is troubled and confused by 'different' immigrant populations of diverse colour, clothing and faith, who more recently have made their country their home. It is probably this anxiety with difference which overpowered their otherwise sterling instincts and social contract for greater equality through interventions by a caring state.

~

Even beyond the question of religion, I believe that political and ethical opposition to ideologies based on hate and difference entails a discourse and practice which is restrained, respectful, pluralist, rational and compassionate. It does not presume the worst in one's opponents and, instead, sets the highest, most uncompromising standards for oneself. It is introspective, open to contradiction and refutation, and also caring about one's opponent.

It is not just the language but the *practice* of one's engagement with protagonists of hate politics which needs to be different in an alternate politics. As Martin Luther King Jr, who I regard to be the greatest Gandhian in the world after Gandhi himself, declared memorably, 'Darkness can never drive out darkness, only light can do that. Hate can never drive out hate, only love can do that.' In many parts of the world, communities live side by side bitterly estranged by conflict, hate and suspicion. The source of conflict may be external or civil war; differences of identity based on the parameters of religion, ethnicity, race and caste; violent political battles between the Right and the Left; battles for self-determination and political independence; and many others. What is common is that unhealed wounds fester and consequently foster legacies of suffering and hatred carried from generation to generation; and the greatest of these burdens are borne by children, women, the aged, disabled people, and the poor.

People of goodwill everywhere, through history, have fashioned strategies to bring about reconciliation, or the meeting of hearts and minds, between people separated by conflict and hate. I will outline here one unusual strategy we deployed in Aman Biradari, initially in the aftermath of the communal violence of 2002 in Gujarat, and the estrangement of people of the Hindu and Muslim faiths which followed. We have also initiated this strategy, of trying to secure 'Reconciliation through Shared Caring', in Assam and Muzaffarnagar, in an attempt to fashion new instruments to battle the politics of hate with an alternate, modest politics of love.

Conventionally, after most conflicts, members of the community which is seen by the victims to have caused harm and perpetrated violence, rarely work on relief and reconstruction programmes for victims of the 'other' community. The dominant 'common sense'—unconsciously accepted often even by humanitarian agencies—is that relief workers from the group which is perceived to have caused harm to people of another community will not be welcomed in efforts to help people after mass violence.

The heart of the strategy of 'Reconciliation through Shared Caring' is to refuse to accept this post-conflict 'common sense'; to swim against the prevailing currents of social estrangement and suspicion by resolving that *all* will work in the aftermath of mass violence—for dialogue, relief, reconstruction, justice, welfare and caring. These groups of workers must *always*, self-consciously and prominently, include members of all the estranged and warring communities. More than what they contribute in tangible terms, the symbolism of mixed teams working together across divides contributes most to healing and rebuilding trust.

Invariably, such proposals are initially rejected as 'impractical', pointless, or even dangerous. Our experience has been quite the contrary. In Gujarat, although the victims were mostly Muslim, teams of aman pathiks and nyaya pathiks of Aman Biradari, from both Hindu and Muslim communities, worked together for a decade, first in relief camps and, later, for reconstruction and justice. We also extended this strategy to other sites of violence like Bhagalpur.

More recently in Assam, after violent conflicts between indigenous Bodo people and Bengali Muslims in the summer of 2012, the climate was charged with hatred and anger between these communities. Yet, when we appealed for shared humanitarian work, people were surprised that many young people came forward from both communities, including Muslim young people such as social work student Abdul Kalam Azad and civil servant Ashiq Zamin, and Raju Narzary, a Bodo postgraduate in social work, whose own property had been burnt down in the violence.

With the help of these young leaders, we constituted a joint platform called Shanti Gazun—which means 'peace' in the Assamese and Bodo tongues respectively. With volunteers from Gujarat, Hyderabad and Delhi, young people from both communities went into camps of the 'other' community. People in the camps—who had suffered betrayal, uprooting and violence at the hands of their neighbours—were initially incredulous, angry and suspicious when they saw persons from the community of their attackers. But when the peace workers humbly persisted in their resolve to serve them, their resistance melted everywhere into a healing appreciation; dialogues were organized for the first time, and estranged neighbours often wept and embraced each other. I will narrate the story of one such activist, Yusuf, at the end of this narrative.

Our experience in Gujarat was that once people start returning to their old damaged homes and habitats, often in the neighbourhood of their attackers' residences, the role of the joint teams becomes even more critical. They began with dialogues between people of different communities sitting together and listening as tentative first steps in the long journey to ultimately re-establish trust. Joint youth and women groups organized recreation activities, including sports, which further helped people across the conflict divide to meet each other again. They aided children to return to mixed schools in hostile pockets, and make up for interrupted schooling; and also jointly extended special support to old people, widows and children who had lost loved ones.

People also need practical assistance in rebuilding their damaged livelihoods and homes. An audacious reconciliation plan was to appeal to people from both communities to contribute voluntary labour, or shramdaan, to help rebuild the houses damaged on both sides of the conflict. We made this appeal for the first time after Godhra. The slogan which we worked with implied that it would be hard to again destroy a house which Hindus and Muslims had jointly built. Defying the hot winds of hate, people offered voluntary labour to rebuild houses of people of the 'other' community in eighty villages in Godhra. Through this simple act, ordinary people of both communities demonstrated remorse and caring.

The peace and trust people rebuild from the ruins wrought by hate and violence endures precisely because they rebuild together.

I recall visiting one village near Godhra one hot summer day, a little over a year after 2002, to observe and share in the joint shramdaan organized by Hindus and Muslims to rebuild the houses of Muslim victims. In this village, I was told that young people of the village had decided to rebuild the home of an old Hindu widow. Her husband had died a few months earlier, and she was too poor to afford a pyre for his last rites. In desperation, she decided to set her own thatch hovel on fire with her husband's body within it. Therefore, along with the riot survivors, she, too, had become homeless. I went to the site where a group of young men were working in the hot summer afternoon. I found among them a young man in a skull cap.

Curious, I sat down with him and talked. He said to me that his home had been looted and gutted by Hindu mobs. This had left him depressed and hopeless. But when a call was made to help rebuild the Hindu widow's home, he decided to join in. In a strange way which he could not explain to himself or to me, it helped heal his spirits. When I was leaving, he said quietly, 'I wanted to thank you for organizing this programme.' This left me in great wonder. This young Muslim man, who had lost everything in the fires lit by his Hindu neighbours, was thanking me for the chance of working for free, on a hot summer afternoon, to build a home for a destitute Hindu widow.

Of Mercy and Justice

In the winter of 2013-14, two men were successively hanged in India's jails, both indicted for grave crimes of terror. I have written here about one, Afzal Guru; the other was Ajmal Kasab, the one surviving assailant in the Mumbai terror attack of 26/11. On 8 August 2013, another man, Maganlal—a little-known tribal farmer charged with killing his five little daughters—was scheduled to hang in Jabalpur Central Jail.[35] Alert human rights lawyers chanced to read of his hanging in a small online news item just the evening before his execution was fixed, and rushed to the bungalow of the chief justice of the Supreme Court, P. Sathasivam. Recognizing this to be literally a matter of life and death, he agreed to hear them that same evening and concurred that even after the President rejects the mercy petition of a death-row convict, he still has one more legal remedy: to challenge the rejection in the Supreme Court.

Maganlal was much too poor to afford a lawyer in the higher courts. He would be dead today but for the intervention by this committed team of human rights lawyers—Yug Mohan Chaudhary, Siddhartha and Colin Gonsalves—and the stay granted by Justice Sathasivam. There are many reasons I oppose his death penalty. The gravity of Maganlal's crime is not one of them, nor the merits of the judgement holding him guilty. My overwhelming consideration is the intense class bias of capital punishment. It can hardly be a coincidence that the overwhelming majority of 414 people who faced the gallows in India at of the end of 2012 are impoverished and dependent, at best, on legal-aid lawyers.[36]

I visited Maganlal's family who live on the outskirts of a tribal hamlet, Barela, outside Kaneria village in the Sehore district of Madhya Pradesh. Their crumbling earthen house, the sickly pallor of the children's skin and hair, and their gaunt frames and tired faces testified to lives of unrelenting struggle and want. Maganlal's brothers and two wives said that the only months in which food is secure are those which follow the occasional good monsoon, when they live off what they grow on their acre of land. Other times, they await uncertain daily-wage employment from the Forest Department, or gather firewood in the forests selling, after a day's labour, a head-load for forty rupees.

After the crime, Maganlal's brothers pooled ₹5,000 and hired a local lawyer. Once he was convicted in the trial court, they had no further idea about the progress of the case until they abruptly received notice of his hanging. Maganlal was represented by legal-aid lawyers who had never met him even once. The Supreme Court unusually refused to even admit his petition—let alone hear it on its merits. I am convinced that his fate could have been different had he been represented by a competent lawyer, and even more so if the lawyer had been a fashionably high-profile one.

Just the few hours we spent in the village threw up many possible arguments which could have been made, if not for his innocence, at least to mitigate his inclusion in the 'rarest of the rare' cases meriting the highest penalty of death. There was, firstly, his abject poverty. Also, not just his wives and brothers, but other villagers testified to his affable nature; the absence of any history of violence and crime; and that he loved his daughters dearly. Villagers said that his behaviour had changed dramatically in the four months preceding the murder. He had suddenly become withdrawn and quiet, and would wander alone for hours in the forests. Villagers explained this as being caused by black magic. A more convincing explanation could be mental illness, perhaps a temporary breakdown because he could not make ends meet.

I later learned that he was receiving psychiatric medication in Jabalpur Prison. The threshold of insanity required if courts are to declare him innocent is very high. But if evidence from villagers and neighbours suggesting mental illness could have been brought before the courts, could this not have persuaded the courts to at least hang him? Additionally, the entire case against Maganlal was based on circumstantial evidence, as there are no eyewitnesses to the crime.

In the infamous case in which a young politician, Sushil Sharma, murdered his wife, Naina Sahni, and tried to dispose off her body in a tandoor oven, a bench headed by the chief justice observed that this was not a 'crime against society', and that the appellant had no criminal antecedents. 'He is not a confirmed criminal and no evidence is led by the State to indicate that he is likely to revert to such crimes in future. It is, therefore, not possible in the facts of the case to say there is no chance of the appellant being reformed and rehabilitated.'[37] Precisely all these same arguments could apply equally to Maganlal's case.

My point is that if only Maganlal's family could have afforded effective legal representation in the trial as well as in the higher courts, it is possible that the trial court's sentence could have been less severe, and the higher courts could have come to similar conclusions about mitigating circumstances: that this was not a crime against society by a man with any criminal record.

Were we then hanging Maganlal only because of his crime of poverty?

There are also larger philosophical questions about why a society chooses to execute those who violate human and social morality. Is our motivation the prevention of further crimes? Do we credibly believe that the next time a father is driven to consider murdering his own children—in a moment of intense rage, despair or madness—he will be deterred only because of the possibility that he may hang? (Maganlal's brother reported that Maganlal tried to hang himself after killing his daughters, and was saved only because his brother cut the rope at the the last spilt second.)

Or is our objective in seeking capital punishment actually retribution; to take the life of a person who outrages and violates what we cherish? It was evident that people most directly violated by the crime—the mothers of the five girls who were killed that summer afternoon in 2010—have forgiven him for what the courts have found him guilty. They recalled to us how he was an affectionate father and kind husband, how he loved his children, would seat them with him when he ate, and that he never raised a hand on any of them before that horrific day. Their fields lie fallow; their older son has had to drop out of school and instead grazes cattle. 'We only wish he could return home and take care of his family,' his wives say.

If they can forgive him, can we not?

Postscript: The Supreme Court did finally grant Maganlal remission, converting his sentence into life imprisonment, on grounds of possible mental illness, his desperate poverty and lack of access to effective legal counsel.

Learning from Mohandas

This world today has much to learn from Mohandas Karamchand Gandhi.

Many young people, born in free India, have never discovered Mohandas. He towered over the twentieth century with the epic leadership he provided to the non-violent struggle against colonial subjugation, but even more for the intensely moral foundations of his politics. The world in the twenty-first century is vastly different from the one which preceded it. It witnesses the global triumph of market economics, the retreat of the state, and the generation of unprecedented wealth. It also sees a planet torn apart by staggering inequalities and by simmering conflict—often over religious identity—within and between nations. Mohandas's relevance is perhaps even greater to this century than to the ones in which he lived.

There are many things that Mohandas lived for. But what he died for was the secular, democratic idea of India. The struggle for India's freedom was not just a battle against imperialism. It was also a bitter contest about the kind of nation India would be when it was reborn into freedom. Central to Mohandas's imagination of India was of a nation of unparalleled diversity in which it would not matter which god you worshipped—or if you chose to worship no god; it would not matter if you were a man or a woman; if you belonged to this caste or that; if you were rich or destitute; or whether you spoke this language or lived in that region. You would be a fully equal human being and citizen, assured of equal rights and protection to pursue your beliefs and chosen way of life. What is important is not just that Mohandas had this dream for India, but that the majority of Indians—Hindu, Muslim and of other faiths—rallied behind this ideal.

Today, in France and many parts of Europe, the ideals of secularism are currently being invoked to ban women from wearing veils in schools and public places. Elsewhere, Sikhs are barred from wearing turbans. But the secularism that we learnt from Mohandas required the opposite—to defend the right of each person to follow their religious and cultural persuasions. I may (and do) oppose the veil, but must fight for your right to choose—as well as my right to oppose. This 'Indian' ideal of secularism is at variance even with hard atheism, which is intolerant of the faith of others. I may personally choose to reject faith but, equally, I must respect the choice of faith of others.

This ideal was one for which Mohandas was ultimately killed. But free India has repeatedly failed him in so many ways. The blood of innocents is spilled relentlessly because of their religious or caste identity; governments have been voted to power because they pulled down a place of worship; Dalit children in between a third and half of our rural schools are still seated separately; temples are still barred to Dalits; and millions of women still carry human excreta on their heads for disposal.

To battle for their vision for a more just world, many dispossessed and idealistic men and women today continue to pick up the gun. But Mohandas reminded us that it is impossible to build a just and humane society by means which are unjust and inhuman. He taught us ways to resolutely fight injustice without hate or bloodshed but, instead, with the timeless instruments of truth, love, self-restraint, voluntary self-suffering, courage, peaceful mass mobilization and, indeed, on occasion, recourse to law and the courts. These instruments of struggle need to be reclaimed and refurbished to be compatible with the challenges and possibilities of our times.

Mohandas also taught us the futility of revenge and anger. There is so little forgiveness in our public life today. Fasting for communal peace during the post-Partition riots in Calcutta, Gandhi is said to have been confronted by a Hindu man nearly crazed by grief and hate, because a Muslim mob had killed his young son. He had responded by battering a young Muslim boy to death. Mohandas gently counselled him that if he really wished to overcome his suffering, he should find a Muslim boy, the age of his son, whose parents had been killed by Hindu mobs. And he should bring the boy up like his own son, but in the faith of his parents.

It is a hundred years since Mohandas wrote in *Hind Swaraj*, his stirring critique of modernity, and those who return to it and his other writings discover many ideas to craft new solutions to many of the contemporary crises of our world. His economics did not aspire to growth and accumulation, but instead to people's 'swaraj' or control over their own destinies. He opposed the deployment of machines if people were out of work. He did not believe in unlimited wants but, instead, reminded us that the world produces enough for the needs but not the greed of every human being. His economics was not founded on assumptions of self-seeking accumulation being central to human nature; instead, he was convinced that human beings were essentially altruistic. The world would be a fairer, kinder and happier place if it adopted many of Gandhi's principles of an alternate 'economics as if people matter'.

Contemporary notions of 'good governance' envisage an ideal state to be one which best facilitates markets. Mohandas instead offered us a 'talisman' to be summoned in times of doubt and confusion. He counselled us to recall the face of the most disadvantaged person we know, and reflect on the implications of our decisions for this person's life, well-being and 'swaraj'. Applied to state policy, this would mean that the quality of governance should be measured by what the state achieves for its most disadvantaged people. By this measure, if a state facilitates rapid economic growth but dispossesses our poorest of their livelihoods, lands and forests, the government has abjectly failed its people.

Mohandas also gave many lessons about how to lead a good life. He taught us to strive always to live and practise our beliefs, to 'be the change we wish to see in the world'. If we believe in equality, can we try to be egalitarian in the ways we relate with people around us? If we believe in love, can we fight impulses of hate and revenge? He taught us to never lose touch with our immediate humanity even while fighting lofty battles. In negotiations for India's freedom, he would take time off to tend to a goat-kid's broken leg. He was not coldly rigid in his convictions. Although passionately vegetarian, when Badshah Khan's children visited, he offered to arrange meat dishes for them. And he never lost his playful sense of mischief. When asked why he went to see the King of England in only a loin cloth and shawl, he famously responded that the monarch was wearing enough for both of them.

Mohandas by no means held a perfect vision or led a perfect life. Indeed, he was the first to acknowledge his faults and remained preoccupied throughout his life with fighting them. Most flawed for me—as I will elaborate in the next chapter—was his condoning of caste even as he passionately opposed untouchability. His notions of trusteeship of big industry clouded ideas of class oppression and class struggle. And, in his personal life, he failed as a father, leaving his son tormented and broken. His beliefs in women's equality were imperfectly reflected in his loving but often domineering relationship with his wife Kasturba.

We learn from Mohandas's triumphs, but also from his failures. We go back to him not because he was perfect. We go back to Mohandas because, in his own words, he obeyed only one dictator—his conscience.

Learning from Babasaheb

Among most secular progressive people in India today there is the belief—indeed, an article of faith—that India has been, through most of its long history, a diverse, pluralist and tolerant civilization—the land of Buddha, Kabir and Nanak; of Ashok, Akbar and Gandhi. It is a culture in which every major faith in the world has found the space and freedom to flourish and grow, where persecuted faiths have received refuge, where heterodox and sceptical traditions have thrived alongside spiritual and mystical traditions, and where ordinary people live and respect faith systems different from their own. In the words of Maulana Azad, 'It was India's historic destiny that many human races and cultures and religious faiths should flow into her, and many a caravan should find rest here...One of the last of the caravans was that of the followers of Islam...'[38]

All of this is true, and this is why the rise of a narrow, monolithic and intolerant interpretations of Indian culture—what Romila Thapar describes as the Right-wing semitization of Hinduism—in new India causes us deep disquiet.[39] But what our analysis does not stress often or deeply enough is that all of India, both old and new, has been also built on the edifice of monumental inequality and the oppression of caste, and that this is equally the story of India, old and new.

I am sometimes asked how I would describe my political beliefs. I clear my throat, a little embarrassed that I cannot offer a concise answer. I am a secular, democratic, humanist, socialist, I sometimes venture. If I had to choose just one of these appelations, it would probably be humanist. I add that there have been many influences on my politics. The earliest influence, in my college days, was Karl Marx, and from reading and discussing him I have absorbed class analysis, belief in an egalitarian society and a redistributive state, and a passion for the equal rights of labour and the oppressed. In my years in government, I was sometimes called—both mockingly and, at times, affectionately—Comrade Collector in the districts where I served, but I think Marxists never know quite where to place me, because I speak of social and economic equality but also, in the same breath, of egalitarian compassion.

From Mohandas, too, I have learned much, but perhaps foremost is the importance of conformity between means and ends—and that no end, however lofty, justifies violent, unjust and untruthful means—his idea of secularism as equal respect for all faiths, an alternate development economics 'as if people matter', non-violence, and the importance of struggling lifelong—even if hopelessly failing, as I have often done—for greater ethical consistency between a person's beliefs and the way she lives her life.[40] From feminist philosophers, I have learnt that biology does not, and cannot be allowed to determine a person's potential, rights, dignity and destiny; about interlocking systems of inequality and privilege; about assertion, nurturing, caring and solidarities.

But, increasingly, as the years pass, I am influenced—and challenged—more and more by Babasaheb Bhimrao Ramji Ambedkar. You cannot change India until you understand India, you cannot understand India until you understand caste, and you cannot understand caste until you read Ambedkar. For those who celebrate Babasaheb, from Mayawati to Arundhati Roy, the assumption appears to be that it is obligatory to pit him against Gandhi, to discredit all that Gandhi stood for so as to install Ambedkar in his due place in modern Indian history. It is as though Ambedkar can stand tall only if his lifelong political adversary, Gandhi is toppled from his pedestal. I do not agree. I feel that history is too complex and pluralist to be reduced to a simple ordering—and reordering—of heroes and villains. History is expansive enough to admit the decisive role of the two vastly different men who most influenced the making of new India in the years of the anti-colonial struggle for freedom and the immediate years after Independence, Mohandas and Babasaheb.

Having said this, I find I agree with many of Babasaheb's major critiques of Mohandas. He rightly rejects Mohandas's idea of trusteeship, which undermines the imperative for redistributive policies and laws, ignores the injustice and oppression which is the invisible fount of a great part of large wealth accumulation, and leaves the dispossessed at the mercy of the 'goodwill' of the wealthy.

Babasaheb is correct in dismissing Mohandas's glorification of 'village republics', which he accurately describes as 'cesspools' of caste injustice, inequity and bigotry. He opposes, with equal justification, Mohandas's defence of tradition, because tradition in India has always been implacably hostile to the rights and dignity of women and people belonging to disadvantaged castes. He rejects acutely, as a 'myth', the idea of a Hindu society or community.[41] He suggests instead that caste Hindus constitute a society devoid of a unifying principle, a conglomeration of an 'amorphous mass of people'.[42] People owe primary loyalty within it to their sub-caste, whose customs and purity have to be maintained through endogamy and restrictions on commensality; he therefore believes that the system automatically pits one sub-caste against another. He observes that the only time one sub-caste feels unified with another, or one caste with another, is during conflict with other communities. The gradation of castes, with greater rights given to higher castes also prevents the formation of a unified front against the caste system, as each caste 'takes pride and consolation' in being graded above certain other castes.[43]

But Mohandas's greatest failing was his vigorous defence of caste. He opposed untouchability and was an influential champion for the dignity of caste-based scavengers who cleaned human excrement with their own hands. He took to cleaning his own toilets, which was a radical and humanist act in the times in which he lived. However his monumental mistake—an error so unjust to millions of India's oppressed castes that it has led to the rejection of his entire legacy by many of India's poorest people—was in insisting that untouchability was an aberration of caste, and that caste was in itself a benign social system for the division of labour.

I cannot understand how Mohandas could defend the idea of caste even if he artificially excised from it the idea of untouchability. How could he defend a system of ordered social hierarchy based on birth? And even more pertinently, how could he have justified a system which traps a child into a profession because she or he was born into a family which belongs to a particular caste. Babasaheb insisted—and I believe accurately—that far from being an aberration of caste, the cruel system of untouchability was intrinsic to the caste system. That caste was not a division of labour but a 'division of labourers', in which certain groups of people are trapped in devalued work, based on their parents' social status.[44] It does not allow mobility—therefore, he viewed caste as a sort of endogamous, enclosed class, which further suppresses individual development by forcing people to work in occupations that they do not necessarily like or choose.⁴⁵ In this respect, he thought that industrialization and capitalism would create conditions for Dalits to escape the stigma of caste, whereas Mohandas was opposed to modernity and industrialization.

Further, Babasaheb was convinced not only that untouchability is intrinsic to the caste system, but that the caste system is inextricable from the Hindu religion. Mohandas was a devout Hindu all his life and is believed to have died with Ram's name on his lips. But Babasaheb declared in 1936, 'I was born a Hindu and have suffered the consequences of untouchability. I will not die a Hindu.' He described Hindu society with what Arundhati Roy aptly terms as a 'chilling metaphor': 'as a multi-storied tower with no staircase and no entrance. Everyone has to die in the storey they were born into.'⁴⁶ This battle against the Hindu faith culminated in his epic conversion to Buddhism in 1956, along with about a million Dalits, a few months before his death.

Babasaheb, born into an indigent, low-caste Mahad family in Mhow, an army cantonment, was able to acquire an education only because his father was a subaltern in the British Army. He studied law at Columbia University on a state scholarship, and returned first to join the Baroda administration but was wounded and angered by the open caste humiliations he endured in office. Instead, he joined as a professor at the Sydenham College in Bombay around the time Mohandas returned to India to lead its freedom struggle.⁴⁷ In 1924, he formed the Bahishkrut Hitkarni Sabha to promote education and socio-economic improvement among the most disadvantaged castes, as well as to provide a forum to voice grievances.⁴⁸

In 1927, he led a movement, known as the Mahad Satyagrah, to assert the rights of traditionally untouchable castes to draw water from public tanks and wells and to enter Hindu places of worship. In Mahad, more than a thousand people marched to the Chavadar Lake and drank water from the tank in the centre of the town. Worried that Babasaheb and his followers were planning to enter a Hindu temple, a riot ensued. Upper-caste Hindus later 'purified' the tank by performing prayers as they believed that the untouchables had polluted the tank by drinking its water. They also filed a case against Babasaheb, claiming that tank was private property. On 25 December, Babasaheb publicly burnt the Manusmriti in protest. Years passed before December 1937, when the Bombay High Court finally ruled that untouchables had the right to use water from the tank.

Decades later, in my many district postings and as the head of the department charged with Scheduled Caste Welfare in Madhya Pradesh and Chhattisgarh, and my later research into the practice of untouchability, I found that in the majority of villages across large swathes of the country, Dalits are still barred from access to common wells and temples. In a village in the Sagar district of Madhya Pradesh in 1991, Dalit youth raised the demand that since the upper-caste enclaves of the village had many hand-pumps from which Dalits were barred, at least one hand-pump should be drilled in the Dalit hamlet. But the upper-caste villagers were outraged at their assertion and punished them with boycott and violence which ultimately brought them to their knees. In Bilaspur, Madhya Pradesh, in 1996, a Dalit man touched a Hanuman statue in gratitude that his wife's life had been saved, and was brutally attacked and exiled from his village. I wrote both their stories in *Unheard Voices* and Shyam Benegal made these into a film, *Samar*. But these stories are far from unusual. They continue to be so commonplace in rural India that they are, for many, unremarkable. Babasaheb's proud words during the Mahad Satyagrah in 1927 still ring in my heart: 'It is not as if drinking the water of Chavadar Lake will make us immortal. We have survived long enough all these days without drinking it. We are not going to the Chavadar Lake merely to drink its water. We are going to the Lake to assert that we too are human beings like others. It must be clear that this meeting has been called to set up the norm of equality...'[49]

I recall also the Marathi poet, L. S. Rokade's fierce lament about the injustice of unequal birth:

Mother, you used to tell me
> when I was born
> your labour was very long.
The reason for your long labour;
I, still in your womb, was wondering
Do I want to be born?
Do I want to be born at all
> in this land?
Where all paths raced horizonwards
> but to me barred...
Mother, this is your land
> flowing with water
Rivers break their banks
Lakes brim over
And you, one of the human race
> must shed blood
> struggle and strike
> for a palmful of water...[50]

~

My other debt to Babasaheb is for leading the writing of India's Constitution, one of the finest in the world, designed to illuminate for governments pathways and precepts of just governance. He negotiated painfully and resolutely a document which no doubt reflected political compromise, but which in its substantive guarantees and even more in its Directive Principles lays out the blueprint of a just and equal state and society.

He was acutely conscious, right up to his death, that political equality as offered by India's Constitution did not in itself guarantee social and economic equality, and for which a much longer struggle would have to be waged. These lines, taken from his speech, 'My Personal Philosophy', an All-India Radio broadcast on 3 October 1954 remain prophetic today: 'Indians today are governed by two different ideologies. Their political ideal set out in the preamble to the Indian Constitution affirms a life of liberty, equality and fraternity. Their social ideal embodied in their religion, denies them.'

He reminded us pertinently that the Constitution establishes a higher morality than all our respective faiths, prejudices and beliefs, and this higher morality is binding on us all even if it conflicts with our personal beliefs. Many years later, when passing their historic judgement which wrote down Section 377 of the Indian Penal Code (that criminalizes homosexuality), Justices A. P. Shah and Murlidhar distinguished between public and constitutional morality. They laid down, implicitly recalling Amebdkar, that when these are at odds or in conflict with each other, the only morality which passes the test of compelling state interest is constitutional morality.[51]

And Babasaheb placed as much stress on fraternity as he did on liberty and equality. Fraternity, he said, nothing other than 'fellow feeling', is an essential element of a just society.[52] It is the 'disposition of an individual' to treat others 'as the object of reverence and love', and the 'desire to be in unity with fellow beings'. He also declared that 'I and my neighbours are all brothers…'[53] He should surely have added '…and sisters'.

His emphasis on fraternity—which recognizes that the foundation of all contemporary liberal Indian ideas of secularism, pluralism, social equality is ultimately the idea and practice of social solidarity, an idea which indeed is the main burden of this book—is contained in his incandescent words, that only '*collective* liberty is true liberty'.[54]

Learning from the Grosmaires

It is estimated that nearly a million people were killed, and more than ten million, possibly fourteen million people were displaced by the cataclysmic Partition of India in 1947. My family was just one among these many millions, uprooted from their village near Rawalpindi and like the many millions of inheritors of this blood-drenched, shared history, we grew up hearing stories of unbelievable brutality and unbearable loss. In our village, Kahuta, women and girls apparently jumped into the village well to save themselves from rape and abduction by the 'enemy'.

What is also extraordinary about these accounts, passed down from generation to generation, is the partition of collective memory, through partial remembering and partial forgetting. We recall what 'they' did to 'us'—the cruelty, the murders, the arson, the rapes and abductions, the bodies dumped in wells, the desecration of shrines, the betrayals—but never what 'we' did to 'them', which in many instances exactly mirrors the same stories. Similar folklore built on selective amnesias follows every new communal and caste riot, every mass uprooting, each contributing more bricks to construct ever-taller fortresses of public rage and hate.

But there are, there always have been other stories—not just of what 'they' did to 'us'; not even of what 'we' did to 'them'—but of lives saved, of courage, compassion, loyalty and forgiveness. Ashis Nandy led a team which recorded memories of Partition from people who had themselves lived through those tumultuous times. They found—on both sides of the religious divide and on both sides of the border—that more than a quarter of the people reported that their lives had been saved by people of the 'other' community.[55]

One remarkable story was recounted by an old woman in Pakistan. Decades earlier, during the Partition, she had been abducted by a young Sikh man who had tried to rape her. The boy's father had intervened, demanding that he release the woman. When he refused, the old man had shot dead his own son.

These stories, though not uncommon, are rarely recounted or celebrated. In Indore, in 1984, where I served as a young district officer during the anti-Sikh carnage, a twenty-two-year-old Jain shopkeeper took his terrified Sikh neighbours into his home. When murderous mobs still tried to force their way into his home, he resolutely stood between them and the Sikh family. They attacked him with knives and he died saving the family. In my work among survivors of the Gujarat massacre of 2002, I have found significantly many more Hindus who saved lives than those who took them.

Public rage also surrounds those who commit heinous crimes. For the rapists and killers of the student in a bus in Delhi in the winter of 2012, we would settle for nothing less than hanging, even for the underage perpetrator. When one of the rapists allegedly hanged himself, people felt cheated. When I, or someone like actor Rahul Bose, suggests that everyone, including even the rapists, should have the chance to reform, this is bitterly attacked. Some ask: what would you have done if your own loved ones had been attacked? Would you then have spoken of forgiveness and reform?

What indeed would I have done? It is hard to say. But writer Amitava Kumar speaks of one couple, the Grosmaires, who were confronted by just such a choice.[56] In March 2010 in Florida, their nineteen-year-old daughter Ann was killed in a moment of blind rage by her boyfriend Conor, who was of the same age as her. The boy was sentenced to spend his entire life in jail. The appeal against this order was filed not just by the boy's parents, but also by the parents of the girl he had killed. They wanted the boy to spend no more than ten to fifteen years in jail, and Conor's father agreed.

They didn't forgive Conor for his sake, but their own, Kumar writes. This is what the Grosmaires said to *New York Times* reporter Tullis. Ann's mother's words were: 'Forgiveness for me was self-preservation.' For his part, Conor told Tullis, 'With the Grosmaires' forgiveness, I could accept the responsibility and not be condemned.' Kumar adds that if Conor 'had simply been turned into an enemy, he could have escaped the human contract, but by accepting him, the Grosmaires had drawn him into the circle of obligation. He was going to have to do good enough for two.'

Closer home, after her husband Graham, a missionary who had served leprosy patients in tribal Odisha for more than three decades, was burnt alive along with their two young sons, Gladys Staines forgave the killers, declaring: 'It is far from my mind to punish the persons who were responsible for the death of my husband Graham and my two children. But it is my desire and hope that they would repent and would be reformed.'[57] In 2000, senior politician Sonia Gandhi petitioned for clemency because Nalini, one of the women charged with the killing of her husband Rajiv Gandhi, had a young daughter.

The last act which the founder of the Arya Samaj, Swami Dayanand Saraswati, performed in 1883 was to forgive his killer, and to help him escape. He had been poisoned by a cook as part of a conspiracy hatched by people who were opposed to the social reforms he propagated. The cook confessed, and Dayanand gave him money to help him escape before he died.

The time has come when all of us, the world over, are being challenged to discover new ways to respond to people who we believe have caused us grave harm. Punishment is important to deter and discourage crime. But we may also find that rage, revenge and hate trap us no less than those who have caused us suffering and loss.

If the survivors of Partition, of innumerable communal and caste riots, of terrorist attacks, of displacement from homelands, and of heinous crimes of rape and murder, are ultimately to find closure and healing, we need to find public spaces for both justice and forgiveness. Justice is critical, but if we learn to temper justice with compassion, the world may become a kinder, fairer, safer place for everyone.

Learning from Zakia and Shameema

Ahmedabad, 28 February 2012. The entire block of houses in the Gulbarg Society still stands in ruins—abandoned, ravaged, charred. Nothing has changed since these homes were assaulted by mobs blinded by hate on that day ten years earlier. It is as though time has stood still for a decade. I tiptoe though the rooms in which sixty-nine people were slaughtered, among them Ehsan Jafri, Parliamentarian, lawyer and poet.

By my side is Ehsan Jafri's daughter Nishrin, composed and gentle. 'This was my father's library,' she says, pointing to a blackened wall. 'He loved books, and they were piled high to the roof.' The winter before he was killed, she had spent a few weeks with her father, on vacation from her home in the US. She had then helped him organize his treasured volumes.

Nishrin's son Tauseef Hussain, now twenty-three years old, also on a pilgrimage to the house where his grandfather was hacked to death, writes about the same library: 'Inside the abandoned house, as I stood silent with shut eyes, for a moment I felt I was sweating another hot summer in my grandfather's beloved library. I could hear the same chirping of the sparrows. Despite the heat, his ceiling fans would remain always off; switches taped over to make sure those birds could safely weave through our house carefree.'[58]

On 28 February 2002, nearly a hundred men, women and children huddled together, terrified, in that same library and the adjacent room which Jafri used as an office. As surging crowds of young men screaming for their blood had surrounded their housing society, these people had run for safety to the house of the former MP, hoping he would save them. But Jafri's frantic calls to senior police officers, and allegedly Chief Minister Narendra Modi himself, were futile. Mobs threw fireballs into the house, and soon the rooms were thick with smoke. Jafri was himself dragged out and his limbs hacked off before he was burned to death, murdered along with nearly seventy others whom he had tried vainly to save.

Nishrin takes me up the flight of stairs of their bungalow, open to the sky. Jafri had sent the women and children to the room upstairs even as the mobs hurled an unending volley of Molotov cocktails and the foulest abuse at them. But Nishrin does not speak of these; instead, she recalls how every Diwali, the entire staircase used to be lit with earthen lamps.

Among those cowering in this room ten years earlier was the domestic help of the Jafri household, Leelabai. Zakia Jafri, Nishrin's mother, took her into the verandah outside with folded hands. 'She is a Hindu,' she pleaded. 'Why should she die?' The crowd let her flee. The building was by then set aflame from all sides; it was the strength of the construction which finally saved those who were hiding in the first storey.

This was not the first riot which their family had lived through. Nishrin and her brother Tanvir recall the first time that their home was razed, not far away, in the riots of 1969. 'The storm came for a day, then passed, as it did again in 1985 and 1992,' Tanvir remembers. 'But not like this time, when the hate does not end.'

In the years before 2002, as the climate of amity in the city rapidly declined, many friends advised Jafri to shift into the safety of Muslim ghettoes. But he would not even consider the option. Everything he believed in would be extinguished if he moved out of this neighbourhood.

After his murder, Jafri's widow Zakia fought an epic battle for justice in the highest courts of the land. Her grandson recounts: 'As I spoke with my grandmother, I realized time had treated her as harshly as it did the home she lost. Beneath every deliberately hopeful conversation, the ravaged foundation shone through the cracks...She did not want to speak of what we lost as a family, only of those who had so little in this world to begin with, and now are the ones rendered truly destitute.'[59]

He takes her lesson to heart: 'I was aware of my family's pain but had never fully realized that our loss in Gujarat's communal riots was only a minor footnote in a vast library of rewritten lives...Even one decade after...so many families still learn daily what it is to be *beghar*...The word "*beghar*" encapsulates the chill of loss and emotional vacuum, pairing homelessness with hopelessness. Though a home can be built, or rebuilt, to become *beghar* is to have a loss of identity and crisis of belonging which compromises the very basis of one's being.'[60]

It is these beghar men and women living 'rewritten lives', who gather ten years later in the ruins of the Gulbarg Society, to share memory and loss, to grieve together, in a memorial organized by the indomitable fighter Teesta Setalvad. Men and women sob as they stand before a wall on which hang blurred pictures of those killed. Among the sombre crowds that gather that day are Rupa Modi, also a resident of Gulbarg, weeping wordlessly as she embraces Rahul Dholakia, whose film *Parzania* told the story of her wait for her son who never returned home; Bilkees Bano who braved the legal battle against those who raped and killed; the gentle professor Bandukwala, still mourning the looting of his home in the university, yet seeking paths for forgiveness. And many others like them.

As twilight falls, Shubha Mudgal sits aloft a neighbouring terrace and sings resonantly of loss and yearning, of blood-drenched gardens, of fighting those who use religion for politics, of the imperative for a new religion which teaches us to be human. And of the need to walk together, even with bloodied feet and wounded hearts.

~

Lest I be misunderstood, it is not my claim that forgiveness entails giving up the search for justice. On the contrary, I regard the quest for justice fundamental to any quest for a better world. In fact, any exercise of the politics of love which is estranged from the pursuit of justice is, to my mind, emptied of value and meaning. But equally, struggles for justice which are not founded on principles of love—non-violence and the absence of rancour—are equally doomed to sour into hate.

Each age creates its own heroes. Two ageing homemakers—Zakia Jafri and Shameema Jahan—who would otherwise have been content to lead useful but unremarkable lives, were transformed into unlikely warriors because of two brutal killings. These dreadful tragedies stirred both to courageously fight epic battles against what they are convinced was the malevolent exercise of state power.

Zakia Jafri was not content to pursue only those who physically slaughtered her husband. She insisted that justice must reach those who had conspired to organize this massacre. At the end of a long legal battle lasting over a decade, she filed a petition on 15 April 2013 before a magistrate alleging a high-level conspiracy to manipulate the Godhra tragedy to organize and fuel the carnage which followed. The first name among the fifty-nine accused was that of Narendra Modi, who was then chief minister of Gujarat.

In the court hearings which followed, Zakia's lawyer Mihir Desai argued that the political head of the state, the home ministry and the administration had been in full knowledge of and had allowed the 'build-up of aggressive and communal sentiments, violent mobilisation, including carrying of arms, and a general outpouring against the minority community...'[61] Relying on documents collected by the SIT itself, Zakia's petition attempted to establish that there was a conspiracy at the seniormost levels of the state administration, not just to generate hatred against Muslims, but also to target Muslim people and their property and religious places and 'aid and abet this process by acts and omissions of persons liable under law to act otherwise'.[62]

Her petition was rejected by the trial court, and she filed an appeal. Zakia Jafri, then in her mid-seventies, declared in an interview with *Frontline* that she recognized that Modi is 'an extremely powerful man', so charges against him cannot be made lightly.[63] Therefore 'we have persevered at collecting every relevant detail to implicate him. One day it will pay off'.[64] She adds, 'My husband was a good and kind man. I will fight for him and for thousands who suffered like us.'[65]

~

Ishrat Jahan was barely seventeen when her father died, leaving behind a large family in a small rented apartment in Mumra, a Mumbai suburb. Ishrat was not the eldest of the six children, but she was the brightest and the most responsible of all the siblings. Still in high school, she started giving tuitions to children in the neighbourhood. The fees the children gave her became the main source of survival for the closely knit family.

Ishrat joined college for a bachelor's degree in science. She would cook breakfast for the family, rush to college, and return to teach two batches of children. Their mother Shameema spent most of her day at the sewing machine, stitching zari borders to saris. They owned no television, and were not allowed to watch films, or even to visit friends. They were caught up in the business of everyday living; content in their routine of studying, working, dreaming; hardly aware of the world outside their home.

The summer months after school examinations were the hardest for the family, because school children would be on holiday and no one would come to Ishrat for tuitions. In March 2004, some relatives introduced the family to a middle-aged man called Javed, who was looking for help with marketing and accounts for his perfume business. He would pay her ₹3,500 a month during the summer months when there was no income from tuitions; the job would involve also some outstation visits, for which he would pay extra. With seven mouths to feed, her mother had little option but to allow Ishrat to accept employment. Ishrat made two short visits to Pune and Lucknow. On 11 June, she left on her last outstation assignment. Her brother left her at the bus stand. Javed was to meet her in Nasik, from where they were to travel by car to other cities.

On the evening of 16 June, a group of young strangers visited their home. They asked them: Have you not heard the news? Don't you watch television? The visitors initially said that they were from Ishrat's college, and they needed her passport photograph for her college forms. Around 8 at night they finally broke the terrible news. They were journalists. Ishrat had been killed in a police encounter. She had been charged with conspiring to kill Narendra Modi. Television channels had been broadcasting the sensational news all day and the young strangers had lied to them; they wanted her picture to flash on the news.

The cold dread and shock Ishrat's family felt was matched only by their utter bewilderment. The younger children had not even heard of Modi. None of them knew what an 'encounter' was. And they could not believe that their beloved Ishrat was suddenly dead, and branded a terrorist. She was just nineteen.

But they had no time even to grieve.

By 9, police came to their home, evacuated and sealed the house, and drove the entire terrified family to the police station. Throngs of journalists and television cameras had by then crowded outside their home. The police dropped them back at 2.30 a.m. Their house was sealed. Shameema and the children sat sleepless the whole night at a nearby shop.

By morning, the journalists had grown virtually into a mob. A team of women policemen arrived, broke open the seal placed on the the house, and searched it, roughly throwing out the contents of cupboards, stripping the beds and overturning all their furniture.

Shameema was then driven to Ahmedabad by some sympathetic neighbours to collect her daughter's body. She was grilled and abused by the senior police officials there. They then finally handed over Ishrat's body to Shameema; stiff, bloodied and defaced with bullet wounds. The assembled media went wild with their cameras and questions. Back in Mumra, they were stunned when literally tens of thousands of people attended the funeral; all their faces were grim and strained, as though it was a personal loss for each.

In a few weeks, the media forgot about them, but the police did not. The neighbours were initially helpful but, if anyone tried to assist the family, they were harassed by the police for being sympathetic to 'terrorists'. The family was soon left almost entirely alone. 'There were times when we wondered why we were still alive,' her sister Mussarat recalls. 'Why were we being punished?'

They moved into a new rented house, but the mundane business of feeding six mouths, without their father and Ishrat, loomed over their lives. Mussarat dropped out of school and helped her mother at sewing. Young Anwar also sewed, and started conducting computer classes. Not everyone abandoned them and there were a few in the local community who collected money for them once in a while.

In the years since, Shameema battled the trauma of her daughter's violent murder, the stigma of being branded a terrorist, resulting in her family's isolation, and the challenge of raising her remaining six children without Ishrat and her husband. A lesser person would have been felled, but not Shameema. She filed a writ in the Gujarat High Court in 2004 and persevered with a prolonged, uncertain legal battle because she was fiercely committed to proving her daughter's innocence. Her petition in the Gujarat High Court sought a CBI enquiry into the deaths. But the case remained dormant.

Then, in 2006, unexpected glimmerings of hope were lit. Their friends came with the news that the same officers of the Gujarat Police, led by Dahyaji Gobarji Vanzara, allegedly involved in Ishrat's death, had been jailed for the killing of Sohrabuddin and his wife in another 'fake encounter'. Shameema wrote a letter to the chief justice of the Gujarat High Court asking who the killers of her daughter were. They did not hear from the court. Shameema persisted, aided by human rights lawyers Vrinda Grover and Mukul Sinha. In 2007, Javed's father filed a petition. Two years later he was advised to go to the Supreme Court.

Unexpected relief came five years after Ishrat's killing when a junior magistrate, S. P. Tamang, charged with an enquiry into the alleged police encounter killings, acted with exceptional and completely unexpected courage and integrity. Hundreds of persons are eliminated in the country by police and security personnel, claiming that the men in uniform killed in self-defence, and their claims are routinely ratified by compliant magistrates. But Tamang was different. Even as the superior courts prevaricated, this unknown, subordinate metropolitan magistrate, responsible for conducting what is almost always an utterly routine statutory enquiry into encounter killings, stood tall, bravely affirming justice and truth. He examined the forensic reports and statements and, in a lucid and tightly argued report stunned everyone on 7 September 2009, by concluding that the police version of how the killings occurred was an 'absolutely false and concocted story'.

The police had claimed that that Ishrat was a member of the terrorist organization, Lashkar-e-Taiba, who had driven into Ahmedabad with three other terrorists, in a plot to kill Chief Minister

Modi. The police had been tipped off, and chased the vehicle Ishrat had been riding in. They had fired at their tyres, puncturing them, and forcing them to halt. The terrorists were then reported to have alighted from the car and fired relentlessly at the police vehicle. In self-defence, the police finally felled all four in a fierce gun battle.

Magistrate Tamang analysed the post-mortem and forensic evidence to conclude, irrefutably, that Ishrat and the three men had actually been killed several hours before the alleged shoot-out, and that too from close range. The police had then taken their bodies to the roadside, themselves fired upon their jeep, and planted an AK-47 in the hands of one of the dead men and explosives in their car. It was cold-blooded murder by the police, including that of an innocent, nineteen-year-old college-going girl. The police cover-up was clumsy and ham-handed, the forensic evidence crystal clear, but no court had until then chosen to look this ugly and explosive truth in the face. This is what Tamang did.

Ishrat's family received the news with complete disbelief, and then a poignant sense of elation. The grim report confirmed the brutal circumstances in which their beloved Ishrat had been killed. However, it also cleared her name and identified her killers to be men in uniform. The family could emerge at last from the dense darkness of isolation and stigma of the last five years which they had thought would never end. After these long years, they could once again step out of their homes with their heads held high. They could begin to live, and hope again. This hope was fragile, frail, tentative.

Shameema was vindicated and was able to erase the label of terrorist attached to her daughter's name. The state predictably challenged Tamang's order, but the High Court directed the CBI to investigate the case. Its findings were even more explosive, suggesting a criminal conspiracy between Gujarat Police officials and the Intelligence Bureau.[66] Its charge-sheet names seven Gujarat Police officers and charged them with abducting, illegally detaining, drugging and finally killing Ishrat and three men along with her.[67]

~

The wars Zakia and Shameema are waging are many. They battle against forgetting, against the arrogance of state power, against the politics of hate and fear, against open state bias against religious minorities during mass violence, against the labelling of Muslim people, against the opacity and unaccountability of security establishments, and against policies of the state which sanction the elimination of people under the excuse of battling terror. They struggle in solidarity with some of the country's finest activists, and with robust faith in the institutions of India's democracy. They fight with determination, but without rancour. They remind us that secular democracy is never given to a people; it needs to be constantly claimed and reclaimed. By fighting so bravely, with dignity, faith and hope—but also with love—they fight for all of us.

Learning from Yusuf

The idea of justice as retribution currently holds the nation in thrall. But there are other, gentler voices, muffled in the clamour for violent public reprisal, voices that speak of mercy and forgiveness, but also of justice not for revenge but for deterrence, and of the possibility of reformation. I relate here the story of Yusuf Mansuri, a young bus driver I met in the Shah Alam relief camp in Ahmedabad just weeks after the carnage in 2002.

Yusuf lived with his parents and three brothers in a small tenement in the working-class Ahmedabad suburb of Naroda Patiya. His father drove a bus for the state transport corporation, and Yusuf, the eldest, supplemented the income of his joint family by standing in for drivers on leave, and apprenticing in an embroidery workshop. In the carnage of 2002, his home was burned down and looted, and more than a hundred people slaughtered and raped in his settlement, including many from his extended family.

The ravaged family, reduced to penury, began its new journey in the Shah Alam dargah. The courtyards of the medieval dargah rapidly filled up with numerous families like Yusuf's, desperately fleeing the violence, until more than ten thousand people were taking refuge there. Yusuf recalls the humiliation of living on charity, wearing used clothes, eating food directly off the floor, and sharing a single toilet with five hundred people.

I first encountered Yusuf in the camp, teaching children in the open spaces of the graveyard with a group of friends. I was looking for volunteers for peace and reconstruction, and Yusuf was among the first to come forward. Six months later, when the camps were shut down and I walked with Yusuf through the alleyways of Naroda as he described to me the horrific slaughter, I remember wondering then—my eyes clouded—that had I suffered what he had, could I have found the same ready spaces in my heart for forgiveness?

Shortly after the camps were disbanded, both Yusuf and his father were arrested, along with more than a hundred other Muslims, and charged with the murder of the one Hindu who had been killed in Naroda. It was a tactic to intimidate the most active witnesses of the slaughter. During the three months he spent in Sabarmati Jail, I often worried how much this injustice would embitter my young friend. But after his release on bail, I found his spirit and morale unbroken. What he had found most difficult was to see his father in prison. But his father had consoled him, saying, 'Do you know who else was confined in this jail, years ago? Mahatma Gandhi. If he could be here, who are you and me?'

After his release, he was summoned by the courts every month for four years, at the end of which his father and he, and all the other accused, were acquitted. Yusuf worked with us as an aman pathik for a couple of years. Then the pressures of supporting his family—he had a young wife and small son—compelled him to accept regular employment as a bus driver.

But during the nights and in the mornings, he would study law. He would call me proudly each year when the results were announced. 'I have passed with 57 per cent,' he said to me the first year. He maintained his grades and in time graduated as a lawyer.

When violence broke out in Assam in the summer of 2012, we called for volunteers to work in the camps. Yusuf joined the Aman Biradari volunteer group and, along with young people from Gujarat, Delhi and Hyderabad, spent two weeks in the relief camps in Lower Assam. Aman Biradari had one condition: that Bodo volunteers would work in Bengali Muslim camps and Muslims in the Bodo camps.

Conventional wisdom was that in the bitterly polarized climate of Assam, after the bloody ethnic violence, this would be impossible. But Yusuf knew it was not. He opted to work in a Bodo camp, and announced to the inhabitants soon after he arrived that he was a Muslim. The residents were at first unbelieving, then enraged. For hours, they vented fury and abuse about the Muslims who had attacked their settlement.

Yusuf looked at them through all of this, never retaliating, but quietly insisting, 'All you say may be true. But you still cannot take away from me my right to care about your suffering.' In the end, they gave him a bed and food. He was hosted by the man who had been his most vociferous critic. In the days he spent with them, he organized meetings for the first time with their estranged Muslim neighbours. After uneasy silences and some recrimination, then much weeping, both sides admitted their longing for peace.

Later, he visited the Muslim camps and told people where he had come from. They were incredulous, and asked him, 'You slept for days in even assigned the Bodo camps and are still alive to tell the story?' Yusuf only smiled. 'Well, here I am. You can see me, unharmed.'

Back in Ahmedabad, Yusuf was a star witness in the Naroda criminal case. Over the years, he never missed a hearing. The Supreme Court armed guards for protection. On the day the judgement sentencing former minister Maya Kodnani and several others to a lifetime in jail was announced, I telephoned Yusuf to ask how he felt. He felt vindicated, he said, that his faith in justice and democracy had been further strengthened, and Judge Jyotsnaben Yagnik had convinced him about human goodness.

And yet, as the men sentenced to spend their life in jail for the slaughter were driven away in the waiting police vans, he watched their young sons weeping piteously.

'Their fathers were guilty, but not the children,' he told me later. 'I longed then to run to Judge Madam,' he said, 'and to beg her…'

To beg her to let the men who had slaughtered his people walk free.

Learning from Those with Nothing

John Steinbeck, who unforgettably recreated the Great Depression of 1920s America in *The Grapes of Wrath*, wrote, 'If you are in trouble, or hurt, or in need—go to the poor people. They're the only ones that'll help—the only ones.'[68] My chosen work—with the hungry, the homeless and the survivors of violence—allows me the privilege of spending a great deal of time with India's most dispossessed persons, and I agree with Steinbeck completely. It is in their giving and solidarities in which I find my greatest hope that the claiming of a caring and just world is possible. It is possible because people who own the least have not forgotten the paramount obligation to care for each other; and that, in the end, it is love which is the essential life-giving principle of human survival.

I have recounted earlier in this book that small local entrepreneurs in Delhi's walled city rent out quilts and mattresses to homeless people during freezing winters, and many people make the choice each chilly night to either rent a quilt or eat an evening meal.

And yet I noticed that the aged, the mentally ill, the critically ill and the disabled among the homeless at Jama Masjid—who would not survive the cold uncovered—were all always sleeping under quilts. I was very curious, and the younger homeless residents helped me solve the mystery. 'We *know* that they would die in this cold in a single night if they had no cover. Therefore when we gather here after work each night, we first pool money between us to hire quilts for the old and infirm among us. After that we see if there is any money left for us.' They told me this without the sense that they had acted in any way that was extraordinary. They told me this as though it is not acting this way which would have been extraordinary.

It set me thinking: what the government should be doing but is not doing, what people's groups and NGOs should be doing but are not doing, what the entrepreneurs should be doing and are not doing, the city's most dispossessed people are doing because they still know no other way.

~

Like the sites of all great catastrophes and suffering, Gujarat after 2002 abounds with thousands of untold stories. But not all these are tales of massacres, of hate, fear, despair and mass graves, of blood congealed on streets and poison within hearts. The stories even less told are those of most extraordinary human compassion and courage. For every narrative of cruelty and oppression that people recount of those tempestuous days of 2002, I discover that there are at least two or three untold stories of the luminous kindnesses of ordinary people, risking their lives and homes to save innocent lives, and generously helping betrayed and shattered people heal and rebuild. American historian Howard Zinn rightly observed that 'human history is a history not only of cruelty, but also of compassion, sacrifice, courage, kindness'.[69]

In Koha, a village not far from Ahmedabad, more than 110 women, men and children cowered many hours in fields of standing crops. They were all Muslim, all belonging to working-class families—landless workers, lorry drivers, tailors in clothing factories—and all were mortally terrified.

As darkness fell, the children became hungry and they wondered how they would survive that night of terror. They knew a Hindu farmer, Dhuraji, to be a compassionate man. They decided to take a chance with him. Thus they made their way under the cover of darkness to the home of Dhuraji and Babuben Thakur. With lowered eyes, they begged for shelter for just one night.

Neither Dhuraji nor Babuben hesitated for even a moment and opened their doors and hearts to all 110 of their traumatized, wearied, now homeless neighbours. The next morning the guests offered to leave for the relief camp, but their hosts would not hear of it. 'This is your home,' they assured them. 'As long as god gives to us, we will share whatever we have with you.' They opened their entire stores of rice and bajra for the whole year and ensured that all were fed for the full ten days that they lived in the sanctuary of their home. The women of the family brought out all their clothes and would form a human wall around their well as the women bathed each day.

Dhuraji gathered his extended family from the village to mount constant guard for their guests for ten nights and days, armed only with sickles. The women and children were persuaded to sleep inside the home, while the Thakur women slept in the open fields and the Thakur men kept vigil through the long cold nights. They were unshaken by threats from their Hindu neighbours, who sent across bangles as taunts, set fire to their haystacks and, one night, even stole in through the darkness to set fire to their house, which they managed to douse just in time.

Still, Dhuraji and his wife Babuben were perfect hosts, as though these were just normal times. They tried to meet every need of their guests and to make them feel constantly welcomed. Dhuraji's grown sons would set out in their tractors and bring back large stocks of bidis for the men, tea for the women and milk for the children. Years later, the refuge-seekers remembered fondly that seeing them in gloom, Dhuraji even hired a VCR and showed them Hindi films to lift up their spirits!

At the end of ten days, it was they who insisted that they must finally shift to the relief camp. Their hosts tried to persuade them to stay as long as they needed to rebuild their own homes. Dhuraji finally organized tractors and a police escort and safely reached them to the camp. He used to visit them regularly at the camp as well, and the women recall that his eyes would often well over when he saw their children lose weight in the austere rigours of the camp and stand in lines for watery tea.

Four years later, when I met Dhuraji and Babuben, they were embarrassed when I told them that what they had done was magnificent. When I pressed them about why they did what they did, Dhuraji thought for a long time before replying simply, 'How could I bear it that people of my village are treated this way?' He added firmly, 'This village belongs to the Muslims as much as it belongs to me.'

I asked if they were frightened during those ten days and nights. Babuben was almost irritated by my question. 'If you are doing the right thing, how can you be afraid?' she asked me.

I then asked if they regretted that they lost their entire year's stock of grain in ten days. Dhuraji replied, 'Our Thakurji ensured that we get a good harvest after our guests left, and since that day, our grain stocks have never fallen empty.' He had no doubt that his Thakurji would reward him for saving the lives of more than a hundred Muslim children, women and men.

Babuben added, 'Their good wishes and prayers have strengthened us. Don't you see greenery everywhere?'

I did.

~

A few hundred kilometres farther, in the remote village of Nanaposhina in the Sabarkantha district, white-haired Walibhai, a stubborn, ageing agricultural worker was helplessly enraged when his house was looted and burnt by his young neighbours, boys who had grown up before his eyes. He fiercely insisted on remaining in the village to guard the scorched walls which were all that was left of his home, although he forced his grown sons and his wife Mariam to the safety of a relief camp.

He sat awake weeping the whole night. The next morning, it hit him afresh that overnight he had been reduced to a pauper—he owned nothing, not even a lota to go to the fields with. A Thakur boy who walked past felt sorry for the old man and quietly gave him his lota and left without a word. Walibhai recalls that it was with this small act of kindness that he was able to begin his life again. His neighbour, a Patel, called him shortly after to say that there was a phone call for him. His daughter-in-law informed him that she had had a son the night before. 'We have lost everything,' he cried to her. She contradicted him firmly, 'You are saved. This means we have everything.'

He found a broken earthen pot on which to make himself some rotis, refusing to hide any more, glowering at people as they threatened him, almost daring them to take his life. But the wife of his Patel neighbour insisted that she would feed him, and for eight days she defied the angry opposition of many in her village to openly bring him food and tea as he stood guard at his home. 'What has happened is wrong,' she said simply to everyone who protested. 'And he is like our elder.'

Later, when I visited him, the walls of his home were still scorched, but there were shining corrugated sheets screwed on to the roof. 'See my good fortune,' he said to me. 'Rambhai Adivasi was not even a close friend. We only used to sit and talk together sometimes. But when he saw my burnt house some months later, he cried. Without a word, he went home, bought these sheets for six thousand rupees, hired workers and a tractor to transport the material. The workers told me they had instructions to not heed my objections, and to fix the iron sheets. That is how I have a roof over my head today! Look at my good fortune, my friend.'

~

In the relief colonies in Juhapara, many people uprooted from the villages of their birth in 2002 live in tiny tenements, with no hope of ever being able to return. My colleagues, nyaya pathiks from Aman Biradari, visit them from time to time, trying to help them fight their legal cases, secure them compensation, rebuild broken pieces of their lives, or sometimes just to talk. On one of these visits with an elderly woman, a faqir came to her door to seek alms. She went into her room and returned with a crushed five-rupee note, which she pressed into his palm. After he left, she began to weep quietly, rubbing her eyes with her faded veil, in a way that the nyaya pathiks had never seen her do on all their visits.

They worried that maybe they had unknowingly said something that stirred painful memories, and tried in vain to console her. At last she began to speak. She spoke of the toofan. 'Beta,' she said, 'before the toofan, had this faqir come to my door, I would never have sent him away without serving him a meal and giving him at least fifty rupees. And look at me now. All I could give him was five rupees, and then I just sent him away.'

The elderly lady did not mourn her loss; rather, she grieved that she no longer had the capacity to give.

Learning from Shahid

On 11 February 2012, four men walked into the office of human rights lawyer Shahid Azmi in Mumbai, and shot him dead.[70] He was just thirty-two years old.

When Shahid was seven, his father died, and in the years that followed, his family survived on the charity of his better-off relatives. In their cramped, single-room home in Mumbai, perched in an attic above a bakery, his mother raised her five sons with an iron hand. His older brother Arif quietly sacrificed his own dreams and aspirations to protect his mother and raise his siblings. It was his steady support which sustained Shahid through his tragically brief and turbulent life and its many trials, and helped enable him to realize his dreams.

Shahid was just fifteen when he watched Mumbai burn for weeks in 1992-93 after the razing of the Babri Masjid. 'Police gathered outside his home in a slum area of Mumbai,' his brother Arif recounted to Hanna Ingber of the *Huffington Post* after his death. 'As he, his brothers and mother huddled inside between the bed and cupboards, police stoned the home and fired shots over the windows.'[71] The teenager was further traumatized and enraged by the openly partisan role the police played. He saw mobs of Hindus burn down homes, destroy businesses and slaughter his Muslim neighbours as policemen looked on and even encouraged the marauding mobs. His brother further recalled that young Shahid saw men in khaki storm a Muslim home in their Shivaji Nagar community, drag women out of the apartment and try to rape them in the street. He witnessed an officer tell a Muslim neighbour to run, only to be shot down by another policeman.

In an interview to *The Times of India* years later, Shahid himself testified: 'I had seen policemen killing people from my community. I have witnessed cold-blooded murders. This enraged me and I joined the resistance.'[72] He was briefly radicalized by what he saw during the Mumbai riots, and crossed the country's borders as a young teenager to join a terrorist formation. But he was quickly disillusioned and returned home within months.

However, these few months changed the course of his short life permanently. Police detained and tortured him, and charged him with terror crimes. The persecution stopped only when he was acquitted of all charges by the Supreme Court after seven long years of incarceration.

Refusing either to lose hope or become embittered, he persisted with his college education during his years in prison, and emerged with a post-graduate degree. Despite his family's strained means, he resolved, after his discharge, to study law. It was his brother Arif who made this possible. After Shahid earned his law degree, he worked for a short time with a senior lawyer but left soon, unable to brook compromises with justice and truth that a large commercial legal firm entails, and instead established his own practice.

His legal practice was mainly devoted to defending Muslim youth unjustly charged with terror crimes, subjected—just as he had been—to torture and long, hopeless years of imprisonment. Paid little or nothing, he won many extraordinary acquittals for several innocent young men in terror cases, bitterly contested by the state. He bravely persisted with his defence of those young men who he believed were innocent, despite many death threats. He constantly fought the tall walls of bias within the criminal justice system, the confessions extracted through torture, the creation of false evidence and witnesses to bolster terror charges, the open hostility of the public prosecutor to the accused, which spilled over sometimes to the lawyer fighting on their behalf. But he also encountered judges—faceless people in the huge judicial machine—who struggle to be humane and fair.

Some years later, he would be invited for guest lectures to the Tata Institute of Social Sciences, Mumbai. His colleague and friend Monica Sakhrani said he would sometimes speak of 'his illegal confinement in the dungeons below Red Fort for over 50 days and the torture he went through there; and his one-year of solitary confinement at Tihar until Kiran Bedi intervened to take him off it. At one point, he pretended to be mentally ill and was in a mental asylum for another year in order to look after the mentally ill'.[73] She adds, 'He would open up and share extremely personal, painful experiences with the students describing his years in the jail and the manner in which he was tortured. When asked about the most painful torture that he went through, he replied, not being given the *Sehr* breakfast during the month of Ramzan. He said that this was more painful than the physical torture that he went through.'[74]

It was his suffering which drove him to defend other young men from the same torment and injustice. Shahid had truly lived by the creed enunciated by Roy Black, an American criminal defence lawyer, who declared, 'By showing me injustice, He taught me to love justice. By teaching me what pain and humiliation were all about, He awakened my heart to mercy. Through these hardships I learned hard lessons. Fight against prejudice, battle the oppressors, support the underdog.'[75]

Monica recalls that he was 'branded a "terrorist" lawyer, which label had a double entendre given his past. He never hid his past, as he believed that it was bound to catch up with him anyway. With infinite patience and humility, he sought to convince people that he was not a terrorist; he tried to explain his standpoint of justice to them'.[76]

He was undeterred by many the death threats he was subjected to continuously because he defended men charged with terror crimes. Ultimately, he was gunned down by four assailants in his office at the tragically young age of thirty-two.

In his brief, brilliant career of seven years, he defended some fifty men charged with terror crimes and succeeded in establishing their innocence in fourteen cases. After Shahid's death, refusing to let his battle die or to be cowed down, his friends continued his last case, of Faheem Ansari, charged as an accomplice in the 26/11 Mumbai terror attack, and Faheem was finally acquitted by the court. The prosecution appealed right up to the Supreme Court but the Supreme Court also upheld the verdict. As Mehtab Alam observes, 'This was only possible because during the argument at the special court, Shahid had built a solid base and demolished the prosecution's accusation on his client of being part of the conspiracy in 26/11 attack.' His younger brother Khalid Azmi took over his brother's work two weeks after Shahid's murder. 'I want to take up my brother's cause (as)…a real tribute to him. I don't fear for my life. The cause is more important than my life…,' he told Alam. Alam also reports that there are hundreds of youth, especially Muslims—both men and women, who have taken inspiration from Shahid and are now either studying or practising law. In fact, there are half a dozen of them in Taximan Colony, Kurla, Mumbai, where he lived.[77]

Over the years, I have met and worked with young men—in Godhra and Hyderabad—who, like Shahid, were held on trumped-up charges of terror. I have written here the stories of Junaid in Hyderabad, and three brothers arrested for the burning of the train in Godhra in 2002.

Shahid's life reminds us of all of the stolen years of these men, but also how this injustice can be battled in ways that are remarkably—

almost miraculously—free of bitterness and despair.

What is extraordinary about Shahid is not just his courage and heroism, but his optimism. Even though he was tortured and had precious years of his youth wasted in unjust incarceration, he firmly rejected radicalism and was, instead, driven by the conviction that India's democratic institutions may delay and block justice, but if you fight hard and doggedly, justice will indeed come your way. For a man who was tortured and spent seven years unfairly in prison, it is extraordinary that such faith in the creaky, flawed and ponderous institutions of criminal justice in India endured, and that he persisted with fighting for justice through these institutions even though it cost him his life.

'Shahid was in love with the idea of justice,' Monica Sakhrani recalls. 'Fighting against injustice was the driving force of his life. This is what cost him his life. Had he looked the other way and treated the testimonials of state oppression, structural violence and systemic injustices as "cases" and not as his crusade for justice, he would have been alive today. The tragedy of Shahid's death is the tragic loss of possibilities of a life that will now never be. His was a brilliant, astute mind, a thirst for knowledge, and a kind, loving heart. He combined moral courage with legal acumen. His work was his politics and his life.'[78]

When students at TISS asked him what he felt were the solutions to the problems he had encountered and fought throughout his life—torture, unjust incarceration, the profiling of Muslim youth, communal violence, and the violence and bias of the state—he would softly reply in just one word, 'justice'.

His short, brilliant burst of a life compels us to introspect if India's democracy deserves the fierce belief and allegiance of valiant warriors for justice like Shahid—whom it so profoundly lets down.

Shahid reminds me of the words of another man in another continent who was also felled for his beliefs, Martin Luther King Jr. 'Never, never be afraid to do what is right,' King said, 'Society's punishments are small compared to the wounds we inflict on our souls when we look away.'

EPILOGUE

Death by starvation was not an uncommon calamity among the tribal Sahariya people living in the Baran district of eastern Rajasthan. Ten years had passed since I first visited Baran, in 2002, to investigate complaints of hunger fatalities. Exactly a decade later, when I was again in Sunvas, the village in which I had first found many children who had succumbed to starvation, I thought it was time to take stock of what had changed, and what had not, for one of India's most dispossessed rural communities.

I found a report card which remains blotted, but is not entirely hopeless. Sahariya children told me stoically that they still sleep hungry three or four times every month. Ten years earlier, it had been closer to ten days.

In a household in which a child had died of hunger ten years earlier, I found the father still in bondage, and the children still frail. His son Ashok, fifteen years old, was listening to our conversation with interest. I turned to him and asked if he was studying. He replied that he was in Class 10. I assumed he studied in the government school, but he startled me.

He had rejected the government school because its teachers, even if present, rarely taught the students. Instead, he had joined a private school which some educated young men had started in their village. I asked how he paid the fees, ₹2,500 a year; by no means a fortune, but unattainable for a boy whose father was a bonded labourer. Ashok answered that he had himself chosen to enter partial bondage to pay his fees, with a landlord who was free to call him for work five days a month. On other days, Ashok would attend school, and the school accepted that he would be absent five days every month.

I asked him what work he wished to do when he grew up. He looked me confidently in the eye and said, 'The same work that you do!'

I asked him then what he thought I did. He said he did not know exactly, but estimated that my work was, in some way, connected with helping people who live with hunger and bondage. This, he said, was what he wanted to do.

I am not a believer but I could not restrain myself from uttering, 'Inshallah!'

I hope I live to see the day this young man realizes his dreams.

NOTES

IN FEEBLE LIGHT

1. Priyanka Borpujari, 'What Is Striking in India Is the Indifference of the Privileged: Chomsky', *Tehelka*, 6 July 2013, accessed 13 January 2014, http://www.tehelka.com/what-is-striking-in-india-is-the-indifference-of-the-privileged/.
2. Borpujari, 'What Is Striking in India Is the Indifference of the Privileged: Chomsky'.
3. Ela Bhatt, speech at the programme, 'India's 25 Greatest Global Living Legends', organized by NDTV in the Rashtrapati Bhavan, 14 December 2013, New Delhi.
4. Jawaharlal Nehru, *The Discovery of India* (New Delhi: Penguin Books India, 2004).
5. Stuart Corbridge and John Harriss, *Reinventing India: Liberalization, Hindu Nationalism and Popular Democracy* (Cambridge: Polity Press, 2000).
6. B. Shiva Rao, ed., *The Framing of the Constitution of India: Select Documents* Vol. 4 (New Delhi: Indian Institute of Public Administration, 1966), pp. 944-45.
7. B. Shiva Rao, ed., *The Framing of the Constitution of India*.
8. See for instance Ronald Herring, 'Agrarian Reform for a Liberal Pattern of Society?' in Gopal Kadekodi, Ravi Kanbur and V. Rao, *Development in Karnataka: Challenges of Governance, Equity and Empowerment* (New Delhi: Academic Foundation, 2008).
9. Tim Hanstad, Robin Nielsen, Darryl Vhugen and T. Haque, 'Learning from Old and New Approaches to Land Reform in India', in Hans P. Binswanger-Mkhize, Camille Bourguignon and Rogier van den Brink, eds., *Agricultural Land Redistribution: Toward Greater Consensus*

(Washington DC: World Bank, 2009), pp. 245-47, https://openknowledge.worldbank.org/handle/10986/2653.
10. Tim Hanstad, Robin Nielsen, Darryl Vhugen and T. Haque, 'Learning from Old and New Approaches to Land Reform in India'.
11. P. S. Appu, *Land Reforms in India: A Survey of Policy, Legislation and Implementation* (New Delhi: Vikas Publishing House, 1996).
12. Ministry of Rural Development, 'Annual Report 2013-14', http://rural.nic.in/netrural/rural/sites/downloads/annual-report/Annual_Report_2013_14_English.pdf
13. Ministry of Rural Development, 'Draft Land Reforms Policy', 24 July 2013, http://rural.nic.in/sites/downloads/latest/Draft_National_Land_Reforms_Policy_July_2013.pdf.
14. Ministry of Rural Development, 'Draft Land Reforms Policy'.
15. Ministry of Rural Development, 'Draft Land Reforms Policy'.
16. Walter Fernandes, 'India's Forced Displacement Policy and Practice: Is Compensation up to its Functions?' in Michael M. Cernea and Hari Mohan Mathur, eds., *Can Compensation Prevent Impoverishment? Reforming Resettlement through Investment and Benefit-Sharing* (New Delhi: Oxford University Press, 2008), pp. 180-207.
17. Jyotsna Kapur and Manjunath Pendakur, 'The Strange Disappearance of Bombay from Its Own Cinema: A Case of Imperialism or Globalization?' *Democratic Communiqué* Vol 21, No. 1, http://journals.fcla.edu/demcom/article/view/76498.
18. Enrique Penalosa, speaking at the 'Delhi Urban Age Conference: Governing Urban Futures', November 2014.
19. Arundhati Roy, *Listening to Grasshoppers: Field Notes on Democracy* (New Delhi: Penguin Books India, 2009).
20. Arundhati Roy, *Listening to Grasshoppers*.
21. Arundhati Roy, *Listening to Grasshoppers*.
22. Arundhati Roy, *Listening to Grasshoppers*.
23. Rajesh Shukla, *How India Earns, Spends and Saves: Unmasking the Real India* (New Delhi: SAGE and NCAER-CMCR, 2010).
24. Sambuddha Mitra Mustafi, 'Why Indian Elites Like to Call Themselves "Middle Class"', 17 May 2013, http://india.blogs.nytimes.com/2013/05/17/why-indian-elites-like-to-call-themselves-middle-class/.
25. Ministry of Labour and Employment, 'Report on Third Annual Employment & Unemployment Survey (2012-13) Vol. 1' (Chandigarh: Government of India), http://labourbureau.nic.in/EUS_2012_13_Vol_1.pdf.

26. Ministry of Labour and Employment, 'Report on Third Annual Employment & Unemployment Survey 2012-13 Vol. 1'. p. 60.
27. Ministry of Labour and Employment, 'Report on Third Annual Employment & Unemployment Survey 2012-13 Vol. 1', p. 10.
28. Ministry of Labour and Employment, 'Report on Third Annual Employment & Unemployment Survey 2012-13 Vol. 1', p. 10.
29. Saeed A. Mirza, 'The Age of Amnesia', unpublished paper presented at the Idea of India Conclave, 4-5 July, New Delhi.
30. 'India's 25 Greatest Global Living Legends', organized by NDTV in the Rashtrapati Bhavan, 14 December 2013, New Delhi.
31. Jawaharlal Nehru, *The Discovery of India* (New Delhi: Penguin Books India, 2004).
32. Stuart Corbridge and John Harriss, *Reinventing India: Liberalization, Hindu Nationalism and Popular Democracy* (Cambridge: Polity Press, 2000).
33. Oxfam International, 'Even It Up: Time to End Extreme Inequality', p. 8, http://www.oxfamamerica.org/static/media/files/even-it-up-inequality-oxfam.pdf.
34. Oxfam International, 'Even It Up', p. 8.
35. Oxfam International, 'Even It Up', p. 8.
36. Seumas Milne, 'The Davos Oligarchs Are Right to Fear the World They've Made', *The Guardian*, 22 January 2015, accessed 7 March 2015, http://www.theguardian.com/commentisfree/2015/jan/22/davos-oligarchs-fear-inequality-global-elite-resist.
37. Thomas Piketty, *Capital in the Twenty-First Century*, trans. Arthur Goldhammer (Harvard: Harvard University Press, 2013).
38. Oxfam International 'Even It Up', p. 4.
39. Kumkum Dasgupta, 'For India, It's Time to Even Up', *Hindustan Times*, 9 Feb 2015.
40. Kumkum Dasgupta, 'For India, It's Time to Even Up'.
41. BBC 4 Series, 'Why Poverty?, http://www.bbc.co.uk/programmes/b01pblv4.
42. Mark Tran, 'Global Poverty Rate Falling, Says UN', *The Guardian*, 7 July 2011, accessed 12 January 2013, http://www.theguardian.com/global-development/2011/jul/07/millennium-development-goals-2011-report.
43. Subodh Varma, 'India Rising, Falling, Stumbling, Speeding', *The Economic Times*, 25 January 2010, accessed 12 January 2013,

http://articles.economictimes.indiatimes.com/2010-01-25/news/27582033_1_steel-production-poverty-line-economic-indicators.

44. Planning Commission, 'Press Note on Poverty Estimates', July 2013, accessed 12 January 2013, http://planningcommission.nic.in/news/pre_pov2307.pdf.
45. Harsh Mander, *Ash in the Belly: India's Unfinished Battle against Hunger*, (New Delhi: Penguin Books India, 2013).
46. J. P. Naik and Syed Nurulla, *A Student's History of Education in India: 1800-1973* (New Delhi: Pan Macmillan Publications, 2000).
47. Office of the Registrar General and Census Commissioner, India, 'Census Report-2011', accessed 12 January 2013, http://www.censusindia.gov.in/.
48. Proceedings of the book launch held in Delhi, Jean Dreze and Amartya Sen, *Uncertain Glory: India and Its Contradictions* (New Delhi: Penguin Books India, 2013).
49. John Baffes, Donald Mitchell, Elliot Riordan, Shane Streifel, Hans Timmer and William Shaw, 'Global Economic Prospects: Commodities at the Crossroads 2009', World Bank, http://documents.worldbank.org/curated/en/2009/01/10158584/global-economic-prospects-commodities-crossroads-2009.
50. Asian Development Bank, 'Key Indicators for Asia and the Pacific', 2014, p. 62, http://www.adb.org/publications/key-indicators-asia-and-pacific-2014.
51. Pedro Olinto, Kathleen Beegle, Carlos Sobrado and Hiroki Uematsu, 'The State of the Poor: Where Are the Poor, Where Is Extreme Poverty Harder to End and What Is the Current Profile of the World's Poor?' *Economic Premise*, World Bank, October 2013, p. 125, http://siteresources.worldbank.org/EXTPREMNET/Resources/EP125.pdf.
52. Oxfam International, 'Even It Up', pp. 2-3.
53. Credit Suisse, 'Global Wealth Databook 2014', October 2014, https://publications.credit-suisse.com/tasks/render/file/?fileID=5521F296-D460-2B88-081889DB12817E02.
54. Institute of Applied Manpower Research, 'India Human Development Report 2011: Towards Social Inclusion' (New Delhi: Oxford University Press, 2011), http://www.iamrindia.gov.in/ihdr_book.pdf.
55. Lucy Dubochet, 'India: Moving Towards Equal Opportunities for All?' (New Delhi: OXFAM International, 2013), p. 2, http://www.oxfam.org/en/research/india-moving-towards-equal-opportunities-all.

56. Lucy Dubochet, 'India: Moving Towards Equal Opportunities for All?'
57. Lucy Dubochet, 'India: Moving Towards Equal Opportunities for All?'
58. Lucy Dubochet, 'India: Moving Towards Equal Opportunities for All?'
59. Lucy Dubochet, 'India: Moving Towards Equal Opportunities for All?'
60. Lucy Dubochet, 'India: Moving Towards Equal Opportunities for All?'
61. Lucy Dubochet, 'India: Moving Towards Equal Opportunities for All?', p. 2.
62. 'Hurun Global Rich List 2015', for the complete list, see http://www.hurun.net/en/ArticleShow.aspx?nid=9607.
63. Amartya Sen, 'Keynote Address', ZEE Jaipur Literature Festival, 2014, http://jaipurliteraturefestival.org/festival-inauguration-and-keynote-address-dr-amartya-sen/.
64. World Bank, 'Perspectives on Poverty in India: Stylized Facts from Survey Data' (Washington DC: World Bank, 2009), accessed 14 January 2014, https://ideas.repec.org/b/wbk/wbpubs/2299.html.
65. Jean Dreze and Amartya Sen, *An Uncertain Glory: India and Its Contradictions* (New Delhi: Penguin Books India, 2014).
66. Jean Dreze and Amartya Sen, *An Uncertain Glory: India and Its Contradictions*.
67. Jean Dreze and Amartya Sen, *An Uncertain Glory: India and Its Contradictions*.
68. Stephanie Nolen, 'A Farewell to India: False Miracles and True Inspiration', *The Globe and Mail*, 10 August 2013, http://www.theglobeandmail.com/news/world/breaking-caste/a-farewell-to-india-false-miracles-and-true-inspiration/article13700792/?page=all.
69. Stephanie Nolen, 'A Farewell to India'.
70. James B. Davies, Susanna Sandström, Anthony B. Shorrocks and Edward N. Wolff, 'The Level and Distribution of Global Household Wealth', National Bureau of Economic Research, http://www.nber.org/papers/w15508.pdf.
71. United Nations Development Programme, The Rise of the South: Human Progress in a Diverse World' (New York: UNDP, 2013), accessed 15 January 2015, http://hdr.undp.org/sites/default/files/reports/14/hdr2013_en_complete.pdf

72. See for instance International Institute of Population Sciences and Macro International, 'National Family Health Survey-3, 2005-06'; Government of India, 'Social, Economic and Educational Status of Muslims in India: A Report', accessed 8 March 2014, http://repository.berkleycenter.georgetown.edu/061100SacharCommitteeSocialEconomicEducationalStatusMuslimCommunityIndia.pdf; Centre for Equity Studies, 'India Exclusion Report 2013-14' (New Delhi: Books for Change, 2014).
73. Ashutosh Varshney, 'India's Moment of Truth', *The Indian Express*, 11 June 2012, accessed 13 January 2014, http://archive.indianexpress.com/news/india-s-moment-of-truth/960277/.
74. Pratap Bhanu Mehta, 'Breaking the Silence', *The Caravan*, 1 October 2012, http://caravanmagazine.in/essay/breaking-silence.
75. Jean Dreze and Amartya Sen, *An Uncertain Glory: India and Its Contradictions*.
76. Premal Balan and Kalpesh Damor, 'Adani Group Got Land at Cheapest Rates in Modi's Gujarat', *Business Standard*, 26 April 2014, http://www.business-standard.com/article/companies/adani-group-got-land-at-cheapest-rates-in-modi-s-gujarat-114042501228_1.html.
77. Oxfam International, 'Working for the Few'.
78. Oxfam International, 'Working for the Few'.
79. Michael J. Sandel, *What Money Can't Buy: The Moral Limits of Markets,* (New York: Farrar, Straus and Giroux, 2013).
80. Oxfam International, 'Working for the Few'.
81. Jean Dreze, '2014 Budget for Beginners', India Resists, http://www.indiaresists.com/bjp-2014-budget-for-beginners-jean-dreze/.
82. Christine Lagarde interviewed by Chris Gelles, 'IMF Warns on Threats of Income Inequality', *Financial Times*, 19 January 2014, http://www.ft.com/cms/s/0/b3462520-805b-11e3-853f-00144feab7de.html.
83. Christine Lagarde 'A New Multilateralism for the 21st Century: The Richard Dimbleby Lecture', 3 February 2014, https://www.imf.org/external/np/speeches/2014/020314.htm.
84. Christine Lagarde 'A New Multilateralism for the 21st Century'.
85. Christine Lagarde 'A New Multilateralism for the 21st Century'.
86. Adapted from 'Subh-e-Azaadi' in *Poems of Faiz Ahmed Faiz*, V. G. Kiernan, trans., (New Delhi: Oxford University Press, 2000).

MANY EXILES OF INDIA'S POOR

1. Akhil Gupta, *Red Tape: Bureaucracy, Structural Violence, and Poverty in India* (North Carolina: Duke University Press, 2012).
2. The method Akhil Gupta uses to make this back-of-the-envelope calculation is to simply take the Human Development Indices of Kerala, which are among the highest in India, and see if they are being achieved in the rest of India.
3. 'The Bengal Famine of 1943, Amartya Sen and Satyajit Ray' http://pooreconomics.com/sites/default/files/14.73_Food_Lecture4.pdf.
4. John Vidal, 'Global Warming Causes 300,000 Deaths a Year, Says Kofi Annan Thinktank', *The Guardian*, 29 May 2009, accessed 8 March 2015, http://www.theguardian.com/environment/2009/may/29/1.
5. BBC News, 'India Aims to End Poverty by 2040', 3 February 2007, http://news.bbc.co.uk/2/hi/south_asia/6326629.stm.
6. BBC News, 'India Aims to End Poverty by 2040'.
7. Akhil Gupta, *Red Tape*, p. 16.
8. Pratap Bhanu Mehta, 'Breaking the Silence', *The Caravan*, 1 October 2012, http://caravanmagazine.in/essay/breaking-silence.
9. Pratap Bhanu Mehta, 'Breaking the Silence'.
10. Jan Breman, Isabelle Guerin and Aseem Prakash, *India's Unfree Workforce: Of Bondage Old and New* (New Delhi: Oxford University Press, 2009).
11. See for instance Palagummi Sainath, 'How to Be an "Eligible Suicide"', *The Hindu*, 19 May 2010, http://www.thehindu.com/opinion/lead/how-to-be-an-eligible-suicide/article428367.ece?ref=relatedNews.
12. See for instance Asian Human Rights Commission, 'India: A Heartless Nation for Women', 16 April 2012, http://www.humanrights.asia/news/ahrc-news/AHRC-PAP-001-2013/?searchterm=16 per cent20april per cent202012.
13. Harsh Mander, 'India's Great Shame', *The Hindu*, 17 November 2012, http://www.thehindu.com/opinion/columns/Harsh_Mander/indias-great-shame/article4097808.ece.
14. Planning Commission of India, 'Report of the Expert Group to Review the Methodology for Estimation of Poverty', 2009, http://planningcommission.nic.in/eg_poverty.htm.
15. Harsh Mander, 'The Troubling Figures of Poverty in India', 26 July

2013, http://www.livemint.com/Opinion/zLVp0Nt6MmnO5hqii5piZK/The-troubling-figures-of-poverty-in-India.html.
16. John Harriss, 'State of Injustice: The Indian State and Poverty', Institute of South Asian Studies, 20 March 2014, accessed 14 January 2014, http://www.jnu.ac.in/sss/csss/images/working-paper/John%20Harriss.pdf.
17. Dhananjay Mahapatra and Nitin Sethi, 'Spend Rs 32 a Day? Govt Says You Can't Be Poor', *The Times of India*, 21 September 2011, http://articles.timesofindia.indiatimes.com/2011-09-21/india/30183983_1_urban-areas-poverty-line-norms
18. Planning Commission of India, 'Report of the Expert Group to Review the Methodology for Measurement of Urban Poverty', June 2014, http://planningcommission.nic.in/reports/genrep/pov_rep0707.pdf
19. Harsh Mander, *Ash in the Belly: India's Unfinished Battle against Hunger*, (New Delhi: Penguin Books India, 2013).
20. Jean Dreze and Amartya Sen, 'Democratic Practice and Social Inequality in India', *Journal of Asian and African Studies* Vol. 37, Issue 6, p. 10.
21. Jean Dreze and Amartya Sen, 'Democratic Practice and Social Inequality in India', p. 26.
22. Jean Dreze and Amartya Sen, 'Democratic Practice and Social Inequality in India', p. 26.
23. For full text of the Act, see http://indiacode.nic.in/acts-in-pdf/202013.pdf.
24. Press Trust of India, 'India's Food Bill Can Set Example for Rest of World', *The Hindu Business Line*, 17 July 2012, accessed 14 January 2014, http://www.thehindubusinessline.com/industry-and-economy/indias-food-bill-can-set-example-for-rest-of-world/article3649594.ece.
25. Ashok Dasgupta, 'Food Bill Leaves Rupee Famished', *The Hindu*, 28 August 2013, accessed 14 January 2014, http://www.thehindu.com/business/markets/food-bill-leaves-rupee-famished/article5065562.ece.
26. Sabina Alkire, 'This Bill Won't Eat Your Money', *The Hindu*, 29 July 2013, accessed 14 January 2014, http://www.thehindu.com/opinion/op-ed/this-bill-wont-eat-your-money/article4963938.ece.
27. Sadanand Dhume, 'New Delhi's Hunger Games', *Wall Street Journal*, 20 June 2013, accessed 14 January 2014, http://online.wsj.com/news/articles/SB10001424127887323393804578557050745156758.

28. Sadanand Dhume, 'New Delhi's Hunger Games'.
29. Sadanand Dhume, 'New Delhi's Hunger Games'.
30. Gurcharan Das, 'Food Security Bill: Corruption by Another Name', 31 March 2013, accessed 14 January 2014, http://gurcharandas.blogspot.in/2013/03/food-security-bill-corruption-by.html.
31. Yashwant Sinha, 'Food Security Bill Is Proof That PM Is Happy to Go along with Sonia Gandhi's Senseless Welfarism', *The Economic Times*, 9 July 2013, accessed 14 January 2013, http://articles.economictimes.indiatimes.com/2013-07-09/news/40469285_1_congress-party-finance-minister-fiscal-deficits.
32. 'Dirty D-word and Unspoken Subsidy', *The Telegraph*, 30 December 2013, accessed 14 January 2014, http://www.telegraphindia.com/1131230/jsp/nation/story_17733538.jsp#.UtWj8tIW2tM.
33. Revised estimates for the year 2012-13 as per the 2013-14 Union Budget, accessed 15 January 2014, http://indiabudget.nic.in/budget.asp.
34. Udit Misra, 'Are Direct Cash Subsidies Better?', *Forbes India*, 21 March 2011, accessed 15 January 2014, http://forbesindia.com/printcontent/23422.
35. See, for example, Jagdish Bhagwati, 'Why Amartya Sen Is Wrong', *LiveMint*, 23 July 2013, accessed 15 January 2014, http://www.livemint.com/Opinion/9Qzg05zypjEUbioqK9N1UM/Why-Amartya-Sen-is-wrong.html.
36. Interviews of Amartya Sen and Jagdish Bhagwati by, respectively, Subhabrata Guha and Surojit Guha, *The Times of India*, 30 April 2014, accessed 15 January 2014, http://timesofindia.indiatimes.com/home/lok-sabha-elections-014/news/Minorities-have-reason-to-fear-Modi-Amartya-Sen-says-Gujarat-CM-has-vision-of-where-he-will-take-us-Jagdish-Bhagwati-argues/articleshow/34392562.cms.
37. David Pilling, 'Lunch with the FT: Jagdish Bhagwati', *Financial Times*, 17 April 2014, accessed 15 January 2014, http://www.ft.com/cms/s/2/f3a22bc8-c3db-11e3-a8e0-00144feabdc0.html#axzz36x8k72uh.
38. Press Trust of India, 'Fiscal Deficit to Slip Up by 50 bps on New Food Scheme: DBS', *The Economic Times*, 4 July 2013, accessed 15 January 2013, http://articles.economictimes.indiatimes.com/2013-07-04/news/40372215_1_food-security-bill-subsidy-bill-crude-prices.
39. Harsh Mander, 'Food Security Bill: Why Blame the Poor and the

Hungry?', *LiveMint*, 26 August 2013, accessed 15 January 2014, http://www.livemint.com/Opinion/LECvGhB8nDmWnX5i9 OTL2H/Blaming-the-poor-and-the-hungry.html?ref=ms.
40. Sabina Alkire, 'This Bill Won't Eat Your Money'.
41. Sabina Alkire, 'This Bill Won't Eat Your Money'.
42. Jean Dreze, 'On the Mythology of Social Policy', *The Hindu*, 8 July 2014, accessed 15 January 2014, http://www.thehindu.com/opinion/lead/on-the-mythology-of-social-policy/article6186895.ece.
43. Sankanath Bandopadhyay, 'Tax Exemptions in India: Issues and Challenges' (New Delhi: Centre for Budget and Governance Accountability, 2013), http://www.cbgaindia.org/files/recent_publications/Tax%20Exemptions%20in%20India.pdf.
44. UNESCO, 'Teaching and Learning: Achieving Quality for All', accessed 15 January 2014, http://www.unesco.org/new/en/education/themes/leading-the-international-agenda/efareport/reports/2013/ EFA Global Monitoring Report 2013-14, p. 10.
45. Oxfam International, 'No Effort in Budget to Close the Gaps',
46. Palagummi Sainath, 'The Feeding Frenzy of Kleptocracy', *The Hindu*, 16 March 2013, accessed 15 January 2014, http://www.thehindu.com/opinion/columns/sainath/the-feeding-frenzy-of-kleptocracy/article4513159.ece.
47. Sankanath Bandopadhyaya, 'Tax Exemptions in India: Issues and Challenges'.
48. Jean Dreze, 'On the Mythology of Social Policy', *The Hindu*, 8 July 2014, http://www.thehindu.com/opinion/lead/on-the-mythology-of-social-policy/article6186895.ece.
49. Gurcharan Das, 'Food Security Bill'.
50. Harsh Mander, 'Abandoning the Right to Food', *Economic and Political Weekly* Vol. 48, No. 8, 23 February 2013.
51. Siddharth Singh, 'Delhi's Opiated Intellectuals', *LiveMint*, 20 May 2014, http://www.livemint.com/Opinion/dNShxc6zqMvTGOcXil E4kO/Delhis-opiated-intellectuals.html.
52. Gurcharan Das, 'Food Security Bill'.
53. Himanshu Kaushik, 'Slums to Be Covered for Vibrant' *The Times of India*, 1 January 2015, http://timesofindia.indiatimes.com/city/ahmedabad/Slums-to-be-covered-for-Vibrant/articleshow/45720435.cms.
54. National Transport Development Policy Committee, 'India Transport

Report: Moving India to 2032', http://planningcommission.nic.in/sectors/index.php?sectors=National%20Transport%20Development%20Policy%20Committee%20%28NTDPC%29.
55. National Transport Development Policy Committee, 'India Transport Report'.
56. For more information see http://www.un.org/esa/population/publications/worldageing19502050/pdf/80chapterii.pdf.
57. T. S. Papola and Partha Pratim Sahu, 'Growth and Structure of Employment in India: Long-Term and Post-Reform Performance and the Emerging Challenge', (New Delhi: Institute for Studies in Industrial Development, 2012).
58. Ministry of Finance, 'Key Features of Budget 2012-13', accessed 8 March 2015, http://indiabudget.nic.in/ub2012-13/bh/bh1.pdf
59. Centre for Equity Studies and Centre for Budget and Governance Accountability, 'India Exclusion Report 2013-14', (New Delhi: Books for Change, 2014), p. 253.
60. Centre for Equity Studies and Centre for Budget and Governance Accountability, 'India Exclusion Report 2013-14'.
61. Centre for Equity Studies and Centre for Budget and Governance Accountability, 'India Exclusion Report 2013-14'.
62. Centre for Equity Studies and Centre for Budget and Governance Accountability, 'India Exclusion Report 2013-14'.
63. Subodh Varma, 'Government Spends Just Rs 124 Each on 10 Crore People Aged 60 Years and Above', *The Times of India*, 21 December 2013, http://timesofindia.indiatimes.com/india/Government-spends-just-Rs-124-each-on-10-crore-people-aged-60-years-and-above/articleshow/27697251.cms.
64. Helpage India, 'Report on Elder Abuse in India', accessed 8 March 2015, http://www.helpageindia.org/pdf/surveysnreports/elderabuseindia2010.pdf
65. Vandana Prasad, 'A Snapshot of the Health and Nutrition of the Ageing/Elderly Poor: Survey of 102 Participants of Pension Parishad Dharna, December 2013, New Delhi', accessed 15 March 2014, http://www.phrnindia.org/researchAdvocacy/REPORT%20ON%20HEALTH%20&%20NUTRITION%20STATUS%20 OF%20ELDERLY%....20PERSONS%.20.pdf
66. Loveleen Kacker, Srinivas Varadan and Pravesh Kumar, 'Study on Child Abuse: India 2007', (New Delhi: Ministry of Women and

Child Development, Government of India), accessed 15 January 2014, http://wcd.nic.in/childabuse.pdf

67. In a survey of street children in Delhi, Save the Children counted at least 50,000 individuals. Smaller informal head counts in other cities lead me to estimate that at least 0.5 percent of the city's population comprises street children. Accordingly, given that India's urban population is 377 million, I estimate the numbers of street children to be close to 1.8 million.

68. For full text of the Act, see Child Labour (Prohibition and Regulation) Act, 1986, http://bba.org.in/sites/default/files/Child percent20Labour percent20_Prohibitionpercent20_percent20Regulation_percent20 Act, percent201986.pdf.

69. Ministry of Statistics and Programme Implementation, 'Children in India 2012: A Statistical Appraisal', (New Delhi: Government of India), p 72, accessed 8 March 2015, http://mospi.nic.in/mospi_new/upload/Children_in_India_2012.pdf.

70. Ministry of Labour and Employment, 'Child Labour FAQ', accessed 8 March 2015, http://labour.nic.in/content/faq/child-labour-faq.php.

71. Ministry of Labour and Employment, 'Census Report 2011', http://labour.gov.in/upload/uploadfiles/files/Divisions/childlabour/Census-2001 percent262011.pdf.

72. World Bank. Data available at http://data.worldbank.org/indicator/SL.TLF.0714.WK.MA.ZS and; http://data.worldbank.org/indicator/SL.TLF.0714.WK.FE.ZS

73. Pia Lindstrom, 'Human Development in India: Analysis to Action', (New Delhi: United Nations Development Programme in Association with the Planning Commission of India, 2010), accessed 8 March 2015, http://www.in.undp.org/content/dam/india/docs/human_development_analysis_to_action.pdf.

74. Institute of Applied Manpower Research, 'India Human Development Report 2011', (New Delhi: Oxford University Press, 2011), p. 224.

75. Institute of Applied Manpower Research, 'India Human Development Report 2011', p. 226.

76. Institute of Applied Manpower Research, 'India Human Development Report 2011', p. 226.

77. Santosh Mehrotra, Ankita Gandhi, Partha Saha and Bimal Kishore Sahoo, 'Joblessness and Informalization: Challenges to Inclusive Growth in India', (New Delhi: Institute of Applied Manpower

Research, 2012), p. 12, https://www.abdn.ac.uk/sustainable-international-development/documents/Joblessness_Informalization_in_India.pdf.
78. 'Report of the Committee on Child Labour (Gurupadswamy Committee)', (New Delhi: Ministry of Labour, 1979).
79. Myron Weiner, *The Child and the State in India: Child Labor and Education Policy in Comparative Perspective* (New Jersey: Princeton University Press, 1991).
80. 'Annual Status of Education Report 2014' (Provisional), accessed 8 March 2015, http://img.asercentre.org/docs/Publications/ASER%20Reports/ASER%202014/fullaser2014mainreport_1.pdf.
81. 'Annual Status of Education Report 2014' (Provisional).
82. Municipal Corporation of Greater Mumbai, 'Mumbai Human Development Report 2009', (New Delhi: Oxford University Press, 2010), accessed 8 March 2015, https://drive.google.com/file/d/0B9w08mnxUvF9NWZlYTUzMmItYjMyNS00OTYwLWJkNTQtMjdiNTMxMTdiYmQ3/view?pli=1.
83. Social and Rural Research Institute, 'All India Survey of Out-of-School Children of Age 5 and in 6-13 Years Age Group', Ministry of Human Resource Development, 2009, accessed 13 January 2015, http://www.educationforallinindia.com/Survey-Report-of-%20out-of-school-children-IMRB-MHRD-EDCil-2009.pdf.
84. 'Statistics of School Education 2010-11', Ministry of Human Resource Development, accessed 13 January 2014, http://mhrd.gov.in/sites/upload_files/mhrd/files/SES-School_201011_0.pdf.
85. Government of India, 'Social, Economic and Educational Status of Muslims in India: A Report', November 2006, http://www.minorityaffairs.gov.in/sachar.
86. 'EFA Global Monitoring Report WIDE 2005', http://www.education-inequalities.org/countries/india.
87. Human Rights Watch, 'They Say We're Dirty: Denying Education to India's Marginalized', 2014, accessed 15 January 2015, http://www.hrw.org/sites/default/files/reports/india0414_ForUpload_1.pdf.
88. Kiran Bhatty, Centre for Policy Research; Annie Namala, Centre for Social Equity and Inclusion; Archana Dwivedi, A. Nirantar and A. Sharma, Ambedkar University; Madhumita Bandyopadhyay, National University of Educational Planning and Administration; Farah Farooqi, Jamia; S. Anant, NEG-FIRE; Naaz Khair, Radhika Alkazi, A. Aastha,

Subrat and Jawed, Centre for Budget and Governance Accountability; S. Hassan, A. Shah and A. Bhasin, Centre for Equity Studies.
89. UNESCO, 'Teaching and Learning: Achieving Quality for All', (Paris: UNESCO, 2014), p. 353, accessed 15 January 2015, http://unesdoc.unesco.org/images/0022/002256/225660e.pdf.
90. UNESCO, 'Teaching and Learning', p. 369.
91. Centre for Equity Studies and Centre for Budget and Governance Accountability, 'India Exclusion Report 2013-14'.
92. Centre for Equity Studies and Centre for Budget and Governance Accountability, 'India Exclusion Report 2013-14'.
93. Ghanshyam Shah, Harsh Mander, Sukhadeo Thorat, Satish Deshpande and Amita Baviskar, *Untouchability in Rural India* (New Delhi: Sage Publications, 2006).
94. Ghanshyam Shah et al, *Untouchability in Rural India*.
95. Arjuna Dangle, ed., and Priya Adarkar, trans., *Poisoned Bread: Translations from Modern Marathi Dalit Literature*, (Noida: Orient Blackswan, 2009), p. 11.
96. Max Lawson, 'Heads of IMF and World Bank Must Support a Global Goal to End Extreme Inequality', *Huffington Post*, 9 April 2014, accessed 15 January 2015, http://www.huffingtonpost.co.uk/max-lawson/global-banks fight-poverty_b_5116582.html.
97. Society for Un-Aided Private Schools of Rajasthan versus U.O.I & Anr, accessed 13 January 2014, http://judis.nic.in/supremecourt/imgs1.aspx?filename=39251.
98. Harsh Mander, 'India's Many Eklavyas', *Hindustan Times*, 23 July 2012.
99. 'Principals Nervous over Reservations for Poor', *Hindustan Times*, 13 April 2012, accessed 13 January 2014, http://www.hindustantimes.com/india-news/mumbai/principals-nervous-over-reservation-for-poor/article1-839775.aspx.
100. 'Principals Nervous over Reservations for Poor'.
101. A. Kumaraswamy and Alok Mathur, 'RTE Act: Private Schools as Catalysts?', *The Hindu*, 28 March 2010, accessed 13 January, 2014, http://www.thehindu.com/features/education/rte-act-private-schools-as-catalysts/article309771.ece.
102. Sonia Singh, 'Dirty Three-letter Words', *Outlook*, 7 May 2012, accessed 14 January 2014, http://www.outlookindia.com/article/Dirty-ThreeLetter-Words/280695.

103. Pavithra S. Rangan, 'An Unequal Childhood', Outlook, 8 September 2014, accessed 14 January 2014, http://www.outlookindia.com/printarticle.aspx?291801.
104. Pavithra S. Rangan, 'An Unequal Childhood'.
105. Pavithra S. Rangan, 'An Unequal Childhood'.
106. Subodh Varma, 'More Students Opt for Higher Education, but Even More Drop Out: Survey', *Economic Times*, 31 August 2013, accessed 15 January 2014, http://economictimes.indiatimes.com/industry/services/education/more-students-opt-for-higher-education-but-even-more-drop-out-survey/articleshow/22178598.cms?curpg=2.
107. Abusaleh Sharrif and Amit Sharma, 'Intergenerational and Regional Differentials in Higher Education in India', (Washington: US-India Policy Institute, 2013).
108. Centre for Equity Studies and Centre for Budget and Governance Accountability, 'India Exclusion Report 2013-14'.
109. Centre for Equity Studies and Centre for Budget and Governance Accountability, 'India Exclusion Report 2013-14'.
110. Centre for Equity Studies and Centre for Budget and Governance Accountability, 'India Exclusion Report 2013-14'.
111. Sean Michael Dougherty, 'Labour Regulation and Employment Dynamics at the State Level in India', *OECD Economics Department Working Papers*, No. 624, 2008.
112. Centre for Equity Studies and Centre for Budget and Governance Accountability, 'India Exclusion Report 2013-14'.
113. Leo Panitch, 'Europe's Left Has Seen How Capitalism Can Bite Back', *The Guardian*, 12 January 2014.
114. Eduardo Porter, 'Americanized Labor Policy Is Spreading in Europe', *The New York Times*, 3 December 2013, accessed 14 January 2014, http://www.nytimes.com/2013/12/04/business/economy/the-americanization-of-european-labor-policy.html?pagewanted=all&_r=0.
115. Atul Sood, Paaritosh Nath and Sangeetha Ghosh , 'Deregulating Capital, Regulating Labour: The Dynamics in the Manufacturing Sector in India', *Economic and Political Weekly*, Vol. XLIX, nos. 26 and 27, 28 June 2014, http://www.epw.in/system/files/pdf/2014_49/26-27/Deregulating_Capital_Regulating_Labour.pdf.
116. Atul Sood et al, 'Deregulating Capital, Regulating Labour'.
117. K. P. Kannan, *The Working People's Charter: A Critique*.
118. Jan Breman, ed., *Footloose Labour: Working in India's Informal Economy* (Cambridge: Cambridge University Press, 1996).

119. Annual Status of Education Report 2012, accessed 13 January 2014, http://www.asercentre.org/education/India/status/p/143.html.
120. Annual Status of Education Report 2014, accessed 13 January 2014, www.asercentre.org/Keywords/p/234.html.
121. Annual Status of Education Report 2013, accessed 13 January 2014, http://www.asercentre.org/Keywords/p/205.html.
122. UNESCO, 'Education for All: Global Monitoring Report', accessed 14 January 2014, http://www.unesco.org/new/en/education/themes/leading-the-international-agenda/efareport/.
123. International Institute for Population Studies and Population Council, 'Youth in India: Situation and Needs 2006-07', (Mumbai: IIPS, 2010).
124. International Institute for Population Studies and Population Council, 'Youth in India: Situation and Needs 2006-07'.
125. International Labour Organization, 'Decent Work for Youth in India', 2012, accessed 16 January 2014, http://www.ilo.org/newdelhi/info/WCMS_175936/lang—en/index.htm.
126. Centre for Equity Studies and Centre for Budget and Governance Accountability, 'India Exclusion Report 2013-14'.
127. Centre for Equity Studies and Centre for Budget and Governance Accountability, 'India Exclusion Report 2013-14'.
128. NSSO data 2001 puts estimates of temporary migrant workers at about 10 million, but this is a gross underestimation as the survey 'does not count short term migration and part-time occupation' (Priya Deshingkar and Shaheen Akhter, 'Migration and Human Development in India', 2012, p.3, accessed 14 January 2013, http://hdr.undp.org/en/content/migration-and-human-development-india). Deshingkar and Akhter argue that the number of circular migrants is about 100 million. A UNESCO report, ('Social Inclusion of Internal Migrants in India', accessed 14 January 2013, http://unesdoc.unesco.org/images/0022/002237/223702e.pdf) estimates that of a total of 400 million internal migrants, the number of circular migrants could lie anywhere between 15 and 100 million. Youth between the ages of fifteen to twenty-nine constitute 30 per cent of the total migrants and fifteen million are children. ('Internal Migrants Make up 1/3rd of India's Population, *The Times of India*, 18 October 2013, accesed 13 January 2014, http://timesofindia.indiatimes.com/india/Internal-migrants-make-up-1/3rd-of-Indias-population/articleshow/24313033.cms.)

129. Centre for Equity Studies and Centre for Budget and Governance Accountability, 'India Exclusion Report 2013-14'.
130. Centre for Equity Studies and Centre for Budget and Governance Accountability, 'India Exclusion Report 2013-14'.
131. Centre for Equity Studies and Centre for Budget and Governance Accountability, 'India Exclusion Report 2013-14'.
132. Kevin Bales, *Disposable People: New Slavery In Global Economy*, (New Jersey: University of California Press, 1999).
133. Rahul Pandita, 'The Nowhere People', *Open*, 13 October 2012, accessed 14 January 2014, http://www.openthemagazine.com/article/nation/the-nowhere-people.
134. Jim Rees, *Surplus People: From Wicklow to Canada*, (Collins Press, 2001), http://archives.gnb.ca/Irish/Databases/Fitzwilliam/text/en-CA/SurplusPeople.pdf.
135. Jan Breman, 'Myth of the Global Safety Net', *New Left Review* 59, September-October 2009, accessed 14 January 2014, http://newleftreview.org/II/59/jan-breman-myth-of-the-global-safety-net.
136. For instance, see Jan Breman, 'On Labour Bondage, Old and New', *The Indian Journal of Labour Economics*, Vol. 51, No. 1, accessed 14 January 2014, http://www.isleijle.org/ijle/IssuePdf/31edd8fe-2ff9-481c-a0d6-44fcd53adda6.pdf.
137. Harsh Mander, 'Workers in a World Class City', *The Hindu*, 1 August 2010, http://www.hindu.com/mag/2010/08/01/stories/2010080150110300.htm.
138. People's Union for Democratic Rights and others versus Union of India and others. For a full description see http://ww3.lawschool.cornell.edu/AvonResources/India-People-s_Union_for_Democratic_Rights_v-_Union_Of_India-1982.pdf.
139. 'Commonwealth Games: Monitoring Committee Report', accessed 17 January 2014, http://www.pudr.org/sites/default/files/pdfs/MC%20report.pdf.
140. CWG-CWC, 'Safety and Social Security of Construction Workers Engaged in Major Projects in Delhi, 2009', accessed 17 January 2014, www.mobilecreches.org/pdf/publications/2009_Safety-Social-Security-of-Construction-Workers-Commonwealth-Games-Delhi.pdf.
141. For full Act, see http://clc.gov.in/Acts/shtm/bocw.php.
142. Centre for Equity Studies and Centre for Budget and Governance Accountability, 'India Exclusion Report 2013-14'.

143. See for instance, 'Govt Call for Social Security of Invisible Women Workers', *The Pioneer*, 19 September, 2009.
144. Centre for Equity Studies and Centre for Budget and Governance Accountability, 'India Exclusion Report 2013-14', p. 127.
145. Centre for Equity Studies and Centre for Budget and Governance Accountability, 'India Exclusion Report 2013-14', p. 11.
146. Harsh Mander, 'Wishes Are Not Horses', *Hindustan Times*, 19 March 2007, http://www.hindustantimes.com/comment/bigidea/wishes-are-not-horses/article1-210778.aspx.
147. Judgement by P. N. Bhagwati on Bandhua Mukti Morcha versus Union of India and Others on 16 December 1983.
148. Lekha Rattanani interviews P. N. Bhagwati, 'It Is for the Benefit of the People', *Outlook*, 6 March 1996, accessed 18 January 2014, http://www.outlookindia.com/article.aspx?200933.
149. For full text of the The Bombay Prevention of Begging Act, (1959) see http://delhi.gov.in/wps/wcm/connect/f2214e0043383b63b2d1f3cf71a315bd/THE+BOMBAY+PREVENTION+OF.pdf?MOD=AJPERES&lmod=-716342930&CACHEID=f2214e0043383b63b2d1f3cf71a315bd.
150. Harsh Mander, 'The War against Begging', *The Hindu Sunday Magazine*, 25 January 2009, http://www.hindu.com/mag/2009/01/25/stories/2009012550090300.htm.
151. Harsh Mander, 'Wishes Are Not Horses'.
152. Harsh Mander, 'The War against Begging'.
153. Harsh Mander, 'The War against Begging'.
154. Harsh Mander, 'Wishes Are Not Horses'.
155. Usha Ramanathan, 'Demolition Drive', *Economic and Political Weekly* 2908-12 (2 July 2005), p. 3607, accessed 18 January 2014, http://www.ielrc.org/content/a0507.pdf.
156. Almitra H. Patel and Anr. vs Union Of India (Uoi) And Ors. on 16 January 1998, accessed 18 January 2014, indiankanoon.org/doc/1513084/.
157. Shantanu Guha Ray and Shoma Chaudhury interview P. Chidambaram, *Tehelka*, 31 May 2008 accessed 18 January 2014, http://archive.tehelka.com/story_main39.asp?filename=Ne310508cover_story.asp.
158. Government of India, 'State of Indian Agriculture 2012-13', accessed 18 January 2014, http://164.100.47.132/paperlaidfiles

AGRICULTURE/State per cent20ofper cent20Indian percent20 Agriculture per cent202012-13 percent20(English) per cent20with per cent20cover.pdf.

159. Dhananjay Mahapatra, 'Half of Delhi's Population Lives in Slums', *The Times of India*, 4 October 2012, accessed 18 January 2014, http://articles.timesofindia.indiatimes.com/2012-10-04/delhi/34258982_1_civic-bodies-municipal-solid-waste-unauthorized-colonies,.

160. Debolina Kundu and Amitabh Kundu, 'Tenurial Security and the Urban Poor: An Overview of Policies with Special Reference to Delhi, India', presented at the Indo-Dutch Conference held on 1-3 June 2006, New Delhi, http://library.tee.gr/digital/m2267/m2267_kundu.pdf.

161. Amitabh Kundu, 'Infrastructure and Financing and Emerging Pattern of Urbanisation: A Perspective', (New Delhi: Planning Commission of India, 2005), accessed 18 January 2014, http://planningcommission.nic.in/reports/genrep/bkpap2020/9_bg2020.pdf.

162. Centre for Equity Studies and Centre for Budget and Governance Accountability, 'India Exclusion Report 2013-14', p. 79.

163. Centre for Equity Studies and Centre for Budget and Governance Accountability, 'India Exclusion Report 2013-14', pp. 78-107.

164. Centre for Equity Studies and Centre for Budget and Governance Accountability, 'India Exclusion Report 2013-14'.

165. Centre for Equity Studies and Centre for Budget and Governance Accountability, 'India Exclusion Report 2013-14', p. 84.

166. Centre for Equity Studies and Centre for Budget and Governance Accountability, 'India Exclusion Report 2013-14'.

167. Centre for Equity Studies and Centre for Budget and Governance Accountability, 'India Exclusion Report 2013-14'.

168. Centre for Equity Studies and Centre for Budget and Governance Accountability, 'India Exclusion Report 2013-14'.

169. Kathryn Stockett, *The Help*, (LondonUK: Penguin, 2009).

170. Surabhi Tandon Mehrotra, 'Domestic Workers: Conditions, Rights and Responsibilities: A Study of Part-time Domestic Workers in Delhi', (New Delhi: Jagori, 2010), accessed 13 January 2014, http://jagori.org/wp-content/uploads/2006/01/Final_DW_English_report_10-8-2011.pdf.

171. Surabhi Tandon Mehrotra, 'Domestic Workers: Conditions, Rights and Responsibilities'.

172. National Commission for Enterprises in the Unorganised Sector, 'Report on Conditions of Work and Promotion of Livelihoods in the Unorganised Sector,' August 2007, accessed 13 January 2014, http://nceuis.nic.in/condition_of_workers_sep_2007.pdf.
173. Jayati Ghosh, 'Domestic Workers Lowly Paid in India on Inequality', *The Economic Times*, 1 March 2014, accessed 13 January 2014, http://articles.economictimes.indiatimes.com/2014-03-01/news/47799406_1_other-workers-ilo-convention-equal-rights.
174. Jayati Ghosh, 'Domestic Workers Lowly Paid in India on Inequality'.
175. Jayati Ghosh, 'Domestic Workers Lowly Paid in India on Inequality'.
176. Sujata Gothoskar, 'New Initiatives in Organizing Strategy in the Informal Economy: Case Study of Domestic Workers' Organizing', (Bangkok: Committee for Asian Women, 2006), http://wiego.org/sites/wiego.org/files/publications/files/Gothoskar_New_Initiatives_Organizing_2005.pdf.
177. National Commission for Enterprises in the Unorganised Sector, 'Report on Conditions of Work and Promotion of Livelihoods in the Unorganised Sector.'
178. This evidence emerged from a survey undertaken by the National Resource Team for the Homeless undertaken by the Centre For Equity Studies in collaboration with Oxfam.
179. 'Death on the Streets', *The Hindu Sunday Magazine*, 3 October 2010, accessed 19 January 2014, http://www.thehindu.com/todays-paper/tp-features/tp-sundaymagazine/death-on-the-streets/article810008.ece.
180. For more information, visit http://zipnet.in/.
181. Data available at http://zipnet.in/.
182. Data taken from https://www.cia.gov/library/publications/the-world-factbook/geos/in.html, accessed 19 January 2014.
183. Vandana Prasad, 'Translating Universal Health Care for the Homeless: Barriers and Potential Facilitating Factors for Accessing Health Care amongst Street Dwellers in India', *Health, Culture and Society*, Vol. 2, No. 1, accessed 19 January 2014, http://hcs.pitt.edu/ojs/index.php/hcs/article/view/74.
184. Vandana Prasad, 'Translating Universal Health Care for the Homeless'.
185. Arundhati Roy, *Listening to Grasshoppers: Field Notes on Democracy*, (UK: Penguin, 2009).
186. World Bank Data, accessed 14 January 2014, http://data.worldbank.org/indicator/SH.XPD.PUBL.ZS.

187. Gerard La Forgia and Somil Nagpal, 'Government-Sponsored Health Coverage in India: Are You Covered?', accessed 19 January 2014, http://documents.worldbank.org/curated/en/2012/08/16653451/government-sponsored-health-insurance-india-covered; Anup K. Saran and Sakthivel Selvaraj, 'Deepening Health Insecurity in India: Evidence from National Sample Surveys since 1980s', *Economic and Political Weekly*, Vol. 44, No. 55, 2009.
188. Indranil De and Rajeev Ahuja, 'Health Insurance for the Poor: An Analytical Study', *Economic and Political Weekly*, Vol 39, No. 41, 2004.
189. Amelia Shepherd-Smith, 'Free Drugs for India's Poor', *The Lancet*, Vol. 380, No. 9845, 2012, accessed 14 January 2014, http://www.thelancet.com/journals/lancet/article/PIIS0140-6736(12)61489-5/fulltext.
190. Max Lawson, 'Heads of IMF and World Bank Must Support a Global Goal to End Extreme Inequality'.
191. Subash Gatade, 'Tsundur Massacre: Normalising Injustice the Judicial Way', Kafila, 30 April 2014, accessed 14 January 2014, http://kafila.org/2014/04/30/tsundur-massacre-normalising-injustice-the-judicial-way/.
192. Subash Gatade, 'Tsundur Massacre'.
193. Jean Dreze and Amartya Sen, 'Democratic Practice and Social Inequality in India', *Asian and African Studies 2002*, Vol. 37, April 2002, pp. 6-37.
194. Jean Dreze and Amartya Sen, 'Democratic Practice and Social Inequality in India'.
195. Ghanshyam Shah et al, *Untouchability in Rural India*.
196. Ghanshyam Shah et al, *Untouchability in Rural India*.
197. See http://www.youthforequality.com/about-us/default.aspx.
198. Harsh Mander, 'Fight, but Not for your Privileges', *Tehelka*, 30 September 2006, accessed 19 January 2014 http://archive.tehelka.com/story_main19.asp?filename=Cr093006Do_bigha.asp.
199. Suresh Kadam in Arjuna Dangle, ed., and Vilas Sarang, trans., *Poisoned Bread: Translations from Modern Marathi Dalit* Literature, p. 38.
200. K. Nagaraj, 'Farmers' Suicides in India: Magnitudes, Trends and Spatial Patterns', Madras Institute of Development Studies, 2008, accessed 19 January 2014, http://www.macroscan.org/anl/mar08/pdf/farmers_suicides.pdf

201. Palagummi Sainath, 'How States Fudge the Data on Declining Farmer Suicides', 1 August 2014, accessed 19 January 2014, http://www.rediff.com/news/column/p-sainath-how-states-fudge-the-data-on-farmer-suicides/20140801.htm.
202. Palagummi Sainath, 'Farmers' Suicide Rates Soar above the Rest', 18 May 2013, accessed 19 January 2014, http://www.thehindu.com/opinion/columns/sainath/farmers-suicide-rates-soar-above-the-rest/article4725101.ece.
203. 'Manmohan Promises "New Deal" for Rural India', *The Hindu*, 24 June 2004, accessed 19 January 2014, http://www.hindu.com/2004/06/25/stories/2004062504930100.htm.
204. Palagummi Sainath, 'Farmer Suicide Rates Soar Above the Rest', *The Hindu*, 18 May 2013.
205. Palagummi Sainath, 'Farmer Suicide Rates Soar above the Rest'.
206. Palagummi Sainath, 'Farmer Suicide Rates Soar above the Rest'.
207. Palagummi Sainath, 'Farmer Suicide Rates Soar above the Rest.
208. Palagummi Sainath, 'Farmer Suicide Rates Soar above the Rest'.
209. Suneetha Kadiyala, P. K. Joshi, S. Mahendra Dev, T. Nanda Kumar and Vijay Vyas, 'A Nutrition Secure India: Role of Agriculture', *Economic and Political Weekly*, Vol. 47, No. 8, 2012, pp. 21-25, accessed 25 September 2013, http://www.righttofoodindia.org/data/research_writing_articles/general_interest/April_2012_nutrition_secure_india_role_of_agriculture_suneetha_pkjoshi_mahendra_nanda_vijay_epw_25_february_2012.pdf.
210. From data quoted on the website http://www.census2011.co.in/.
211. 'Agricultural Land Holdings Pattern in India', *NABARD Rural Pulse*, Issue 1, 2014, p.1, accessed 20 January 2015, https://www.nabard.org/Publication/Rural_Pulse_final142014.pdf.
212. Purnamita Dasgupta and Smitha Sirohi, 'Indian Agricultural Scenario and Food Security Concerns in the Context of Climate Change: A Review', Munich Personal RePEc Archive, 2010, accessed 25 September 2013, http://mpra.ub.uni-muenchen.de/24067/1/MPRA_paper_24067.pdf; Deepak Gopinath, 'India's Agriculture on the Brink', YaleGlobal Online, 27 March 2013, accessed 25 September 2013, http://yaleglobal.yale.edu/content/indias-agriculture-brink.
213. Vandana Shiva, *Soil Not Oil: Climate Change, Peak Oil and Food Insecurity*, (London: Zed Books, 2009).
214. S. Mahendra Dev, 'Agriculture-Nutrition Linkages and Policies in

India', International Food Policy Research Institute Discussion Paper 01184, 2012, accessed 25 September 2013, http://www.ifpri.org/sites/default/files/publications/ifpridp01184.pdf.

215. Shambhu Ghatak, 'Clear and Present Challenges before 21st Century Bharat' in Shambhu Ghatak, ed., *Access to Food* (Mumbai: Iris Knowledge Foundation, 2014), e-book edition, http://www.esocialsciences.org/eSS_essay/Food_Essays/Clear%20and%20Present%20Challenge_Shambhu%20Ghatak.pdf.

216. Shambhu Ghatak, 'Clear and Present Challenges before 21st Century Bharat'.

217. National Academy of Agricultural Sciences, 'Value Added Fertilizers and Site Specific Nutrient Management, accessed 25 September 2013, http://naasindia.org/Policy%20Papers/policy%2057.pdf.

218. National Academy of Agricultural Sciences, 'Value Added Fertilizers and Site Specific Nutrient Management'.

219. Deepak Gopinath, 'India's Agriculture on the Brink'; Vandana Shiva, *Soil Not Oil*.

220. Rajwinder Kaur and Manisha Sharma, 'Agricultural Subsidies in India: Boon or Curse', *IOSR Journal of Humanities and Social Science*, Vol. 2, No. 4, 2012, pp. 40-46; S. Mahendra Dev, 'Agriculture-Nutrition Linkages and Policies in India'.

221. CNN-IBN, 'Wages under MGNREGA Per Day Have Almost Doubled', 24 May 2013, http://ibnlive.in.com/news/wages-under-mgnrega-per-day-have-almost-doubled-tweets-pmo/393575-37-64.html.

222. Sukhadeo Thorat, M. Mahamallik and S. Venkatesan, 'Human Poverty and Socially Disadvantaged Groups in India', Human Development Resource Centre, United Nations Development Programme, 2007), p. 34., http://www.in.undp.org/content/dam/india/docs/human_poverty_socially_disadvantaged_groups_india.pdf.

223. Sukhadeo Thorat et al., 'Human Poverty and Socially Disadvantaged Groups in India'.

224. Sukhadeo Thorat et al., 'Human Poverty and Socially Disadvantaged Groups in India'.

225. Sukhadeo Thorat et al., 'Human Poverty and Socially Disadvantaged Groups in India'.

226. Sukhadeo Thorat et al., 'Human Poverty and Socially Disadvantaged Groups in India'.

227. 'The Survival Disadvantage: Mortality among Adivasi Children', *Poverty and Social Exclusion in India*, (Washington: World Bank, 2012), p. 48, https://openknowledge.worldbank.org/bitstream/handle/10986/2289/613140PUB0pove158344B09780821386903.pdf?sequence=1.
228. 'The Survival Disadvantage: Mortality among Adivasi Children', p. 53.
229. 'The Survival Disadvantage: Mortality among Adivasi Children', p.52.
230. Data as published by the National Institute of Rural Development and Panchayati Raj, accessed 25 September 2013, http://www.nird.org.in/Rural%20Development%20Statistics%202011-12/data/sec-10.pdf.
231. 'Overview', *Poverty and Social Exclusion in India*, (Washington: World Bank, 2012), p. 11.
232. 'Overview', *Poverty and Social Exclusion in India*, p. 11.
233. National Institute of Nutrition, 'Diet and Nutritional Status of Tribal Population and Prevalence of Hypertension among Adults', 2009, p. 11, accessed 25 September 2013, http://nnmbindia.org/NNMBTribalReport.pdf.
234. National Institute of Nutrition, 'Diet and Nutritional Status of Tribal Population and Prevalence of Hypertension among Adults'.
235. National Institute of Nutrition, 'Diet and Nutritional Status of Tribal Population and Prevalence of Hypertension among Adults'.
236. National Institute of Nutrition, 'Diet and Nutritional Status of Tribal Population and Prevalence of Hypertension among Adults'.
237. 'The Survival Disadvantage: Mortality among Adivasi Children', p. 58.
238. 'Other Processes Related to Higher Mortality among Adivasi Children', *Poverty and Social Exclusion in India*, p. 60.
239. 2012: People's Union of Civil Liberties versus Union of India and Others, Civil Writ Petition 196 of 2001, accessed 25 September 2013, http://www.hrln.org/hrln/right-to-food/pils-a-cases/1262-2012-pucl-vs-union-of-india-and-others-civil-writ-petition-196-of-2001.html.
240. Virginius Xaxa, 'The Status of Tribal Children in India: A Historical Perspective', 2011, p. 17, accessed 25 September 2013, http://www.ihdindia.org/IHD-Unicefwp-PDF/IHD-UNICEF%20WP%207%20virginius_xaxa.pdf.
241. Virginius Xaxa, 'The Status of Tribal Children in India: A Historical Perspective', p.17.

242. 'The Survival Disadvantage: Mortality among Adivasi Children', p. 60.
243. Verrier Elwin, *The Tribal World of Verrier Elwin: An Autobiography* (Delhi: Oxford University Press, 1965)
244. Planning Commission, 'Tenth Five-Year Plan' Vol. 2 (New Delhi: Government of India) p. 458, accessed 15 January 2014, http://planningcommission.nic.in/plans/planrel/fiveyr/10th/volume2/10th_vol2.pdf.
245. 'Other Processes Related to Higher Mortality among Adivasi Children', *Poverty and Social Exclusion in India*, p.67.
246. Tridip Suhrud, 'Modi and Gujarati "Asmita"', *Economic and Political Weekly* Vol. 43, No.1, 2008, pp. 11-13.
247. K. Alan Kronstadt, Paul K. Kerr, Michael F. Martin and Bruce Vaughn, 'India: Domestic Issues, Strategic Dynamics and U.S. Relations', Congressional Research Service, accessed 19 January 2014, https://www.fas.org/sgp/crs/row/RL33529.pdf.
248. Press Trust of India, 'Vibrant Gujarat 2011: India Inc All Praise for Narendra Modi', *The Economic Times*, 12 January 2011, accessed 19 January 2014, http://articles.economictimes.indiatimes.com/2011-01-12/news/28423442_1_narendra-modi-vibrant-gujarat-vibrant-gujarat.
249. Siddharth Varadarajan, 'The Cult of Cronyism', *Seminar*, April 2014,
250. Siddharth Varadarajan, 'The Cult of Cronyism'.
251. Press Trust of India, 'Vibrant Gujarat 2011: India Inc All Praise for Narendra Modi',
252. Interviews of Amartya Sen and Jagdish Bhagwati by, respectively, Subhabrata Guha and Surojit Guha, *The Times of India.*
253. Interviews of Amartya Sen and Jagdish Bhagwati by, respectively, Subhabrata Guha and Surojit Guha, *The Times of India.*
254. Arvind Panagariya, 'What Amartya Sen Doesn't See', *The Times of India*, 27 July 2013.
255. Press Trust of India, 'Lessons to be Learnt from Gujarat's Business Experience: Amartya', *The Times of India*, 23 July 2013.
256. Arvind Panagariya, 'What Amartya Sen Doesn't See'.
257. Arvind Panagariya, 'What Amartya Sen Doesn't See'.
258. Lyla Bavadam, 'Going Beyond the Narmada Valley', *Frontline* Vol. 17, No. 23, 2000, accessed 19 January 2014, http://www.frontline.in/static/html/fl1723/17230400.htm.
259. According to data provided by the Ministry of Commerce and Industry,

accessed 19 January 2014, http://dipp.nic.in/English/Publications/FDI_Statistics/FDI_Statistics.aspx.
260. Atul Sood, *Poverty amidst Prosperity: Essays on the Trajectory of Development in Gujarat* (New Delhi: Aakar Books, 2012).
261. Paranjoy Guha Thakurta, 'INDIA: Cheapest Car Rides on Govt Subsidies', Inter Press Service, 5 June 2009, accessed 21 January 2014, http://www.ipsnews.net/2009/06/corrected-repeat-india-cheapest-car-rides-on-govt-subsidies/.
262. 'Congress Files RTI on Nano Deal', 14 October 2008, accessed 15 January 2014, http://articles.economictimes.indiatimes.com/2008-10-14/news/28400835_1_nano-car-tata-motors-sanand.
263. Paranjoy Guha Thakurta, 'INDIA: Cheapest Car Rides on Govt Subsidies'.
264. Indira Hirway, 'Selective Development and Widening Disparities in Gujarat', *Economic and Political Weekly*, Vol. 30, Nos. 41-42, 1995, pp. 2603-2618.
265. 'Big Corporates Got Govt. Land Cheap: CAG', *The Indian Express*, 13 April 2013, http://archive.indianexpress.com/news/big-corporates-got-govt-land-cheap-cag/1097019/.
266. Premal Balan and Kalpesh Damor, 'Adani Got Land at Cheapest Rates in Modi's Gujarat', *Business Standard*, 26 April 2014, http://www.business-standard.com/article/companies/adani-group-got-land-at-cheapest-rates-in-modi-s-gujarat-114042501228_1.html.
267. 'Probe Rs. 1,100 Land Allocation Scam', *The Indian Express*, 20 January 2015, http://indianexpress.com/article/news-archive/web/probe-rs-1-100-cr-land-allocation-scam/.
268. Atul Sood, 'Poverty amid Prosperity', *The Hindu*, 30 November 2012.
269. Ashutosh Varshney, '2014, like 1952', *The Indian Express*, 19 May 2014, http://indianexpress.com/article/opinion/columns/2014-like-1952/.
270. K. S. Chalam, 'Gujarat: Whose State Is It Anyway?', *Janata* Vol. 67, Issue 45, 2 December 2012.
271. 'India Faces Urgent Hunger Situation', press release from the International Food Policy Research Institute, 2008, accessed 14 January 2014, http://www.ifpri.org/pressrelease/india-faces-urgent-hunger-situation?print
272. 'Gujarat's Social Progress Yet to Match Economic Progress', India

Spend, 30 October 2012, accessed 15 January 2014, http://www.indiaspend.com/states/gujarats-economic-success-yet-to-match-social-progress.
273. 'Gujarat's Social Progress Yet to Match Economic Progress'.
274. 'Gujarat's Social Progress Yet to Match Economic Progress'.
275. Indira Hirway, 'Selective Development and Widening Disparities in Gujarat'.
276. Harsh Mander, 'Worshipping False Gods in India', *Livemint*, 6 April 2014, http://www.livemint.com/Opinion/N3Pxc4L3QCOqe9TkYlFQeL/Worshipping-false-gods-in-India.html.
277. Reserve Bank of India, 'State Finances: A Study of Budgets' (New Delhi: RBI, 2013).
278. Shipra Nigam, 'Gujarat and the Illusion of Development', posted online by Nivedita Menon, Kafila, 23 May 2013, http://kafila.org/2013/05/23/gujarat-and-the-illusion-of-development-shipra-nigam/.
279. Shipra Nigam, 'Gujarat and the Illusion of Development'.
280. Shipra Nigam, 'Gujarat and the Illusion of Development'.
281. Institute of Applied Manpower Research, *India Human Development Report*, (New Delhi: Oxford University Press, 2011), p. 24, http://www.iamrindia.gov.in/ihdr_book.pdf.
282. National Nutrition Monitoring Bureau, 'Diet and Nutritional Status of Rural Population, Prevalence of Hypertension and Diabetes among Adults and Infant and Young Child Feeding Practices', http://nnmbindia.org/1_NNMB_Third_Repeat_Rural_Survey___Technicl_Report_26.pdf.
283. Rukmini S., 'In Gujarat, PDS Is Exclusionary, Leaky, Getting Worse', *The Hindu*, 17 August 2013, , accessed 21 January 2014, http://www.thehindu.com/todays-paper/tp-national/in-gujarat-pds-is-exclusionary-leaky-getting-worse/article5030732.ece
284. NSSO, 'Level and Pattern of Consumer Expenditure 2009-2010', (New Delhi: MoSPI, 2011).
285. Martha Nussbaum, 'Development Is More Than Growth', *The Hindu Centre for Politics and Public Policy*, 8 May 2014, http://www.thehinducentre.com/verdict/commentary/article5985379.ece.

THE LEGITIMIZATION OF PREJUDICE

1. Aditi Raid Malhotra, 'In Khirki Extension, Tensions Rise after Attempted', *Wall Street Journal*, 26 January 2014.
2. Aditi Raid Malhotra, 'In Khirki Extension, Tensions Rise after Attempted'.
3. Max Fisher, 'A Fascinating Map of The World's Most and Least Racially Tolerant Countries', *The Washington Post*, 15 May 2013, http://www.washingtonpost.com/blogs/worldviews/wp/2013/05/15/a-fascinating-map-of-the-worlds-most-and-least-racially-tolerant-countries/.
4. Harsh Mander, *Fear and Forgiveness: The Aftermath of the Massacre*, (New Delhi: Penguin India, 2009).
5. Salman Rushdie, Imran Khan, John McDonnell, Fiona Mactaggart, Pragna Patel, Jayati Ghosh, Suresh Grover, 'If Modi is Elected, it will Bode Ill for India's Future', *The Guardian*, 10 April 2014, accessed 20 February 2015, http://www.theguardian.com/commentisfree/2014/apr/10/if-modi-elected-india-future-gujarat.
6. Independent Voices, 'Letters: The Idea of Modi in Power Fills us with Dread', *The Independent*, 21 April 2014, accessed 20 February 2015, http://www.independent.co.uk/voices/letters/letters-the-idea-of-modi-in-power-fills-us-with-dread-9273298.html.
7. 'Author Amitav Ghosh Joins Amartya Sen, says Modi "Deeply Destabilishing"', *India Today*, 17 September 2013, , accessed 20 February 2015, http://indiatoday.intoday.in/story/author-amitav-ghosh-says-modi-deeplydestablishing/1/310214.html.
8. Press Trust of India, 'Narendra Modi-run Government would be a "Bullying" One, Salman Rushdie says', *The Times of India*, 14 May 2014, accessed 20 February 2015, http://timesofindia.indiatimes.com/home/lok-sabha-elections-2014/news/Narendra-Modi-run-government-would-be-a-bullying-one-Salman-Rushdie-says/articleshow/34726866.cms.
9. Interviews of Amartya Sen and Jagdish Bhagwati by, respectively, Subhabrata Guha and Surojit Guha, *The Times of India*, 30 April 2014, accessed 20 February 2015, http://timesofindia.indiatimes.com/home/lok-sabha-elections-014/news/Minorities-have-reason-to-fear-Modi-Amartya-Sen-says-Gujarat-CM-has-vision-of-where-he-will-take-us-Jagdish-Bhagwati-argues/articleshow/34392562.cms.

10. Jean Dreze, 'The Gujarat Muddle', *The Hindu*, 11 April 2014, accessed 20 February 2015, http://www.thehindu.com/opinion/op-ed/the-gujarat-muddle/article5896998.ece.
11. Press Trust of India, 'I Wouldn't Want to Live in India if Modi Becomes PM, author Ananthamurthy Says', *The Times of India*, 19 September 2013, accessed 20 February 2015, http://timesofindia.indiatimes.com/india/I-wouldnt-want-to-live-in-India-if-Modi-becomes-PM-author-Ananthamurthy-says/articleshow/22763087.cms.
12. Saurabh Gupta, 'Anti-Modi Appeal from Bollywood Personalities Leaves Film Industry Divided', 17 April 2014, accessed 20 February 2015, http://www.ndtv.com/elections/article/election-2014/anti-modi-appeal-from-bollywood-personalities-leaves-film-industry-divided-509616
13. Jason Burke, 'A Narendra Modi Victory Would Bode Ill for India, Say Rushdie and Kapoor', *The Guardian*, 10 April 2014, accessed 20 February 2015, http://www.theguardian.com/world/2014/apr/10/indian-artists-letter-guardian-worry-election.
14. Faizan Ahmad F., 'Those Opposed to Narendra Modi Should Go to Pakistan, BJP Leader Giriraj Singh Says', *The Times of India*, 20 April 2014, accessed 20 February 2015, http://timesofindia.indiatimes.com/news/Those-opposed-to-Narendra-Modi-should-go-to-Pakistan-BJP-leader-Giriraj-Singh-says/articleshow/33971544.cms.
15. Mihir Sharma, 'Why Narendra Modi Doesn't Want a Manifesto', *Business Standard*, 4 April 2014, accessed 20 February 2015, http://www.business-standard.com/article/elections-2014/mihir-sharma-why-narendra-modi-doesn-t-want-a-manifesto-114040400588_1.html.
16. 'Modi Kicks off Gujarat Gaurav Yatra', *The Times of India*, 8 September 2002, accessed 20 February 2015, http://articles.timesofindia.indiatimes.com/2002-09-08/ahmedabad/27299133_1_phagvel-post-godhra-bhathiji-maharaj.
17. Ramachandra Guha, 'The Man Who Would Rule India', *The Hindu*, 8 February 2013, accessed 18 May 2014, http://www.thehindu.com/opinion/lead/the-man-who-would-rule-india/article4390286.ece.
18. Press Trust of India, '2002 Riots: Modi's "Puppy" Remark Kicks up Political Storm', *The Times of India*, 12 July 2013, accessed 18 May 2014, http://articles.timesofindia.indiatimes.com/2013-07-12/india/40535468_1_2002-riots-narendra-modi-political-storm.

19. Amy Kazmin, 'Narendra Modi Rode Wave of Money to India Victory', *Financial Times*, 19 May 2014, accessed 18 May 2014, http://www.ft.com/cms/s/0/ce68abf0-df3f-11e3-86a4-00144feabdc0.html#axzz34tAIuEZB.
20. 'SIT Report Contains Evidence on Conspiracy to Target Minorities,' *The Hindu*, 10 July 2013, accessed 20 February 2015, http://www.thehindu.com/news/national/sit-report-contains-evidence-on-conspiracy-to-target-minorities/article4899065.ece.
21. 'SIT Report Contains Evidence on Conspiracy to Target Minorities'.
22. Manoj Mitta, *The Fiction of Fact Finding: Modi and Godhra* (New Delhi: HarperCollins, 2014).
23. Manoj Mitta, 'Don't Ask, Don't Tell', *Outlook*, 17 February 2014, accessed 20 February 2015, http://www.outlookindia.com/article/Dont-Ask-Dont-Tell/289455.
24. For full text of the report see, Raju Ramachandran, 'Report by the Amicus Curiae Dated 25.07.2011 Submitted Pursuant to the Order of This Hon'ble Court Dated 05.5.2011', http://www.scribd.com/doc/92667736/Final-Report-Raju-Ramachandran.
25. Raju Ramachandran, p. 4.
26. Raju Ramachandran, p. 4.
27. Raju Ramachandran, p. 4.
28. Raju Ramachandran, p. 4.
29. 'SIT Clean Chit to Modi Challenged in Court', *Business Standard*, 16 April 2013, accessed 14 January 2014, http://www.business-standard.com/article/current-affairs/sit-clean-chit-to-modi-in-2002-riots-challenged-in-court-113041500420_1.html.
30. Fareed Kazmi and Sanjeev Kumar, 'The Politics of Muslim Identity and the Nature of Public Imagination In India: Media and Films as Potential Determinants', *European Journal of Economic and Political Studies*, Vol 4, No. 1, accessed 20 February 2015, http://ejeps.fatih.edu.tr/docs/articles/121.pdf.
31. Javed Anand, 'Why Modi cannot shake off 2002', *The Indian Express*, 10 August 2012, accessed 20 February 2015, http://archive.indianexpress.com/news/why-modi-cannot-shake-off-2002/986180/
32. Saeed A. Mirza, 'The Age of Amnesia', unpublished paper presented at Idea of India Conclave, New Delhi, 4-5 July.
33. Arjumand Bano, 'Muslims Need Not Be Scared of Modi: Bajpai', *The*

Times of India, 17 April 2014, http://timesofindia.indiatimes.com/india/Muslims-need-not-be-scared-of-Modi-Bajpai/articleshow/33872890.cms.

34. Siddharth Mazumdar, '2014 Heralds a New Era in Indian Politics', *Tehelka*, 24 May 2014, accessed 20 February 2015, http://www.tehelka.com/2014-heralds-a-new-era-in-indian-politics/.
35. Communal Incidents up 30% in 2013, UP Tops List', *Indian Express*, 4 February 2015, accessed 20 February 2015, http://indianexpress.com/article/india/communal-incidents-up-30-in-2013-up-tops-list/.
36. Jay Mazoomdar, 'The Saffron Coup', *Tehelka*, 24 May 2014, accessed 20 February 2015, http://www.tehelka.com/the-saffron-coup/.
37. 'Amit Shah Booked for "Revenge" Remark on Muzaffarnagar Riots', *India Today*, 6 April 2014, accessed 20 February 2015, http://indiatoday.intoday.in/story/amit-shah-booked-muzaffarnagar-riots-mulayam-singh-yadav-narendra-modi/1/3539285.html.
38. Ayeshea Perera, 'Modi Live: SP Made Congress' Vote Bank Politics Its Own', Firstpost, 21 November 2013, accessed 20 February 2015, http://www.firstpost.com/politics/modi-live-sp-made-congress-vote-bank-politics-its-own-1241447.html.
39. Vijaysinh Parmar, 'Evict Muslims from Hindus Areas: Pravin Togadia', *The Times of India*, 21 April 2014, accessed 20 February 2015, http://timesofindia.indiatimes.com/india/Evict-Muslims-from-Hindu-areas-Pravin-Togadia/articleshow/34017292.cms.
40. Roshan Kumar, 'Modi Targets "Pink Revolution"', *The Telegraph*, 3 April 2014, accessed 20 February 2015, http://www.telegraphindia.com/1140403/jsp/frontpage/story_18149409.jsp#.VNHMD52UdqU.
41. Press Trust of India, 'Won't Appeal to Hindus or Muslims but to All; Ready to Face Defeat,' *Hindustan Times,* accessed 20 February 2015, http://www.hindustantimes.com/the-big-story/will-not-appeal-to-hindus-or-muslims-ready-to-face-defeat-modi/article1-1209629.aspx.
42. See for instance, Nilim Dutta, 'The Myth of the Bangladeshi and Violence in Assam', Kafila, 16 August 2012, accessed 20 February 2015, http://kafila.org/2012/08/16/the-myth-of-the-bangladeshi-and-violence-in-assam-nilim-dutta/.
43. Press Trust of India, 'People in Assam Govt Conspiring to Eliminate Rhinos: Modi', *Business Standard*, 31 March 2014, accessed 20

February 2015, http://www.business-standard.com/article/pti-stories/people-in-assam-govt-conspiring-to-eliminate-rhinos-modi-114033100661_1.html]
44. Samar Halarnkar, 'Globally Narendra Modi's Rise Is Hardly Unique', *The Hindustan Times*, 21 May 2014, accessed 20 February 2015, http://www.hindustantimes.com/comment/analysis/globally-narendra-modi-s-rise-is-hardly-unique/article1-1221623.aspx.
45. Samar Halarnkar, 'Globally Narendra Modi's Rise Is Hardly Unique'.
46. Amitav Ghosh, 'Erdogan and Modi: Parallel Journeys?', *The Times of India*, 30 November, 2014.
47. Prem Shanker Jha, 'What Really Happened in Gujarat?', *Tehelka*, 17 April 2014, accessed 20 February 2015, http://www.tehelka.com/what-really-happened-in-gujarat/.
48. 'Muslims Are Not a Minority, Parsis Are: Najma Heptullah', *The Times of India*, 28 May 2014, accessed 20 February 2015, http://timesofindia.indiatimes.com/india/Muslims-are-not-minorities-Parsis-are-Najma-Heptullah/articleshow/35651799.cms.
49. Mukul Kesavan, ' What about 1984?: Pogroms and Political Virtues', *The Telegraph*, 26 July 2013, accessed 20 February 2015, http://www.telegraphindia.com/1130726/jsp/opinion/story_17155627.jsp#.U4oMo_mSxvE.
50. Prashant Jha, 'BJP Win Blow to Muslim Politics: Singhal', *Hindustan Times*, 17 July 2014, accessed 20 February 2015, http://www.hindustantimes.com/india-news/bjp-win-blow-to-muslim-politics-vhp-chief-patron-ashok-singhal/article1-1241242.aspx.
51. Prashant Jha, 'BJP Win Blow to Muslim Politics: Singhal'.
52. Gopal Krishna Gandhi, 'An Open Letter to Narendra Modi', *The Hindu*, 19 May 2014, http://www.thehindu.com/opinion/lead/an-open-letter-to-narendra-modi/article6022900.ece.
53. 'Anger Aspiration and Apprehension', *Economic and Political Weekly* Vol. 49, No. 21, 24 May 2014.
54. Ashutosh Varshney, *Ethnic Conflict and Civic Life: Hindus and Muslims in India,* (New Haven: Yale University Press, 2002), p. 67
55. Hasan Suroor, 'Chaining 1200 Years,' *Outlook*, 7 July 2014, http://www.outlookindia.com/article/Chaining-1200-Years/291200.
56. Gyanendra Pandey, *The Construction of Communalism in Colonial North India* (Delhi: Oxford University Press, 1990).
57. Mahtama Gandhi was assassinated by Nathuram Godse, a Hindu

nationalist. Indira Gandhi was killed by two of her bodyguards, Satwant Singh and Beant Singh, who were Sikhs. The bomb blast that killed Rajiv Gandhi was carried out by Thenmozhi Rajaratnam, also known as Dhanu and the attack was blamed on the Liberation Tigers of Tamil Eelam (LTTE), a separatist organization from Sri Lanka.

58. Nivedita Menon, 'Some Myths about Muslims', Kafila, 12 April 2014, accessed 20 February 2015, http://kafila.org/2014/04/12/some-myths-about-muslims/.
59. For more information, see www.satp.org.
60. Nivedita Menon, 'Some Myths about Muslims', Kafila, 12 April 2014, accessed 20 February 2015, http://kafila.org/2014/04/12/some-myths-about-muslims/.
61. Praveen Swami, 'Bias and the Police', *Frontline* Vol. 23, Issue 24, December 2006, accessed 18 June 2014, http://www.frontline.in/static/html/fl2324/stories/20061215002503300.htm.
62. Rahi Gaekwad, 'Malegaon Blast; Three Remanded to Custody', *The Hindu*, 25 October 2008, accessed 18 June 2014, http://www.hindu.com/2008/10/25/stories/2008102561761400.htm.
63. Elisa Mala and J. David Goodman, 'At least 80 Dead in Norway Shooting', *New York Times*, 22 July 2011, accessed 18 June 2014, http://www.nytimes.com/2011/07/23/world/europe/23oslo.html?pagewanted=2&_r=1&hp.
64. Mohan Rao, 'Explaining Neo-Malthusianism', accessed 23 September 2011, http://www.consilium.europa.eu/uedocs/cmsUpload?TE-SAT percent202010.pdf.
65. Charles Kurzman, 'Muslim-American Terrorism: Declining Further', Triangle Center on Terrorism and Homeland Security, 1 February 2013, accessed 18 June 2014, http://sites.duke.edu/tcths/files/2013/11/Kurzman_Muslim-American_Terrorism_final2013.pdf.
66. 'Non-Muslims Carried Out More Than 90 per cent of All Terrorist Attacks in America', Centre for Research on Globalization, 1 May 2013, accessed 18 June 2014, http://www.globalresearch.ca/non-muslims-carried-out-more-than-90-of-all-terrorist-attacks-in-america/5333619.
67. DNA News Report, 'Excerpts from the Justice U C Banerjee Committee Report', 23 February 2011, accessed 20 February 2015, http://www.dnaindia.com/india/report-excerptsfrom-the-justice-u-c-banerjee-committeereport-1016092.

68. Ram Puniyani, 'Riot with Many Contrasts', *Countercurrents*, 28 August 2012, accessed 18 June 2014, http://www.countercurrents.org/puniyani280812.htm.
69. Praveen Swami, 'Bias and the Police'.
70. Concerned Citizens Tribunal-Gujarat 2002, 'Violence against Women', *Crime against Humanity* Vol. 2 (Mumbai: Citizens for Justice and Peace) pp. 38-39, accessed 18 June 2014, http://www.sabrang.com/tribunal/tribunal2.pdf.
71. Omar Rashid, 'Now, Victims in Shamli Camps are Thrown Out in the Cold', *The Hindu*, 3 January 2014, accessed 18 June 2014, http://www.thehindu.com/news/national/other-states/now-victims-in-shamli-camps-are-thrown-out-in-the-cold/article5533536.ece.
72. 'SC Expresses Concern at Death of Children in Relief Camps', *The Hindu* 12 December 2013, accessed 18 June 2014, http://www.thehindu.com/news/national/sc-expresses-concern-at-death-of-children-in-relief-camps/article5451945.ece.
73. Sandeep Unnithan and Neeraj Mishra, 'Sachar Committee: Congress Minority Agenda Comes under Scrutiny', *India Today*, accessed 18 June 2014, http://indiatoday.intoday.in/story/sachar-committee-congress-minority-agenda-comes-under-scrutiny/1/181892.html.
74. Ajaz Ashraf, 'Dear Anti-Muslim Commenters, Here Is What Islam Is Really About', *Firstpost*, 8 July 2014, http://www.firstpost.com/living/dear-anti-muslim-commenters-here-is-what-islam-is-really-about-1606503.html.
75. Syeda Saiyidain Hameed, *Maulana Azad, Islam and Indian Nationalism*, (New Delhi: Oxford University Press, 2014).
76. The comments were made by her on a popular TV show. Her apology was later recorded by the IANS 'I Say Sorry and Stand Corrected: Simi Garewal', accessed 18 June 2014, http://www.hindustantimes.com/news-feed/chunk-ht-ui-entertainmentsectionpage-bollwood/i-say-sorry-and-stand-corrected-simi-garewal/article1-355521.aspx.
77. Harsh Mander, 'Barefoot: To Be a Muslim in India Today', *The Hindu*, 7 August 2010, http://www.thehindu.com/opinion/columns/Harsh_Mander/barefoot-to-be-a-muslim-in-india-today/article37959.ece.
78. Ashish Khetan, 'In the Words of a Zealot,' *Tehelka*, 15 January 2011, accessed 16 June 2014, http://archive.tehelka.com/story_main48.asp?filename=Ne150111Coverstory.asp.

79. Ayesha Pervez, 'Persistent Exclusion of Muslims in India', *Infochange News & Features*, accessed 18 June 2014, http://infochangeindia.org/human-rights/analysis/persistent-exclusion-of-muslims-in-india.html.
80. Some banks have identified a number of Muslim concentration areas as 'negative geographical zones' where bank credit and other facilities are not easily provided—Sachar Report highlights.
81. Ashok Sowmiya and Mohammad Ali, 'Housing Apartheid Flourishes in Delhi', *The Hindu*, accessed 18 June 2014, http://www.thehindu.com/news/national/housing-apartheid-flourishes-in-delhi/article3613994.ece.
82. Ather Farouqui, 'Living Together Separately: Ghettoization of Muslims', 2012, accessed 20 February 2015, http://twocircles.net/2010apr14/living_together_separately_ghettoization_muslims.html.
83. Rahi Gaekwad, 'In Mumbai, a "No Rent, No Sale" Policy', *The Hindu*, 8 July 2012, accessed 18 June 2014, http://www.thehindu.com/news/national/other-states/in-mumbai-a-no-rent-no-sale-policy/article3613986.ece.
84. Harsh Mander, *Fear and Forgiveness: The Aftermath of the Massacre*, (New Delhi: Penguin, 2009).
85. Basharat Peer, 'Being Muslim under Narendra Modi', *New York Times*, 18 April 2014, accessed 18 June 2014, http://www.nytimes.com/2014/04/19/opinion/being-muslim-under-narendra-modi.html?_r=0.
86. Basharat Peer, 'Being Muslim under Narendra Modi'.
87. Ather Farouqui, 'Living Together Separately: Ghettoization of Muslims'.
88. Government of India, 'Social, Economic and Educational Status of Muslims in India: A Report', November 2006, p. 136, http://www.minorityaffairs.gov.in/sachar.
89. 'Social, Economic and Educational Status of the Muslim Community of India', p. 165.
90. S. L. Rao, 'Discrimination against the Muslims', *The Telegraph*, 9 April 2007, accessed 18 June 2014, http://slrao.com/Muslim per cent20discrimination.doc.
91. Shaikh Azizur Rahman, 'Indian Muslims Pose as Hindus to Get Jobs', *Australia Network News*, 31 October 2012, accessed 18 June 2014, http://www.abc.net.au/news/2012-10-31/an-indian-muslims-dress-as-hindus-to-avoid-discrimination/4343462.

92. Sukhadeo Thorat and Paul Attewell, 'The Legacy of Social Exclusion: A Correspondence Study of Job Discrimination in India', *Economic and Political Weekly*, (13-19 October, 2007): 4141-4145.
93. Sukhadeo Thorat and Paul Attewell, 'The Legacy of Social Exclusion'.
94. Shaikh Azizur Rahman, 'Indian Muslims Pose as Hindus to Get Jobs'.
95. This has to be 15 per cent
96. Bindu Shajan Perapaddan and Rana Siddiqui Zaman, 'In Delhi's Nursery Classes, Muslim Children Are a Rarity', *The Hindu*, 18 March 2012, accessed 18 June 2014, http://www.thehindu.com/news/national/in-delhis-nursery-classes-muslim-children-are-a-rarity/article3009826.ece.
97. Hem Borker, 'Shutting the School Doors on the Muslim Child', *The Hindu*, 5 April 2012, accessed 18 June 2014, http://www.thehindu.com/opinion/op-ed/shutting-the-school-doors-on-the-muslim-child/article3281463.ece.
98. Hem Borker, 'Shutting the School Doors on the Muslim Child'.
99. Hem Borker, 'Contesting Dilemma's: Muslim Identity and Education: A Case Study of Jamia Nagar', *National Cry Research Fellowship*, CRY, 2011, New Delhi.
100. Election Commission of India, 'Statistical Report on General Elections, 1984 to the Eight Lok Sabha, Vol. 1', p. 87, accessed 18 June 2014, http://eci.nic.in/eci_main/statisticalreports/LS_1984/Vol_I_LS_84.pdf.
101. Harsh Mander, 'Barefoot under the Rubble', *The Hindu*, 7 August 2010, http://www.thehindu.com/opinion/columns/Harsh_Mander/barefoot-under-the-rubble/article60493.ece.
102. 'Timeline: Ayodhya Holy Site Crisis', BBC News South Asia Report, 2012, accessed 18 June 2014, http://www.bbc.co.uk/news/world-south-asia-11436552.
103. 'The Tragedy of Ayodhya', *Frontline* Vol. 17, Issue 13, 24 June-7 July 2000, http://www.frontline.in/static/html/fl1713/17130170.htm.
104. '1990-L.K. Advani's Rath Yatra: Chariot of Fire', *India Today*, 2009, accessed 18 June 2014, http://indiatoday.intoday.in/story/1990-L.K.+Advani's+rath+yatra:+Chariot+of+fire/1/76389.html.
105. Shenali Waduge, 'Why Buddhism Prospered in Asia but Died in India', *Asian Tribune*, 2012, accessed 20 February 2015, http://www.asiantribune.com/news/2012/06/09/why-buddhism-prospered-asia-died-india.

106. Siddharth Vardarajan, 'Searing Indictment of RSS, BJP, but Action to be Taken: Nothing', *The Hindu*, 25 November 2009, accessed 20 February 2015, http://www.thehindu.com/todays-paper/searing-indictment-of-rss-bjp-but-action-to-be-taken-nothing/article147701.ece.
107. Siddharth Vardarajan, 'Searing Indictment of RSS, BJP, but Action to be Taken: Nothing'.
108. Preamble to the Constitution of India.
109. 'Highlights of the Judgements', *The Hindu*, 1 October 2010, accessed 20 February 2015, http://www.thehindu.com/todays-paper/tp-opinion/highlights-of-the-judgments/article805584.ece.
110. Christophe Jaffrelot, 'Communal Riots in Gujarat: The State at Risk?', *Heidelberg Papers in South Asian and Comparative Politics*.
111. Concerned Citizens Tribunal-Gujarat 2002, 'Annexure 10' *Crime against Humanity* Vol. 1 (Mumbai: Citizens for Justice and Peace) pp. 259-262, accessed 18 June 2014, http://www.sabrang.com/tribunal/tribunal1.pdf.
112. Ram Puniyani, *Communal Politics: Facts versus Myths*, (New Delhi: Sage, 2003).
113. Ram Puniyani, 'Demonisation through Demography', 2002, accessed 13 January 2014, http://www.nilacharal.com/news/view/v71.html.
114. Nivedita Menon, 'Some Myths about Muslims'.
115. Mohan Raomohan Rao, 'Saffron Demography', *The Times of India*, 20 April 2006, accessed 13 January 2014, http://articles.timesofindia.indiatimes.com/2006-04-20/editpage/27805824_1_hindus-muslim-growth-rate-muslim-population.
116. U. N. Mukherji, *Hindus: A Dying Race*, 1909, Calcutta.
117. For more see www.sanghparivar.org/blog/rkm/false-portrayal-of-islam-and-muhammad-by-hindu-monks.
118. Mohan Raomohan Rao, 'Saffron Demography'.
119. Mohan Raomohan Rao, 'Love Jihad, a Tool to Create Communal Divide and Fear', *The Hindu*, 3 November 2013, accessed 13 January 2014, http://karnatakamuslims.com/portal/love-jihad-a-tool-to-create-communal-divide-and-fear/.
120. Mohan Raomohan Rao, 'Abiding Appeal of Neo-Malthusianism'.
121. Mohan Raomohan Rao, Ish Mishra, Pragya Singh and Vikas Bajpai, 'Communalism and the Role of the State: An Investigation into the Communal Violence in Muzaffarnagar and its Aftermath', *Economic*

       and Political Weekly, 22 December 2013, accessed 13 January 2014, http://www.epw.in/system/files/Muzaffarmagar%20Report%20-%20Final%20%281%29.pdf

122. Tanika Sarkar, 'Semiotics of Terror: Muslim Children and Women in Hindu Rashtra', *Economic and Political Weekly*, Vol. 37, No. 28, 13 July 2002.

123. Mohan Raomohan Rao, 'Love Jihad, a Tool to Create Communal Divide and Fear'.

124. Voice for Justice, *Love Jihad!: Myth or Reality*, accessed 13 January 2014, http://samvada.org/files/Voice-for-Justice-Book.pdf.

125. Prashant Jha, 'Where Sangh Spins Narratives of Victimhood, Belligerence', *The Hindu*, 13 September 2013, accessed 13 January 2014, http://www.thehindu.com/news/national/where-sangh-spins-narratives-of-victimhood-belligerence/article5113769.ece.

126. Mohan Raomohan Rao, 'Love Jihad, a Tool to Create Communal Divide and Fear.'

127. Mohan Raomohan Rao, 'Love Jihad, a Tool to Create Communal Divide and Fear.'

128. Mohan Raomohan Rao, 'Love Jihad, a Tool to Create Communal Divide and Fear.'

129. 'Cracking Down on Violations of Moral Code in Dakshin Kannada', *The Hindu*, 7 September 2008, accessed 13 January 2014, http://www.thehindu.com/todays-paper/cracking-down-on-violations-of-moral-code-in-dakshina-kannada/article1333074.ece.

130. Sudipto Mondal, 'Schoolgirl Commits Suicide', *The Hindu*, 12 February 2009, http://www.thehindu.com/todays-paper/schoolgirl-commits-suicide/article352908.ece

131. People's Union for Civil Liberties, 'Cultural Policing in Dakshina Kannada: Vigilante Attacks on Women and Minorities, 2008-09', accessed 17 January 2014, http://www.sacw.net/DC/CommunalismCollection/ArticlesArchive/CulturalPolicing-Karnataka.pdf.

132. People's Union of Civil Liberties, 'Cultural Policing in Dakshina Kannada'.

133. Mohan Raomohan Rao, 'Love Jihad, a Tool to Create Communal Divide and Fear'.

134. Mohan Raomohan Rao et al, 'Communalism and the Role of the State'

135. According to data published by the National Crime Records Bureau, http://ncrb.nic.in/PSI-2012/Graphs-2012.pdf.

136. According to data published by the National Crime Records Bureau, http://ncrb.nic.in/PSI-2012/Graphs-2012.pdf.
137. Zeeshan Shaikh, 'Muslims Comprise 21 per cent of Undertrials but Only 17.75 Per Cent of Convicts: NCRB', *The Indian Express*, 23 September 2013, accessed 13 January 2014, http://archive.indianexpress.com/news/muslims-comprise-21—of-undertrials-but-only-17.75—of-convicts-ncrb/1172814/.
138. Zeeshan Shaikh, 'Muslims Comprise 21 per cent of Undertrials but Only 17.75 per cent of Convicts: NCRB'.
139. Shuriah Niazi, 'Muslims Languish in India Jails', *Indian Muslim Observer*, 7 June 2013, accessed 13 January 2014, http://www.indianmuslimobserver.com/?p=430.
140. Vijay Raghavan and R. Nair, 'Over-representation of Muslims: The Prisons of Maharashtra', *Economic and Political Weekly* Vol. 47, No. 11, 2013.
141. Vijay Raghavan and R. Nair, 'Over-representation of Muslims: The Prisons of Maharashtra'.
142. Centre for Equity Studies and Centre for Budget and Governance Accountability, 'India Exclusion Report 2013-14', (New Delhi: Books for Change, 2014), p. 253
143. Harsh Mander, 'In Kakhi Terror', *The Hindu Sunday Magazine*, 6 April 2008, http://www.thehindu.com/todays-paper/tp-features tpsundaymagazine/in-khaki-terror/article1437178.ece.
144. Harsh Mander, 'In Kakhi Terror'.
145. Ashish Khetan, 'In the Words of a Zealot.'
146. Ram Puniyani, *Contours of a Hindu Rashtra: Hindutva, Sangh Parivar and Contemporary Politics* (New Delhi: Kalpaz Publications, 2006), p. 93; see also, Human Rights Watch, 'Attacks across the Country', accessed 20 January 2014, http://www.hrw.org/reports/1999/indiachr/christians8-05.htm.
147. Harsh Mander, 'A Heavy Cross to Bear,' *Hindustan Times*, 27 June 2007.
148. Human Rights Watch, 'Politics by Other Means: Attacks against Christians in India', October 1999, accessed 15 March 2014, http://www.hrw.org/reports/1999/indiachr/.
149. Angana Chatterji and Mihir Desai, 'Communalism in Orissa: Report of the Indian People's Tribunal on Environment and Human Rights' (Mumbai: IPTEHR), accessed 16 March 2014, http://

www.iptindia.org/wp-content/pdf/report/COMMUNALISM-IN-ORISSA.pdf.
150. Uday Mahurkar and Sheela Raval, 'Politics by Other Means', *India Today*, 25 January 1999, accessed 13 January 2014, http://indiatoday.intoday.in/story/champions-of-reconversion-dominate-amid-debate-over-gujarat-violence-against-christians/1/252973.html.
151. Arun Shourie, *Harvesting Our Souls: Missionaries, Their Designs, Their Claims* (New Delhi: Rupa Publications India, 2006).
152. John Dayal, *A Matter of Equity: Freedom of Faith in Secular India* (New Delhi: Anamika Publishers and Distributors).
153. John Dayal, *A Matter of Equity*.
154. John Dayal, *A Matter of Equity*.
155. http://censusindia.gov.in/Census_And_You/religion.aspx
156. http://censusindia.gov.in/Census_And_You/religion.aspx
157. Ram Puniyani, ed., *The Politics behind Anti-Christian Violence: A Compilation of Investigation Committee Reports into Acts of Violence against the Christian Minorities* (Delhi: Media House, 2006).
158. Suchandana Gupta, 'Jhabua Tense after Rape, Murder of Minor,' *The Times of India*, 15 January 2004, accessed 18 January 2014, http://timesofindia.indiatimes.com/india/Jhabua-tense-after-rape-murder-of-minor/articleshow/423735.cms.
159. Hartosh Singh Bal, 'Police Are Silent Watchers as Terror Returns to Jhabua', *The Indian Express*, 21 January 2004.
160. T. K. Rajalakshmi, 'Terror in Jhabua'. Frontline Vol. 21, Issue 04, February 2004, accessed 18 January 2014, http://www.frontline.in/static/html/fl2104/stories/20040227008113000.htm
161. According to data published by the Jhabua administration, http://jhabua.nic.in/factfile.htm.
162. Suhrid Sankar Chattopadhyay, 'Saffronising the Tribal Heartland', *Frontline*, Vol. 21, Issue 6, March 2004, accessed 18 January 2014, http://www.frontline.in/static/html/fl2106/stories/20040326004601900.htm
163. National People's Tribunal on Kandhamal, 'Final Report', August 2010, http://www.sabrang.com/cc/archive/2012/jan2012/citizens%20tribunal%20Kandhamal%20Report%20Full.pdf
164. National People's Tribunal on Kandhamal, 'Final Report', p. 23.
165. National People's Tribunal on Kandhamal, 'Final Report', p. 23.
166. National People's Tribunal on Kandhamal, 'Final Report', p. 24.

167. National People's Tribunal on Kandhamal, 'Final Report', p. 22.
168. National People's Tribunal on Kandhamal, 'Final Report', p. 16.
169. National People's Tribunal on Kandhamal, 'Final Report', p.26.
170. National People's Tribunal on Kandhamal, 'Final Report', p.51.
171. National People's Tribunal on Kandhamal, 'Final Report', p. 31.
172. National People's Tribunal on Kandhamal, 'Final Report', p. 20.
173. National People's Tribunal on Kandhamal, 'Final Report', p. 21.
174. Vrinda Grover, ed., *Kandhamal: The Law Must Change Its Course* (New Delhi: Multiple Action Research Group, 2010) p. 33.
175. National People's Tribunal on Kandhamal, 'Final Report', p. 119.
176. National People's Tribunal on Kandhamal, 'Final Report', p. 44.
177. National People's Tribunal on Kandhamal, 'Final Report', pp. 77-91.
178. National People's Tribunal on Kandhamal, 'Final Report', p. 60.
179. Vrinda Grover, ed., *Kandhamal*, p. 99.
180. Vrinda Grover, ed., *Kandhamal*, p. 99.
181. Vrinda Grover, ed., *Kandhamal*, p. 103.
182. Constituent Assembly of India Debates (Proceedings), Vol. 2, accessed 18 January 2014, http://164.100.47.132/LssNew/cadebatefiles/C06121948.html.
183. According to data available at http://socialjustice.nic.in/pdf/tab18.pdf.
184. Constituent Assembly of India Debates (Proceedings), Vol. 7, accessed 18 January 2014, http://164.100.47.132/LssNew/constituent/vol7p20.html.
185. 'Anti-Christian Violence: The Chronology of Events', Ram Puniyani, ed., *The Politics behind Anti-Christian Violence*.
186. Nilanjana Roy in Gauri Gill, '1984', 31 October 2014, *Outlook*, accessed 14 January 2015, http://www.outlookindia.com/articlefullwidth.aspx?292448.
187. Pradip Krishen in Gauri Gill, '1984', 31 October 2014, *Outlook*, accessed 14 January 2015, http://www.outlookindia.com/articlefullwidth.aspx?292448.
188. Gauri Gill, '1984', 31 October 2014, *Outlook*, accessed 14 January 2015, http://www.outlookindia.com/articlefullwidth.aspx?292448.
189. Darshan Kaur in Gauri Gill, '1984', 31 October 2014, *Outlook*, accessed 14 January 2015, http://www.outlookindia.com/articlefullwidth.aspx?292448.
190. Nilanjana Roy in Gauri Gill, '1984', 31 October 2014, *Outlook*, accessed 14 January 2015, http://www.outlookindia.com/articlefullwidth.aspx?292448.

191. Darshan Kaur in Gauri Gill, '1984', 31 October 2014, *Outlook*, accessed 14 January 2015, http://www.outlookindia.com/articlefullwidth.aspx?292448.
192. Gopi Kaur in Gauri Gill, '1984', 31 October 2014, *Outlook*, accessed 14 January 2015, http://www.outlookindia.com/articlefullwidth.aspx?292448.
193. Gurdayal in Gauri Gill, '1984', 31 October 2014, *Outlook*, accessed 14 January 2015, http://www.outlookindia.com/articlefullwidth.aspx?292448.
194. Bhaggi Kaur in Gauri Gill, '1984', 31 October 2014, *Outlook*, accessed 14 January 2015, http://www.outlookindia.com/articlefullwidth.aspx?292448.
195. Suddhabrata Sengupta in Gauri Gill, '1984', 31 October 2014, *Outlook*, accessed 14 January 2015, http://www.outlookindia.com/articlefullwidth.aspx?292448.
196. Uma Chakravarti and Nandita Haksar, *The Delhi Riots: Three Days in the Life of a Nation* (New Delhi: Lancer International, 1987).
197. See http://www.youthforequality.com/.
198. Harsh Mander, 'Fight, but Not for Your Privileges', Tehelka, 30 September 2006, accessed 15 January 2014, http://archive.tehelka.com/story_main19.asp?filename=Cr093006Do_bigha.asp.
199. Suresh Kadam, 'My Dear Aana', Vilas Sarang, trans., in Arjuna Dangle, ed., *Poisoned Bread: Translations from Modern Marathi Dalit Literature*, (Noida: Orient Blackswan, 2009), p. 38.
200. Vinod K Jose, 'Mulakat Afzal', *The Caravan*, 2006, accessed 13 January 2014, http://caravanmagazine.in/reportage/mulakat-afzal?page=1 per cent2C1.
201. Tarique Anwar, 'Afzal Guru in Last Letter to Family: Take Care of My Wife and Son', *Daily Bhaskar*, 16 February 2013, http://daily.bhaskar.com/news/NAT-TOP-afzal-guru-in-last-letter-to-family-take-care-of-my-wife-and-son-4181457-NOR.html
202. Kehar Singh and Others versus Union of India and Others, accessed 14 January 2014, http://indiankanoon.org/doc/1152284/?type=print.

THE IMPERATIVE FOR PUBLIC COMPASSION

1. Elie Wiesel in an interview with Alvin P. Sanoff, 'One Must Not Forget', *U.S. News and World Report*, 27 October 1986.
2. Amartya Sen, *The Idea of Justice*, (Massachusetts: Harvard University Press, 2009).
3. Saira Kurup, 'Four Women India Forgot', *The Times of India*, 7 May 2006, accessed 10 January 2014, http://articles.timesofindia.indiatimes.com/2006-05-07/special-report/27825117_1_child-marriage-caste-medical-report.
4. Sabrina Buckwalter, 'Just Another Rape Story', *The Times of India*, 29 October 2006, accessed 10 January 2014, http://timesofindia.indiatimes.com/india/Just-another-rape-story/articleshow/222682.cms.
5. Human Rights Watch, 'Overview of the Attacks against Muslims', accessed 10 January 2014, http://www.hrw.org/reports/2002/india/India0402-03.htm.
6. Nirmala Carvalho, 'Orissa: Hindu Extremists Burn One Nun Alive, Rape Another', *AsiaNews*, 25 August 2008, accessed 10 January 2014, http://www.asianews.it/view4print.php?l=en&art=13056.
7. Human Rights Watch, 'The Killing of Thangjam Manorama Devi', accessed 10 January 2014, http://www.hrw.org/reports/2008/india0908/3.htm.
8. Harsh Mander, 'Night of Horror', *The Hindu*, 29 June 2013, http://www.thehindu.com/opinion/columns/Harsh_Mander/night-of-horror/article4862902.ece
9. Research across countries in different regions shows that men who have suffered household violence (psychological/emotional/physical) when young are more likely to be violent to their partners. In India, of the men sampled, over 40 per cent who have experienced violence perpetrated violence on a partner, whereas just over 20 per cent who had never experienced violence perpetrated acts of violence on their partners.
10. Kunal Pradhan and Kaushik Deka, 'India's Most Hated', *India Today*, 5 August 2013, accessed 12 January 2014, http://indiatoday.intoday.in/story/delhi-gangrape-december-16-juvenile-accused-mother-juvenile-justice-act/1/296567.html.
11. Julian W. Mack, 'The Juvenile Court', *Harvard Law Review* Vol. 23, pp. 105-126.

12. Minna Kabir, 'Need to Tackle Crime Constructively: Minna Kabir in an Open Letter', *Hindustan Times*, 15 January 2013, accessed 12 January 2014, http://ww...hindustantimes.com/india-news/newdelhi/need-to-tackle-crime-constructively-minna-kabir-in-an-open-letter/article1-990201.aspx.
13. National Crime Records Bureau, 'Crime in India: 2011 Statistics', accessed 12 January 2014, http://ncrb.nic.in/CD-CII2011/cii-2011/Table per cent2010.9.pdf.
14. Pratap Bhanu Mehta, 'Why We Don't Talk about Inequality and How to Start Again', *Cetri*, 16 October 2012, accessed 12 January 2014, http://www.cetri.be/spip.php?article2792&lang=fr.
15. Ashish Khetan, 'Conspirators and Rioters', *Tehelka*, 12 August 2007, accessed 12 January 2014, http://archive.tehelka.com story_main35.asp?filename=Ne031107The_RSS_will.asp.
16. Concerned Citizens Tribunal-Gujarat 2002, 'Violence against Women', *Crime against Humanity* Vol. 1 (Mumbai: Citizens for Justice and Peace) p. 39, accessed 18 June 2014, http://www.sabrang.com/tribunal/tribunal1.pdf.
17. 'The Joy of Giving', *The Hindu Sunday Magazine*, 19 May 2013, http://www.thehindu.com/todays-paper/tp-features/tp-sundaymagazine/the-joy-of-giving/article4728929.ece, accessed 13 January 2014.
18. James Charlton, *Nothing about Us without US*, (London: University of California Press, 2002).
19. Robert Chambers, 'Poverty and Livelihoods: Whose Reality Counts?', *Environment and Urbanization*, accessed 17 January 2014, http://eau.sagepub.com/content/7/1/173.full.pdf.
20. Constituent Assembly of India Debates (Proceedings), Vol. 11, accessed 18 January 2014, http://164.100.47.132/LssNew/cadebatefiles/C06121948.html.
21. Constituent Assembly of India Debates (Proceedings), Vol. 11.
22. Noam Chomsky, 'The State-Corporate Complex: A Threat to Freedom and Survival', text of lecture given at the University of Toronto, 7 April 2011, accessed 17 January 2014, http://www.chomsky.info/talks/20110407.htm.
23. Michael J. Sandel, 'What Isn't for Sale?', *The Atlantic*, 27 February 2012, accessed 13 January 2014, http://www.theatlantic.com/magazine/archive/2012/04/what-isnt-for-sale/308902/.

24. Ernst Friedrich Schumacher, *Small Is Beautiful: Economics As if People Mattered*, (New York: Harper & Row Publishers, 2010).
25. Noam Chomsky, 'The State-Corporate Complex: A Threat to Freedom and Survival'.
26. Human Rights Watch, 'Abuses by Salwa Judum', accessed 13 January 2014, http://www.hrw.org/reports/2008/india0708/6.htm.
27. 'Nandini Sundar and Others versus the State of Chhatisgarh', accessed 13 January 2014, http://www.thehindu.com/multimedia/archive/00679/Supreme_Court_judgm_679794a.pdf.
28. See for instance 'Declining Population Trend in Naxal-hit Chhattisgarh Districts', *The Hindu*, 1 April 2013, accessed 13 January 2014, http://www.thehindu.com/news/national/other-states/declining-population-trend-in-naxalhit-chhattisgarh-districts/article4567542.ece.
29. Nirmalangshu Mukherji, 'Charu Mazumdar's Vision', *Outlook*, 1 June 2010, accessed 13 January 2014, http://www.outlookindia.com/article.aspx?265655.
30. See for instance R. K. Raghavan, 'Human Rights Concerns', *Frontline* Vol. 20, Issue 7, 29 March-11 April 2003, accessed 13 January 2014, http://www.frontline.in/static/html/fl2007/stories/20030411003610800.htm.
31. Planning Commission, 'Development Challenges in Extremist Affected Areas: Report of an Expert Group to Planning Commission', 2008, accessed 13 January 2014, http://planningcommission.gov.in/reports/publications/rep_dce.pdf.
32. Harsh Mander, 'Burning Baskets of Shame', *The Hindu*, 9 May 2010.
33. Saiyidain Hameed, *Maulana Azad, Islam and Indian Nationalism*, (New Delhi: Oxford University Press, 2014).
34. Ramachandra Guha, 'The Commanding Heights of Nehru', *The Hindu*, 13 November 2012, accessed 13 January 2014, http://www.thehindu.com/opinion/lead/the-commanding-heights-of-nehru/article4091296.ece.
35. P. Naveen and Ankur Sirothia, 'Man Who Beheaded 5 Daughters to be Hanged by Kasab's Executioner Today', *The Times of India*, 7 August 2013, accessed 13 January 2014, http://articles.timesofindia.indiatimes.com/2013-08 07/bhopal/41166656_1_central-jail-jail-superintendent-sehore.
36. Ch. Sushil Rao., 'India has 414 death row convicts: National Crime Records Bureau', *The Times of India*, 24 October 2013, accessed 13

January 2014, http://articles.timesofindia.indiatimes.com/2013-10-24/india/43361442_1_death-row-death-penalty-death-sentence.
37. Dhananjay Mahapatra, 'Tandoor Case: Killer Gets Lifeline from Supreme Court', *The Times of India*, 9 October 2013, accessed 23 January 2014, http://timesofindia.indiatimes.com/city/delhi/Tandoor-case-Killer-gets-lifeline-from-Supreme-Court/articleshow/23751321.cms.
38. Ashutosh Varshney, *Ethnic Conflict and Civic Life: Hindus and Muslims in India*, (New Haven: Yale University Press, 2002), p. 67
39. Romila Thapar, 'A Historical Perspective on the Story of Rama', in Sarvepalli Gopal, ed., *Anatomy of a Confrontation: Ayodhya and the Rise of Communal Politics in India* (New Delhi: Palgrave Macmillan, 1993) p. 141-163.
40. A phrase adapted from E. F. Schumacher's *Small Is Beautiful*, a collection of his essays first published in 1973. One of the major themes he discusses is the dehumanization of work occurring because of the replacement of craft or skill-based work with techniques of mass-production and the development of economies based on profit rather than need.
41. Bhim Rao Ambedkar, *Annihilation of Caste: The Annotated Critical Edition* (New Delhi: Navayana, 2014), p. 241.
42. Bhim Rao Ambedkar, *Annihilation of Caste*, p. 243.
43. Bhim Rao Ambedkar, *Annihilation of Caste*, p. 243.
44. Bhim Rao Ambedkar, *Annihilation of Caste*, p. 233.
45. Bhim Rao Ambedkar, 'Castes in India: Their Genesis, Mechanism and Development', paper presented at the Columbia University on 9 May 1916), accessed 13 January 2014, https://ia600508.us.archive.org/22/items/castesinindia035140mbp/castesinindia035140mbp.pdf.
46. Arundhati Roy, 'The Doctor and the Saint' in Bhim Rao Ambedkar, *Annihilation of Caste*, p. 104.
47. Gail Omvedt, *Hinduism as Counter-revolution: B. R. Ambedkar in Understanding Caste,* (New Delhi: Orient Blackswan, 2011), pp. 47-48.
48. National Campaign on Dalit Human Rights, http://www.ncdhr.org.in/ncdhr/general-info-misc-pages/dr-ambedkar.
49. Bhim Rao Ambedkar, 'Dr. Ambedkar's Speech in Mahad' in Arjuna Dangle, ed., *Poisoned Bread: Translations from Modern Marathi Dalit Literature*, (Noida: Orient Blackswan, 2009), p. 259.

50. L. S. Rokade, 'To Be or Not to Be Born' in in Arjuna Dangle, ed., *Poisoned Bread*, p. 4.
51. For full text of the judgement see http://www.nazindia.org/judgement_377.pdf.
52. Badal Sarkar, 'Dr. B.R. Ambedkar's Theory of State Socialism', *International Research Journal of Social Sciences*, Vol. 2, Issue 8, 38-41, August 2013, p. 39.
53. Badal Sarkar, 'Dr. B.R. Ambedkar's Theory of State Socialism'.
54. Badal Sarkar, 'Dr. B.R. Ambedkar's Theory of State Socialism'.
55. 'A Psychological Study of India's Partition, and Some Surprising Results' 21 March 2009, accessed 27 February 2014, http://sanhati.com/articles/1299/.
56. Amitava Kumar, 'The Restoration of Faith', *The Caravan*, 1 February 2013, accessed 13 January 2014, http://caravanmagazine.in/perspectives/restoration-faith.
57. Ram Puniyani, ed., *The Politics behind Anti-Christian Violence: A Compilation of Investigation Committee Reports into Acts of Violence against the Christian Minorities* (Delhi: Media House, 2006), p. 265.
58. Tauseef Hussain, 'Gujarat Revisited', *Outlook*, 28 February 2012, accessed 13 January 2014, http://www.outlookindia.com/printarticle.aspx?280084.
59. Tauseef Hussain, 'Gujarat Revisited'.
60. Tauseef Hussain, 'Gujarat Revisited'.
61. 'SIT Report Contains Evidence on Conspiracy to Target Minorities,' *The Hindu*, 10 July 2013, accessed 13 January 2014, http://www.thehindu.com/news/national/sit-report-contains-evidence-on-conspiracy-to-target-minorities/article4899065.ece.
62. 'SIT Report Contains Evidence on Conspiracy to Target Minorities.'
63. Anupama Katakam, 'Glimmer of Justice', *Frontline* Vol. 27, Issue 8, accessed 13 January 2014, http://www.frontline.in/static/html/fl2708/stories/20100423270803600.htm.
64. Anupama Katakam, 'Glimmer of Justice'.
65. Anupama Katakam, 'Glimmer of Justice'.
66. Sunetra Choudhury, 'Ishrat Jahan Killing: CBI Charges Former Gujarat Intelligence Bureau Chief with Murder', http://www.ndtv.com/india-news/ishrat-jahan-killing-cbi-charges-former-gujarat-intelligence-bureau-chief-with-murder-549947.
67. 'SC Denies Bail Plea of NK Amin in Ishrat Jahan Case', *Deccan*

Herald, 10 February 2015, http://www.deccanherald.com/content/453623/sc-dismisses-bail-plea-n.html.
68. John Steinbeck, *The Grapes of Wrath* (New York: Penguin, 1939).
69. Howard Zinn, *A Power Governments Cannot Suppress* (California: City Lights, 2006) p. 270.
70. Shahid Azmi's life has been sensitively and authentically recreated in the National Award-winning film *Shahid*, directed by Hansal Mehta.
71. Hanna Ingber, 'India: The Meaning of Shahid Azmi', *Huffington Post*, 18 March 2010.
72. Somit Sen, 'Lawyer Who "Piqued" Salian Was Once Pursued by Law', *The Times of India*, 15 August 2004, accessed 22 February 2014, http://timesofindia.indiatimes.com/city/mumbai/Lawyer-who-piqued-Salian-was-once-pursued-by-law/articleshow/815657.cms?referral=PM.
73. Monica Sakrani, 'Remembering Shahid Azmi', *Economic and Political Weekly*, Vol. 45, Issue 11, (13 March 2010).
74. Monica Sakrani, 'Remembering Shahid Azmi'.
75. Mahtab Alam, 'The Advocate of the Terrorised: Remembering Shahid Azmi, on the Day He Was Murdered', 11 February 2015, accessed 13 January 2014, http://www.youthkiawaaz.com/2015/02/shahid-azmi-murder-case/.
76. Monica Sakrani, 'Remembering Shahid Azmi'.
77. Mahtab Alam, 'The Advocate of the Terrorised'.
78. Monica Sakrani, 'Remembering Shahid Azmi'.

ACKNOWLEDGEMENTS

Three hundred former street children in Delhi call me Harsh Papa, and I write this book in part for them and about them, and for the privilege of their love. I write to speak of what I have learnt from them about life and this unequal world—of violence, betrayal, cruelty, resilience, survival, bare-faced courage, cheekiness, an unbending spirit, forgiveness, healing, the human potential and love. I also write in the hope that the world in which they will grow up in, and I, will live up to their faith and expectations.

There are many people I loved and admired greatly who left the world in the years that this book was in the making. This book is also dedicated to them. They are the outstanding humanists S. R. Sankaran and G. Narendranath, scholar and civil servant P. S. Appu, philanthropist Ferdinand van Koolwijk, human rights workers Ram Narayan Kumar, Balagopal, Vinod Raina and Mukul Sinha, champion for secular democracy Asghar Ali Engineer, and artist activist Bindia Thapar.

Many friends—Nina Ellinger, Vinay Lal, Ghanshyam Shah, Jan Breman, Zoya Hasan, Navsharan Singh, Yasmeen Arif, Shailaja Fennel and Patrick Heller—gave me generous advice and feedback on early drafts of this book and helped me think critically about my arguments.

I received strong research assistance and advice for portions of this book from many young colleagues: Anamika Lahiri—who helped me patiently and diligently with many rounds of editing—Jeevika Shah, Shikha Sethia, Amod Shah, Saba Sharma, Ashwin Parulkar, Agrima Bhasin, Gitanjali Prasad, Anna Piccarda Lazzarin and

Karl-Axel Lindgren. Punit Goyal, Manish Bansal, Ankita Dhakre and Rikhiya Banerjee also assisted with research and referencing.

This book is filled also with insights which I have gained while working with my wonderful colleagues in Aman Biradari and the Centre for Equity Studies, in our small, shared efforts to grapple together against hate, violence, hunger, homelessness, discrimination and despair. Their idealism, intelligence and compassion taught me a great deal, and gave me the gift of much hope, even in difficult and bewildering times. This book is theirs as well. They include my colleagues who work with children, K. Anuradha, Bahadur, Satya Pillai, Anwar ul Haque, Suroor Mander, Afsar Alam, Farzana Sagheer, Mahenaz Khan, Asghar Sharif, Rashmi Singh, Preeti Mathew, Mansi Chaturvedi, Robin Rai and Divya Jain among others; Biraj Patnaik, Sejal Dand, Dipa Sinha, Sandeep Chachra, Aditya Shrivastava, Tanveer Dar, M. Kumaran, Ashish Soni and Ravinder Rawat, among others, who work in the office of the Supreme Court Commissioners. Sajjad Hassan, Pritarani Jha, Warisha Farasat, Mallika Begum, Mangla Varma, Mehmood, Pravir, Sunitha, Usman Sheikh, Yusuf Mansuri, Abdul Kalam Azad, Aman Wadud, Surabhi Chopra and Amar Nijhawan, among others, who work with survivors of communal violence. Shikha Sethia, Amod Shah, Anamika Lahiri, Gitanjali Prasad, Agrima Bhasin, Saba Sharma, Vipul Kumar, Faraz Ahmed, Sandeep Ranjana and Rajanya Bose, among others, who conduct research into exclusion and the state. Ashwin Parulkar, Pradeep, Shaguna Kanwar, Phuntsok Tsering, Deepak Das, Javed Khan, Satyabir, Firoze, Gufran, Imaan, Anhad Imaan, Prachi Priyam, Chandan Aman, Rakesh Aman, Shabana, Godhan and Chunchun, among others, who work with homeless people. Sveta Dave, Shashi Mendiratta, Rohan Preece, Mahesh Gopalan, Alia Farooqui, Divya Murali, among others, who work with education for social justice and citizenship. Avi Singh, Nandita Rao, Karuna Nandy, Anup Surendranath and Mathew John, among others, who work with the Aman Legal Action Group.

I am grateful to my colleagues in the Aman Biradari Trust—

Sharmila Tagore, Admiral R. H. Tahiliani, Ram Puniyani, Dr Bandukwala, Navsharan Singh, Rahul Bose, and Vijay Pratap—and the Board of the Centre for Equity Studies—including Satish Deshpande, N. C. Saxena, Gopal Pillai, Bejwada Wilson, Ritu Priya, S. Parasuraman, Anshu Vaish and Chingmak Kejong, because much of the work from which the insights of this book were gathered over the years were undertaken as part of these organizations. My fine colleagues in the Right to Food campaign include Kavita Shrivastava, Jean Dreze, Arundhati Dhuru, Anuradha Talwar, Rajkishor Mishra, Gangabhai, Balram, Rama Melkote, Gurjeet Singh, Roopesh, Sunil Kaul, Ashok Khandelwal; in our anti-communal work Anhad founder Shabnam Hashmi, with Mohd Aamir, Dhruv Sangari, Bhavana Sharma, Mansi Sharma and Manan Trivedi; and colleagues in the National Campaign for the People's Right to Information include Aruna Roy, Nikhil Dey, Shankar Singh, Shekhar Singh, Anjali Bhardawaj, Inayat Sabhikhi, Nandini Dey, Ruchi Gupta, Rakshita Swamy, Amrita Johri, Venkatesh Nayak, Suchi Pande, Nachiket Udapa and Ankita Anand, and Baba Adhav of the Pension Parishad. I owe them all a special debt.

I quote many times in this book from the 'India Exclusion Report' being coordinated by the Centre of Equity Studies, in collaboration with many researchers and centres, including Coen Kompier, Kiran Bhatty, Annie Namala, Gautam Bhan, Warisha Farasat, Sajjad Hassan, Arvind Narrain and Shubha Chacko, Subrat Das and Jawed Khan. They brought to me many invaluable insights into inequality and prejudice, which enriched this book.

Apart from these many friends and collaborators, I learn a great deal from the work of many outstanding scholars, writers and practitioners. These include Abhijit Sen, A. K. Shiv Kumar, Aditya Nigam, Akhil Gupta, Akhila Sivadas, Amartya Sen, Amlanjyoti Goswami, Amirullah Khan, Amita Baviskar, Amita Dhanda, Amita Joseph, Amitabh Behar, Amitav Ghosh, Amitava Kumar, Amod Kumar, Amrita Chhachi, Anand Grover, Anant Asthana, Anita Agnihotri, Anita Rampal, Angana Chatterjee, Anita Ghai, Annie

Koshy, Annie Namala, Anu Aga, Anurag Behar, Apoorvanand, Arjan De Haan, Arundhati Roy, Ashish Khaitan, Ashis Nandy, Ashok Bharti, Ashwani Kumar, Atul Sood, B. N. Yugandhar, Barbara Harriss-White, Binalakshmi Nepram, Bipan Chandra, Biraj Swain, Bharat Dogra, Bharti Chaturvedi, Bhaskar Veer, Bunker Roy, Chaman Lal, Chenniah, Clifton D' Rozario, Colin Gonsalves, Daniel Bradley, Daniel Umi, David Rieff, Deborah Padgett, Deep Joshi, Deepak Nayyar, Devaki Jain, Devaki Nambiar, Devika Singh, Ela Bhatt, Farah Naqvi, Flavia Agnes, Frederika Meijer, Gagan Sethi, Ganesh Devy, Gauri Gill, Ghanshyam Shah, Githa Hariharan, Gopal Guru, Gudmunder Erikson, H. S. Phoolka, Harsha Hegde, Hargopal, Indira Hirway, Indira Jaising, Indira Khurana, Indu Prakash Singh, Ira Bhaskar, Irfan Habib, John Harris, Jayati Ghosh, Jean Dreze, Jenny Liang, Jim Withers, John Dayal, Justice A. K. Shah, Justice Leila Seth, Justice Murlidhar, K. B. Saxena, K. N. Pannikar, Kailash Satyarthi, Kalyani Menon, Kamla Bhasin, Kanak Dixit, Kanika Gill, Kancha Ilaiah, Karamat Ali, Karan Thapar, Kavitha Kuruganthi, Kavita Krishnan, Keshav Desiraju, Kim Hopper, Dr Kishore, Krishna Kumar, Kshama Metre, Kuldip Nayar, Lakshmi Lingam, Lakshmidhar Mishra, M. S. Swaminathan, Madhu Bhaduri, Mahesh Bhatt, Maja Daruwala, Mallika Sarabhai, Miloon Kothari, Manohar Agnane, Manoj Jha, Mark Tully, Mary John, Mathew Cherian, Medha Patkar, Meera Dewan, Mihir Shah, Mirai Chaterjee, Mohan Rao, Mridula Mukherjee, Mukul Kesavan, Mujibur Rahman, N. C. Saxena, Nadira Chaturvedi, Nandini Sundar, Nandita Das, Neera Chandoke, Nikhil Dey, Nirija Jayal, Nishirin Jafri, Nitin Sethi, Nitya Ramakrishna, Nivedita Menon, P. Sainath, Pamela Schumer-Smith, Pattabhi Somayaji, Paul Divakar, Penny Vera-Sova, Peter Kenmore, Phaniraj, P. G. Thakurta, Poonam Mattreja, Prabhat Patnaik, Prabir Purkayastha, Pradeep Prabhu, Prakash Amte, Prashant Bhushan, Praveen Kumar, Praveen Jha, Radhika Alkazi, R. Kumaran, R. Subramaniam, Rahul Bose, Rajni Bakshi, Raju Narzary, Ramachandra Guha, Reetika Khare, Renana Jhabwala, Richard Shapiro, Ritu Priya, Robert Chambers, Rohinton Mistry, Romila

Thapar, Ruchir Joshi, S. Parasuraman, S. Thorat, S. Nolen, Saeed Mirza, Sagari Ghosh, Samar Harlankar, Samvartha Sahil, Santosh Mathew, Sara Ahmed, Satish Agnhotri, Satish Deshpande, Seema Mustafa, Shabana Azmi, Shankar Singh, Shantha Sinha, Sharmila Tagore, Shashi Buleshwar, Shiv Visvanathan, Shekhar Singh, Shiraz Balsara, Shyam Benegal, Shyam Menon, Siddharth Sharma, Siddharth Varadarajan, Sister Cyril Mooney, Sister Lellis, Sonia Singh, Srinivas Murthy, Sreenivasan Jain, Sukumar Muralidharan, Suneeta Dhar, Sunil Kaul, Sutapa Deb, Swami Agnivesh, Syeda Hameed, T. Sundararaman, Tanika Sarkar, Tarique, Teesta Setalvad, Tejinder Sandhu, Tempa Tsering, Tushar Gandhi, U. R. Ananthamurthy, Uma Chakraborty, Uma Shankari, Umakant, Upendra Baxi, Urvashi Butalia, Usha Ramanathan, V. Suresh, Vandana Gopikumar, Vandana Prasad, Vatsala Subramaniam, Ved Kumari, Veena Shatrughan, Venkat Krishnan, Venkat Reddy, Vidya Rao, Vijay Pratap, Vijayanand, Vijay Kumar, Vijay Mahajan, Vikram Chandra, Vikram Seth, Virginius Xaxa, Vrinda Grover, Yogendra Yadav, Yug Mohit Chaudhry, among many, many others.

I owe many debts to the newspaper editors who have hosted my columns over the years, in *The Hindu*, *Hindustan Times*, *Dainik Bhaskar* and the *Mint*, where portions of this book have appeared from time to time. These include Nirmala Lakshman, N. Ram, Indrajit Hazra, Kumkum Dasgupta, Krithika R., Shravan Garg, Lalita Panikar, and also C. Rammanohar Reddy, of the *Economic and Political Weekly*.

I am fortunate to have for this book the finest editor I could look for in the world—and I mean that literally—in Ravi Singh. I feel that my book—flawed in many ways, but very close to my heart—is safe in his hands. Senior editor Anurag Basnet went through the entire manuscript with great care and insight, and ironed out many rough edges. I thank O. P. Jain for his generous hospitality in giving me space in Anandgram, surely the most aesthetic piece of real estate in Delhi; whenever I need solitude and birdsong to be able to write, I head for Anandgram, and it is here that many parts of this book were written.

I thank my family for sharing my journey: my mother, a strong, feisty and caring matriarch who held us together with fierce protectiveness and love, and who left us in September 2013, my gentle father, battling old age so bravely and with much dignity, my wife and partner for thirty years, my daughter who gives me great pride and shares so much of my life's work, and my elder brother who sat by my mother's bedside for three years when she could hardly move and gave us all a gift of great love. My friends are the starlight which brightens the darkest days of my life, and gives me strength and love through all my foolhardy enterprises.